Risk in business decision

Risk in business decision

Peter G. Moore

Professor of Statistics and Operational Research
London Graduate School of Business Studies

A Halsted Press Book

John Wiley & Sons
New York

658.4
M 823

Published in the U.S.A., Possessions, Dependencies, and Philippine Islands only by
Halsted Press, a Division of John Wiley & Sons, Inc. New York

© Longman Group Limited 1972

First published 1973

ISBN 0 470 61440 4

Library of Congress Catalog Card no: LC 72–11307

Printed in Great Britain

Contents

Preface

During recent years interest in the quality of decisions made, in both the public and private sectors of the economy, has grown tremendously. Two dramatic examples amongst many, namely the siting of the third London airport and the acceptance of the ill-fated RB 211 contract that led to the Rolls-Royce collapse, bear witness to the intense concern felt amongst managers about the procedures by which decisions are reached. In particular, it is clear that traditional approaches to decision making are lacking in certain dimensions, particularly in the manner in which they commonly fail to link together initial and consequential alternatives, the way that uncertainties are dealt with on an informal basis and the evaluation of information in an arbitrary manner.

This book develops an analytical approach to the consideration of risk in business decisions that is coherent and consistent. It is argued that this will enable the relevant expertise of advisers and managers to be better utilized and hence better decisions to be made. No method, short of eliminating uncertainty, will guarantee success in every situation, but an increase in the percentage of correct decisions made can have a dramatic effect on an organization's overall results. Who, in a period that has seen the collapse of so many household names in business, can deny that a more rational approach to uncertainty is needed? This is contrary, however, to a widely held view that intuition and judgment form the crucial elements for success in business. Of course, the truth lies somewhere in between the two extremes. Analysis will not generate, in itself, the possible ideas for action in the first place—these must continue to be derived from the creativity and vision of those concerned. Rational analysis will, however, enable the necessarily scarce availability of creativity and judgment amongst managers to be better exploited.

The nucleus of this book is in Chapters 5 to 12 inclusive which, for many readers, will provide the development of statistical decision analysis they seek. Since a proper understanding does, however, require a knowledge of basic probability the nucleus is buttressed by a preliminary three chapter development of the concepts and applications of probability theory. Similarly it is desirable to show the relationships of the theory developed in this book with that of classical statistics and the nucleus is therefore buttressed on the other side by a two-chapter synopsis and comparison of classical statistics. In this way the book can be used, either to provide an account of decision analysis, or to provide a more comprehensive development of statistical methods of inference as a whole that is particularly suitable for students of business studies.

The way in which the material is developed contains some novel features, although few of the ideas are themselves new. In particular Thomas Bayes, the Nonconformist clergyman from Tunbridge Wells who died in 1761, would be amazed to see how his essay on probability, found amongst his papers after his death, has become a cornerstone of modern thinking on the formal incorporation of uncertainty in business, medicine, the law and elsewhere. Howard Raiffa at Harvard, and Dennis Lindley at University College, London are responsible for many of the developments discussed in this book, but my own debt is much wider and includes those from many professions with whom I have discussed these ideas, and who have consciously or unconsciously provided me with illustrative material. Three cohorts of postgraduate students at the London Business School have helped in numerous ways to sharpen up the development.

The mathematics in the text has been kept to the lowest possible level consistent with the adequate development and illustration of the appropriate conceptual arguments. As such, it should be within the competence of all those seriously interested in the subject. No attempt is made to use mathematics for its own sake, and the few proofs of formulae given can be omitted without detriment to an understanding of the book as a whole. All the principles enunciated are illustrated by copious non-mathematical examples and exercises and the non-mathematically inclined reader should concentrate his attention on these. The data in the examples and exercises have been drawn from (or suggested by) a very wide range of reports, journals, magazines and books. In many cases the original material has been greatly tampered with so as to illustrate a particular concept. In these cases the source has not been given for fear of misrepresentation of the original author's intentions. Where the material is substantially in the original form, due acknowledgement has been made. The tables in Appendices B and D are extracted from rather fuller tables in *Biometrika Tables for Statisticians* with the permission of Professor E. S. Pearson, whilst the table in Appendix C and the extracts in exercise 8.5 from the *Acme Company Case* are reproduced by permission of the President and Fellows of Harvard University.

It is a pleasure to acknowledge the help received from many quarters in the preparation of this book. Dr H. Thomas and Mrs Mary Middleton read and commented upon an earlier draft. Mr S. M. Schaefer gave much help compiling the exercises and their answers. My successive secretaries, Mrs Sheila Ewart and Miss Beverley Godden, wrestled ably with the typing of numerous drafts of a far from easy manuscript and my wife, Mrs Sonja Moore, gave invaluable assistance with the proof reading and compilation of the index. Nevertheless, the ultimate responsibility for the contents of any book must rest with the author and comments from readers will be welcomed.

P. G. MOORE

London, May 1972

1 The case for statistical decision analysis

1.1 Introduction

Much of life is concerned with the making of decisions. Many, possibly the majority, of the decisions that you make in your personal or professional life can be made without a lot of fuss. Either your best choice of action is clear to you without much analysis of the situation, or the decision is not important enough to warrant any great amount of attention on your part. From time to time, however, you will find yourself in situations where you will feel it is worth your time and effort to think systematically and hard about the different courses of action that you might pursue. You may even be willing to plan and collect some information and to push a few numbers around, on the assumption that this will help you to make a better decision than would be the case with pure guesswork. This book deals primarily with the development of methods for drawing conclusions from information of a numerical kind, in situations where we have to decide between alternative courses of action, and the outcomes contain elements of risk or uncertainty.

Decisions can range widely in importance and far-reaching effect. At one extreme you may have to decide whether to go from Victoria to Charing Cross by 'Underground', bus, taxi or on foot; at the opposite extreme whether or not to build a £5 million factory for making plastic containers and, if so, where. In both these cases certain information is likely to be available: for the journey the usual frequency of 'underground' trains or buses, the amount of walking to be done at each end, the likelihood of a delay due to traffic, the relative costs, the need to be on time at the other end, etc. In the capital investment situation, there would be information regarding potential markets, costs of equipment and building, costs of raw materials and selling, costs of raising capital, availability and cost of labour, etc. At the end of the day, however, with all this information available, some of it known to be good, some believed to be bad, and some indifferent, a decision or choice has to be made. An important part of everybody's life is to make these kinds of decisions or choices.

To make such decisions, what should we do? Well, first of all we could 'intuit' the decision. That is, faced with the investment decision, we can sit back in our chair, close our eyes and think about the problem on the basis of a combination of experience, hunch and judgment. We finally decide how and where to build or else decide 'don't build', or 'build with a partner', or 'wait a while and get more information'. Alternatively, the decision-maker can approach the problem rather differently and systematically sort out various elements contained in the decision and then use certain decision rules to help him decide what to do.

'Statistical decision analysis' is the term commonly used for a formal approach to the analysis of decision-making under uncertainty. It is an unfortunate title since it evokes in many people's minds unpleasant associations with the older concept of statistics as the study of great masses of data, columns of figures galore, percentages, ratios, indices and the lot. Further, until fairly recently, statistical analysis was mostly concerned with drawing inferences from limited data, without helping a person decide what to do with the inferences. Today, however, a new breadth has been given to statistics. Using concepts and techniques from such fields as mathematics, logic, economics, psychology and accounting, statisticians have designed a whole new way of thinking about decisions to help a person choose the most reasonable course of action under uncertainty. The principles adopted are relatively simple, but what statistical decision does is to formalize the many mental assumptions, facts and goals that go into making up a complex decision under uncertainty. By so doing, and by allowing certain logical principles to guide action, the chances of error and inconsistent action are reduced.

1.2 Success rate

When any decision is made, the complete set of information that would be desirable is never completely available. We have to guess about unknown future outcomes that will follow a course of action by using information derived largely from a collection of historical facts. We can, however, become better at guessing. This need not come only from having practice at making the same decision on a number of occasions. We do not usually get very much experience of putting up £5 million factories (and it would be an expensive form of practice), even if we do have plenty of experience of travelling from Victoria to Charing Cross. Instead, we have to supplement the lack of such practical experience with the use of logical methods in order to sharpen the guessing process[To say that there is no point in formally studying decision-making on a systematic and scientific basis, since it cannot be taught in its entirety due to the non-repetitive nature of many decisions, could lead to an assertion that decision-makers cannot be taught anything[Surely nobody would really accept the latter as being a logical deduction, and hence we are driven to the conclusion that we have something to go for in aiming to improve the bases of decision-making. Of course, we may not be entirely successful in our efforts and may not be able to raise our success rate to 100 per cent.) But even a small rise may have dramatic effects. If companies engage in large-scale enterprises, they will occasionally make very costly mistakes[The aim of any kind of formal decision analysis must be to reduce both the costs of these mistakes and their frequency] By this means the benefits of the successes are enhanced.

As a simplified version of the kind of problems that we shall be concerned with in this book, suppose that a chemical manufacturer has accepted an order for a specially manufactured chemical to be delivered by a certain date. He realizes, at an early stage in the manufacturing process, that there is a substantial chance that he may be late in delivery. If the chemical delivery is late, the manufacturer has to pay a penalty at a rate of £2000 per week that the delivery is late. At this stage, too, it is still open to the manufacturer to use an alternative, but more expensive, process to fulfil the order. He reckons that if he does so, there is virtually no chance that he will miss the delivery date, but it will cost him an extra £5000. Should he go ahead or should he change to the alternative process? On what basis should he make this decision? What factors should he consider?

The definition of a success rate in decision-making sometimes causes problems. A newspaper survey a few years ago reported, with glowing approval from the appropriate authorities, that when a broker confronted a jobber in the Stock Exchange the latter could correctly divine which way the former wished to trade (i.e. buy or sell) on a little more than 59 per cent of occasions. But, of course, guesswork should give us a 50 per cent correct assessment over a period. (Incidentally, the conclusion drawn in the newspaper was that jobbers were good psychologists.) Hence, while statistical decision analysis cannot guarantee to make a successful decision in any one particular decision problem, its utility must be judged against the overall level of the success rate achieved through its use when taken over a number of decisions.

1.3 Numeracy

To answer the sorts of question just posed demands not only analytical thought, but the handling of data expressed in numerical terms, some being of a probabilistic nature. Now literacy has long been regarded as of some importance in our concept of the educated manager, and its value is as great as ever. However, when speaking of 'literacy', in this context, we mean much more than its dictionary sense of the ability to read and write. Similarly, when speaking of 'numeracy' we mean more than mere ability to manipulate the simple rules of arithmetic. When we say a scientist is 'illiterate', we mean that he is not skilled enough to be able to communicate effectively with other scientists or with those who have had a literary rather than a scientific education. When we say that a historian or linguist is 'innumerate', we mean that he cannot begin to understand what scientists or mathematicians are talking about, not so much the jargon as such, but the approaches to problems that such experts use. Is this just a matter of language and terminology, or is it something rather deeper?

It is perhaps possible to distinguish two different aspects of numeracy. On the one hand, there is an understanding of the scientific approach to the study of phenomena: observation, hypothesis, experiment, verification. On the other hand, there is the need in the modern world to think quantitatively, to realize how far many of our problems are problems of degree, even when they appear as problems of kind. Statistical ignorance and statistical fallacies are quite as widespread and quite as dangerous as the logical fallacies which come under the heading of illiteracy. The man who is innumerate is cut off from understanding some of the relatively new ways in which the human brain is now most busily at work. Numeracy has come to be an indispensable tool to the understanding and mastery of all phenomena, and not only of those in the relatively close field of the traditional natural sciences. Today, the way in which we think, marshal our evidence and formulate our arguments in every field, is influenced by techniques first applied in science. The educated man of action needs, therefore, to be numerate as well as literate, and to obtain a feel for numbers, orders of magnitude, probabilities, and so forth. Side by side with this need for understanding a new and essential approach to knowledge, such men also require a general acquaintance with the directions in which science is most rapidly advancing and with the nature of the new knowledge that is being acquired.

1.4 Classification

To place statistical decision analysis in perspective, it is necessary to summarize briefly the main avenues of development of the subject of statistics. The subject, once called *political arithmetic*, dates back some three centuries and was originally concerned with obtaining the necessary information for the raising of taxes, manpower for armies and so forth. The field has considerably broadened since the turn of this century, and statistical problems encountered today by the professional statisticians fall into three reasonably distinct categories. These three categories can be labelled 'data handling and analysis', 'decision', and 'inference'.

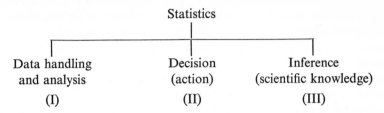

Category I deals with the collection and analysis of masses of data, the data being thought of essentially as forming the population or universe of all data available on the subject. For example, all public companies in the United Kingdom have to file their annual accounts with the Department of Trade and Industry Registrar each year. To produce concise meaningful tabulations of the salient features of this mass of material for Government publications, such as the *Annual Abstract of Statistics* or *Financial Statistics,* is a tough problem in data analysis. The statistician here is not concerned with problems of drawing inferences about all companies from a handful of companies; rather, he is bringing order to what might seem to many people to be chaos. His mission in such circumstances is to glean fundamental insights into the data, to explore relationships that help structure and thereby explain the data. In other words, he reports without himself making any inferences. To do this he must work over the body of the data or, as a colleague of mine once picturesquely expressed it, massage the data. After he comes to understand what the data seem to say, he must report the results in such a way that the data are self-explanatory. Notice, too, that the statistician carrying through such work will not always be aware of the uses to which the data may ultimately be put. Hence, he has to be careful to give precise definitions, and not to compress the data so severely that their utility is thereby unduly constrained. The advent of computers in the last decade has naturally revolutionized the ability to carry out this form of data analysis. However, it has made the statistician's task harder in one sense, in that it has become all too easy to swamp by quantity instead of trying to compress with quality.

Category II, dealing with decisions for action, is concerned with the kind of problem involving the chemical plant that was described in the previous section. It seeks to develop procedures for the weighing up of alternative courses of action and deciding upon the criterion or criteria which you would use to decide between them. The argument for having a systematic approach to such decision-making procedures is threefold. First, it forces a decision-maker to be explicit concerning his problem, the constraints and the criteria by which he is to judge alternatives; second, it introduces uniformity and consistency both between alternative decision-makers who may be faced with similar problems, and the same decision-makers facing a variety of decisions over time; and third, it helps to narrow down those areas where real and scarce managerial skills are needed. Decision analysis will never completely eliminate judgment but, by isolating those parts of the decision-making process where judgment is essential from those parts that can be handled on a more routine basis, scarce managerial skills can be more effectively employed.

Against these arguments the contention is sometimes made that the 'best' decisions are often intuitive, and therefore cannot be taught or dealt with in a cold, scientific and analytical manner. Of course, it is true that many great successes of the world have been the result of inspired hunches. We should, however, also take into account the many hunches that have failed, before we condemn all forms of analysis and suggest replacing them by hunch for all decisions and all parts of the decision process. But, more importantly, in any area of business, be it big or small, there are a whole sequence of decisions that need to be taken, and it is unrealistic to expect to make them all by intuition and be 100 per cent correct all the time. What is needed is the right balance between analysis and hunch, and the contention of this book is that there are relatively few decisions in the lives of most businessmen that should best be left completely to hunch, and that most decisions will benefit from the formal discipline of statistical decision analysis. A paper-mill manager in a large paper manufacturing group complained to the author a few years ago that he had always been used to appraising his capital investment projects on the back of an envelope, and now he was forced to complete a complex questionnaire and perform a detailed analysis before being allocated the money he required. 'Wasn't this', he asked, 'bureaucracy gone mad?' I had to point out to him a number of past investments that had gone sour in the group, and the sad but pertinent fact that the industry now, with the removal of various tariffs, needed to be much more competitive than it had been, so that the margin of fat available as a cushion for poor investment decisions was that much less. Furthermore, he was now in a situation where there was considerable competition for the limited amount of capital available and for the managerial skills available to supervise the spending of funds, so that only highly productive propositions could be entertained. The spate of financial collapses among large well-known firms in British industry in 1971 suggests that further scope exists for the assessment of risk and its handling in relation to decision-making.

Category III of statistical work concerns inference. Here, we are not so much concerned with a specific decision or choice between alternative courses of action, but with establishing a piece of information or knowledge. At the time that the investigation is being made, it is not always known precisely for what purpose this particular piece of information is required, and by whom it will be used. Many scientific research investigations would fall into this category, in that only at a much later stage is a very positive decision procedure required. For example, suppose a paper firm decides to investigate the relative effects of adding certain resins to papers used to manufacture paper sacks and other wrapping papers. To do this, a series of experiments is set up, from which experimental determinations are made of the effects, using a number of different criteria. Certain resins may be found to be significantly better than others in a statistical sense on some or all of the criteria. There may, however, also be some factors whose effects on the customers of paper sacks are simply not quantifiable, e.g. colour, smell, feel of the paper, etc. Now this information may not be used immediately, but may be part of an ongoing programme of research whereby alternative forms of raw materials and chemicals are explored. Subsequently, pieces of the research results may be picked out for further development and exploitation on a commercial basis. This kind of thing is going on all the time, in all industries. The task here is to develop methods for assimilating complete bodies of factual information and for assessing the uncertainties of inferences drawn from such bodies of information.

1.5 Present approach

This book is concerned basically with the second category of statistical methods, but it is inevitable that a considerable amount of material that is directly applicable to the third category will creep in, and this is by no means a bad thing, as these two categories of statistical analysis rest very much on the same basic premises. No attempt is made to cover systematically the first category of statistics, which is well covered elsewhere, and for which some references are given in Appendix G.

The plan of the book is as follows. Chapters 2, 3 and 4 are concerned with the development of probability and the concept of random variables, both discrete and continuous. These chapters cover a great deal of basic material which is essential for a proper understanding of the book as a whole (or indeed for more advanced work in statistics, operational research and other functional applications). In Chapter 5 approaches to some simple one-stage decision problems using some of this earlier material are discussed. Chapter 6 develops the concept of a decision tree for showing up the logic and structure of a multistage decision problem. Chapter 7 then deals with the revision of initial (prior) probabilities of possible outcomes in the light of subsequent information coming to hand. This is a key concept in the so-called 'Bayesian' approach to decision-making that underlies much of the later analysis in this book. Chapter 8 reconsiders the multistage decision problems discussed in Chapter 6 with the benefit of the concept of probability revision outlined in Chapter 7. Chapter 9 provides a brief discussion of some of the problems involved in the assessment of probabilities, when subjective elements enter the assessment.

Chapters 10 and 11 are concerned with the choice as to how much information it is worth while to obtain in a given decision problem, bearing in mind both costs and the value of the information obtained. Chapter 12 develops the concept of utility, which is necessary and applicable when the decision-maker's attitude towards money is not strictly linear (linearity implies that an extra unit of money has equal worth to him, whatever his present capital may be). Chapters 13 and 14 provide a link with the third category of statistical work mentioned earlier, namely, statistical inference. These chapters also provide a background to sampling methods, which is of considerable importance in decision analysis, since so much effort is necessarily made in practice to obtain worthwhile sample information.

The book contains numerous worked examples of all the main concepts discussed. Some readers, with high mathematical aptitude, or already possessing a basic knowledge of probability concepts, may find that it is unnecessary to work through all the examples given in the text. A high pace of progression, without loss of comprehension, can be kept up by judicious skipping of examples, particularly with the earlier chapters. To aid such accelerated progress a number of worked examples are marked with a dagger (†) and it is suggested that these should be omitted by such readers, unless the worked examples remaining provide difficulties. The daggered examples introduce no new concepts.

Readers are advised to study the book carefully in the correct order, and not to jump to what appears to them to be the more interesting and practically oriented chapters. (Chapters 13 and 14 are the possible exceptions to this rule.) This is because, in general, the need in statistics is to build one concept upon another. Once the reader has left out a substantial chunk of the development, he will find it hard to understand fully the later work. An analogy can be made here between a *chain* which is broken on the failure of a single link, and a *mesh* which may still be effective with many of its individual links broken. Statistical analysis is a chain subject, economics is possibly both a chain and a mesh subject, while organizational behaviour is very much a mesh subject. On this analogy, it is important that the reader follows the development in this book step by step.

1.6 Justification

Business would not be as difficult as it has commonly turned out to be if it did not involve risks. The aim of the businessman must be to take the risks he faces in such a way that he can ensure that the balance of correct versus incorrect decisions is in his favour. There will always be businessmen, very much a minority, who will have the flair of intuition that enables them to cut through the dense undergrowth of complex problems they encounter and reach good conclusions. But these occasions will occur only rarely and there will also always be a vast majority who, if they follow such methods, will court ultimate disaster. For them we can point to the encouragement which decision analysis gives to the scrutiny of the problem as a whole, and the manner in which it allows the experts to give evidence about their own area of expertise in unambiguous quantitative terms that can be put on a par with the information and evidence from other experts. Systematic evaluation helps to suggest those areas where it would be meaningful to gather new information and how much it would be worth paying for such information. It can help to distinguish the decision-maker's preferences for consequences from his judgment about uncertainties. It gives a stimulus for all the viable, alternative actions to be listed and examined. It helps a decision-maker to communicate his decisions and to mediate where differences arise. Finally, it looks to the future and shows the areas of contingency planning that should be undertaken, thus giving a framework for continuous reassessment of the situation.

We can sum up at this stage by pointing out that, if you are faced with a given decision situation, you must act. How will you decide on the action to be taken? If you reject the kind of approach that is outlined in this book, you must put something in its place and be able to justify your approach in terms of a greater success rate in decision-making. In some special circumstances your alternative approach may be correct, but the methods outlined in this book provide a logical and consistent framework for decision-making and the range of problems to which the methods are applicable is ever widening. While it is unlikely that a major business organization would agree at present to put all its formal decision-making on the kind of bases discussed here, many organizations now consider that these ideas are too promising to be ignored completely. Such organizations are encouraging their management to experiment with the ideas and to use them on selected medium-sized problems, while at the same time monitoring on paper some really important decisions. For the latter, the final decisions will often still be taken by the 'seat-of-the-pants' approach, while possibly comparing the consequences with the more formal decision analysis approach. As time goes on, it should be possible to delineate more firmly the precise types of problem for which these methods are or are not relevant.

FURTHER READING

A good summary of modern views on the second and third categories of statistical analysis outlined above is given in a monograph by L. J. Savage, *The Foundations of Statistical Inference*. Methuen, 1962. This is a report of a two day conference on the subject and contains contributions by many distinguished statisticians of all shades of opinion.

2 Probability concepts

2.1 Introduction

For many years I have discussed, argued and taught probability with people of all ages and backgrounds. Among the great welter of different reactions that I receive to the basic concepts, none arises so consistently as the view that people feel they are talking about concepts that do not really concern them in their real lives; the discussion is, to them, about happenings in an intellectual arena for which they are merely observers on the sidelines. They talk as though somebody else were involved in the problems concerned, somebody who is usually thought of as a not too bright and a rather disembodied character. And yet we all continuously make decisions that have within them elements of uncertainty: trivial ones like selecting from the lunch menu, or deciding whether to go to a shop by bus or 'underground', more important ones like choosing a lecture course or a book to study and, occasionally, very major ones such as the acceptance of a job that may turn out in retrospect to be a life career.

If we are to treat probability on a scientific basis, it is necessary as a first step to establish a scale of measurement that we can use. This scale is conventional, but it is vitally important to have a general acceptance of some scale. Hence we customarily measure probability by providing ourselves with a numerical scale that is marked zero at one end and unity at the other, no values outside these limits having any meaning. The top end of the scale (see Fig. 2.1) is marked unity or 1, and represents absolute certainty. Any proposition about which there is absolutely no doubt at all would find its place at this point on the scale. For example, the probability that you will die one day is equal to unity, because everybody accepts that it is absolutely certain that you will die some day. We accordingly write $p = 1$ for this event, the letter p denoting the probability of the occurrence of the event concerned. At the other end of the scale, the probability that I should succeed in an attempt to swim the Atlantic is zero, because failure would be absolutely certain. Here we would write $p = 0$ for this happening or event.

If all the affairs of life were as clear-cut as these two examples, life would be very simple indeed, although possibly rather boring. Human beings are presented daily with a whole stream of problems concerning events to which it is not possible to give a clear-cut $p = 0$ or $p = 1$ answer. A doctor may know that a certain drug is excellent for your symptoms, but he cannot completely guarantee that you will be cured by using it. At most he can be very sure and put $p = 1$ for practical purposes. But this is an approximation and we have already slipped from the realms of absolute certainty. In this instance, it may be more realistic and meaningful to put p equal to 0·99, not 1 itself. Figure 2.1 shows the position of some other possible events on this kind of scale. How, though, do we arrive at actual measures of probability of any real life events? This is something we will return to at later stages in this book. Meanwhile, much of probability theory is concerned with deriving probabilities for complex situations, on the basis of the probabilities given for simpler events. Let us, therefore, start this chapter by posing four problems in each of which derived probabilities are required, and asking you to guess solutions. Make a note of your guesses; later in this book methods will be described by which you, the reader, will be able to analyse these problems in more detail and check your guesses.

Problem 2.1

A group of twenty-five unrelated students are in a classroom. What is the (approximate) probability that there is at least one duplication of birthday (month and day) among them?

Problem 2.2

Electronic components are made in large batches by a supplier, and previous experience has shown that approximately 4 per cent of the individual components are defective. You purchase a fresh batch from the supplier and, to check on quality, take a handful of fifty components from the well-mixed-up batch, testing each one of the fifty selected. Of the 50 thus tested, 4 fail and 46 pass. We would expect to find $50 \times 0·04$, or 2 defectives, but the observed number of 4 is twice that expected. Does the difference indicate that there has been a rise in the overall defective rate? To answer this, we pose the ancillary question: what is the probability that, given a sample of 50 from a large batch of components, in which 4 per cent are defective, 4 or more components in such a sample are found to be defective?

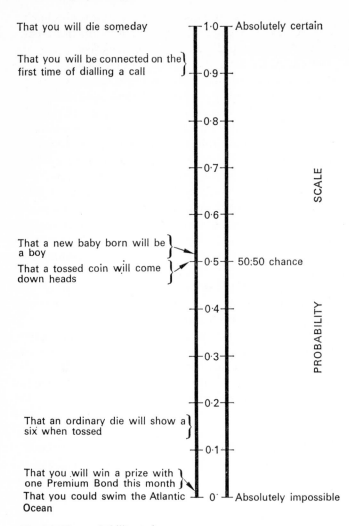

Fig. 2.1. The probability scale

Problem 2.3

I have two apparently identical canvas bags labelled inside A and B respectively, and each filled with similarly sized small beads. Bag A contains 7000 white beads and 3000 red beads, while bag B contains 7000 red beads and 3000 white beads. The beads in each bag have been well mixed. I now move the two bags around so that you do not know which is which, and I ask you to choose one of the bags.

(*i*) What do you assess to be the probability that the bag is the predominantly white bag, i.e. bag A?

(*ii*) Before asking you to assess the probability that the bag is A, you are allowed to draw out 50 beads one at a time, replacing the bead drawn after each drawing: 27 of these beads are white and 23 are red. What do you now assess as the chance that the bag selected is the predominantly white bag?

(*iii*) Instead of drawing 50 beads as in (*ii*), a sample of 4 beads is drawn in the same manner, and all 4 are white. What do you now assess as the probability that the bag is the predominantly white bag?

Problem 2.4

A diagnostic test for cancer is being applied to individuals selected from a large population in which the overall incidence of cancer among the individuals in the population is known to be 5 per cent. A test has been devised to detect cancer but it is, like many such tests, not entirely accurate. Previous experience has shown that there is a 90 per cent chance, if the person does not have cancer, that the test will be negative, whilst if the person does have cancer there is a 90 per cent chance that the test will be positive. An individual is selected by lot from the population and undergoes the test. What is the probability that, if the test gives a positive result, the person concerned has cancer?

What would be the revised chance if the person underwent two separate and quite independent tests of this kind and both tests indicated the presence of cancer?

2.2 The classical theory

In the next two sections we outline briefly the two main schools of thought and definition concerning probability, namely, the classical theory and the relative-frequency theory. Much of the discussion in later sections and other chapters is independent of the particular basis of definition that is accepted, but it does affect the assessment and interpretation of basic probabilities and we return to this topic in Chapter 9.

The classical theory of probability is founded upon the indefinable concept of equally likely events. Suppose that the possible outcomes of an experiment, reduced to their simplest cases, are $c_1, c_2, c_3, \ldots, c_n$, these being mutually exclusive and exhaustive (no other possibilities exist and one of the outcomes must occur). Then, under the classical theory, the statement that these cases are equally likely is understood to mean that:

$$P(c_1) = P(c_2) = \ldots = P(c_n) = \frac{1}{n},$$

where $P(c_i)$ represents the probability of the occurrence of case c_i. Suppose that an event E is said to occur when any one of a particular subset of the cases c_i occurs. By the use of this device, the definition of probability is now extended beyond equally likely events. For example, if a number, a, of the equally likely cases, $c_1, c_2, \ldots, c_n$ favour E, then $P(E)$ is defined as a/n. As the number a varies from its minimum of 0 to its maximum of n, the mathematically possible range of values of $P(E)$ goes from 0 to 1. If any of the c's are favourable to E, then $n-a$ must be unfavourable and hence favourable to the complementary event $\bar{E}$. Thus

$P(\bar{E})=(n-a)/n$, and

$P(E)+P(\bar{E})=1$.

As an example of the classical approach, consider the probability that a six will turn up on the toss of a single die. The six faces of the die constitute six mutually exclusive, exhaustive cases; thus, assuming these cases to be equally likely, we have $P(6)=1/6$. Alternatively, what is the probability of turning up an even number? Representing this event by E, we see that there are three favourable cases: two, four, and six. Hence $P(E)=3/6=\frac{1}{2}$.

The assumption that the faces are equally likely is physically justified only to the extent that the balance of the die and the method of throwing do not favour one face rather than another. The practical impossibility of manufacturing a perfect die, or of making a truly unbiased throw is ignored. On the other hand, when the die and tossing are idealized, equal likelihood or probability is the only reasonable assumption, and in a real situation the effect of imperfections may be negligible.

The so-called subjectivists have taken the classical definition of probability one stage further and defined probability simply as a number, between zero and unity, which represents a degree of belief concerning the occurrence of some future event. A useful way to view such subjective probabilities is to relate them to betting odds. If you were willing to give odds of 4 to 1 that it will rain tomorrow, you implicitly assess the probability of rain at 4 out of 5, or 0·8. Note that, while today's weather may be a factor in assessing these odds, it can hardly be the sole determinant. Tomorrow is another day, and conditions will not necessarily be the same as today. Weather forecasts will therefore lack accuracy to varying degrees.

In much the same way, business men, on the combined basis of historical record, current conditions, and perhaps hunch, may formulate the probability of success of some business venture. This probability basis is not irresponsible subjectivity, but rather a subjective assessment based on a realistic appraisal of the empirical world.

2.3 Relative-frequency theory

The relative-frequency theory of probability is founded upon an observational concept. A record is kept of the number of times (say n_1) that a certain event E occurs in n trials of some appropriate experiment. The ratio n_1/n is called the relative frequency of the event E, and the complementary ratio $(n-n_1)/n$, the relative frequency of $\bar{E}$. Denoting the two relative frequencies by $R(E)$ and $R(\bar{E})$ respectively, we see that each can go from 0 to 1 and that $R(E)+R(\bar{E})=1$.

As an illustration, suppose we have a very large lot of corrugated cases, from which individual cases are drawn at random and each is tested for strength at some defined high pressure. The relative frequency of failures can be calculated as the number of cases examined increases, and Fig. 2.2 shows

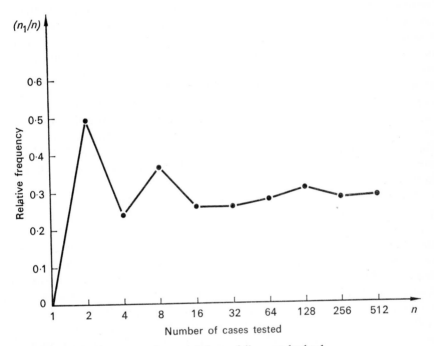

Fig. 2.2. Relative frequency of corrugated case failures under load

a typical result, where n is the number of cases examined and n_1 the number failing. A logarithmic scale is used for n as the oscillations for large n are very small. It is an empirical fact that the proportion of failures stabilizes about some fixed amount as more and more cases are tested. This tendency has been verified experimentally on many occasions and seems to be inherent in the nature of all kinds of random phenomena. Therefore, the existence of a limiting value can be postulated, and the probability $P(E)$ of the event E is defined as the limit approached by the relative frequency when the number of trials increases indefinitely:

$$P(E)=\lim_{n\to\infty}\frac{n_1}{n}=\lim_{n\to\infty}R(E).$$

Similarly,

$$P(\bar{E}) = \underset{n \to \infty}{\text{limit}} \frac{n - n_1}{n} = \lim_{n \to \infty} R(\bar{E})$$

and

$$P(E) + P(\bar{E}) = 1.$$

A definition of this type is known as an operational definition, in that the term defined by it is the result of a prescribed operation or a series of operations. Such definitions have proved very useful in ridding experimental science of a great deal of ambiguity and confusion. From the mathematical standpoint, however, an operational definition is decidedly awkward, because mathematical rigour demands immutable classifications. Therefore, an axiomatic development is more appropriate for the mathematical theory, although empirical estimates of probability are obtained from relative frequencies. A limit in the ordinary sense of mathematics would be more satisfactory as the basis of a mathematical theory, since an operational limit does not have the same rigorous definition as a mathematical one. This difference, between mathematical convergence and the convergence described here as operational, will become increasingly clear as subsequent material is developed.

To illustrate the relative-frequency definition of probability, consider a market research survey of the readership of newspapers which found that, out of 1500 randomly selected adults questioned in the AB social class in one particular area of England, 720 read the *Daily Telegraph*. Hence the relative-frequency of *Daily Telegraph* readers is 0·48 in this particular sample. In so far as the adults questioned constituted a valid and representative cross-section of all AB adults in that area, we may regard the stated relative frequency as an estimate of the probability of reading the *Daily Telegraph* among all AB adults. A true probability really exists only for an instantaneous moment of time, because of changes in both the population itself and in adults' choice of newspaper. It can, however, be estimated to a greater degree of accuracy by taking larger samples at that single instant of time. Strictly speaking, by taking samples over a finite stretch of time, we are not estimating a quantity which is actually the limit of n_1/n as $n \to \infty$, since this limit itself will change over the finite stretch of time. The existence of this limit is, of course, essential to the definition and this example illustrates one of the practical difficulties in empirical estimates of probability. However, empirical estimates are necessary, and we have to accept their inherent limitations.

The two concepts of probability impose philosophical contradictions that have yet to be resolved. For us, however, the crucial question is whether they impose contradictions from the perspective of the decision-maker in business. If a businessman has encountered a particular problem enough times to have available the relative frequencies of similar past events he would be foolish not to use them as probabilities of similar events occurring in the future. On the other hand, if no such relative frequencies are available because the situation is new or unique, he must rely on whatever related and general experience he has had, in addition to whatever specific observations he can make to formulate the probabilities of possible outcomes.

2.4 Properties of relative frequencies

Both theories of probability define probability as a ratio and yield the same basic rules of probability. We now examine some of these rules. We have already seen the first rule, which defines the general character of probability.

RULE 1 (COMPLEMENTARY EVENTS)

For every event E and its complementary event $\bar{E}$,

$$P(E)+P(\bar{E})=1.$$

This rule implies that both $P(E)$ and $P(\bar{E})$ are in the range 0 to 1.

Example 2.1

Two fair dice are tossed. What is the probability that the two dice show different numbers? If E represents the event 'two dice show different numbers', then the complementary event $\bar{E}$ will be that the 'two dice show the same number'. We will first calculate $P(\bar{E})$. If we label the two dice X and Y, there are 36 possible combinations, all equally likely, e.g. (X=1, Y=1), (X=1, Y=2), etc. Of these 36 combinations, 6 will have both X and Y showing the same number, viz., X and Y=1, 2, 3, 4, 5 or 6. Hence

$P(\bar{E})=\frac{6}{36}=\frac{1}{6}$. Then, from rule 1,

$P(E)=1-P(\bar{E})=1-\frac{1}{6}=\frac{5}{6}$.

Note that by calculating here the probability of the complementary event, a great deal of tedious enumeration was avoided.

Consider next two different kinds of event A and B, which may exist simultaneously. The set of all possible basic outcomes can be illustrated in terms of a *sample space* which, in turn, can be subclassified into four mutually exclusive categories:

$(A, B)\ (A, \bar{B}),\ (\bar{A}, B),\ (\bar{A}, \bar{B})$

These categories represent the simultaneous occurrence of events A and B, the simultaneous occurrence of events A and $\bar{B}$, etc. Suppose, for illustration, that employees of a firm are classified, first, by sex (A denotes male) and, second, according to whether they are under 35 years of age (B denotes under 35). Then Fig. 2.3 gives a symbolic representation (sometimes referred to as a *Venn diagram*) of the possibilities in the form of a sample space. The

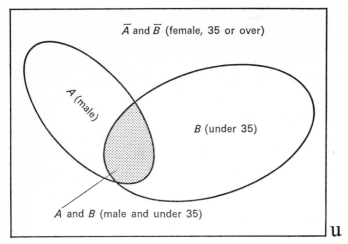

Fig. 2.3. Representation of two events

area marked (A, B) refers to those employees who are both male and under 35 years of age; the area marked $(A, \bar{B})$ represents those employees who are male and at least 35 years of age, etc. The whole area enclosed in the rectangle is referred to as the sample space denoted by (u), and represents all employees. The Venn diagram is only descriptive and areas should not be taken to be precisely proportional to the frequencies of occurrence involved. Denote the respective number of employees in each category as follows:

Category	(A, B)	$(A, \bar{B})$	$(\bar{A}, B)$	$(\bar{A}, \bar{B})$	Total
Number of occurrences	n_1	n_2	n_3	n_4	n

The total number of occurrences of A is $n_1 + n_2$ and of B is $n_1 + n_3$. The corresponding probabilities are:

$$P(A) = \frac{n_1 + n_2}{n} \quad \text{and} \quad P(B) = \frac{n_1 + n_3}{n}$$

By these expressions it is meant that if an employee is selected at random the probability that he is male will be $P(A) = (n_1 + n_2)/n$ and similarly for B, $P(B) = (n_1 + n_3)/n$.

Suppose we now define the composite event $A \cup B$ as the occurrence of either A or B alone or both together. This composite event is then called the *union* of A and B. In the context of the employees, this would imply that we were concerned with the composite event 'either male or under 35 or both male and under 35' and is represented by the area inside either of the ellipses in Fig. 2.3. The definition of event $A \cup B$ is satisfied by each of the categories (A, B), $(A, \bar{B})$, $(\bar{A}, B)$. Hence, we obtain:

Rule 2 (Addition rule)

$$P(A \cup B) = \frac{n_1 + n_2 + n_3}{n}$$

$$= \frac{n_1 + n_2}{n} + \frac{n_1 + n_3}{n} - \frac{n_1}{n}$$

$$= P(A) + P(B) - P(A \cap B),$$

where $P(A \cap B)$ represents the probability of both events A and B occurring, and $A \cap B$ is referred to as the *intersection* of events A and B. In Fig. 2.3 this is represented by the shaded area.

Example 2.2

Alpha and Omega are two weather stations in Wales. Let A and W represent the occurrence of rain at Alpha and Omega respectively, during any randomly selected twenty-four hour period in August. It is found that $P(A) = P(W) = 0.4$ whilst the probability of rain at both places is 0.28. What is the probability of rain at either Alpha or Omega or at both places?

   We require the probability of rain at either A or W, or both A and W. This probability is represented by $P(A \cup W)$. The information we have gives $P(A) = P(W) = 0.4$ and $P(A \cap W) = 0.28$.

   From Rule 2 we have:

$$P(A \cup W) = P(A) + P(W) - P(A \cap W).$$

   Hence,

$$P(A \cup W) = 0.4 + 0.4 - 0.28$$

$$= 0.52.$$

In other words, the probability of rain at A or W, or at both, on a given day is 0.52.

2.5 Conditional probabilities

We now introduce the concept of conditional frequencies. This implies restriction to a particular class, as opposed to the unconditional inclusion of all possibilities. A conditional relative frequency is calculated in the same way as an ordinary (unconditional) relative frequency, except that the calculation is confined to those events which satisfy the prescribed criterion (condition). Thus, suppose people in Kent are classified, first, as to whether they are male or female and, second, as to whether they are employed or not. Then, the relative frequency of males, given that the persons considered are employees, will be the proportion of males among all employed persons in Kent, and not among all persons in Kent whether employed or not.

Put formally, the conditional relative-frequency of A, given B, denoted by $R(A \mid B)$ is simply the proportionate number of occurrences of A among all occurrences of B, and is hence the ratio of the number of simultaneous occurrences of A and B to the total number of occurrences of B:

$$R(A \mid B) = \frac{n_1}{n_1 + n_3} = \frac{n_1/n}{(n_1 + n_3)/n} = \frac{R(A \cap B)}{R(B)}.$$

This leads to the third rule of probability, the so-called multiplication rule.

RULE 3 (MULTIPLICATION RULE)

If neither $P(A)$ nor $P(B)$ is zero, then:

$$P(A \cap B) = P(A)P(B \mid A) = P(B)P(A \mid B).$$

If either $P(A)$ or $P(B)$ is zero, then $P(A \cap B) = 0$.

The expression $P(A \mid B)$ is known as a *conditional probability* and represents the probability of event A occurring, given that event B has occurred. In terms of Fig. 2.3 this is represented by the proportion that the shaded area bears of the whole area in the ellipse B.

Example 2.2 (continued)

For Example 2.2 above, find the two conditional probabilities $P(A \mid W)$ and $P(W \mid A)$. (Note that $P(A \mid W)$ requires the probability of rain at A, given that it is raining at W, and vice versa for $P(W \mid A)$).

$$P(A \mid W) = \frac{P(A \cap W)}{P(W)} = \frac{0 \cdot 28}{0 \cdot 40} = 0 \cdot 70,$$

$$P(W \mid A) = \frac{P(A \cap W)}{P(A)} = \frac{0 \cdot 28}{0 \cdot 40} = 0 \cdot 70.$$

2.6 Extensions

If two events A and B are *mutually exclusive*, then their simultaneous occurrence is impossible and $P(A \cap B) = 0$. This situation is illustrated in Fig. 2.4. For example, if the two events were, first, that a person selected at random from the UK population should be under 21 years of age and, second, that he be a qualified doctor, these events are mutually exclusive, as no one person possesses both these properties. On the other hand, if the two events were 'under 30 years of age' and 'a qualified doctor', these events would not be mutually exclusive and the kind of situation shown in Fig. 2.3 would be relevant.

With mutually exclusive events, we can immediately see that:

(*i*) $P(A \cap B) = 0$, and hence

(*ii*) $P(A \cup B) = P(A) + P(B)$.

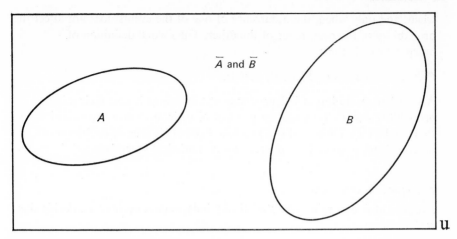

Fig. 2.4. Mutually exclusive events

Example 2.3

A student has to choose two elective courses of study: one from subjects A, B and C, the other from subjects D, E and F. He cannot choose to take A with D, or B with E, or C with F; otherwise the choice is unrestricted. Among a group of students the proportions taking each subject are as follows:

Subject A 0·2   Subject D 0·3
Subject B 0·2   Subject E 0·4
Subject C 0·6   Subject F 0·3

What is the probability that a student chosen at random:

(*i*) is doing either A or D as one of his electives?
(*ii*) is doing A and E as his two electives?

For (*i*) we need:

$$P(A \cup D) = P(A) + P(D),$$

since A and D are mutually exclusive events.

Now $P(A) = 0·2$ and $P(D) = 0·3$, hence $P(A \cup D) = 0·5$.
For (*ii*) we need:

$$P(A \cap E) = P(A)P(E \mid A) \quad \text{or} \quad P(E)P(A \mid E).$$

While we know the value of $P(A)$, or $P(E)$, we do not know the value of $P(E \mid A)$ or $P(A \mid E)$ from the data given. Hence, we cannot obtain the required probability from the data given.

Another case of special importance arises when the events are *independent*. In the probability sense, two events A and B are said to be independent

B

when, and only when, the occurrence of one of the events does not affect the probability of the occurrence of the other. The formal definition of independence is that:

$$P(B \mid A) = P(B) \quad \text{or} \quad P(A \mid B) = P(A).$$

A sufficient definition of independence of two events is that their joint probability $P(A \cap B)$ equals the product of their respective probabilities, $P(A)$ and $P(B)$. Thus, $P(A \cap B) = P(A).P(B)$. This type of definition of independence is sometimes referred to as 'statistical independence'.

Example 2.2 (continued)

Are rain at A and rain at W statistically independent events? To decide this we calculate:

$$P(A).P(W) = 0.4 \times 0.4 = 0.16,$$

and note that this is not equal to the value of $P(A \cap W)$ calculated earlier as 0·28. Hence, the two events A and W are not statistically independent.

Example 2.4

An electronic device has two independent components A and B in series. The device will not work if either, or both, of the components are defective. The probability that A is defective is 0·05 and that B is defective is 0·02. What is the probability that the device fails?

Let $P(A) = 0.05$ and $P(B) = 0.02$. Then $P(\bar{A}) = 0.95$ and $P(\bar{B}) = 0.98$.

Since defectives among the two components are independent, the probability that both components are good is:

$$P(\bar{A} \cap \bar{B}) = P(\bar{A})P(\bar{B})$$

$$= 0.95 \times 0.98$$

$$= 0.931.$$

Hence, the required probability will be:

$$1 - P(\bar{A} \cap \bar{B}) = 1 - 0.931 = 0.069.$$

(Note that this is not equal to the sum or the product of the separate probabilities of the two components being defective.)

2.7 Generalizations

The various probability rules stated above for two events can be generalized for more than two events. These generalizations will now be given without formal proof, but their method of derivation is briefly indicated.

RULE 4 (ADDITION RULE FOR MUTUALLY EXCLUSIVE EVENTS)

$$P(A \cup B \cup \ldots \cup M) = P(A) + P(B) + P(C) + \ldots + P(M)$$

This is a straightforward generalization of Rule 2 and states that, for a series of mutually exclusive events, the probability that one of them occurs is the sum of the separate probabilities that each occurs by itself. Thus, if the four mutually exclusive events were that, on drawing a card at random from an ordinary pack, it was a club (A), diamond (B), heart (C) or spade (D) respectively, then $P(A \cup B \cup C)$ would represent the probability of drawing a club or a diamond or a heart and would equal:

$$P(A) + P(B) + P(C) = \tfrac{1}{4} + \tfrac{1}{4} + \tfrac{1}{4} = \tfrac{3}{4}.$$

RULE 5 (ADDITION RULE FOR MANY EVENTS)

From Rule 2, we can write for three events A, B and C:

$$P(A \cup B \cup C) = P(S \cup C) \quad \text{where } S = A \cup B$$
$$= P(S) + P(C) - P(S \cap C)$$
$$= P(A) + P(B) - P(A \cap B) + P(C) - P(S \cap C).$$

Now the symbol $(S \cap C)$ means that C occurs in conjunction with A or B or both, and has the same logical import as the expression $(A \cap C) \cup (B \cap C)$, since the simultaneous occurrence of $(A \cap C)$ and $(B \cap C)$ implies no more nor less than the simultaneous occurrence of A, B, C. Consequently:

$$P(S \cap C) = P[(A \cap C) \cup (B \cap C)] = P(A \cap C) + P(B \cap C) - P(A \cap B \cap C),$$

and, hence,

$$P(A \cup B \cup C) = P(A) + P(B) + P(C) - P(A \cap B) - P(A \cap C) - P(B \cap C) +$$
$$+ P(A \cap B \cap C).$$

This can be generalized still further so that, with t events, $A_1, A_2, \ldots A_t$, the probability $P(A_1 \cup A_2 \cup A_3 \ldots \cup A_t)$ is equal to the algebraic sum of the probabilities of the events in all distinct combinations: singles, pairs, triples, $\ldots$ t-tuples. The sign is plus for the odd combinations (singles, triples, etc.) and minus for the even combinations (pairs, quadruples, etc.). The general expression can be written as:

$$P(A_1 \cup A_2 \cup \ldots \cup A_t) = \sum_i P(A_i) - \sum_{\substack{\text{all } i,j \\ i \neq j}} P(A_i \cap A_j) + \sum_{\substack{\text{all } i,j,k \\ i \neq j \neq k}} P(A_i \cap A_j \cap A_k)$$

$$\ldots (-1)^{t-1} P(A_1 \cap A_2 \cap \ldots \cap A_t).$$

Example 2.5

Three letters are written and three matching envelopes are prepared. The letters are placed in the envelopes at random. What is the probability that at least one of the letters gets into the correct envelope?

Denote the event that the ith letter ($i=1, 2, 3$) gets into the correct envelope by A_i. Then,

$P(A_i)=\frac{1}{3}$ (given no other information)

$P(A_i \cap A_j)=\frac{1}{3}\cdot\frac{1}{2}$ (assuming $i\neq j$)

$P(A_1 \cap A_2 \cap A_3)=\frac{1}{6}$.

These probabilities can all be readily established by enumerating the possible cases. For example, the second probability arises because $P(A_i)=\frac{1}{3}$ and $P(A_j \mid A_i)=\frac{1}{2}$, since at the second stage there are then two envelopes left and an equal chance of putting the letter in either.

The event required, of at least one letter in the correct envelope, is denoted by $(A_1 \cup A_2 \cup A_3)$, and, hence, the required probability is:

$$P(A_1 \cup A_2 \cup A_3)=\sum_i P(A_i)- \sum_{i\neq j} P(A_i \cap A_j)+P(A_1 \cap A_2 \cap A_3)$$

$$=3\times\frac{1}{3}-3\times\frac{1}{6}+\frac{1}{6}=\frac{2}{3}.$$

The probability that all the letters go into the wrong envelopes will be $1-\frac{2}{3}$, or $\frac{1}{3}$. The reader is left to demonstrate for himself that the latter probability does not vary very much, whatever the number of letters and envelopes concerned. As the number of letters increases, the probability approaches the value 0·368.

RULE 6 (GENERAL COMPOUND PROBABILITY)

Consider three events A, B, C which can occur either singly or in combination, and let X denote the simultaneous occurrence of A and B. Then the two compound events $(A \cap B \cap C)$ and $(X \cap C)$ are equivalent, or:

$(A \cap B \cap C)\equiv(X \cap C)$

and $P(A \cap B \cap C)=P(X)P(C \mid X)=P(A)P(B \mid A)P(C \mid A \cap B)$.

Continuing in the same vein, we can express the joint probability of the occurrence of any finite number M of events $A, B, C, \ldots M$ as the product of M terms. The first term is the unconditional probability of any particular one of the events chosen arbitrarily; the second is the conditional probability of any particular one of the remaining events, given the occurrence of the one first selected; and so on, for the remaining events. Thus, the general term will be the conditional probability of any particular one of the remaining events given the occurrence of those already chosen. In all, there are $M(M-1)(M-2)(M-3)\ldots 3.2.1$, or $M!$ (pronounced 'M factorial') equivalent expressions for this same joint probability, according to the order in which we place the various events. The general rule thus states:

$$P(A \cap B \cap C \ldots M)=P(A)P(B \mid A)P(C \mid A \cap B)\ldots P(M \mid A \cap B \cap C \ldots L)$$

where $A, B, C \ldots M$ can be placed in any order desired, so that equivalent expressions can be obtained by interchanging the letters A, B, C, etc.

If the events are all independent, then the expression for the joint probability reduces to the product of the individual probabilities, giving:

$$P(A \cap B \cap C \ldots M) = P(A)P(B)P(C) \ldots P(M).$$

2.8 Illustrations of principles

The ideas developed thus far equip us to solve a wide variety of basic problems. The following examples are presented in order to put the ideas and definitions to work and to demonstrate the application of the general principles of probability.

Example 2.6

In a survey of 100 middle-class families, the numbers that had read recent monthly issues of *Homes and Gardens* were found to be:

June only	18	April	48
June but not May	23	April and May	8
April and June	8	None of the	
June	26	three months	24

(*i*) How many read the May issue?
(*ii*) How many read at least two consecutive issues?
(*iii*) How many read the April issue, but not the May issue?
(*iv*) How many read the May and June issues, but not the April issue?

Figure 2.5(a) gives an appropriate Venn diagram for this problem with the data listed above inserted. These data can then be reduced to that shown in Fig. 2.5(b) by simple addition and/or subtraction of numbers. The data are now in a suitable form to answer the questions posed.

(*i*) $10+3+5=18$.
(*ii*) April/May $=5+3=8$.
    May/June $=3$, but none of these are new readers.
    Hence, required answer is 8.
(*iii*) $35+5=40$.
(*iv*) None.

†*Example 2.7*

The letter A denotes that a family has a car, $\bar{A}$ that it does not; B, $\bar{B}$, $\bar{\bar{B}}$ denote that the family has an annual income under £1200, between £1200 and £2000, or over £2000 respectively. Certain probabilities are known:

$P(A)=0.60$ $P(B \mid A)=0.35$

$P(\bar{B})=0.50$ $P(\bar{B} \mid \bar{A})=0.50$

$P(\bar{\bar{B}})=0.10$

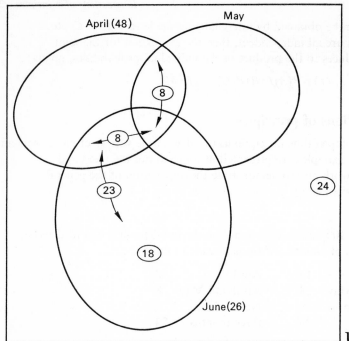

Fig. 2.5(a). Venn diagram for readership survey

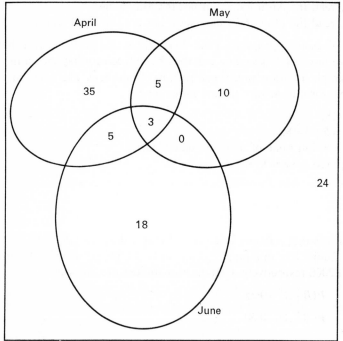

Fig. 2.5(b). Readership survey data reduced

(*i*) Find the probability that a family has either a car or an income in the top range, or both.

(*ii*) Find the probability that a family has both a car and an income in the middle band.

(*iii*) Find the probability that a family does not have a car given that it has an income in the middle range.

It is probably simplest to start by finding the probabilities of all the possible classifications and then picking out those required. Figure 2.6 gives a Venn

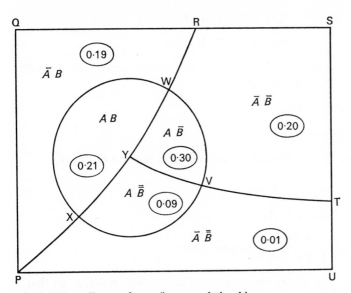

Fig. 2.6. Venn diagram for car/income relationships

diagram with all the possible classifications included, this time as probabilities (or proportions) rather than numbers. The universal set in this instance will be unity. Thus, area RSTY represents $P(\bar{B})$, which can be subdivided into RSTVW representing $P(\bar{A} \cap B)$, and YWV representing $P(A \cap \bar{B})$. Now:

$$P(\bar{A} \cap \bar{B}) = P(\bar{A})P(\bar{B} \mid \bar{A})$$

$$= 0 \cdot 40 \times 0 \cdot 50$$

$$= 0 \cdot 20,$$

and $P(\bar{A} \cap \bar{B}) + P(A \cap \bar{B}) = P(\bar{B})$

or $0 \cdot 20 + P(A \cap \bar{B}) = 0 \cdot 50$

giving $P(A \cap \bar{B}) = 0 \cdot 30.$

The probabilities for the top right-hand sector of Fig. 2.5 can now be entered. For the left-hand sector we have:

$$P(A \cap B) = P(A)P(B \mid A)$$

$$= 0.60 \times 0.35 = 0.21,$$

and $P(\bar{A} \cap B) + P(A \cap B) = P(B)$

or $P(\bar{A} \cap B) = 0.4 - 0.21 = 0.19.$

Hence, $P(A \cap \bar{B}) = P(A) - P(A \cap B) - P(A \cap \bar{B})$

$$= 0.60 - 0.21 - 0.30 = 0.09$$

and $P(\bar{A} \cap \bar{\bar{B}}) = P(\bar{A}) - P(\bar{A} \cap B) - P(\bar{A} \cap \bar{B})$

$$= 0.40 - 0.19 - 0.20 = 0.01.$$

The answers for the specific problems posed may now be picked out. Item (*i*) requires $P(A \cup \bar{\bar{B}})$. This can be expressed as:

$$P(A \cup \bar{\bar{B}}) = P(A) + P(\bar{\bar{B}}) - P(A \cap \bar{\bar{B}})$$

$$= 0.60 + 0.10 - 0.09 = 0.61.$$

Item (*ii*) requires $P(A\bar{B})$. From the Venn diagram this can be directly read off as 0.30.

Item (*iii*) requires $P(\bar{A} \mid \bar{B})$. Now:

$$P(\bar{A} \cap \bar{B}) = P(\bar{B})P(\bar{A} \mid \bar{B})$$

Hence, $P(\bar{A} \mid \bar{B}) = \dfrac{P(\bar{A} \cap \bar{B})}{P(\bar{B})} = \dfrac{0.20}{0.50} = 0.40.$

In other words, the probability that a family does not have a car, given that it has an income in the middle range, is 0.40.

Example 2.8

There are six directors on the board of a company, including the managing director who has an extra casting vote in the event of a tie when the board votes on some issue. Although each member of the board makes up his own mind, each usually agrees independently of the others with the managing director on three-quarters of the issues on which it is found necessary to vote.

(*i*) What is the probability that the managing director will be defeated on a given issue?

(*ii*) If two other members, X and Y, agree always to vote as X decides, what is now the probability of the managing director's defeat on a given issue?

(*i*) The two situations where the managing director loses are *FAAAA* and *AAAAA* where *F*=for and *A*=against, and the five letters indicate the other five members of the board (order not being taken into account).

The one F member can be one of five, and hence the overall probability of defeat is:

$$5\{(\tfrac{3}{4}) \times (\tfrac{1}{4}) \times (\tfrac{1}{4}) \times (\tfrac{1}{4}) \times (\tfrac{1}{4})\} + \{(\tfrac{1}{4}) \times (\tfrac{1}{4}) \times (\tfrac{1}{4}) \times (\tfrac{1}{4}) \times (\tfrac{1}{4})\} = 5(\tfrac{3}{4})(\tfrac{1}{4})^4 + (\tfrac{1}{4})^5 = \tfrac{1}{64}.$$

(*ii*) The possible arrangements for defeat are similar to (*i*), namely, $F\overline{A}\overline{A}AA$ and $\overline{A}\overline{A}AAA$, where the two barred As indicate voting agreement. In the first arrangement, three of the board members can be the one member of the board who is going to vote for the managing director. In the second arrangement, the four board members, excluding Y, must decide to vote against the managing director, whereupon Y will also vote against. The revised probability will now be:

$$3\{(\tfrac{3}{4}) \times (\tfrac{1}{4}) \times (\tfrac{1}{4}) \times (\tfrac{1}{4})\} + \{(\tfrac{1}{4}) \times (\tfrac{1}{4}) \times (\tfrac{1}{4}) \times (\tfrac{1}{4})\} = 3(\tfrac{3}{4})(\tfrac{1}{4})^3 + (\tfrac{1}{4})^4 = \tfrac{5}{128},$$

which is some $2\tfrac{1}{2}$ times the previous probability. This result can be generalized to show how a small minority on a committee or board can exercise great, and apparently disproportionate, power over the group decisions if they decide to act together consistently when the other members of the committee are acting independently of each other.

Example 2.9

Suppose there are n different applicants for a certain job. Three interviewers are asked independently to rank the applicants according to their suitability for the job. It is decided that an applicant will be hired if he is ranked first by at least two of the three interviewers. If this criterion is not met, none of the applicants will be hired. What fraction of the sets of possible rankings would lead to the filling of the job from among the n men applying?

We solve this problem by first finding the converse, namely, the fraction of possible rankings which do not lead to an acceptance, and then subtracting this result from 1. The total number of possible rankings is $(n!)^3$ since each interviewer can rank the men in $n!$ possible orders. If a particular set of rankings does not lead to the acceptance of any applicant, it must imply that each interviewer has put a different man in first place. This can be done in $n(n-1)(n-2)$ different ways. For each possible first choice there are then $\{(n-1)!\}^3$ ways in which the remaining $n-1$ men can be ranked by the interviewers. Thus, the number of rankings which do not lead to acceptance is the product of these two numbers, namely:

$$n(n-1)(n-2)\{(n-1)!\}^3.$$

Dividing by the total number of possible rankings gives:

$$\frac{(n-1)(n-2)}{n^2}$$

as the fraction of rankings which fail to accept a candidate, giving:

$$1 - \frac{(n-1)(n-2)}{n^2} \quad \text{or} \quad \frac{3n-2}{n^2}$$

as the fraction which lead to acceptance. For three applicants this fraction
is $\frac{7}{9}$; for five applicants it is $\frac{13}{25}$; for ten applicants it is $\frac{28}{100}$. Hence, with few
applicants, this kind of procedure would be very haphazard for selection
purposes, since even if the interviewers are ranking completely at random,
so that each ranking arrangement is equally likely, there is a good chance of
some candidate being accepted on the basis of the reports. Only when n is
very large indeed does this probability of selecting an applicant through
random rankings become negligible.

†*Example* 2.10

An unbiased coin is tossed n times. What is the probability that no two
consecutive tossings give the same result, assuming that at each tossing the
coin is equally likely to come down heads or tails?

If the first tossing is a head (H), the second must be a tail (T), etc., giving
the order $HTHT\ldots$ for n tosses. Alternatively, and mutually exclusively,
the order $THTH\ldots$ for n terms would satisfy the conditions laid down.
Now the probability of either of these sequences is:

$\frac{1}{2} \times \frac{1}{2} \times \frac{1}{2} \ldots$ for n terms

and, hence, the required probability is twice this amount, or:

$2 \times (\frac{1}{2})^n = (\frac{1}{2})^{n-1}$.

†*Example* 2.11

The probability of a salesman making a sale at a single customer call is $\frac{1}{6}$.
What is the probability that he will make at least one sale in the next five
calls? What is the probability that he will make four or more sales in these
same five calls? (Assume that the calls are independent of each other as
regards outcome.)

The probability of making at least one sale is equal to one minus the
probability of no sales being made. The probability of the latter is $(1 - \frac{1}{6})^5$

or $(\frac{5}{6})^5$; and hence the required probability is:

$1 - (\frac{5}{6})^5 = 0 \cdot 598$.

The event of 'four or more sales' is the sum of two mutually exclusive
events: namely, exactly four sales (and one no-sale) and exactly five sales. The
probability of the former is $5 \times (\frac{1}{6})^4 \times (\frac{5}{6})$, since the no-sale can be on any one
of the five calls. The probability of the latter is $(\frac{1}{6})^5$. Hence, the required
probability is the sum of these two, namely, $0 \cdot 0033$.

Example 2.12

A large square board is divided into a series of equal squares in the fashion
of a chessboard, each square having a side of 2 in. A circular coin, of diameter
$1 \cdot 5$ in. is dropped at random on the board and is wholly contained within it.

What is the probability that the coin is wholly within one of the small 2 in. squares?

For the coin to be wholly within a square, its centre must fall within one of a set of smaller squares of side 0·5 in. that are centrally positioned inside each 2 in. square (see Fig. 2.7). This is true of every square over the whole

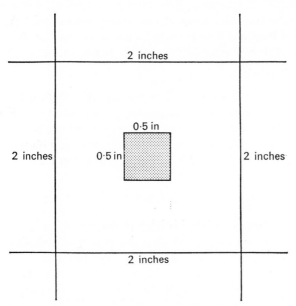

Fig. 2.7. Permitted region for centre of coin

board. Suppose there are n squares on the board, then the required probability of the coin being inside a square is:

$$\frac{\text{Total area of small 0·5 in. squares}}{\text{Total area of 2 in. squares}} = \frac{n(\frac{1}{2})^2}{n2^2} = \frac{1}{16},$$

the number of squares on the board being immaterial.

The probability is surprisingly small. Indeed, if the ratio of the diameter of the coin to the side of the squares on the board is k (where $k < 1$) then the probability of the coin falling wholly inside a square is $(1-k)^2$. If k is near 1, this probability is very small indeed—a result that is well known to those who organize charity fêtes and funfairs!

†*Example* 2.13

Which event has the greater probability: throwing at least one six in four throws of a single six-sided die, or at least one double six in twenty-four throws of two such dice? This problem is known as 'Chevalier de Méré's paradox' because he was an inveterate gambler and thought, from straightforward proportionality, that the two probabilities ought to be the same. He blamed mathematics for his gambling losses which resulted from the unequal probabilities of the two events.

The first probability is one minus the probability of throwing no sixes with the four tossings of the die. This probability is $(\frac{5}{6})^4$ and, hence, the required probability is $1-(\frac{5}{6})^4=\frac{671}{1296}=0.5177$.

The probability of a double six with a single throw of two dice is $\frac{1}{6}\times\frac{1}{6}=\frac{1}{36}$. Hence, the probability of at least one double six in 24 throws of two dice is one minus the probability of throwing no double sixes in 24 throws, or:

$$1-(1-\tfrac{1}{36})^{24}=1-(\tfrac{35}{36})^{24}=0.4914.$$

Hence the probability of at least one six within four tossings of a single die is the more likely event, and de Méré's idea that the two probabilities were the same is false. Incidentally, the difference between the two probabilities is very small (0.0263), which gives some indication of the volume of gambling that must have been indulged in by de Méré if he was able to detect the existence of a difference.

Example 2.14

This problem is sometimes referred to as the birthday problem and is a generalization of Problem 2.1 posed on page 11. In a group of n individuals, what is the probability that there is at least one duplication of birthday (month and day)? For simplicity, we will ignore the existence of leap years and will consider a year of 365 days, assuming that an individual's birthday is equally likely to fall on each day of the year.

Attacking the problem head on is rather tricky, but we can avoid a lot of difficulty by calculating the converse probability, namely the probability that there are no duplicates, implying that all the n birthdays are on different dates. The required probability is then one minus this probability. If n is 366 or greater, there must be at least one duplication and, hence, the required probability is 1. We will, therefore, consider only the case where n is 365 or less.

The 'no duplication' event is a multiple event. For the n individuals there are 365^n ways in which the n birthdays can be selected. If the n birthdays are all different, then the first can be selected in 365 ways, the second in 364 ways, the third in 363 ways, and the nth in $(365-n+1)$ or $(366-n)$ ways. Hence, the total number of ways of choosing n birthdays with no duplication is:

$$365\times364\times363\ldots\times(366-n)=\frac{365!}{(365-n)!}$$

This expression is sometimes referred to as the *permutation* of 365 objects n at a time. In general the permutation of N objects n at a time is equal to $N!/(N-n)!$

The probability of at least one duplicate birthday is accordingly:

$$1 - \frac{365!}{(365-n)! \, 365^n}$$

Specimen values of this probability for various values of n are as follows:

n	Probability	n	Probability
10	0·1169	35	0·8143
15	0·2529	40	0·8912
20	0·4114	50	0·9704
25	0·5687	75	0·9996
30	0·7063	100	1·0000

(to 4 decimal places)

The probabilities are much higher than most people guess on the basis of pure intuition, and it becomes an even money chance that there will be at least one duplication of birthday when n reaches 23, and for 25 individuals, as in Problem 2.1, the probability is approximately 0·57. These results seem surprising to most people, but experiments with groups of students, or pages of the *Army List*, or *Who's Who*, will rapidly show that the result is not inconsistent with practical observations.

Example 2.15

There is at present only one brand (X) of tinned dog food on the market in Utopia. A manufacturer is considering the introduction of a new tinned brand (Y) of dog food and wants to estimate the proportion of the dog food market that the new brand will succeed in capturing. To do this he puts the new brand Y on sale in a small test market area and observes through market research the way in which consumers switch from one brand to another. This brand-switching pattern is described by the probabilities in Table 2.1.

Table 2.1

Switch from brand	Switch to brand	
	X	Y
X	0·4	0·6
Y	0·3	0·7

This table shows, for example, that if a consumer buys brand X on one occasion, the probability that he buys brand Y on the next occasion is 0·6.

Now, if these probabilities remain constant, the market will eventually settle down into a state of equilibrium. We can estimate the equilibrium shares as follows:

Initially brand X has 100 per cent of the market. After the first round of purchases, 40 per cent will be with brand X (and 60 per cent with brand Y). After the next round brand X will have:

$$40 \times 0{\cdot}4 + 60 \times 0{\cdot}3 = 34 \text{ per cent}$$

and brand Y will accordingly have 66 per cent.

The following round gives brand X with:

$$34 \times 0{\cdot}4 + 66 \times 0{\cdot}3 = 33{\cdot}4 \text{ per cent.}$$

A further round gives brand X with:

$$33{\cdot}4 \times 0{\cdot}4 + 66{\cdot}6 \times 0{\cdot}3 = 33{\cdot}3 \text{ per cent,}$$

and it is fairly clear that the equilibrium position is going to leave brand X with a third of the market and hence, brand Y with two-thirds. Note that this has been a very much over simplified example, as it is unlikely that the transition probabilities would remain constant, even for a relatively short period of time.

Example 2.16

A sample of three precision-made engineering pieces is drawn from a lot of ten such pieces containing two defectives. Figure 2.8 shows the possible

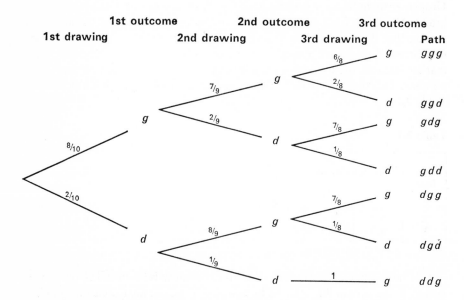

Fig. 2.8. Probability tree for defectives

arrangements drawn in the form of a probability tree. The first piece drawn can be either good (*g*) or defective (*d*), so that there are again two branches. This is the case at each drawing, except a drawing which follows the initial drawings of two defectives in succession. The latter situation arises in that there are only two defectives in the lot, and hence there is only one possible outcome on the third drawing in this situation.

On the first drawing we assign $P(g) = \frac{8}{10}$, and hence $P(d) = \frac{2}{10}$ as $d \equiv g$. For the second drawing we assign $P(d \mid g) = \frac{2}{9}$ for the probability that the second piece chosen is defective, given that the first piece chosen was good. This is because in the second drawing there are only nine pieces remaining, of which, under these conditions, two are defective. The other probabilities are enumerated in a similar manner.

The probability that the sample will consist of three good pieces is the combined probability that the first, second and third pieces will all be good. This is simply the product:

$$\frac{8}{10} \times \frac{7}{9} \times \frac{6}{8} = \frac{7}{15}.$$

To obtain the probability that the sample contains exactly one defective, we must obtain the combined probability of all paths which result in two good pieces and one defective. There are three such paths, *ggd* (path 2), *gdg* (path 3) and *dgg* (path 5). The respective probabilities are:

$$\frac{8}{10} \times \frac{7}{9} \times \frac{2}{8} = \frac{7}{45}, \quad \frac{8}{10} \times \frac{2}{9} \times \frac{7}{8} = \frac{7}{45}, \quad \text{and} \quad \frac{2}{10} \times \frac{8}{9} \times \frac{7}{8} = \frac{7}{45}.$$

Therefore the probability of exactly one defective in the sample is:

$$\frac{7}{45} + \frac{7}{45} + \frac{7}{45} = \frac{7}{15}.$$

2.9 Comment

This chapter has been concerned with the basic notions of probability and, as such, provides a foundation for much of the later work in this book. The next two chapters are concerned with *random variables*. In most of the problems we will meet we are interested in a particular numerical aspect or aspects of an investigation. It may be the income of an interviewee, the number of bars of soap he bought last month, or the breaking strength of a steel wire. All these quantities are what we term random variables in that they are a particular number associated with the outcome of an event. In some instances the variable is discrete (e.g. the number of bars of soap bought), while in others it is continuous (e.g. the breaking strength of the steel wire). These two types of random variable are discussed in Chapters 3 and 4 respectively.

Exercises on Chapter 2

1 A committee is composed of four men and six women. A subcommittee of five is to be chosen at random. What is the probability that it will be composed of:

(*i*) two men and three women?
(*ii*) four men and one woman?

2 In a code such as morse, letters and numbers are formed by sequences of symbols that are either dots or dashes. Suppose that all letters or numbers have either one, two, three or four symbols. How many letters and numbers can be represented?

3 Three men and three women are available for tennis. In how many different ways can a game of mixed doubles be made up from the players available? (In mixed doubles one man and one woman are partnered against another man and woman pair.)

4 A machine shop has three milling machines, five lathes, six drill presses and four grinders. In how many ways can a part be routed through the machine shop if it must first be ground, then milled, then turned on a lathe and then drilled? In how many ways can a part be routed if these four operations can be performed in any order?

5 A company wants to obtain three tenders for a subcontract and there are five possible suppliers, A, B, C, D, E. The general manager decides to pick three of the five suppliers at random and invite each of them to tender. Subsequently he discovers that the suppliers have certain interlocking directorships which might lead to collusion and higher tenders. The suppliers in question are A and B; C and D; C, D and E. What is the probability that at least one of these combinations would arise among a randomly chosen set of three companies?

6 Twenty identical boxes, each containing a dozen wine glasses, were sent by post from a departmental store. The number of glasses broken in each box was recorded at the end of the journey to give the following figures:

0, 0, 1, 0, 0, 2, 3, 0, 1, 1, 4, 0, 2, 1, 0, 0, 0, 1, 3, 0.

Calculate the relative frequencies of the following events in these 20 trials:

(*i*) E_1: at most one glass is broken;
(*ii*) E_2: exactly 2 glasses are broken;
(*iii*) E_3: at least 3 glasses are broken;
(*iv*) E_4: an odd number of glasses is broken;
(*v*) $(E_1 \cup E_2 \cup E_3)$;
(*vi*) $(E_1 \cup E_4)$.

7 There are two types of battery M and N. Type M has eight cells and type N six cells. Exhaustive tests on a large number of batteries show that after twelve months of intensive use the relative frequency of the number of active cells, k, left is as shown in Table 2.2.

Table 2.2

	k Relative frequency	0	1	2	3	4	5	6	7	8
Type M		0·01	0·03	0·04	0·07	0·13	0·18	0·30	0·21	0·05

	k Relative frequency	0	1	2	3	4	5	6
Type N		0·06	0·09	0·12	0·20	0·25	0·19	0·09

Type M operates satisfactorily with five or more active cells, type N with three or more active cells. A piece of equipment contains two batteries, one of type M and one of type N. What is the probability that after twelve months of intensive use:

(*i*) Both batteries are operating satisfactorily?
(*ii*) At least one battery is operating satisfactorily?

8 On one particular day, five residents in a town telephone for a local electrician, of whom three are listed in the local directory. If each resident selects an electrician at random from the directory, what is the probability that all three electricians are telephoned at least once?

9 Thirty light bulbs are on display in a supermarket, and three are defective. A customer picks out four bulbs at random. What is the probability (*i*) that all four are good? (*ii*) that exactly two are defective?

10 An electrical mechanism containing four switches will fail to operate unless all of them are closed. In the probability sense, the switches are independent with regard to closing or failure to close, and for each switch the probability of failure to close is 0·1. Find the probability of failure of the whole mechanism (neglecting all sources of failure except switches).

11 In a computer punch room with a large number of operators, 5 per cent of the cards which are punched contain errors. A spot check is made on the work of a certain operator by taking four cards at random from her output. Two of these cards are found to contain errors. Would you consider that this is convincing evidence that the operator's work is substandard?

12 Suppose that the probability of failure of a valve mechanism on a spacecraft is 0·1. How many valve mechanisms, operating independently, would one need to install to be 99·9 per cent sure that at least one of them would operate satisfactorily?

13 A industrial inspection rule reads: 'Draw a random sample of four items from the batch. Test each item for breaking strength and accept the entire batch provided that all four items break above 1000 lb.' A batch comes along which has 10 per cent of its items with breaking strength (unknown to the buyer) below 1000 lb. What is the probability that such a batch will be accepted under the inspection procedure? Assume that the batch size is so large that we can ignore the effect that a small depletion of four items will have on the probability that an individual item will fail the test.

14 A lift starts with seven passengers and stops at each of ten succeeding floors at one of which each passenger will get out. A passenger is equally likely to get out at any of the floors and the passengers are independent of each other. Find the probability that all the passengers leave the lift at different floors.

15 Two inspectors A and B independently inspect the same lot of items. Four per cent of the items are actually defective. It turns out that:

5 per cent of the items are called defective by A.

6 per cent of the items are called defective by B.

2 per cent of the items are correctly called defective by A.

3 per cent of the items are correctly called defective by B.

4 per cent of the items are called defective by both A and B.

1 per cent of the items are correctly called defective by both A and B.

   (*i*) Draw a Venn diagram showing percentages of items in the eight possible disjoint classes generated by the classification of the two inspectors and the various classifications of the items.

   (*ii*) What proportion of the items that are not defective are classified as defective by either A or B or both?

   (*iii*) What proportion of the items that are really defective are missed by both the inspectors?

16 Individuals are classified according to whether or not they possess a house, a car and a washing machine. Some key information is as follows:

30 per cent own both house and car.

40 per cent own a car, but not a house.

10 per cent own a house, but not a car.

60 per cent own a washing machine.

40 per cent own both a car and a washing machine.

5 per cent own a house and a washing machine, but not a car.

20 per cent own a house and a car, but not a washing machine.

What is the probability that an individual drawn at random owns:

(*i*) All three items?
(*ii*) None of the three items?

17 A, B and C agree that the odd man out when they each toss a coin will pay for the drinks. (If they all show the same side of their coins, the tossing will be repeated.) After tossing their coins B has the only tail, but in handing back A's coin notices that it has heads on both sides. B is naturally very upset and angrily demands a retossing with fresh (and inspected) coins. What are the relative chances, before tossing commences, of A, B and C losing and having to pay for the drinks if B and C both use 'fair' coins, and A uses his double-headed coin?

18 The probability of winning a prize on a single toss of a die is p. There are n contestants for the prize. The first contestant tries and, if he fails, he passes the die to the second contestant. The second contestant then tries to win with a single toss of the die, and, if he fails, passes the die to the third contestant, etc. This procedure continues until somebody wins, while if all n contestants fail, the process is repeated with the same order of contestants until a winner emerges. What is the probability that the kth contestant $(k \leqslant n)$ is the ultimate winner?

19 Suppose that, in flight, aeroplane engines fail with probability q, independently from engine to engine, and that a plane makes a successful flight if at least half of its engines run. For what values of q is a two-engine plane to be preferred to a four-engine one? (The probability that an engine does not fail is $p = 1 - q$.)

20 In a multiple choice examination there are four possible answers to each question, of which only one is correct. If a student knows the right answer, he has a probability of one of choosing correctly; if he does not know and guesses at random, he has a probability of 0·25 of choosing correctly. Assume that a good student will know 90 per cent of the answers, a poor student only 50 per cent.

(*i*) If a good student has given the correct answer, what is the probability that he was only guessing?
(*ii*) If a poor student has given the correct answer, what is the probability that he was only guessing?

21 A series of parallel straight lines, a distance d apart from each other, are ruled on a large horizontal table. A needle of length k (less than d) is tossed at random on the table. What is the probability that it crosses a line?

(Hint: Assume that all positions of the centre of the needle are equally likely and also that all angles which the needle makes to some fixed direction are equally likely. The solution requires the use of integral calculus.)

22 A ball of diameter c inches is thrown at random against a trellis composed of bars of width b inches crossing one another at right-angles so as to leave openings of a inches square. What is the chance of the ball passing clear through the trellis? (It is assumed that c is less than a.)

3 Discrete random variables

3.1 Introduction

A *random variable* is any variable quantity whose precise value cannot be completely predicted in advance of the event to which the variable refers. Some examples of discrete random variables, i.e. random variables which can only take a finite number of distinct values, are:

(*i*) the number of absentees from an office tomorrow;
(*ii*) the number of lorries arriving at a warehouse in the next hour;
(*iii*) the number of shares quoted on the Stock Exchange whose prices will rise tomorrow;
(*iv*) the number of defective valves in a batch of 1000 valves;
(*v*) the number of building contractors bidding for a contract.

All these are random variables only before the event concerned; the actual values that occurred can be obtained after the event, and probability ceases to be relevant. For planning and decision-making purposes before the event, however, they are random variables in that the precise value that the variable concerned will take is unknown. They are all discrete variables in the examples given because they can only change in whole units; we cannot sensibly talk about 9·81 absentees or 4·2 lorries. Notice, too, that they are all integer discrete random variables which can only take non-negative values.

If a number of observations of each of these random variables is made, the frequency with which each possible value of the variable occurs is referred to as a *frequency distribution*. (Readers unfamiliar with the concept of a frequency distribution are recommended at this stage to consult one of the elementary statistical texts given in Appendix G.) Where a large number of trials have been made, the relative frequencies with which the various values of the variable concerned occur provide us with a *probability distribution*.

Let us now state this result in more formal terms. Suppose that corresponding to the n exhaustive and mutually exclusive results that may result from some trial, a variable x can assume the value x_i with corresponding probability p_i, where $i = 1, 2 \ldots n$. Then the set of values x_i, with their probabilities p_i, constitutes the probability distribution of the variable x. Any variable x, which possesses a probability distribution of this kind is called a random variable.

3.2 Probability functions

In connection with random variables, we are usually interested in numerical relationships such as $x \geqslant a$, or $b < x < c$, and we adjust our probability notation accordingly. Thus, the expressions $P(x \geqslant a)$ and $P(b < x < c)$ are read, respectively, as 'the probability that x is greater than or equal to a' and 'the probability that x lies between b and c, both b and c excluded'. For convenience we will adopt the notation, for discrete random variables, that: $f(x_i) \equiv P(x = x_i)$, and refer to $f(x)$ as the probability distribution of the random variable x. The distribution of x can then be defined simply by stating the equation or expression for $f(x)$, and indicating the allowable values which x may assume, or alternatively by giving the appropriate numerical values for $f(x)$ for all possible values of x. (Note that $f(x)$ is sometimes referred to as the *probability density function* or pdf.)

Example 3.1

The maximum number of lorries that can arrive at a warehouse in the next hour is 12. Then, x, the random variable corresponding to the number of arrivals in the next hour, can only take one of the 13 integer values from 0 to 12 inclusive. Assume that the probability distribution is then defined as shown in Table 3.1.

Table 3.1

x	0	1	2	3	4	5	6	7	8	9	10	11 or 12
$f(x)$	0	0·11	0·18	0·24	0·20	0·12	0·08	0·03	0·02	0·01	0·01	0

These results are shown graphically in the form of a *histogram* in Fig. 3.1. Notice that:

$$\sum_{x=0}^{x=12} f(x) = 1,$$

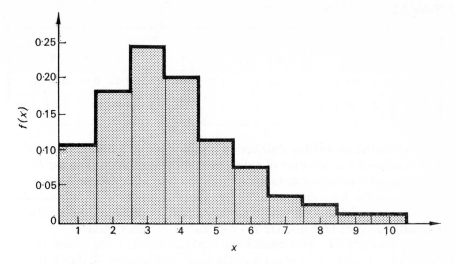

Fig. 3.1. Histogram of probability distribution

where Σ represents the sum of all $f(x)$ for x from 0 to 12 inclusive. The shaded area in the histogram is accordingly exactly one (since the width of each strip is one unit). This also indicates that a value from among the defined set of x values must occur. If this were not so, the distribution has been incorrectly defined.

Now suppose that we wish to find the probability that more than two lorries arrive in the next hour. The required probability is:

$$f(3)+f(4)+f(5)\ldots+f(12).$$

This is a lengthy arithmetic calculation, but can be short-circuited as it is equal to the simpler expression:

$$1-f(0)-f(1)-f(2)$$

or

$$1-0-0\cdot11-0\cdot18=0\cdot71.$$

The probability that the number of lorries arriving is less than, or equal to, some general value x is:

$$f(0)+f(1)+f(2)\ldots+f(x).$$

Such a sum is referred to as a *cumulative probability distribution* and is referred to by the symbol $F(x)$. In words, $F(x)$ represents the probability that the random variable concerned is less than or equal to x. The cumulative probabilities corresponding to each value of x in the lorry arrival situation are shown in Table 3.2.

Table 3.2

x	0	1	2	3	4	5	6	7	8	9	10	11 or 12
$f(x)$	0	0·11	0·18	0·24	0·20	0·12	0·08	0·03	0·02	0·01	0·01	0
$F(x)$	0	0·11	0·29	0·53	0·73	0·85	0·93	0·96	0·98	0·99	1·00	1·00

This cumulative probability distribution is shown in Fig. 3.2. Instead of using $f(x)$ to define the distribution of a discrete random variable, we can use $F(x)$, together with a statement as to the admissible values of x. Although this latter alternative form may not seem very appealing at first sight, it is actually the more powerful tool when, in the next chapter, we come to integrate the relevant theory for both discrete and continuous random variables.

If the least possible value which some random variable x can assume is denoted by A, while the greatest possible value is denoted by B, then it is evident that the graph of $F(x)$ will coincide with the x-axis for all values of x less than A, and will coincide with the horizontal line for which $F(x)=1$ for all values of x greater than or equal to B. Discrete values necessarily yield cumulative distribution functions of the discontinuous and increasing type (step function) shown in Fig. 3.2. The reason is that values of x which cannot

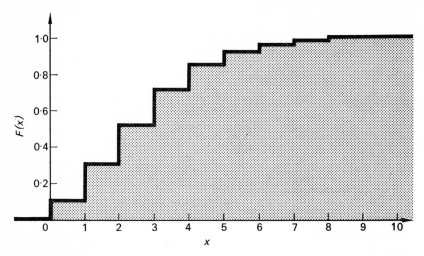

Fig. 3.2. Cumulative probability distribution

occur in reality add nothing to the probability that a random variable of the variate will lie in a stated range. Consequently, the graph of $F(x)$ is horizontal between admissible values, but takes a finite upward step at each point on the x-axis that corresponds to an admissible value. Since $F(x)$ is discontinuous in this case, its value at an admissible value of x is not defined explicitly. For convenience $F(x)$ is everywhere defined so that it is always continuous on the right, i.e. $F(x+\Delta x)=F(x)$, where Δx is a small positive increment in x.

Example 3.2

As an example of a discrete random variable having only a small number of admissible values, consider the tossing of an unbiased six-sided die and let the occurrence of a 5 or a 6 uppermost be considered a success. If the die is tossed three times, the total number of successes can assume any one of four possible values: 0, 1, 2 or 3. From the classical theory of probability we would put the probability of success at a single trial as $\frac{1}{3}$. Hence, the respective probabilities of 0, 1, 2 or 3 successes are, from reasoning similar to that in Chapter 2, given by

$$f(0)=\left(\frac{2}{3}\right)^3=\frac{8}{27}; \qquad f(1)=3\left(\frac{2}{3}\right)^2\left(\frac{1}{3}\right)=\frac{12}{27};$$

$$f(2)=3\left(\frac{2}{3}\right)\left(\frac{1}{3}\right)^2=\frac{6}{27}; \qquad f(3)=\left(\frac{1}{3}\right)^3=\frac{1}{27}.$$

The sum of the four probabilities is one, as it must be, since the sum of the probabilities of all admissible values is unity. The cumulative probabilities will therefore be:

$$F(0)=\frac{8}{27};$$

$$F(1)=\frac{8}{27}+\frac{12}{27}=\frac{20}{27};$$

$$F(2)=\frac{20}{27}+\frac{6}{27}=\frac{26}{27};$$

$$F(3)=\frac{26}{27}+\frac{1}{27}=\frac{27}{27} \text{ or } 1.$$

Figure 3.3 shows this cumulative distribution and, in terms of the discussion earlier in this section, A is equal to 0 and B is equal to 3.

3.3 Expected value

In succeeding chapters we will be specially interested in certain derived functions of random variables. Of these, the most important is the *expected value* (or mean). We begin by explaining the term on a pragmatic basis. Suppose that you go to a bus stop on your way to work each morning and you find, almost invariably, a queue of people waiting. On five successive mornings there are 2, 5, 1, 5, 3 people respectively ahead of you. The number

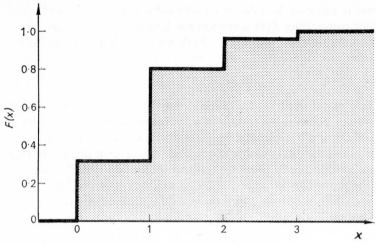

Fig. 3.3. Cumulative probability distribution for die tossing

waiting can be regarded as a random variable, each day giving rise to some value of the random variable. Assume now that we add up the values of the random variable so obtained and divide by the number of days (5) on which we have observed the queue. This gives us a figure of 3·2 and is commonly termed the *arithmetic average* or *mean* of the values taken. Such a calculation is something all readers will have done time and time again in many different situations.

Now if we repeat the experiment of waiting for a bus unendingly, instead of for a limited and finite number of times, the average we have calculated will come closer and closer to the average of the probability distribution of x, the random variable concerned, a unique value which is referred to as the *expected value* of the random variable x. Formally, we define the expected value, μ or $E(x)$, of a random variable as:

$$E(x) = \Sigma x \cdot f(x) \tag{3.1}$$

where the summation is taken over all values of the random variable x, and $f(x)$ is the probability of each value being taken. Effectively, we take each value of x and weight it by the proportion of occasions on which this particular value of x occurs. The term *mean* is commonly used interchangeably with expected value.

Example 3.2 (*continued*)

Using the same data as for Example 3.2, what is the expected number of successes?

$$E(x) = 0 \times \frac{8}{27} + 1 \times \frac{12}{27} + 2 \times \frac{6}{27} + 3 \times \frac{1}{27}$$

$$= 1.$$

† *Example* 3.3

A jeweller is considering stocking seven of a special tie clip for the Christmas season at a total cost of £42. He will sell back any unsold stock at £3 per clip, thus incurring a loss. The demand may turn out to be for 0, 1, 2, ... 7, 8 (or more) clips. The owner estimates the probabilities of each of these events, at a selling price of £10 per clip, to be 0·05, 0·10, 0·10, 0·10, 0·10, 0·20, 0·20, 0·15, The corresponding profits will be − £21, − £14, − £7, £0, £7, £14, £21, £28, £28 respectively. What is his expected profit if seven clips are stocked?

Let x be the profit. Then we have:

$$f(-21)=0·05 \qquad f(7)=0·10$$
$$f(-14)=0·10 \qquad f(14)=0·20$$
$$f(-7)=0·10 \qquad f(21)=0·20$$
$$f(0)=0·10 \qquad f(28)=0·15$$

Hence, $E(x)=(-21)\times 0·05+(-14)\times 0·10+ ...+28\times 0·15$

$$=11·90-3·15=8·75.$$

Thus, his expected profit will be £8·75. Note that on this one Christmas he will not, indeed cannot, achieve precisely £8·75 profit. The most likely profit (sometimes called the *modal profit*), would be £14 or £21, since these particular profits both have the highest probability of occurring.

The reader must differentiate clearly between *expectation* and *probability*. To highlight the difference, consider the following situation, which is analogous to investing in the premium bonds issued through the Post Office, although with different probabilities. Suppose the purchase of a £1 bond entitles you to take part in a monthly draw in which the prize is £5. The draw is carried out by putting a very large number of beads in a drum, 20 per cent are red and 80 per cent are white. A bead is drawn out at random; if it is red you receive a prize of £5, if it is white you get nothing. The probability of your winning a prize is clearly 0·2, your expected gain being given by

$$E(x)=0·2\times 5+0·8\times 0=1.$$

Now suppose that you purchase two £1 bonds, which entitles you to two draws from the drum. Denote a prize on the first draw by d_1, no prize by $\bar{d}_1$, and similarly for the second draw. Then there are four possibilities:

Outcome	Probability	Prize
$d_1\, d_2$	$0·2\times 0·2=0·04$	$5+5=10$
$\bar{d}_1\, d_2$	$0·8\times 0·2=0·16$	5

$d_1 \; \bar{d_2}$ $0 \cdot 2 \times 0 \cdot 8 = 0 \cdot 16$ 5

$\bar{d_1} \; \bar{d_2}$ $0 \cdot 8 \times 0 \cdot 8 = 0 \cdot 64$ 0

Hence the probability of winning a prize is $0 \cdot 04 + 0 \cdot 16 + 0 \cdot 16 = 0 \cdot 36$. The expected gain is now:

$$E(x) = 0 \cdot 04 \times 10 + 0 \cdot 16 \times 5 + 0 \cdot 16 \times 5$$
$$= 2 \cdot 0.$$

Hence, the expectation has doubled ($2 \cdot 0$ versus $1 \cdot 0$), while the probability of winning has not ($0 \cdot 36$ versus $0 \cdot 2$). This effect would be repeated as the number of bonds held was increased further, the expected gain being proportional to the number of bonds held, while the probability of winning at least one prize would rise somewhat less than proportionally. This basic difference, between expectation of gain and probability of winning, has led to some misunderstandings with the premium bond system, where bondholders may hold very different numbers of bonds.

3.4 Variance

Consider a random variable x, with probability distribution $f(x)$ and expected value μ (the Greek letter mu). Introduce the alternative random variable $z = x - \mu$ which measures the deviation of x from its expected value. Now $E(z)$ must, by definition, be zero, but it is frequently of interest to know something about the magnitude of the individual deviations of the possible values of x from μ that will occur. Thus our interest centres around the probability distribution of z. In this section we introduce a numerical measure of these deviations.

An obvious type of measure to use for this purpose would be the average absolute deviation from the mean, the average being obtained by weighting deviations by the appropriate probabilities. This measure has gained a limited acceptance, but its exceedingly poor combinative properties render it useless for many purposes, practical and theoretical alike. The simplest measure which satisfies both intuitive and analytical requirements is the mean squared deviation from the expected value; referred to as the *variance* and denoted by the symbol σ^2 (the Greek letter sigma). Formally, we have:

$$\sigma^2 = E(x - E(x))^2$$
$$= \Sigma(x - E(x))^2 f(x). \tag{3.2}$$

It is often more convenient to express this as:

$$\sigma^2 = \Sigma \{x^2 - 2xE(x) + (E(x))^2\} f(x)$$
$$= \Sigma x^2 f(x) - (E(x))^2$$
$$= E(x^2) - (E(x))^2. \tag{3.3}$$

The variance of x is commonly abbreviated to var(x) instead of σ^2.

Example 3.4

Using the data of Example 3.3, the variance of the expected profit will now be found. The steps are laid out in detail in Table 3.3 below. From this table the variance of the expected profit is 220.

Table 3.3

Calculation of variance

x	$x-E(x)$	$(x-E(x))^2$	$f(x)$	$f(x)(x-E(x))^2$
-21	$-29{\cdot}75$	$885{\cdot}1$	$0{\cdot}05$	$44{\cdot}3$
-14	$-22{\cdot}75$	$517{\cdot}6$	$0{\cdot}10$	$51{\cdot}8$
-7	$-15{\cdot}75$	$248{\cdot}1$	$0{\cdot}10$	$24{\cdot}8$
0	$-8{\cdot}75$	$76{\cdot}6$	$0{\cdot}10$	$7{\cdot}7$
7	$-1{\cdot}75$	$3{\cdot}1$	$0{\cdot}10$	$0{\cdot}3$
14	$5{\cdot}25$	$27{\cdot}6$	$0{\cdot}20$	$5{\cdot}5$
21	$12{\cdot}25$	$150{\cdot}1$	$0{\cdot}20$	$30{\cdot}0$
28	$19{\cdot}25$	$370{\cdot}6$	$0{\cdot}15$	$55{\cdot}6$
			Total	$220{\cdot}0$

Sometimes the *standard deviation*, which is the positive square root of the variance, is found to be more useful than the variance since it is in the same units as the original variable x, rather than in squared units. In this instance the standard deviation is $\sigma = \sqrt{220} = £14{\cdot}8$.

The standard deviation provides us with some indication of how widely the values of x are scattered about μ. Its precise quantitative significance in a measurement sense will become clearer as the book develops. For the moment, it is sufficient to realize that the standard deviation provides a linear measure of the spread of a distribution; if the standard deviation doubles, so does the spread.

3.5 Functions of a random variable

There are some general properties of random variables which it is useful to have available for help in problem-solving. These will be listed, without formal proof, and used in this and subsequent chapters of the book.

(*i*) If a is constant and x is a random variable, then

$$E(ax) = aE(x) \tag{3.4}$$

and

$$E(x+a) = E(x) + a \tag{3.5}$$

(*ii*) If $\phi(x)$ represents some function of a random variable x (e.g. x^2, $x+2$, $\frac{1}{2}x$, $\log x$, etc.) then,

$$E(\phi(x)) = \Sigma \phi(x) f(x) \tag{3.6}$$

For example, if the random variable x represents the running time in hours of a machine until breakdown and the costs of running the machine consist of a fixed set-up cost of α for each run, together with a variable cost β per run, then the total cost per run is:

$$y = \alpha + \beta x,$$

and

$$E(y) = \sum(\alpha + \beta x) f(x) = \alpha + \beta E(x)$$

(*iii*) $\mathrm{Var}(ax) = a^2 \, \mathrm{var}(x)$, where a is a constant $\hspace{2cm}$ (3.7)

(*iv*) Two random variables, x and y, are said to be independent if $P(x = X, y = Y) = P(x = X) P(y = Y)$. If now x_i ($i = 1, 2, \ldots k$) are a series of independent random variables and a_i ($i = 1, 2, \ldots k$) are constants, then:

$$X = a_1 x_1 + a_2 x_2 + \ldots + a_k x_k = \sum_{i=1}^{k} a_i x_i$$

has

$$E(X) = \sum_{i=1}^{k} a_i E(x_i) \hspace{3cm} (3.8a)$$

$$\mathrm{Var}(x) = \sum_{i=1}^{k} a_i^2 \, \mathrm{var}(x_i). \hspace{2.5cm} (3.8b)$$

Example 3.5

Three ordinary six-sided dice are tossed, the first being coloured red, the second yellow and the third blue. You are to receive from a banker as many pounds as shown on the red die, and as many pence as shown by the yellow die, and to give to the banker ten times as many pence as shown by the blue die. Find the expected value and standard deviation of what you will receive.

Let the number shown on the ith die ($i = 1, 2, 3$) be denoted by x_i. Then:

$$f(x_i) = \tfrac{1}{6} \text{ for } x_i = 1, 2, \ldots 6.$$

$$E(x_i) = 1 \times \tfrac{1}{6} + 2 \times \tfrac{1}{6} + \ldots + 6 \times \tfrac{1}{6} = 3 \cdot 5.$$

$$\mathrm{Var}(x_i) = 1^2 \times \tfrac{1}{6} + 2^2 \times \tfrac{1}{6} + \ldots + 6^2 \times \tfrac{1}{6} - (3 \cdot 5)^2 = \tfrac{35}{12}.$$

Your gain, in pence, will be:

$$X = 100 x_1 + x_2 - 10 x_3$$

Hence, using Eq. 3.8a we have:

$$E(X) = (100 + 1 - 10)3 \cdot 5 = 91 \times 3 \cdot 5 = 318 \cdot 5,$$

showing that the expected gain is £3·185.

Using Eq. 3.8b we have:

$$\mathrm{var}(X) = (100^2 + 1^2 + 10^2)\tfrac{35}{12} = 29{,}461 \cdot 25,$$

giving the standard deviation of X as $\sqrt{29{,}461{\cdot}25}$, equal to 171·6 pence or £1·716. It is interesting to notice for further consideration later the high value of the standard deviation in relation to the expected value.

3.6 Binomial distribution

The remainder of this chapter will be devoted to the introduction of certain discrete distributions, each of which is important enough from the standpoint of general use to be regarded as a basic item of equipment for practical applications of probability theory. The first of these is closely related to the binomial series in algebra and is referred to as the *binomial probability distribution*.

Assume that the occurrence of an event E at a series of trials is subject to chance, so that the number x of occurrences of E in n independent trials is a discrete random variable, the possible values of which are 0, 1, 2, ... n. If the probability p of the occurrence of E on each individual trial is constant, then x is called a *binomial variable*, and its distribution is known as the *binomial probability distribution*. Since the failure of E to occur on a given trial automatically implies the occurrence of the complementary event $\bar{E}$, the probability of which is $q=1-p$, any possible sequence of n trials is necessarily made up of x instances of E (successes) and $n-x$ instances of $\bar{E}$ (failures), where x may take on one of its admissible values 0, 1, 2, ... n. Now the probability of any one particular sequence of x successes and $(n-x)$ failures is $p^x(1-p)^{n-x}$ or p^xq^{n-x}. The number of distinct sequences of x successes and $n-x$ failures is:

$n!/x!(n-x)!$, written as $\binom{n}{x}$ or, sometimes, ^nC_x, and referred to in words as

'n combinatorial x'. This result follows since one can arrange n distinct items in $n!$ ways, but in this instance x are like in one sense and $(n-x)$ alike in another sense, so that $n!$ has to be divided by $x!$ and $(n-x)!$, in turn, to give the revised number of ways. Hence, the required probability, denoted here by b_x for convenience, is:

$$b_x = \binom{n}{x} p^x q^{n-x} \tag{3.9}$$

Note that the symbol b_x will only be used as a convenient shorthand when the values of n and p are self-evident.

Figure 3.4 gives some illustrations of the shapes that the binomial distribution can take for various values of n and p. Adjustable constants, such as n and p in the binomial distribution, are called *parameters*, and any empirical estimates that may be made of parameters are called *statistics*. In Fig. 3.4(a) the parameter n is held constant ($n=9$) and the parameter p is allowed to vary ($p=0\cdot2$, $0\cdot5$, $0\cdot8$). In Fig. 3.4(b) p is held constant and n

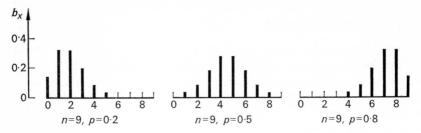

Fig. 3.4(a). Binomial distribution with fixed n

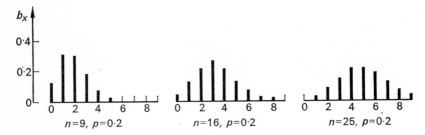

Fig. 3.4(b). Binomial distribution with fixed p

is allowed to vary ($n=9$, 16, 25). The figures illustrate the symmetry of the binomial distribution when $p=0\cdot5$, but the non-symmetry otherwise. However, for a given value of p, the skewness (which is a technical expression implying non–symmetry) of the binomial distribution becomes less pronounced as n increases.

In Appendix A, page 331, cumulative probability values of the binomial distribution are given for $n=5$, 10, 15, 20, 25, 50 and $p=0\cdot05$, $0\cdot1$, $0\cdot15$, $0\cdot2$, $0\cdot25$, $0\cdot3$, $0\cdot35$, $0\cdot4$, $0\cdot45$ and $0\cdot5$. The tables can be used in the straightforward manner explained in the Appendix. When p has a value greater than $0\cdot5$, the appropriate value can be found by using the table in a converse manner. For example, suppose we require the probability of 8 or more successes in 10 trials, with a probability of $0\cdot6$ of success at each trial. This is numerically identical to one minus the probability of 7 or fewer successes, with a probability of $0\cdot6$ of success at each trial. We now look in the righthand columns of the table for $n=10$ and, against $1-p=0\cdot40$ and $r=7$, find the probability $0\cdot8327$. Hence, our required probability is equal to $1-0\cdot8327$, or $0\cdot1673$.

The mean and variance of the binomial distribution are important quantities. First, let us find the mean. From Eq. 3.1,

$$E(x) = \sum_{x=0}^{n} x f(x)$$

$$= \sum_{x=0}^{n} x \binom{n}{x} p^x q^{n-x}$$

$$= \binom{n}{1} pq^{n-1} + 2\binom{n}{2} p^2 q^{n-2} + 3\binom{n}{3} p^3 q^{n-3} + \ldots$$

$$= np\left\{ q^{n-1} + \binom{n-1}{1} pq^{n-2} + \binom{n-1}{2} p^2 q^{n-3} + \ldots \right\}$$

$$= np \sum_{x=1}^{n} \binom{n-1}{x-1} p^{x-1} q^{n-x}.$$

Now

$$\sum_{x=1}^{n} \binom{n-1}{x-1} p^{x-1} q^{n-x}$$

represents the successive terms of the binomial expansion $(q+p)^{n-1}$ and, since $q+p=1$, this equals 1^{n-1} or 1. Hence, we have:

$$E(x) = np. \tag{3.10}$$

Therefore, the mean number of successes is np. For the variance we use Eq. 3.3 to evaluate:

$$\mathrm{var}(x) = E(x^2) - (E(x))^2.$$

Now

$$E(x^2) = \sum_{x=0}^{n} x^2 f(x)$$

$$= \sum_{x=1}^{n} \{x(x-1) + x\} f(x).$$

Now

$$\sum_{x=1}^{n} x(x-1) f(x) = \sum_{x=1}^{n} x(x-1) \binom{n}{x} p^x q^{n-x}$$

$$= n(n-1) p^2 \sum_{x=2}^{n} \binom{n-2}{x-2} p^{x-2} q^{n-x},$$

and the summation portion represents the successive terms of the expansion of $(q+p)^{n-2}$ which is equal to 1. The second term of $E(x^2)$ has already been shown to be equal to np. Hence, we have:

$$E(x^2) = n(n-1) p^2 + np.$$

C

Hence:

$$\text{var}(x) = n(n-1)p^2 + np - (np)^2 = np - np^2$$

$$= npq. \tag{3.11}$$

The standard deviation is thus $\sqrt{(npq)}$.

Summarizing, for a binomial probability distribution, where there are n independent trials at each of which the probability of a success is p, the mean and standard deviation of the total number of successes are np and $\sqrt{\{np(1-p)\}}$ respectively.

Example 3.6

In a large town 60 per cent of the households own a washing machine. Ten households are chosen at random to form a sample of households. Suppose this procedure was followed a large number of times. What would be the mean and standard deviation of the number of households in the sample possessing washing machines?

Here let x be the number of households in the sample possessing a washing machine. Then $p = 0.6$ and $q = 1 - 0.6 = 0.4$, with $n = 10$. From Eqs. 3.10 and 3.11 we have:

$$\text{Mean} = np = 10 \times 0.6 = 6.$$

Standard deviation $= \sqrt{(npq)} = \sqrt{(10 \times 0.6 \times 0.4)} = 1.55$. Hence, the mean number of households with a washing machine is 6 and the standard deviation is 1.55.

We will now go on to consider some more general problems involving the binomial distribution.

Example 3.7

In a large factory, observations over a long period have shown that 20 per cent of the workmen succumb to an occupational disease within a year of commencing work. To try to improve conditions, considerable alterations were made to a particular part of the factory and, of the fifty workmen in this part, only six succumbed to the disease during the year following the alterations. Can it be reasonably deduced that a significant improvement has been effected?

To answer this question, consider first the situation if the alterations had effected no improvement. Under these conditions, the probabilities of $0, 1, 2, \ldots 50$ workmen getting the disease in a sample of fifty from a population in which each man has a chance of 0.2 of getting the disease, are the successive terms of the binomial expansion: $(0.8 + 0.2)^{50}$. Thus $b_0 = (0.8)^{50}$ and is zero to four decimal places, where b_i stands for the probability that exactly i of the men get the disease. Similarly, from the binomial expansion in Eq. 3.9 or from Appendix A, $b_1 = 0.0002$, $b_2 = 0.0011$, $b_3 = 0.0044$, $b_4 = 0.0128$, $b_5 = 0.0295$ and $b_6 = 0.0554$.

Hence, the probability that exactly six men get the disease in the sample of fifty is equal to 0·0554. It might be argued that, as this probability is reasonably small, the true probability of a man getting the disease is smaller than 0·2. This is a logical argument because if it were 0·15, say, the observed sample result of six men with the disease becomes a more likely happening. Before accepting this result, however, it must be borne in mind that if such a decision were to be made when just six of the men in the sample get the disease, an identical decision would be made, only more strongly so, if five or four or fewer of the men get the disease, since:

$$b_5 = 0·0295, \ b_4 = 0·0128, \ b_3 = 0·0044, \text{ etc.,}$$

and all these probabilities are even less than b_6. Hence, the decision to say that there is an improvement if only six men get the disease implies that the same decision would be made if five or even fewer got the disease. The probability that one of these eventualities occurs in the sample, when there is really no improvement, is therefore:

$$b_0 + b_1 + b_2 + b_3 + b_4 + b_5 + b_6 = 0·1034.$$

Thus, in about 10 per cent of cases, such a result could occur by chance, and this represents in probability terms a sufficiently common occurrence for there to be doubt as to whether a significant improvement had in fact been effected.

On the other hand, suppose that only three of the fifty men got the disease. The probability of three or fewer of the men getting the disease if there has been no improvement is:

$$b_0 + b_1 + b_2 + b_3 = 0·0057,$$

and such a result would thus only occur about once in 180 times by chance. This would throw considerable doubt on the theory that 20 per cent of the men get the disease, and would suggest that the true proportion was now somewhat lower, so that some improvement has been made.

First, it should be noted that the smallness of the individual probabilities does not by itself prove or disprove the statement to be examined. It is essential to include the probabilities of all results which would lead to the same decision. Second, it is necessary for the sample result to be more likely on the alternative theory if the original theory is to be rejected. For example, if out of the fifty men considered above, twenty got the disease, it will be found that $b_{20} = 0·0006$, if the probability that each man gets the disease is 0·2. The expected number of men getting the disease is np or 10, so that more extreme values than 20 would be 21, 22, and so on. Adding up the appropriate probabilities gives:

$$b_{20} + b_{21} + b_{22} + \ldots = 0·0009,$$

and shows that such an extreme result would only occur about once in a thousand times or even less. But to reject the proposition that each man has a probability of 0·2 of getting the disease, in favour of the alternative that the new conditions have made an improvement, would be foolish. This follows because, if the probability of getting the disease were actually lower than 0·2, the probability of getting twenty men with the disease would be even smaller and it would be a still more unlikely event than before.

† *Example 3.8*

The probability that a person will positively respond to a mailed advertisement for a book and place an order is estimated at 0·1. What is the probability that, if the mailed advertisement is sent to 20 persons, there will be:

(*i*) exactly two orders,
(*ii*) more than two orders?

For (*i*) the required probability will be:

$$b_2 = \binom{20}{2} (0·1)^2 (0·9)^{18} \text{ or } 0·2852.$$

For (*ii*) the required probability is:

$$b_3 + b_4 + \ldots b_{20}$$

$$= \binom{20}{3} (0·1)^3 (0·9)^{17} + \binom{20}{4} (0·1)^4 (0·9)^{16} + \ldots + (0·1)^{20}$$

It is simpler to calculate the latter as:

$$1 - b_0 - b_1 - b_2$$

$$= 1 - (0·9)^{20} - \binom{20}{1} (0·1)(0·9)^{19} - \binom{20}{2} (0·1)^2 (0·9)^{18}$$

which is identical, since the sum of the probabilities of the twenty-one possible outcomes must be unity. Calculation then gives the result as 0·3231.

Both these results can also be readily obtained from the tables in Appendix A. For (*i*) we find the probability of two or more orders and subtract from it the probability of three or more orders. This gives us $0·6083 - 0·3231 = 0·2852$ as the required probability. The probability for (*ii*) can be directly read off as 0·3231.

3.7 Poisson distribution

The Poisson distribution is named after Simeon Poisson, a Frenchman who lived from 1781–1840, who first enunciated the distribution in 1837. The distribution arises as a limiting form of the binomial distribution in the particular situation when n tends to infinity and p tends to zero in such a manner that np remains constant and finite. Under these conditions it can be shown that:

$$b_x = \binom{n}{x} p^x q^{n-x} \rightarrow \frac{m^x e^{-m}}{x!} \text{ for } x = 0, 1, 2 \ldots \tag{3.12}$$

where $m = np$ and e is the base of natural logarithms (having the value 2·71828). It is the latter expression, which we denote by p_x for convenience when there is no possibility of confusion, which is commonly referred to as the *Poisson distribution*. Note that:

$$\sum_{x=0}^{\infty} p_x = \sum_{x=0}^{\infty} \frac{m^x e^{-m}}{x!} = e^{-m} \sum_{x=0}^{\infty} \frac{m^x}{x!} = e^{-m} e^m = 1,$$

as it should be for a probability distribution.

For the mean and variance of the Poisson distribution, we calculate:

$$E(x) = \sum_{x=0}^{\infty} x \frac{m^x e^{-m}}{x!} = m e^{-m} \sum_{x=1}^{\infty} \frac{m^{x-1}}{(x-1)!} = m. \tag{3.13a}$$

$$\text{Var}(x) = \sum_{x=0}^{\infty} x^2 \frac{m^x e^{-m}}{x!} - m^2 = \sum_{x=1}^{\infty} \{x(x-1) + x\} \frac{m^x e^{-m}}{x!} - m^2$$

$$= m^2 + m - m^2 = m. \tag{3.13b}$$

Hence, both the mean and variance are equal to m. This is not the case with the binomial distribution where the values were, in general, rather different. The distinctive feature of the Poisson distribution, and the main reason for its great practical utility, is that it only depends upon one parameter, m, and hence is rather simpler to handle than the binomial distribution which depends upon the two parameters, n and p.

To assist in computations involving the Poisson distribution, a small table of values of e^{-m} is given in Table 3.4. Values of m not given in the table can usually be obtained by the multiplication of appropriate values taken from the table. For example, $e^{-2·5} = e^{-2·4} \times e^{-0·1} = 0·0907 \times 0·9048 = 0·0821$.

Table 3.4

Values of e^{-m}

m	e^{-m}	m	e^{-m}	m	e^{-m}
0·00	1·0000	1·80	0·1653	4·20	0·0150
0·01	0·9901	2·00	0·1353	4·40	0·0123
0·05	0·9512	2·20	0·1108	4·60	0·0101
0·10	0·9048	2·40	0·0907	4·80	0·0082
0·20	0·8187	2·60	0·0743	5·00	0·0067
0·40	0·6703	2·80	0·0608	5·20	0·0055
0·60	0·5488	3·00	0·0498	5·40	0·0045
0·80	0·4493	3·20	0·0408	5·60	0·0037
1·00	0·3679	3·40	0·0334	5·80	0·0030
1·20	0·3012	3·60	0·0273	6·00	0·0025
1·40	0·2466	3·80	0·0224	6·20	0·0020
1·60	0·2019	4·00	0·0183	6·40	0·0017

Example 3.9

Two per cent of the very large number of screws made by a machine are defective, the defectives occurring at random during production. If the screws are packaged 100 per box, what is an appropriate expression for the probability that a given box will contain just x defectives?

The probability that the box contains precisely x defectives is given by the binomial distribution:

$$b_x = \binom{100}{x} (0 \cdot 02)^x (0 \cdot 98)^{100-x} \quad \text{for } x = 0, 1, 2 \ldots 100$$

Since $n = 100$, $p = 0 \cdot 02$ and $np = 2$, the Poisson approximation to b_x seems likely to be reasonable in this instance and is given by:

$$b_x \to p_x = \frac{2^x e^{-2}}{x!} \quad \text{for } x = 0, 1, 2 \ldots.$$

Theoretically, p_x is defined for all positive integer values of x, whereas from the conditions of the problem x cannot exceed 100. The numerical values concerned when x exceeds 100 are, however, so infinitesimal that this discrepancy is of no real significance. Calculation of p_x is much simpler than for b_x, and Table 3.5 gives a comparison of the results from the two distributions in this example. The agreement between the exact binomial probability and the (approximate) Poisson probabilities is seen to be extremely good, the maximum error in an individual term being $0 \cdot 0027$. If the cumulative probabilities, shown in brackets, are considered, the maximum error of $0 \cdot 0027$ only occurs at $k = 0$, and otherwise the agreement is extremely close. Hence, the use of the Poisson approximation in these circumstances seems well justified.

Table 3.5

Comparison of b_x and p_x for n $= 100$, p $= 0 \cdot 02$

(cumulative probabilities are given in brackets)

x	b_x	p_x
0	0·1326 (0·1326)	0·1353 (0·1353)
1	0·2707 (0·4033)	0·2707 (0·4060)
2	0·2734 (0·6767)	0·2707 (0·6767)
3	0·1823 (0·8590)	0·1804 (0·8571)
4	0·0902 (0·9492)	0·0902 (0·9473)
5	0·0353 (0·9845)	0·0361 (0·9834)
6	0·0114 (0·9959)	0·0120 (0·9954)
7	0·0031 (0·9990)	0·0034 (0·9988)
8	0·0007 (0·9997)	0·0009 (0·9997)
9	0·0002 (0·9999)	0·0002 (0·9999)

† *Example* 3.10

A factory has 500 nominally identical machines in use. Examination of past records suggests that the chance of a machine breaking down on any given day is 0·01. A repair mechanic can mend up to seven broken machines in a day without working overtime. What is the probability that, on a given day, he will have to work overtime in order to have all machines running before the next day?

We have $n = 500$, $p = 0·01$ and $np = 5$, giving again the conditions for a Poisson approximation. Hence, the probability we require will be:

$p_8 + p_9 + p_{10} + \ldots$

$$= e^{-5} \left[\frac{5^8}{8!} + \frac{5^9}{9!} + \frac{5^{10}}{10!} + \frac{5^{11}}{11!} + \ldots \right]$$

$$= 0·133$$

Hence, he could expect to have to work overtime on about one day in seven. Note that there would also be days when fewer than seven machines break down and he will not be fully occupied.

† *Example* 3.11

The average number of misprints in a column of a certain newspaper is three. If five or fewer misprints are found in a column during proof-reading (which is assumed to be 100 per cent accurate) no action is taken. If six or more misprints are found, the column is reset. What proportion of columns can be expected to require resetting?

Even though we do not know n (the number of letters per column) and p (the probability a letter is wrong) separately, we can deduce that $m = np = 3$. Hence the required probability is:

$1 - p_0 - p_1 - p_2 - p_3 - p_4 - p_5$ where $m = 3$

This expression is equal to:

$$1 - e^{-3} \left[1 + \frac{3}{1!} + \frac{3^2}{2!} + \frac{3^3}{3!} + \frac{3^4}{4!} + \frac{3^5}{5!} \right]$$

$$= 1 - 0·0498 \times 18·4 = 0·0837.$$

Hence, the proportion of columns expected to need resetting will be 0·0837, or about one column in twelve.

3.8 The hypergeometric distribution

So far we have assumed that successive trials are independent, and this is realizable in many situations. But other situations occur when it is not, particularly when sampling is taking place from a relatively small population. The *hypergeometric distribution* applies to sampling from a finite population without replacement. Consider a population of N items, of which a are of type A and the remaining $(N-a)$ items are of type non-A. Suppose that a random sample of n items is drawn from the population without replacement between the drawings from the population. Then the probability of getting exactly x items of type A in the sample is:

$$h_x = \binom{a}{x}\binom{N-a}{n-x} \Big/ \binom{N}{n} \quad \text{for } x=0, 1, 2 \ldots a \tag{3.14}$$

and is zero for x greater than a.

The numerator represents the total number of ways of selecting x items of type A and $(n-x)$ items of type non-A, while the denominator gives the total number of ways of selecting a sample of n from the population of N items.

The mean and variance of x for the hypergeometric distribution are given, without formal proof, as:

$$E(x) = n\frac{a}{N}. \tag{3.15a}$$

$$\text{Var}(x) = \left(\frac{N-n}{N-1}\right) n\frac{a}{N}\left(1-\frac{a}{N}\right). \tag{3.15b}$$

Note that if we let N get very large, keeping a/N constant and equal to p, say, then these expressions will tend to $E(x) = np$ and $\text{var}(x) = np(1-p)$. These results are then the same as those given in Eqs. 3.10 and 3.11 for the binomial distribution. For this reason, the factor $(N-n)/(N-1)$ in Eq. 3.15b is sometimes referred to as the *finite population correction*, since the one difference in principle between the two types of sampling is that the hypergeometric distribution refers to sampling from a finite rather than an infinite population.

† *Example* 3.12

A worker opens a box containing ten axle bearings, six of which were made on machine No. 1 and the remaining four on machine No. 2. If the worker selects four axle bearings at random from the carton, what is the probability that all four were made on machine No. 1?

Here, $N=10$, $n=4$, $a=6$, $x=4$. Hence:

$$h_4 = \binom{6}{4}\binom{4}{0} \Big/ \binom{10}{4}$$

$$= \frac{6!}{4!\,2!} \times \frac{4!\,6!}{10!} = 0 \cdot 0714.$$

Hence, the required probability is $0 \cdot 0714$.

Example 3.13

A lot of ten components includes three defective items. A random sample of four components is drawn from the lot. Suppose the number of defective items in the sample is x. What is the expected value and standard deviation of x?

From Eqs. 3.15a and 3.15b we have:

$$E(x) = 4 \times \frac{3}{10} = 1\cdot2$$

$$\text{Var}(x) = \frac{10-4}{10-1} \times 4 \times \frac{3}{10} \times \left(1 - \frac{3}{10}\right) = \frac{42}{75} = 0\cdot56,$$

and the standard deviation of x is $\sqrt{0\cdot56}$ or $0\cdot75$.

It is worth remarking that, had the drawing of the sample of four components been from an infinitely large lot with 30 per cent defective, we would have the binomial situation with:

$$E(x) = 4 \times \frac{3}{10} = 1\cdot2$$

Standard deviation of $x = \sqrt{\left(4 \times \frac{3}{10} \times \frac{7}{10}\right)} = 0\cdot92.$

Hence, by drawing from a finite group, without replacement of each individual after it is drawn, the expected value of the number of defectives is left unchanged, but the standard deviation is diminished.

Exercises on Chapter 3

1 Assess probability distributions (drawing a graph of their cumulative probability density functions) for the following variables:

   (*i*) the number of cars you will buy in the next fifteen years;
   (*ii*) the number of astronauts who will land on the moon in the next two years;
   (*iii*) the number of new motor cars registered in the UK in the next twelve months;
   (*iv*) the number of giro accounts there will be one year from now.

2 A soap company distributes blank entry forms for a lottery requiring nothing more than filling in one's name and posting the form. The prize schedule is:

1st prize	£5000	Next 10 prizes	£100 each
2nd prize	£2000	Next 50 prizes	£50 each
3rd prize	£1000	Next 100 prizes	£20 each
Next 5 prizes	£200 each	Next 1000 prizes	£5 each

Assume that half a million entry forms are returned. Let the random variable x be your gain from participation with a single entry.

(i) What is $E(x)$?
(ii) What is the standard deviation of x?
(iii) Suppose it costs you $2\frac{1}{2}$p to post each entry. Give reasons why it does, or does not, make sense to participate.

3 The XYZ Company produces a product that is divided into three different grades. With raw material from one supplier the proportion of units falling into each of the three grades is:

Grade	I	II	III
Probability	0·80	0·15	0·05

Grade I units sell for £2·50, grade II for £2·00 and grade III for £1·75.

(i) What is the expected revenue per unit produced from this source of raw material? How do you interpret this expected revenue?
(ii) What is the expected revenue for a lot of 1000 units? Will this be the amount actually received?
(iii) If the company modifies its production process, which would cost £0·25 per unit, the proportions would be changed to 0·87, 0·10 and 0·03 respectively. Would this modification be desirable if the company still purchased its raw material from the same source?

4 The distribution of defective tyres among a batch of four tyres moulded at the same time is as shown in Table 3.6.

Table 3.6

x	0	1	2	3	4
$f(x)$	0·70	0·20	0·05	0·03	0·02

(i) Find the expected value of x and its standard deviation.
(ii) Suppose a defective tyre represents a loss of £4. Let $y=4x$. What does y represent?
(iii) Find the expected value and standard deviation of y.

5 A factory produces nuts and bolts on separate processes in packets of six. If satisfactory, the nuts and bolts can be matched in pairs. The number of defective nuts and bolts varies from packet to packet. Past experience has shown that reasonable estimates of the probability distribution of the number of defectives per packet, x or y respectively, are as shown in Table 3.7.

Table 3.7

Nuts	x	0	1	2	3	4	5	6
	$p(x)$	0·83	0·12	0·03	0·02	0	0	0
Bolts	y	0	1	2	3	4	5	6
	$p(y)$	0·89	0·05	0·03	0·02	0·01	0	0

A customer purchases one packet of nuts and one packet of bolts. What are the probabilities:

(*i*) That the packet will provide six satisfactory nut-bolt combinations?

(*ii*) That the packet will provide at least four satisfactory nut-bolt combinations?

(*iii*) That there will only be one unsatisfactory nut-bolt combination in the packet?

6 A classroom quiz has ten multiple choice questions, each with four possible answers, the student being required to tick the one correct answer. If a student completes the test entirely by guesswork, what is the probability that he gets seven or more of the questions correct?

7 The number of defects (x) on first assembly in a certain model of television set are distributed as shown in Table 3.8.

Table 3.8

x	0	1	2	3	4	5
$p(x)$	0·60	0·22	0·10	0·05	0·02	0·01

If the production cost of a set is £30 and the average cost of removing each defect found is £3, what is the expected cost of producing a defect-free set? Find also the expected cost, and the standard deviation of that cost, for producing ten defect-free sets. (Assume that sets are independent as regards the occurrence of faults.)

8 It is estimated that 95 per cent of school children are righthanded and 5 per cent lefthanded. A classroom for twenty children has twenty tablet armchairs, all with the tablet on the right arm of the chair. Assume that the twenty children assigned to this room are a random sample of all school children.

(*i*) What is the probability of one or more lefthanded children in a class of 20?

(*ii*) Suppose one of the chairs is exchanged for a leftarmed one. What is the probability that the chairs precisely match the children's needs?

(*iii*) It is suggested that the classroom should have 21 chairs, one leftarmed and 20 rightarmed for the 20 children. What is the revised probability that everyone's handedness is provided for?

9 Two people each toss an unbiased coin n times. Find the probability that they will score the same number of heads.

10 A married couple, both aged 65, makes a proposal for a policy with the undermentioned benefits to an insurance company. The benefits are (*i*) £1000 if the wife, but not the husband, dies within five years, (*ii*) £2000 if the husband, but not the wife, dies within five years, (*iii*) £500 if both die within five years. The company assesses from life tables the independent probabilities of the proposers dying as shown in Table 3.9.

Table 3.9

	Husband	Wife
Dying within five years	0·15	0·10
Surviving at least five years	0·85	0·90

Estimate a suitable premium for the insurance company to charge for this policy. Assume that the office expenses are £4 per policy written, and that it aims to make a profit per policy equal to 25 per cent of the premium charged. (Ignore any discounting of the sums of money involved.)

11 A certain process turns out articles of which a proportion θ are defective. The process is inspected by choosing randomly over a period of time a large number of samples of four articles and inspecting them. The following information is known: in 60 per cent of the samples selected, none of the four was defective, while in 30 per cent of the samples just one of the four was defective. What fraction of the articles produced by this process would you estimate to be defective, i.e. what estimate would you make for θ?

12 An insurance company estimates that 0·01 per cent of the insured males die from a certain kind of accident each year. What is the probability that the insurance company must pay off in more than 3 of 10 000 insured risks against such accidents in a given year?

13 A large restaurant, for costing purposes, is developing a probability model to describe the lifetime of the cups it uses. For this purpose, it assumes that, at each serving where the cup is used, there is a constant probability p of the cup being damaged and that servings are independent. Once damaged, a cup is thrown away.

(*i*) On this model what is the probability that a cup newly purchased
  (*a*) is damaged before the fifth serving;
  (*b*) is damaged on the fifth serving;
  (*c*) survives its first five servings?
(*ii*) If x is the number of servings before a newly purchased cup is scrapped, what is the expected value of x and its standard deviation?

14 A small carhire firm has two cars which it rents out by the day. Suppose that the number of demands for a car each day is distributed as a Poisson distribution with mean 1·5.

(*i*) On what proportion of days is neither car required?
(*ii*) On what proportion of days is the demand in excess of the firm's capacity?

15 A seed distributor finds that, on average, 5 per cent of his seeds fail to germinate. He puts the seeds in packets of 100 for sale and guarantees 90 per cent germination. Estimate the probability that a man who buys a packet of the seeds finds the guarantee violated.

16 A process for making plate glass produces an average of four 'seeds' (small bubbles) scattered at random in the glass per 100 square feet. Use the Poisson distribution to estimate the probability that:

(*i*) a piece of plate glass 5 ft × 10 ft will contain more than two seeds,
(*ii*) six pieces of plate glass 5 ft × 5 ft will all be free of seeds.

17 In a community of 20 households, 5 of whom take *Punch*, what is the probability of finding that, in a random sample of 10 households, exactly 2 take the magazine? What is the probability of more than 2 households in the sample having the magazine? How would the former probability be affected if the sample of 10 households came from a larger community of 2000 households, of whom 500 took *Punch*?

18 Look again at Problem 2.2 on page 11 and calculate the probability that, with a random sample of fifty components from a large batch in which 4 per cent are defective, four or more of the sample components are found to be defective. Compare the answer with your previous subjective guess at the probability.

19 A golf course consists of eighteen holes, each of which has a par score of four shots. Two shots are allowed to reach the green, namely, a drive and an iron shot. Assume that the probability of a certain player having a good drive is 0·8, and of having a good iron shot is 0·7. The two shots are independent of each other. If either shot is a bad one an extra shot is required at that hole (if both basic shots are bad, two extra shots are required). Find the expected total number of shots required to reach the eighteen greens in the round, together with the standard deviation of that number. Assume performance at each hole is independent of the other holes.

4 Continuous random variables

4.1 Introduction

In the last chapter we were concerned with random variables which could only take a limited set of values, e.g. integer values, and then not always every possible integer. These were referred to as discrete random variables. In this chapter we shall be concerned with random variables which can take any value, although sometimes only within a defined range. These are referred to as *continuous random variables*. Thus a man's height is, in theory, a continuous random variable. Within certain limits, say from 4 ft to 7 ft, he can have any height and is not limited to exact inches (or exact centimetres, etc.). Or again, the time I have to wait at a bus stop until the next bus comes along is, in theory, a continuous variable that could take any value from zero upwards and does not necessarily have to be an exact number of minutes (or seconds). Thus, in both these instances we could associate possible values of these measures (height or time) with all the points on a defined interval of a line that represents a scale of measurement. We want then to assign probabilities to points on the line, not in chunks as in discrete distributions, but more smoothly. An example will show the need more clearly.

Imagine the second hand on an electric clock that stops instantly at your blindfold command. What is the chance that it stops at *exactly* 10 seconds after a full minute? By 'exactly' we mean 10·000 . . . seconds with zeros carried on forever. A moment's thought will suggest that there is no chance at all. And the same thing is true for every possible number of seconds, whether an exact integer or not, between 0 and 60. Yet the clock must stop somewhere, since the probability that it stops is 1. Thus, if we tried to add probabilities as usual, taking each separate point of time over the 60 second interval, we would have nothing but zeros to add. They cannot add to 1, though common sense suggests that they must do so.

But this difficulty is insoluble, and the mathematical notions of areas and intervals signal a way round this problem. We assign probabilities to intervals, rather than to single points, and thus represent probabilities as the appropriate area over some interval. Suppose again that a clock stops at a random time; what is the probability that the minute hand stops between the numerals 1 and 5? The space between the numerals 1 and 5 is $\frac{4}{12}$ of the circumference, and so most people would agree that the appropriate probability is $\frac{1}{3}$. Here we have a random variable, x, which has a numerical value in the range from 0 to 12, indicating the instant when the clock stopped. Any real value of x between 0 and 12 is possible. There is an infinite number of possibilities; we wish to treat them all alike in assigning probabilities, but there is a difficulty that we have not met before in trying to assess and count the equally likely cases in such a situation. However, there is a way out of the difficulty by assigning to each interval of values of x between 0 and 12, a probability proportional to the length of the interval. Since the entire interval from 0 to 12 has probability 1, an interval of unit length is assigned probability $\frac{1}{12}$, an interval of length 4 is assigned probability $\frac{4}{12}$, etc. Thus, as stated above, the probability that x will fall between 1 and 5 is $\frac{4}{12}$, or:

$$P(1 \leqslant x \leqslant 5) = \frac{5-1}{12-0} = \tfrac{1}{3}.$$

This is shown graphically in Fig. 4.1, which illustrates the probability density function, $f(x)$, appropriate to this example. The base extends from 0 to 12 along the x-axis. Because the clock can stop at random at any point between 0 and 12, we want to assign equal probabilities to any two equal time intervals. If the probabilities relating to the time intervals are to be

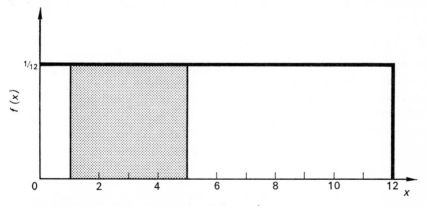

Fig. 4.1. Probability density function for clock stopping

measured by areas, the altitudes of the corresponding rectangles should be equal. Thus, since the total area under the rectangle has to be 1, as the clock must stop at some point, the density function is bounded by a line parallel to the x-axis and at a distance $\frac{1}{12}$ above the axis. The shaded area in Fig. 4.1 represents the probability that the clock stops between 1 and 5. The area of the rectangle is then $(5-1)/12 = \frac{4}{12}$.

As a different illustration, consider a commuter who drives to work from his home in the suburbs of London and aims to reach his office by 9.00 a.m. Because of fluctuations in traffic and other factors, he actually arrives between 8.45 and 9.05, with 8.55 as his average time of arrival. The relative frequencies of his various arrival times seem to him to be in the form of an isosceles triangle with the apex at 8.55 a.m. Hence the probability graph for his time of arrival can also be approximated very well by an isosceles triangle. If this is true, what is the probability that he will arrive at work on time?

Let the time of arrival in minutes be represented by x, a continuous random variable. To simplify matters, let $x=0$ correspond to 8.55 a.m., the mid-point of his arrival times. Then his density function is an isosceles triangle with base from $x=-10$ to $x=+10$, and altitude above $x=0$ at a distance h that will make the total area of the triangle equal to 1. Hence $\frac{1}{2} \times h \times 20 = 1$, or $h = \frac{1}{10}$. Put formally in symbols, we now have:

$$f(x) = \frac{1}{10}\left(1 + \frac{x}{10}\right) \quad -10 \leqslant x \leqslant 0$$

$$= \frac{1}{10}\left(1 - \frac{x}{10}\right) \quad 0 \leqslant x \leqslant 10$$

$$= 0 \quad \text{elsewhere.}$$

Figure 4.2 shows the completed probability density function. The area of the small shaded triangle represents the probability of the commuter arriving after 9 o'clock; the altitude is $\frac{1}{20}$ and the shaded area is $(\frac{1}{2})5(\frac{1}{20}) = \frac{1}{8}$. Therefore, the probability that he will arrive on, or before, time is $1 - \frac{1}{8} = \frac{7}{8}$.

4.2 Cumulative density functions

The previous section showed how the probability density function of a continuous variable can be defined. The probability density function (or pdf) is the analogue for continuous random variables of the probability distribution for discrete random variables. The concept can be extended to define the cumulative density function (or cdf) of a random variable x in the terms that:

$F(a) \equiv$ Probability that $x \leqslant a$

where a is any value whatsoever. Since we are going to allow a to take on all possible values, and thus serve much the same purpose as the symbol x,

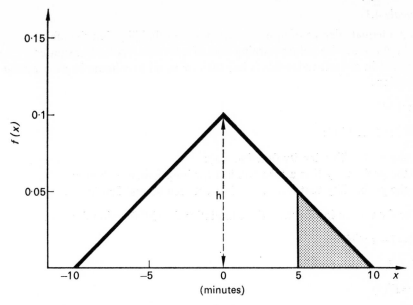

Fig. 4.2. Probability density function for time of arrival

it is more sensible to adopt the notation $F(x)$ rather than $F(a)$. That is, $F(x)$ denotes the probability that the random variable in question assumes any value less than or equal to x. A table, graph or mathematical formulae giving $F(x)$ for all possible values of x uniquely defines the distribution of x as a random variable. Note, therefore, the distinction between $f(x)$, the probability density function, and $F(x)$, the cumulative density function. In mathematical terms:

$$F(x) = \int_{-\infty}^{x} f(x)\, dx \qquad (4.1)$$

where $-\infty$ is taken as the lower bound of the values that x can take. (In many instances the effective lower bound for x will be considerably higher.) By differentiation:

$$\frac{d}{dx} F(x) = f(x)$$

or

$$F'(x) = f(x) \qquad (4.2)$$

This implies that we can readily turn one form of density function into the other form. The cdf is the continuous variable analogue to the cumulative probability distribution for discrete variables.

Example 4.1

To an adequate degree of approximation, the probability that the life (i.e. hours of service before burning out) of a certain type of transmitter tube used in aircraft radar sets is less than or equal to x hours is given by the expression:

$1 - e^{-x/180}$

for $0 \leqslant x \leqslant \infty$. Find:

(*i*) the probability density function $f(x)$;
(*ii*) the probability that a tube will last for longer than 90 hours;
(*iii*) the probability that a tube will last between 90 and 360 hours.

The data given implies that the cumulative density function for x is:

$F(x) = 1 - e^{-x/180}$

For (*i*) we have:

$f(x) = F'(x)$

and, hence:

$f(x) = \dfrac{1}{180} e^{-x/180}$ for $0 \leqslant x \leqslant \infty$.

Figure 4.3(a) shows the cumulative density function $F(x)$ and Fig. 4.3(b) the the probability density function $f(x)$.

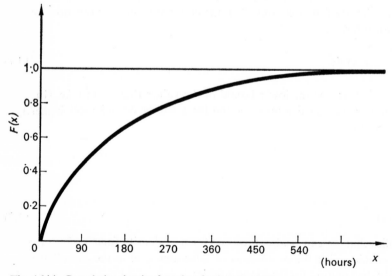

Fig. 4.3(a). Cumulative density function for length of life

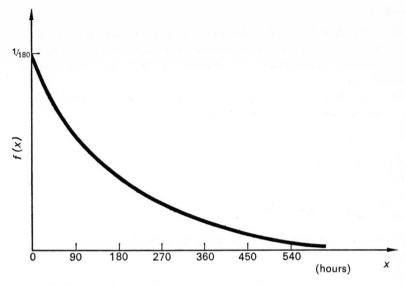

Fig. 4.3(b). Probability density function for length of life

For (*ii*) we require to evaluate the expression:

$1 - F(x)$ when $x = 90$.

This is equal to:

$1 - \{1 - e^{-90/180}\} = e^{-\frac{1}{2}} = 0.393.$

For (*iii*) we require to evaluate either the expression:

$F(x_1) - F(x_2)$ where $x_1 = 360$, $x_2 = 90$,

or the expression:

$$\int_{90}^{360} f(x)\, dx.$$

The former is probably simpler to handle and is equal to:

$$e^{-90/180} - e^{-360/180} = e^{-\frac{1}{2}} - e^{-2}$$

$$= 0.472.$$

The form of distribution considered in this example is a particular case of an *exponential* distribution. It is quite commonly met with in practice as it provides a reasonably practical approximation to the probability density function of a number of frequently observed phenomena, e.g. the length of life of electronic components, the time spent in a queue waiting to be served, etc.

† *Example 4.2*

Form the cumulative density function $F(x)$ for the commuter illustration used earlier in the chapter. Use the function $F(x)$ to evaluate the probability that the commuter arrives within three minutes of the correct office starting time of 9.00 a.m.

Again using 8.55 a.m. as an origin, and minutes as units, the probability density function was derived earlier as follows:

$$f(x)=0 \quad x<-10 \quad \text{or} \quad x>10$$

$$f(x)=\frac{1}{10}\left(1+\frac{x}{10}\right) \quad -10\leqslant x\leqslant 0$$

$$f(x)=\frac{1}{10}\left(1-\frac{x}{10}\right) \quad 0\leqslant x\leqslant 10$$

By integration we can now form $F(x)$, using the general definition:

$$F(x)=\int_{-\infty}^{x} f(x)\, dx.$$

Clearly, for $x<-10$, $F(x)=0$; while for $x>10$, $F(x)=1$.
Consider next the case of $-10\leqslant x\leqslant 0$. Here:

$$F(x)=\int_{-10}^{x} \frac{1}{10}\left(1+\frac{x}{10}\right) dx=\left[\frac{1}{200}(10+x)^2\right]_{-10}^{x}$$

$$=\frac{(10+x)^2}{200}.$$

Similarly, for the case when $0\leqslant x\leqslant 10$, we have:

$$F(x)=\int_{-10}^{0} f(x)\, dx+\int_{0}^{x} f(x)\, dx$$

$$F(x)=\tfrac{1}{2}+\int_{0}^{x}\frac{1}{10}\left(1-\frac{x}{10}\right) dx=\tfrac{1}{2}+\left[\frac{-1}{200}(10-x)^2\right]_{0}^{x}$$

$$=\tfrac{1}{2}+\tfrac{1}{2}-\frac{(10-x)^2}{200}$$

$$=1-\frac{(10-x)^2}{200}.$$

The graph of this cumulative density function is shown in Fig. 4.4. The probability that the commuter arrives within three minutes of 9.00 a.m. will be equal to $F(8)-F(2)$, or:

$$\left(1-\frac{2^2}{200}\right)-\left(1-\frac{8^2}{200}\right)=\frac{60}{200}=0\cdot 3.$$

Hence, the probability of arrival between 8.57 and 9.03 a.m. is 0·3.

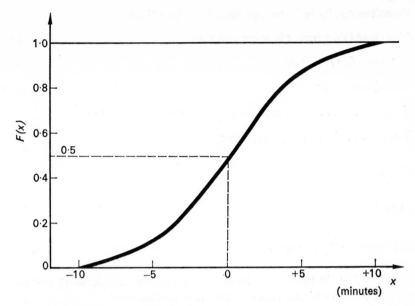

Fig. 4.4. Cumulative density function for commuter arrival

4.3 Properties

Basically the same kind of properties hold for continuous random variables as for discontinuous random variables. Thus:

(i) $E(\phi(x)) = \int \phi(x) f(x) \, dx.$ (4.3)

(a) If $\phi(x) = x$, then

$$E(x) = \int x f(x) \, dx$$ (4.4)

and is referred to as the mean or expected value.

(b) If $\phi(x) = (x - \bar{x})^2$, then

$$E(\phi(x)) = \text{var}(x) = E(x - \bar{x})^2$$

$$= \int (x - \bar{x})^2 f(x) \, dx$$

$$= \int (x^2 - 2x\bar{x} + \bar{x}^2) f(x) \, dx$$

$$= E(x^2) - [E(x)]^2$$

giving rise to the commonly used result:

$$\text{var}(x) = E(x^2) - [E(x)]^2.$$ (4.5)

(*ii*) From the results in (*i*) we can directly deduce that:

$$E(ax)=aE(x), \text{ where } a \text{ is some constant} \tag{4.6}$$

$$E(x+a)=E(x)+a, \text{ and} \tag{4.7}$$

$$\mathrm{var}(ax)=a^2 \, \mathrm{var}(x) \tag{4.8}$$

(*iii*) If x_i ($i=1, 2, \ldots k$) are a series of random variables and a_i

($i=1, 2, \ldots k$) are constants, then:

$$X= \sum_{i=1}^{k} a_i x_i$$

has
$$E(X)= \sum_{i=1}^{k} a_i E(x_i) \tag{4.9a}$$

and
$$\mathrm{var}(X)= \sum_{i=1}^{k} a_i^2 \, \mathrm{var}(x_i), \tag{4.9b}$$

provided that the random variables x_i are mutually independent. For the statistical independence required here it is implied that:

$$P(x_i \leqslant X_i, \; x_j \leqslant X_j)=P(x_i \leqslant X_i) \, P(x_j \leqslant X_j)$$

for all values of i and j ($i \neq j$). The lefthand side of this equation is symbolic shorthand for the probability that x_i is less than, or equal to, X_i, simultaneously with x_j less than or equal to X_j. This requirement for statistical independence is necessary for Eq. 4.9b, but is not a necessary condition for Eq. 4.9a.

Example 4.3

A defective spot (point) occurs in a glass disc R inches in radius and is equally likely to occur anywhere on the disc. Let x be a random variable representing the distance between the centre of the disc and the point of occurrence of the defective spot.

(*i*) Find an expression for $F(x)$ and $f(x)$.
(*ii*) Find the mean and standard deviation of the random variable x.

For the evaluation of $F(x)$ we need the probability that the spot falls within a circle of radius x (less than R). This probability is equal to $\pi x^2 / \pi R^2$ by straightforward geometrical considerations of the ratio of the concentric circles with radii x and R respectively. Hence:

$$F(x)=x^2/R^2 \quad 0 \leqslant x \leqslant R$$

and

$$f(x)=2x/R^2 \quad 0 \leqslant x \leqslant R. \tag{From 4.2}$$

From the latter result we can in turn evaluate:

$$E(x) = \int_0^R x \cdot \frac{2x}{R^2} dx = \frac{2}{3R^2} \left[x^3 \right]_0^R = \frac{2}{3} R. \qquad \text{(From 4.4)}$$

and $\text{var}(x) = \int_0^R x^2 \frac{2x}{R^2} dx - \left(\frac{2}{3} R \right)^2 = \frac{1}{18} R^2.$ (From 4.5)

Hence, the standard deviation of x is $R/3\sqrt{2}$ or $0 \cdot 235R$.

Example 4.4

A resistor is composed of three component parts soldered together in series; the total resistance of the resistor equals the sum of the resistances of the component parts. The first part is randomly drawn from a production lot having a mean of 200 ohms and a standard deviation of 2 ohms, while the second and third parts are each randomly drawn from a large lot of components having a mean of 150 ohms and a standard deviation of 3 ohms. Find the mean and standard deviation of the resistance of the assembled resistor.

Let x_1, x_2, x_3 be the resistance of the three component parts.

Then $E(x_1 + x_2 + x_3) = E(x_1) + E(x_2) + E(x_3)$ (From 4.9a)

$$= 200 + 150 + 150$$

$$= 500 \text{ ohms.}$$

$\text{Var}(x_1 + x_2 + x_3) = \text{var}(x_1) + \text{var}(x_2) + \text{var}(x_3)$ (From 4.9b)

$$= 2^2 + 3^2 + 3^2 = 22.$$

Hence, the standard deviation of the resistor is $\sqrt{22}$ or $4 \cdot 7$ ohms.

† *Example 4.5*

A product has to go through three processes A, B and C in turn. The times taken in each process are independent random variables and the cost per hour in each process is different. Find the mean and standard deviation of the total cost of processing the product, given the information shown in Table 4.1.

Table 4.1

Process	Mean time (hr)	Standard deviation (hr)	Cost (£/hr)
A	1	0·1	6
B	3	0·2	5
C	2	0·25	8

Let x_i ($i=1, 2, 3$) be the times taken in the three processes. Then we require the expected value and standard deviation of:

$$X=6x_1+5x_2+8x_3.$$

From Eq. 4.9a we have:

$$E(X)=6\times1+5\times3+8\times2=£37.$$

From Eq. 4.9b we have:

$$\text{Var}(X)=6^2\times(0\cdot1)^2+5^2\times(0\cdot2)^2+8^2\times(0\cdot25)^2$$

$$=5\cdot36.$$

Hence, the standard deviation is $\sqrt{5\cdot36}$ or £2·3.

Example 4.6

The length of life of electric light bulbs being purchased in a large lot has a mean of 1000 hours with a standard deviation of 150 hours. A sample of 4 bulbs is randomly drawn from this lot and the bulbs burnt until they fail. If $\bar{x}$ is the mean (or average) length of life in the sample of four bulbs, what is the mean and standard deviation of $\bar{x}$?

Let x_i, $i=1, 2, 3, 4$, be the lengths of life of the four bulbs in the sample. Then:

$$\bar{x}=\tfrac{1}{4}\sum_{i=0}^{4}x_i$$

where, in the terms of Eq. 4.9a and 4.9b, we have $k=4$ and $a_i=\tfrac{1}{4}$. Hence:

$$E(\bar{x})=\tfrac{1}{4}\sum_{i=1}^{4}E(x_i)=\tfrac{1}{4}\times4\times1000$$

$$=1000 \text{ hours.}$$

$$\text{Var}(\bar{x})=\tfrac{1}{16}\sum_{i=1}^{4}\text{var}(x_i)=\tfrac{1}{16}\times4\times(150)^2$$

$$=22\ 500/4$$

and the standard deviation of $\bar{x}$ is $\sqrt{(22\ 500/4)}$ or 75 hours.

Note that we can generalize the particular result of this example as follows: if we have drawn a random sample of size n from some population, where the mean and variance of each individual are μ and σ^2 respectively, then the mean, $\bar{x}$, of the sample has an expected value given by:

$$E(\bar{x})=\mu \tag{4.10a}$$

and variance given by:

$$\text{Var}(\bar{x})=\sum_{i=1}^{n}\frac{1}{n^2}\cdot\sigma^2=\frac{\sigma^2}{n}$$

so that the standard deviation of $\bar{x}$ is $\sigma/\sqrt{n}$. $\tag{4.10b}$

These results imply that, if repeated random samples of size n are drawn from some population, the mean of the sample means is the same as that of the population from which the individuals were drawn, and the standard deviation of the sample means decreases inversely with $\sqrt{n}$. These are important results, since, as will be discussed later, they have implications as to the amount of information it is worth obtaining by sample investigation for any particular decision situation.

4.4 Normal distribution

The normal distribution plays a fundamental role in all facets of mathematical statistics, and many important statistical techniques are based on the properties of this particular distribution. The distribution was discovered by de Moivre, whose published works as early as 1733 contained a derivation of it as the limiting form, when the number of trials is very large, of the binomial distribution discussed earlier. It was also known to Laplace no later than 1774 but, through historical error, it has been commonly attributed to Gauss, whose earliest published reference to it did not appear until 1809. For this reason, some books refer to the distribution as the *Gaussian distribution*. During the eighteenth and nineteenth centuries, various attempts were made to establish this distribution as some underlying natural and universal law governing all continuous variates—hence the name 'normal'. Although these attempts failed, being based on what we now accept to be a false premise that such a law exists, the normal distribution rightly occupies a preeminent place in the field of probability. Besides having exceptionally convenient properties of its own, it also serves as a useful approximation to many other distributions which are less tractable. In particular, the average or mean of n observations taken at random from almost any population tends to become more nearly normally distributed as n increases.

A random variable x is said to be normally distributed if its probability density function $f(x)$ is given by an expression of the form:

$$f(x) = \frac{1}{\sigma\sqrt{(2\pi)}} \exp\left\{-\frac{1}{2}\left(\frac{x-\mu}{\sigma}\right)^2\right\} \quad -\infty \leqslant x \leqslant \infty, \tag{4.11}$$

where μ can be any real number, positive or negative, σ any real positive number, and $\exp\{z\}$ is written to indicate e^z, e being as before the base of natural logarithms ($e = 2\cdot71828$).

The distribution is unimodal, with the mode at $x = \mu$, and it has two points of inflexion, each located at a distance σ on either side of the mode. By inspection of the expression in Eq. 4.11, it is evident that the density function is symmetrical about $x = \mu$, and falls off rapidly as the magnitude of $(x - \mu)$ increases. Although the normal distribution has an infinite range in both directions, the probability $f(x)$ of very large deviations from μ is small enough to be neglected for most practical purposes; hence, the distribution is capable of approximating others for which the true range is finite. Figure 4.5(a) shows the distribution for three values of μ and a constant value of σ; while in Fig. 4.5(b) μ is held constant and three values of σ are illustrated. Clearly,

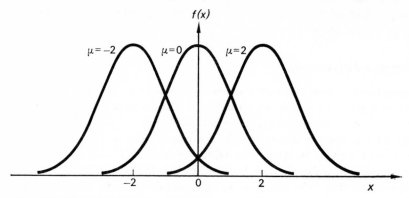

Fig. 4.5(a). Normal distributions with $\sigma=1$

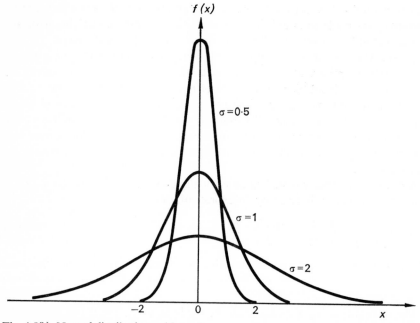

Fig. 4.5(b). Normal distributions with $\mu=0$

a shift in μ displaces the curve as a whole, whereas a change in σ, for a fixed value of μ, alters the relative proportions falling in differing intervals along the fixed scale of x.

Such a normal distribution obviously has a mean equal to μ due to its symmetry about $x=\mu$. It can also be deduced mathematically that the variance of x is equal to σ^2. Hence, the two parameters μ and σ, which define the distribution, are respectively the mean and standard deviation of the random variable x.

A normal distribution with $\mu=0$ and $\sigma^2=1$ is termed a unit (or standard) normal distribution. The formula for the probability density function will then be the rather simpler expression:

$$f(x)=\frac{1}{\sqrt{(2\pi)}}\exp\{-\tfrac{1}{2}x^2\}\quad -\infty\leqslant x\leqslant\infty. \tag{4.12}$$

Since the probability density function of the normal distribution cannot be integrated explicitly, the evaluation of probabilities whenever they were required would entail numerical integration, were it not for extensive tables already available. These tables have been constructed for the unit normal distribution only, but can be adapted to any other normal distribution by the substitution:

$$u=(x-\mu)/\sigma.$$

For example, if x is a normal random variable with the general parameters, μ and σ, then:

$$P(a\leqslant x\leqslant b)=\int_a^b \frac{1}{\sqrt{(2\pi)}\sigma}\exp\left\{-\frac{1}{2}\left(\frac{x-\mu}{\sigma}\right)^2\right\}dx$$

$$=\int_{a'}^{b'} \frac{1}{\sqrt{(2\pi)}}\exp\{-\tfrac{1}{2}u^2\}\,du,$$

where a simple substitution of $u=(x-\mu)/\sigma$ is made with $a'=(a-\mu)/\sigma$ and $b'=(b-\mu)/\sigma$. The unit normal distribution as expressed in the second integral above will be used so often in this book that, to avoid writing down explicit expressions for its probability density function and cumulative density function each time they arise, the symbols $f_N(x)$ and $F_N(x)$, respectively, will be used. A concise tabulation of $f_N(x)$ and $F_N(x)$ for the unit normal distribution is provided in Appendix B, where only positive values of x are given, since $f_N(-x)=f_N(x)$, and $F_N(-x)=1-F_N(x)$, thus enabling the probabilities for negative values of x to be readily evaluated.

A study of Appendix B shows that the standard deviation, σ, provides us with a yardstick of the proportion of a normal distribution falling within various bands, viz.,

Mean $\pm\,1\times$ standard deviation covers 68·3 per cent of the distribution.

Mean $\pm\,2\times$ standard deviation covers 95·4 per cent of the distribution.

Mean $\pm\,3\times$ standard deviation covers 99·7 per cent of the distribution.

These yardsticks give a rough but ready means of comparing the variabilities of two or more distributions and indicate the meaning of the expression 'standard deviation' in physical terms.

Example 4.7

A college entrance test taken by a large number of students is scaled so that the scores approximate to a normal distribution with mean 500 and standard deviation 100. What is the probability that:

(*i*) A randomly selected student will score 750 or more?
(*ii*) A randomly selected student will score between 550 and 700?
(*iii*) Three randomly selected students all score over 600?

For (*i*) we require $1 - F_N(x)$ where $x = (750 - 500)/100 = 2 \cdot 5$. From Appendix B, $F_N(2 \cdot 5) = 0 \cdot 9938$, and hence $1 - F_N(2 \cdot 5) = 0 \cdot 0062$.

For (*ii*) we require $F_N(x_1) - F_N(x_2)$, where $x_1 = (700 - 500)/100 = 2 \cdot 0$ and $x_2 = (550 - 500)/100 = 0 \cdot 5$. From Appendix B, $F_N(x_1) - F_N(x_2) = 0 \cdot 9772 - 0 \cdot 6915 = 0 \cdot 2857$.

For (*iii*) we require first the probability that one student scores over 600. This is given by $1 - F_N(x)$ where $x = (600 - 500)/100 = 1 \cdot 0$. From Appendix B, the value is $1 - 0 \cdot 8413$, or $0 \cdot 1587$. Hence, the required probability is $(0 \cdot 1587)^3$ or $0 \cdot 0040$.

† *Example* 4.8

Bags of sugar, when filled by a machine with a fixed setting, vary in weight, following a normal distribution with a mean equal to the nominal fixed setting and a standard deviation of $0 \cdot 02$ lb. What setting (or average weight) should be selected for weighing out nominal 2 lb bags of sugar if it is desired that not more than one bag in 500 of the sugar bags produced will, on average, have less than the nominal 2 lb of sugar in it?

Let the nominal setting be μ. Then the probability that a bag will have less than 2 lb of sugar in it will be $F_N(x)$, where $x = (2 - \mu)/0 \cdot 02$. Now from inspection of Appendix B, x must be equal to $-2 \cdot 88$ if $F_N(x)$ is to be equal to $0 \cdot 0020$. Hence:

$$-2 \cdot 88 = \frac{2 - \mu}{0 \cdot 02} \quad \text{or} \quad \mu = 2 \cdot 058.$$

Thus it will be necessary to give an average of about 3 per cent overweight if the probability of a 'rogue' bag of sugar is to be kept down to $0 \cdot 002$. To decrease the amount of excess sugar that must be given away without increasing the probability of rogue bags of sugar, it would be necessary to make the standard deviation of the weighing procedure rather lower than $0 \cdot 02$ lb.

4.5 Normal approximation to binomial

The normal distribution is the limiting form of a great many distributions. In particular, as de Moivre demonstrated as long ago as 1733, it is the limiting form approached by the binomial distribution for large values of n. Thus, if x is a random variable that is binomially distributed, we know that

$$f(x) = \binom{n}{x} p^x q^{n-x} \quad x = 0, 1, 2, \ldots n,$$

with n and p as the parameters concerned and $q = 1 - p$. Then, as n increases

$$f(x) \to \frac{1}{\sqrt{(2\pi)}\sqrt{(npq)}} \exp\left\{-\frac{1}{2}\frac{(x-np)^2}{npq}\right\} \quad -\infty \leqslant x \leqslant +\infty \tag{4.13}$$

which is of normal form with $\mu = np$, $\sigma^2 = npq$. For moderately large values of n, the binomial distribution is adequately approximated for most purposes by this normal distribution with $\mu = np$, $\sigma^2 = npq$, provided that $np \geqslant 5$. However, in applying the normal approximation, a compensation needs to be made for the fact that the binomial variable is actually discrete and n is finite. The conventional correction consists of changing the numerical deviation from μ by one-half unit before dividing by σ, on the grounds that the discrete value $x = a$ should correspond on a continuous scale to the interval $a - \frac{1}{2} \leqslant x \leqslant a + \frac{1}{2}$. The rationale of this correction is illustrated in Fig. 4.6,

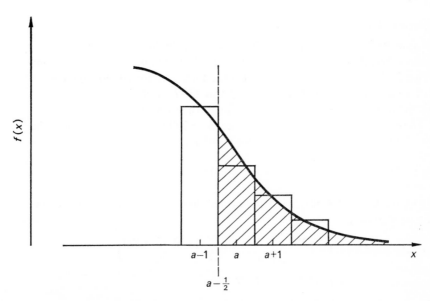

Fig. 4.6. Normal approximation to binomial

where the blocks represent part of the discrete binomial probabilities and the curve the approximating normal distribution. Thus, to estimate the probability:

$$P(x \geqslant a) = \sum_{x=a}^{n} \binom{n}{x} p^x q^{n-x};$$

where a is $\geqslant np + \frac{1}{2}$, we first set:

$$u = \frac{a - \frac{1}{2} - \mu}{\sigma},$$

where $\mu = np$ and $\sigma = \sqrt{(npq)}$.
Then,

$$P(x \geqslant a) \doteqdot 1 - F_N(u),$$

where $F_N(u)$ is the unit normal variable.

Again, to estimate the probability:

$$P(x \leqslant a) = \sum_{x=0}^{a} \binom{n}{x} p^x q^{n-x}$$

where $a \leqslant np - \frac{1}{2}$, we set:

$$u' = \frac{\mu - (a + \frac{1}{2})}{\sigma}$$

where $\mu = np$ and $\sigma = \sqrt{(npq)}$, and look up $F_N(u')$. Finally, to estimate $P(a \leqslant x \leqslant b)$, we extend the interval one half unit to either side before dividing by σ.

Example 4.9

In a defined large conurbation, 20 per cent of the households possess a dishwasher. A market research survey selects 1000 households at random. What is the probability (*i*) that not more than 230 households possess a dishwasher, and (*ii*) that between 170 and 230 households possess a dishwasher among the 1000 households in the sample? Here $n = 1000$, $p = 0.2$, $q = 0.8$. Hence, $np = 200$ and $npq = 160$. Using the normal approximation, we have, for (*i*), that:

$$P(x \leqslant 230) = F_N \left(\frac{230 + \frac{1}{2} - 200}{\sqrt{160}} \right) = F_N(2 \cdot 41)$$

From the table in Appendix B the probability is 0·992. For (*ii*) we require the probability:

$$P(170 \leqslant x \leqslant 230) = F_N \left(\frac{230 + \frac{1}{2} - 200}{\sqrt{160}} \right) - F_N \left(\frac{170 - \frac{1}{2} - 200}{\sqrt{160}} \right)$$

$$= F_N(2 \cdot 41) - F_N(-2 \cdot 41)$$

$$= 0 \cdot 992 - 0 \cdot 008 = 0 \cdot 984.$$

† *Example* 4.10

It is believed that the incidence of mortgage protection assurance policies among householders is approximately 10 per cent, and a market research survey is commissioned to verify (or disprove) this statement. It is accordingly desired to estimate the percentage of households having such a policy to within ±2 per cent. How many households should be sampled if we want to be 95 per cent sure of the result being accurate to the desired limits?

Assume that n households are sampled and that $p=0\cdot10$. Then, if x is the number of households in the sample found to have a policy, we require the minimum value of n such that:

$$P(p-0\cdot02 \leqslant \frac{x}{n} \leqslant p+0\cdot02)=0\cdot95$$

With an assumed value of $p=0\cdot1$ and $q=0\cdot9$, we need:

$$P(0\cdot08n \leqslant x \leqslant 0\cdot12n)=0\cdot95,$$

or

$$F_N\left(\frac{0\cdot12n+\frac{1}{2}-0\cdot1n}{\sqrt{(0\cdot09n)}}\right)-F_N\left(\frac{0\cdot08n-\frac{1}{2}-0\cdot1n}{\sqrt{(0\cdot09n)}}\right)=0\cdot95,$$

or

$$F_N\left(\frac{0\cdot02n+\frac{1}{2}}{\sqrt{(0\cdot09n)}}\right)-F_N\left(\frac{-0\cdot02n-\frac{1}{2}}{\sqrt{(0\cdot09n)}}\right)=0\cdot95 \qquad (4.14)$$

Now we would usually aim to have

$$F_N\left(\frac{0\cdot02n+\frac{1}{2}}{\sqrt{(0\cdot09n)}}\right)$$

equal to 0·975, since in this way

$$F_N\left(\frac{-0\cdot02n-\frac{1}{2}}{\sqrt{(0\cdot09n)}}\right)$$

will be equal to 0·025 and thus give a difference of 0·95. Hence, from the unit normal tables in Appendix B:

$$\frac{0\cdot02n+\frac{1}{2}}{\sqrt{(0\cdot09n)}}=1\cdot96 \quad \text{and} \quad n=865 \text{ approximately.}$$

Hence, a sample of 865 or thereabouts seems to be necessary to achieve the required precision.

In the above analysis we set a 95 per cent degree of certainty. Suppose, alternatively, that we only wanted to be 90 per cent certain that the result was accurate to the desired limits. In this instance we will have, in place of

Eq. 4.14 above, the expression:

$$F_N \left(\frac{0 \cdot 02 + \frac{1}{2}}{\sqrt{(0 \cdot 09n)}} \right) - F_N \left(\frac{-0 \cdot 02 - \frac{1}{2}}{\sqrt{(0 \cdot 09n)}} \right) = 0 \cdot 90.$$

From the unit normal tables in Appendix B we now have:

$$\frac{0 \cdot 02n + \frac{1}{2}}{\sqrt{(0 \cdot 09n)}} = 1 \cdot 645$$

Hence, a sample of 557 or thereabouts will be necessary to achieve the revised level of precision. Notice that a relaxation of the degree of certainty required in the result has led to a considerably lower minimum sample size. This provides an illustration of the trade-off between confidence and sample size.

4.6 Linear functions of normal random variables

We saw earlier in Eq. 4.9a and 4.9b how to obtain the mean and standard deviation of a linear sum of independent random variables. There is one further extension of these results that is of great use; it is stated without proof. This result is that if there are k independent random variables x_i, each normally distributed with mean μ_i and variance equal to σ_i, then the random variable

$$X = \sum_{i=1}^{k} a_i x_i$$

where the a_is are constants, is also normally distributed with

$$\text{mean} = \sum_{i=1}^{k} a_i \mu_i \qquad (4.15a)$$

$$\text{and variance} = \sum_{i=1}^{k} a_i^2 \sigma_i^2. \qquad (4.15b)$$

This is a powerful result. It implies, for example, that the mean of a random sample drawn from a population which follows a normal distribution will itself be normally distributed. This follows because the sample mean, as we have already seen, is a linear function of the sample values. There is yet another extension of the latter result that is even more powerful. This extension states that the means of random samples drawn from *any* population tend to be more and more nearly normally distributed as the sample size increases. This result, the proof of which is beyond our scope here, will be much used in later chapters.

† *Example* 4.11

A small aircraft will take four passengers in addition to the pilot, and the mean weight of the passengers must not exceed 180 lb. Assuming that the passengers are selected at random from a population where weights are normally distributed with mean 150 lb and standard deviation 32 lb, how often will the four passengers overload the plane?

The mean weight of the four passengers will be normally distributed with mean 150 lb and standard deviation of $32/\sqrt{4}$ or 16 lb. Hence, the required probability will be:

$$1 - F_N \left(\frac{180 - 150}{16} \right) = 1 - F_N(1\cdot875) = 0\cdot0305.$$

Hence, in approximately 1 in 33 occasions the plane will be overloaded.

Example 4.12

The distribution of gross weights of 8-ounce boxes of cornflakes has mean 9·60 ounces and standard deviation 0·80 ounces respectively. If the boxes are packaged 24 per carton, and if the population of weights of empty cartons is normally distributed with mean 24·00 ounces, and standard deviation 2·20 ounces, what are:

(*i*) the mean and standard deviation of the weight of filled cartons, and
(*ii*) the percentage of the filled cartons with weights between 250 and 260 ounces?

Let X be the total weight of 24 boxes of cornflakes. Then:

$$X = x_1 + x_2 + x_3 \ldots + x_{24}.$$

Using Eqs. 4.9a and 4.9b we have:

$$E(X) = 24 \times 9\cdot60 = 230\cdot40$$

and

$$\text{var}(X) = 24 \ \text{var}(x_i) = 24 \times 0\cdot80^2 = 15\cdot36.$$

If Y is the weight of an empty carton, then:

$$E(X + Y) = E(X) + E(Y) = 230\cdot40 + 24\cdot00 = 254\cdot40$$

This is the mean weight of the filled cartons.

Also $\text{var}(X + Y) = \text{var}(X) + \text{var}(Y) = 15\cdot36 + (2\cdot20)^2 = 20\cdot20$, giving a standard deviation of the weight of filled cartons of $\sqrt{20\cdot20}$, or 4·5 ounces. This answers part (*i*). For part (*ii*) we need:

$$P(250 < X + Y < 260).$$

In the light of the discussion earlier in the chapter it is reasonable to assume that the weight of filled cartons is normally distributed. Hence, in terms of a unit normal variable, u say, the required probability is equivalent to:

D

$$P\left(\frac{250-254{\cdot}4}{4{\cdot}5}<u<\frac{260-254{\cdot}4}{4{\cdot}5}\right)$$

or

$$P(-0{\cdot}979<u<1{\cdot}246)$$

or

$$F_N(1{\cdot}246)-F_N(-0{\cdot}979)$$

$=0{\cdot}8936-0{\cdot}1641$ (from the table of the unit normal distribution)

$=0{\cdot}7295.$

Hence, approximately 73 per cent of the filled cartons have weights between 250 and 260 ounces.

4.7 Populations and samples

We have already seen that statistics are largely concerned with populations, and samples drawn from those populations. To help to fix the ideas put forward, let us summarize some of the notation and concepts that have been used so far. First, the constants in a probability distribution which represents a population are referred to as *parameters*. Thus, with a sampling situation that is described by a binomial distribution, n and p would be termed *parameters*. Again, with a population described by a normal distribution, the constants μ and σ that correspond to the mean and standard deviation would be termed *parameters*. If sample information is used to estimate parameters of a distribution, the quantities so used are referred to as *statistics*. Thus, should we use the mean of a sample drawn from a normal population as an estimator of the population mean, the sample mean is referred to as a statistic.

Second, it is usual to distinguish between equivalent quantities calculated from a population and from a sample, by using Greek letters for the former and Roman letters for the latter. Thus we usually write:

	Population	Sample
Mean or expected value	μ	$\bar{x}$
Standard deviation	σ	s

A considerable part of statistical work involves the use of sample information to obtain estimates of population parameters. This aspect will be developed in Chapter 8 onwards. The next three chapters, however, give a basic introduction to decision analysis concepts.

Exercises on Chapter 4

1 A continuous random variable has the probability density function:

$f(x)=3x^2 \quad 0\leqslant x\leqslant 1$

$\quad =0 \qquad$ otherwise.

(*i*) Find the cumulative density function.

(*ii*) Obtain numerical values for $F(x=\frac{1}{3})$, $F(x=\frac{9}{10})$ and $P(\frac{1}{3} \leqslant x \leqslant \frac{1}{2})$.

(*iii*) Find the value of a, such that $P(x \leqslant a) = \frac{1}{4}$ (a is then referred to as the 25th percentile of x).

(*iv*) Find the mean and variance of x.

2 The probability density function for the operating life of a TV tube is:

$$f(x) = 0 \quad x \leqslant 80$$

$$= \frac{80}{x^2} \quad x > 80$$

You buy a TV set containing three of these tubes. Assuming the tubes were selected at random, what is the probability that all three tubes will still be functioning after 120 hours?

3 You intend to contract with a carhire firm for a daily journey across town of 4 miles. The contract offered by a firm involves a charge of 10p per mile and 3p per minute of the journey. Experience of the route to be followed suggests the points shown in Table 4.2 on the cumulative density function for the time of the journey.

Table 4.2

Number of minutes (x)	7	8	9	10	11	12
Probability that journey takes less than x minutes	0·10	0·22	0·54	0·80	0·93	1·00

Estimate the average cost per journey.

A second firm offers a contract based on 15p per mile and 1p per minute of the journey. Which contract will be the more advantageous in the long run?

4 A baker's shop sells cake by the pound. The profit on each pound of cake sold on the day it is baked is 40p, and the loss on each pound not sold on the day it is baked is 15p. Daily demand has the probability density function:

$$f(x) = \frac{1}{100} \quad 100 \leqslant x \leqslant 200$$

$$= 0 \quad \text{elsewhere.}$$

Assuming the baker wishes to maximize the expected profit, what quantity should be baked per day?

5 The distribution of a defined characteristic of a certain electrical component is normal with a mean of 200 units and a standard deviation of 8 units. A transmitter with one of these components needs it to have a characteristic of 188 or greater to obtain full power. The loss of power, in arbitrary units, from the use of a component with a lower characteristic is equal to the square of the difference between the characteristic and 188. What is the mean loss of power, expressed in the arbitrary units, of transmitters using the given components? (Hint: divide the range characteristic below 188 into a number of discrete intervals; an answer to two significant figures is acceptable.)

6 Mass-produced articles are each fitted into a cardboard container and are then packed in wooden boxes, 12 containers per box. Suppose the mean and standard deviation of the weights of the population of articles are 20·6 lb and 0·8 lb respectively, those of the cardboard containers are 1·8 lb and 0·1 lb respectively, and those of the wooden boxes are 3·6 lb and 0·4 lb respectively.

(*i*) What are the values of the mean and standard deviation of the population of weights of filled boxes ready to ship?

(*ii*) What are the mean and standard deviation of the total weight of 16 filled boxes selected at random?

7 A process for making ¼ in. ball-bearings yields a population of ball-bearings with diameters having a mean of 0·2497 in. and standard deviation of 0·0002 in. If we assume a normal distribution of diameters, and if specifications call for bearings with diameters within 0·2500 ± 0·0003 in.;

(*i*) What fraction of the bearings turned out under the set-up are defective (i.e. do not meet specification)?

(*ii*) If minor adjustments of the process can be made to change the mean diameter, but not the standard deviation, what mean should be aimed at in the process set-up so as to minimize the percentage of defectives? What will be the percentage of defectives in such a set-up?

8 A bag of 500 new 5p pieces is emptied on a table and the coins spread out flat.

(*i*) What is the probability of getting between 230 and 270 heads?
(*ii*) What is the probability of getting more than 260 heads?
(Use the normal approximation to the binomial distribution.)

9 A resistor is composed of eight component parts soldered together in series, and the total resistance of the resistor equals the sum of the resistances of the component parts. Three of the components are drawn from a production lot having a mean of 200 ohms and a standard deviation of 2 ohms; four components from a lot having a mean of 150 ohms and a standard deviation of 3 ohms; and one component from a lot having a mean of 250 ohms and a standard deviation of 1 ohm. If we assume (approximate) normality of the distribution of total resistances:

(*i*) What value of the total resistance is such that only 5 per cent of resistors would be below that value?

(*ii*) What is the probability that a sample of four such resistors, manufactured from these components, will have an average resistance in excess of 1443 ohms?

10 Pipes (for tobacco-smoking) are to be packed in fancy plastic boxes. The length of the pipes is normally distributed with a mean of 4·5 in. and a standard deviation of 0·04 in. The internal length of the boxes is normally distributed with a mean of 4·6 in. and a standard deviation of 0·03 in. On what proportion of occasions will the box be too small for the pipe?

11 Three dice are thrown simultaneously, the highest number, x_1, noted, and the die put on one side. (If two or three dice show the same highest number, the throw is not valid and the experiment is repeated.) The two remaining dice are thrown simultaneously until they show different numbers and the higher number, x_2, is noted. Find the expectation and standard deviation of $x_1 + x_2$.

12 A random variable x has probability density function:

$$f(x) = \frac{x}{b^2} \exp\left(-\frac{x^2}{2b^2}\right) \qquad 0 \leqslant x \leqslant +\infty$$

(*i*) Find the distance between the quartiles (the 25th and 75th percentiles) of the probability function.
(*ii*) Evaluate the standard deviation of x.
(*iii*) Show that the ratio of (*i*) to (*ii*), both of which are measures of spread, is independent of b.

13 X_1 and X_2 are independent random variables, each with probability density function:

$$f(X) = 1 \quad \text{if } 0 \leqslant X \leqslant 1$$

$$= 0 \quad \text{otherwise.}$$

Suppose that $X_{(1)}$ is the lower of the values X_1 and X_2. Find the probability density function of $X_{(1)}$ and determine its mean and variance.

14 Two aptitude tests A and B are each given to a large number of applicants seeking admission to a college. Each test is separately scaled so as to give a normalized score distribution with mean of 500 and a standard deviation of 100. A combined score is obtained for each applicant by combining the scores from A and B in the ratio $\frac{2}{3} : \frac{1}{3}$. The applicants' scores on the two tests are assumed to be statistically independent.

(*i*) Calculate the probability that an applicant's combined score exceeds 600;
(*ii*) Calculate the combined score that will be exceeded by 15 per cent of the applicants;

(*iii*) Calculate an applicant's chance of acceptance if the score under (*i*) is the minimum admittance level and it is already known that he has a score of 540 on test A.

15 There are M men, all of whom must die in the next r years, but each of whom is equally likely to die at any instant within this time. The men are independent of each other in this respect. Show that, if x is the expected duration of life of the last survivor, then:

$$E(x)=rM/(M+1),$$

and find the standard deviation of x.

16 The Shockville Laboratory is a government-supported test centre whose objective is to verify manufacturer's adherence to contents stated on product labels. Table 4.3 shows the observations on the percentage of active bleaching ingredients in a household cleanser:

Table 4.3

Percentage of active ingredients	No. of units
5·2	1
5·3	2
5·4	4
5·5	6
5·6	3
5·7	4

The 20 containers were selected at random from a manufacturer's delivery to retail stores in the area. How large a sample would be required if the estimate of the average percentage of active ingredients in the company's production is to have a 95 per cent chance of being within the band of sample mean ± 0.05? (Assume that quality control investigations at the manufacturer's plant show that the distribution of percentage of active ingredients is normal.)

17 On a piece work operation, the Webster and Sons Company pays a bonus if an employee processes 320 or more acceptable pieces in a day. The daily number of acceptable pieces processed by Barry and Kemp, two employees in the department, is normally distributed with the characteristics shown in Table 4.4.

Table 4.4

Employee	Mean	Standard deviation
Barry	290 pieces	20 pieces
Kemp	300 pieces	10 pieces

(*i*) On what percentage of days will (*a*) Barry and (*b*) Kemp get the bonus?

(*ii*) Assume that the outputs of Barry and Kemp are statistically independent and find the probability that their combined total daily output will exceed 600 pieces.

18 A rod AB of unit length is broken at a random point X and thus gives rise to two pieces AX and XB. The piece XB is again broken at a random point Y and this gives rise to form two pieces XY and YB. What is the probability that the three pieces of rod, AX, AY and YB can be used to form a triangle?

19 A time and motion study expert makes a survey of customers arriving at a big store. The times of arrival at one entry door for a forty minute period are noted in Table 4.5 (friends or relatives out shopping together are considered as one customer).

Table 4.5

Minutes	Seconds	Minutes	Seconds
0	0, 5, 9, 12, 31, 49	20	17, 21, 23, 25
1	5, 25, 37, 57	21	8, 24, 45, 58
2	30, 32, 34, 37, 40, 45, 50, 53	22	2, 30, 56
3	46	23	6, 9, 12, 31, 43
4	12, 33, 42	24	9, 25, 39
5	20, 22	25	49
6	8, 20, 59	26	23
7	40	27	40
8	5, 8, 9, 17, 36, 39	28	5, 55
9	1, 19, 28, 31, 34, 44, 55	29	36, 47
10	31, 51, 54	30	0, 46, 50, 53
11	28, 59	31	24, 54
12	30	32	10, 16, 26, 48
13	33, 50, 55	33	18
14	1	34	17
15	31	35	39, 43, 46, 49, 56
16	6, 59	36	—
17	3, 40, 42	37	13, 39
18	9, 49	38	16, 45
19	25, 55	39	30, 55

(*i*) Fit an appropriate distribution to the observations of arrivals per minute on the assumption that arrivals can reasonably be considered random with a constant probability.

(*ii*) Assuming that (*i*) provides a reasonable fit, estimate the probability that, in any given minute, more than three groups of customers will enter the store.

20 The distribution of length x of telephone calls, in minutes, between two cities was found to be exponential, i.e.

$$f(x) = \frac{1}{\beta} \exp\left(-\frac{x}{\beta}\right) \quad 0 \leqslant x \leqslant \infty$$

(*i*) Find the mean and standard deviation of x in terms of β.

(*ii*) A random sample of telephone calls provides a mean length of call of 2·26 minutes. Find the probability that a further call will exceed 5 minutes in length.

(*iii*) Find the approximate probability that the total combined length of 25 further calls selected at random will exceed 60 minutes.

(Assume that the sum of the twenty-five random variables concerned is normally distributed.)

5 Single-stage decision problems

5.1 Introduction

Before considering the effects of uncertainty on the making of decisions—the
main theme of this book—it is worth discussing briefly the problem of choice
under conditions of certainty, or situations which are regarded as
deterministic. As an illustration, suppose that, on 1 August 1971, you have
£500 to invest, money which you want to realize in five years' time when you
expect to have to repay some debt. Three alternatives have been suggested
to you. First, you could invest the money in a building society at $5\frac{1}{4}$ per cent
net per annum and allow the interest to accumulate. Second, you could buy
500 £1 National Savings Certificates which mature at £1·25 each in five years'
time. Third, you could buy British Government 3 per cent Savings Bonds
1965–75 standing at 88 (per £100 nominal) on 1 August 1971 and reinvest all
dividends received in a building society account.

Given these three possibilities, you could work out, under each
alternative, precisely how much would have accumulated by 1975. Income
tax is only payable on the savings bond interest. Surtax, if relevant to you,
is payable both on the savings bond interest and on the grossed up building
society interest which is free of income tax. The National Savings Certificates
are free of all taxes, and no capital gains tax is payable on any of the three
investments. As a consequence you could (and this is left as an exercise for
the reader, taking into account his personal tax position) ascertain which
possible action would give the largest accumulated sum at the end of the
five-year period, and hence which is the best decision to take.

But even this apparently deterministic situation involving the future contains some elements of uncertainty. If the level of interest rates changes, this would affect the yield under the first alternative, investment in a building society, but not the yield of the other two. (Strictly speaking, the reinvestment of interest under the third option of savings bonds would be affected, but the overall effect would be very small.) If taxation levels change, this would affect the yield from the savings bonds and also, indirectly, the yield from the building society. There could be other changes as well, and hence our original model, with its very precise assumptions, only approximates to the real-world situation. The approximation may, however, be very good for practical purposes.

5.2   Single-stage problems

Virtually every situation which involves the future contains an element of uncertainty. This uncertainty is caused because the decision-maker, when he makes the relevant decision, does not have knowledge or control of all the relevant factors which affect the outcomes of the decision. We refer to procedures over which the decision-maker has control as *actions* or *decisions*, while the possible consequences which he cannot completely control are called *events* or *outcomes*. The attractiveness of a particular action/event combination is referred to as the *pay-off* corresponding to that combination. As general notation, we let a_i represent the ith action, r_j the jth event and u_{ij} the pay-off corresponding to the ith action and the jth event.

To illustrate these terms, consider the manager of a small factory which has received an order for twenty-five special castings made from a particular alloy. The specifications are very tight and the allowable tolerances on the finished work correspondingly small. The company makes its own castings, but some of them will probably turn out to be below the standard required. If, after he has completed his batch of castings, he has too few of adequate standard to supply the order, he will have to buy out from a larger manufacturer sufficient castings to make it up. The cost will inevitably be higher than his own castings. How many castings should the manager make?

In this situation, the a_i correspond to the possible size of batch that is made. Then the r_j correspond to the possible numbers of good castings that result from the batch. The pay-offs u_{ij} will then correspond to the total cost of providing the order of twenty-five castings, i.e. the factory costs plus the cost of buying in any extra castings that may be needed.

Note that here we have just one decision to make, namely, the number of castings to be made. When there is a series of decisions, a deterministic sequence can always be formulated from the outset as a series of unique choices. When it is a probabilistic sequence, however, as most such sequences are, the decision corresponding to the second and subsequent stages may be dependent upon what occurred in the first stage.

5.3 Decision criteria

Before we discuss complex problems where there is more than one set of
possible decisions or actions involved we will, in this chapter, look at examples
where there is only one stage in the decision process. In so doing, we must
decide upon the decision criterion that is to be used to choose among
alternatives. To fix ideas we do this through a simple example.

Example 5.1

Our friend Brown is at Euston station about to catch a train to go to a
meeting in Birmingham. On inquiry at the ticket office, he finds that there is
a day return ticket to Birmingham at £3. Alternatively, a single ticket costs
£1·75 (and the same fare would have to be paid to come back again). Brown
has to make up his mind as to which kind of ticket to purchase, bearing in
mind that the railway will not give a refund on an unused half of a day return
ticket. Brown intends to return to London by train, but there is a chance
that he will meet some friend at the meeting who is coming back to London
by car and will offer him a lift. Quite apart from financial considerations,
Brown would prefer to come back by car and, hence, would accept the
offer of a lift whether or not he already had a ticket for the return journey.
The situation as regards the costs of alternatives is as shown in Table 5.1
(the £ sign is omitted):

Table 5.1

		Outcome	
	Action	r_1 Friend shows up with car	r_2 No friend shows up
a_1	Return ticket	3	3
a_2	Single tickets	1·75	3·50

Let us now attempt to analyse this problem for Brown. To decide between
the possible actions, a number of alternative criteria are available. First, we
could choose the so-called *minimax loss* (or maximin gain) approach. This
is a very conservative or pessimistic approach, as it assumes that, whatever
decision we make, the outcome which is the worst for us, given the decision
we have made, will turn up. To safeguard ourselves we choose the action for
which the worst outcome is the least bad for us. Thus, to use this approach,
find, for each row in Table 5.1, the highest cost. Then choose that action
for which the maximum cost is minimized. The necessary steps are shown in
Table 5.2.

Table 5.2

	Action	Max. cost	Min. of max. costs
a_1	Return ticket	3	③
a_2	Single tickets	3·50	

The recommendation will be that Brown should take action a_1, namely, to purchase a return ticket. Under this action, the worst possible cost he incurs is 3, whereas the alternative action could lead to a higher total cost of 3·50. Note that when this approach is applied to many business problems it is likely to protect the decision-maker against large losses, but it takes no account whatsoever of possible large profits to be made, and some attractive opportunities might be foregone.

If Brown had followed the preceding approach and bought a return ticket, and then a friend with a car turned up at the meeting, he would regret the 1·25 that he had lost by having bought a return ticket. This suggests that one should look at such regrets leading to an alternative criterion, namely, the so-called *minimax regret criterion*. Regret is defined formally as the difference between the profit (or cost) of any particular action and the profit (or cost) that would have arisen had you chosen the best action for that particular outcome. Thus, in the current example, suppose that the outcome 'Friend shows up' occurs, the better action then would have been to take a single ticket. Hence, there would be no regret if action a_2 had been taken. If action a_1, however, had been taken then the regret would have been $3 - 1·75$, or 1·25. Similarly, for the event 'Friend doesn't show up', the better action would be to take a return ticket. Hence, there would be no regret if action a_1 had been taken. If action a_2, however, had been taken, then the regret would be $3·50 - 3$, or 0·50. The table of regrets accordingly is as shown in Table 5.3.

Table 5.3

	Action	Friend shows up	Friend does not show up	Max. regret	Min. of max. regrets
a_1	Return ticket	1·25	0	1·25	
a_2	Single tickets	0	0·50	0·50	⓪·50

Again we seek, for each action, the maximum regret, which in this problem is 1·25 or 0·50 respectively. Of these, we now pick the action which has the minimum of the maximum regrets. This is action a_2 with a regret of 0·50. Hence, under the minimax regret rule, we would recommend action a_2.

This decision, it will be noticed, is a different result from that obtained by the use of the minimax criterion. Some readers may be surprised to find that different criteria lead to different actions and may feel that there must be something wrong. But a few moments' reflection will show that this is not really surprising. If the same decision were always reached, whatever the criterion employed to reach the decision, this would be tantamount to saying that you could think of any criterion you liked and it would not affect the answer. You might as well then choose a criterion that is easy to handle, such as spinning a coin or taking the top action on a list, etc. This is clearly absurd, and hence we must not be surprised if the use of different criteria leads to different decisions.

However, minimax regret suffers a further disadvantage in that it is not really consistent within itself. To illustrate this, suppose that a product can be made by either of two processes, a_1 and a_2, for which the discounted pay-offs for the two possible levels of demand, denoted by r_1 and r_2, are given in Table 5.4(a), together with the appropriate regrets in brackets.

Table 5.4(a)

Alternative processes decision

Action	Demand level		Max. regret	Min. of max. regrets
	r_1	r_2		
Process a_1	7(3)	25(0)	3	③
Process a_2	10(0)	20(5)	5	

Analysis as before leads to action a_1 being selected as the better action under the minimax regret criterion. Now suppose that your chief chemist comes along with a third possible process, a_3, and a corresponding new set of pay-offs is as given in Table 5.4(b). The regrets are again given in

Table 5.4(b)

Revised alternative processes decision

Action	Demand level		Max. regret	Min. of max. regrets
	r_1	r_2		
Process a_1	7(7)	25(0)	7	
Process a_2	10(4)	20(5)	5	⑤
Process a_3	14(0)	15(10)	10	

brackets. From the final columns we see that the best action is now a_2. But this seems unreasonable, even though the logic has been carried through correctly. The implication is that, starting with two alternative actions a_1 and a_2 we have, by introducing a third possible action a_3, switched the optimum action from a_1 to a_2. A colleague of mine once put this apparent illogicality rather more colourfully when he described going to a cocktail party and being asked to choose between sherry and pink gin. After a moment's thought he chose sherry. When the host returned from the sideboard he confided that whisky was also available, whereupon my colleague decided— after an appropriate interval for assessment of alternatives—to change from sherry to pink gin.

Both the criteria we have employed have disadvantages, the main one being that they seem to be somewhat extreme in their approach and look at things from a somewhat defensive and pessimistic point of view. Both are slanted towards avoiding the worst outcomes and take no account of opportunities for profit. This defensiveness is clearly demonstrated from the realization that the choice, under either criterion, does not in any way reflect our beliefs as to whether a friend is likely to show up or not. We may have relevant evidence or information (past parties attended, having spoken to somebody who may be going, etc.) and it seems reasonable that the decision criterion adopted should be capable of taking into account this kind of knowledge.

5.4 Expected monetary value

Suppose that for the ith action in conjunction with the jth outcome the pay-off or profit is u_{ij}. Assume, furthermore, that the probability of the jth outcome for the ith action is assessed at p_{ij}, where

$$\sum_{\text{all } j} p_{ij} = 1.$$

Then a very reasonable way to proceed would appear to be to select that action a_i for which

$$\sum_{\text{all } j} u_{ij} p_{ij}$$

is a maximum (or, in the case where the u_{ij} are costs rather than profits, a minimum). This approach is commonly referred to as the *expected monetary value* (or EMV) approach. We will illustrate the approach through a number of examples.

Example 5.1 (continued)

Suppose that we ask Brown to summarize all his information and beliefs concerning the outcome r_1, 'friend turns up', into a single figure, w, between 0 and 1. This figure will represent his overall assessment (partly objective and partly subjective) that a friend will show up and offer him a lift. Then, for each action, a_1 or a_2, we can calculate a mean or expected cost. Thus, action a_1 has an expected cost of:

$$w \times 3 + (1-w) \times 3 = 3.$$

Action a_2 has an expected cost of:

$$w \times 1{\cdot}75 + (1-w) \times 3{\cdot}5 = 3{\cdot}5 - 1{\cdot}75w.$$

To follow an EMV approach, we now recommend that action which gives us the lower expected cost (or higher expected gain). Hence, in this instance, we would recommend action a_1 (the return ticket) if $3 < 3{\cdot}5 - 1{\cdot}75w$ or $w < \frac{2}{7}$. We would, by the same reasoning, recommend action a_2 if $w > \frac{2}{7}$. If $w = \frac{2}{7}$, either action is equally acceptable.

Suppose that Brown assesses w as being equal to 0·4. On the above reasoning we would recommend action a_2 as having the greater expected value. In precise terms, the expected cost for action a_1 is calculated as 3, while that for action a_2 is 2·8. Hence, action a_2 is to be preferred. Note, however, that the specific cost incurred will never actually be 2·8; it must be either 1·75 or 3·5. Hence, the expected cost of a single action may not, indeed in general cannot, be the actual cost. If a long series of actions is considered, however, the total actual cost will approach the total of the expected costs.

Example 5.2

A sales agent is considering whether he should take on a new product which can be sold to his existing customers during the coming selling season. The product is such that only one can be sold to each customer. The salesman is considering three possible strategies or actions. The first, a_1, is to operate as normal, selling the new item along with his regular lines. In the second strategy, a_2, he could add an extra secretary to the staff in his office to distribute literature and handle inquiries about the product, thus increasing his effectiveness, but adding to his costs at the same time. In the third, strategy a_3, he could hire a new assistant to make calls to promote the new item. This would be more productive than the second alternative, but more costly as well, since a large fixed salary and travelling expenses would be involved. The pay-off from each of the three strategies depends upon whether the immediate acceptability of the product to his customers is high or low. Given the two possible outcomes and the three strategies, the pay-offs are as shown in Table 5.5. If immediate acceptability is low, the cost of having a a new assistant under strategy a_3 is greater than the income it creates, leaving a negative pay-off of -40. If immediate acceptability is high, then the more attention paid to the product the higher the pay-off.

Table 5.5

Salesman's pay-off table (£)

Strategy	Acceptability	
	Low	High
a_1	40	140
a_2	20	170
a_3	−40	210

The sales agent does not know in advance which of the two outcomes will prove to be true. No strategy is dominant over the others in the sense that it will always produce the higher pay-off, whichever acceptability outcome occurs. Consequently, we cannot disregard any of the strategies at this point in the discussion. Suppose that the sales agent assesses the probability that there will be low acceptability as p, and hence the probability of high acceptability as $1-p$. Then the expected pay-offs or EMVs for the three strategies are:

a_1 $\quad 40p + 140(1-p) = 140 - 100p;$

a_2 $\quad 20p + 170(1-p) = 170 - 150p;$

a_3 $\quad -40p + 210(1-p) = 210 - 250p.$

These results are illustrated graphically in Fig. 5.1. From this graph it can be seen that, if we use the maximum expected pay-off as our method of choice, then the three strategies are each best for different ranges of values of p, but no single strategy is best for the whole range of values of p. For low values of p, strategy a_3 is best; for high values of p, strategy a_1 is best; while strategy a_2 is optimal for some intermediate values of p. The precise range of values for which each is optimum can easily be obtained by finding the values of p where the expected pay-offs are equal for neighbouring strategies. This gives:

Strategy a_1 optimal $0.6 \leqslant p \leqslant 1.0$

Strategy a_2 optimal $0.4 \leqslant p \leqslant 0.6$

Strategy a_3 optimal $ 0 \leqslant p \leqslant 0.4$

We have tacitly assumed here that the sales agent would be willing, and able, to give a subjective value for the probability p, and that this value does not depend upon the strategy adopted. Even accepting the latter assumption, he might, however, wish to obtain some further information before giving a numerical value. We will discuss later the problem of using sample information to assist in giving an appropriate numerical value to p. The reader

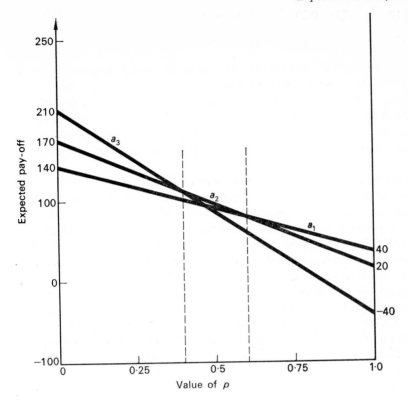

Fig. 5.1. Choice of strategy

is, however, left at this stage to investigate the decisions which would be reached if maximin gain or minimax regret were used to make the choice of optimum strategy in this particular situation.

Example 5.3

Every Saturday a high-class baker in a large town stocks a few very special and expensive cakes which appeal to some of his customers. Unfortunately, these customers do not necessarily come every Saturday, nor do they always buy one of these cakes when they are in the bakery. There is no way of finding out ahead of time precisely how many cakes will be demanded. Over the past two years, however, the baker has kept a record of the number of cakes demanded each Saturday. He feels justified in using these figures to provide historical relative frequencies which can serve as the probabilities of various demand levels. These data show that the number of cakes demanded on a Saturday was always less than or equal to five. The relative frequencies with which the different numbers of cakes have been purchased in in the past give the following probabilities of having x cakes demanded:

$$f(0)=0{\cdot}10 \qquad f(1)=0{\cdot}20 \qquad f(2)=0{\cdot}20$$

$$f(3)=0{\cdot}30 \qquad f(4)=0{\cdot}15 \qquad f(5)=0{\cdot}05$$

where $f(x)$ represents the probability of the random variable concerned taking the value x. We will refer to these outcomes or events with the symbols r_0, r_1, r_2, ... The actions possible correspond to the number of cakes made and we let a_j represent the action 'make j cakes'. Clearly j will never exceed five, since there is no probability of more than five cakes being demanded, and there are thus six possible actions, a_0, a_1, ... a_5, that may be taken.

Next we have to consider the pay-offs and we assume that, for the sums of money involved, the baker is willing to choose the number of cakes which he should stock by maximising his expected pay-off. The cakes sell for £1·30 and cost the bakery 75p. Any cakes left over on Saturday evening will be sold at half-price, i.e. 65p, on Monday and, at this price, are always sold. If a customer comes in and requests a cake when the bakery is out of stock, the baker has observed that the customer usually becomes somewhat annoyed, and as a consequence buys less than usual of other things. The owner feels that, on average, each time a cake is demanded when he is out of stock, it costs him 40p in lost profits on other sales. However, the baker has observed that the inability to supply a customer's demand has no carryover effect to future weeks, since his is the only high-quality bakery in the area. Therefore, the only effect of not being able to meet a customer's request for a cake is the 40p loss on other sales.

We must now determine the pay-off (or profit) if he stocks i cakes and the demand turns out to be for j cakes. When $i>j$, all demands will be met and there will be $i-j$ cakes left over at the end of the day for sale on Monday. The pay-off in pence will be:

$$130j+65(i-j)-75i, \quad \text{or} \quad 65j-10i.$$

When $i=j$, all demands will be met and there will be no cakes left over. The pay-off will be:

$$130j-75j, \quad \text{or} \quad 55j.$$

When $i<j$, all cakes made will be sold and there will be $j-i$ unsatisfied demands. The pay-off will be:

$$130i-75i-40(j-i), \quad \text{or} \quad 95i-40j.$$

The pay-offs obtained from these calculations are shown in the body of Table 5.6. The final column of this table gives the expected pay-off for each act; thus for action a_i the expected pay-off is:

$$\sum_{\text{all } j} f(r_j)u_{ij}$$

Table 5.6

Pay-off table for baker's problem

Outcome		r_0	r_1	r_2	r_3	r_4	r_5	
No. of cakes demanded		0	1	2	3	4	5	Expected profit
$f(r_j)$		0·10	0·20	0·20	0·30	0·15	0·05	
Action	No. of cakes made							
a_0	0	0	−40	−80	−120	−160	−200	−94
a_1	1	−10	55	15	−25	−65	−105	−9·5
a_2	2	−20	45	110	70	30	−10	54
a_3	3	−30	35	100	165	125	85	96·5
a_4	4	−40	25	90	155	220	180	107·5
a_5	5	−50	15	80	145	210	275	102·75

where u_{ij} is the profit or pay-off for the combination of action a_i with outcome r_j. For example, the expected profit for baking 3 units (action a_3) is:

$$-30 \times 0·10 + 35 \times 0·20 + 100 \times 0·20 + 165 \times 0·30 + 125 \times 0·15 + 85 \times 0·05$$

$$= 96·5.$$

If the baker now selects that action for which the expected pay-off is a maximum, he should stock four cakes, since this has the highest pay-off. Note, however, that the expected pay-offs for stocks of both four and five cakes are nearly equal, so that it makes little difference which action is selected. Note, too, that we have assumed once again that the probabilities of the six outcomes concerned will not depend on which particular strategy was selected, that is demand is independent of availability. This is commonly, but by no means invariably, a reasonable assumption to make.

5.5 Incremental analysis

The last example studied was a special case of a type of problem that arises fairly frequently. In this section we will discuss this type of problem in a more general way and show how, by some additional analysis, it is possible to develop much simplified procedures for determining optimal decisions for this type of problem without explicitly constructing the complete pay-off table as was done in Example 5.3.

We illustrate the procedure by discussion of a scrap allowance problem. Consider a jobbing workshop which makes batches of a variety of products to special orders. Usually a product, such as a particular type of gear, must undergo operations on several machines, such as lathes, drills, etc. Jigs are used on each of the machines, and the set-up operation can be both time-consuming and expensive. Jobs on one machine may be finished before later work in the sequence is even started and, by that time, the jigs on the initial machines may have been taken down and the machines themselves be working on different products. As defectives are occasionally produced during each operation, some allowance for them has to be built in at each stage, so as to meet the batch order, particularly as the defectives may not be located until the final quality control inspection.

Let us consider one particular operation and assume that we need to produce at least m good pieces. The two types of information we require are, first, the incidence rate of failures (or defectives) and, second, the various costs involved. To define the probability density function for the incidence of defectives, suppose that we were to go on producing units until we get m good units and that this occurs after exactly x units have been produced. This implies that there are exactly $m-1$ good units in the first $x-1$ units produced, and that the xth unit is also a good one. Denote the probability density function of x by $f(x)$. We will not discuss in detail here how this function could be obtained in practice, except to note that, if we can assume independence between units, it is likely to be more straightforward to assess than if we are unable to make this assumption. Notice, too, as the analysis proceeds, that the random variable x is a more convenient one to use than an alternative random variable, y, the number of good pieces obtained if we schedule i units for production. The difficulty of the latter would be that the distribution of y will change as i is changed, whereas the distribution of x is independent of the number of units scheduled.

For costs we assume that the raw materials, plus the variable production costs (variable referring to those production costs which change with the number of units produced) amount to C per unit scheduled for production, independently of the number of units scheduled. If units are produced in excess of the number m ordered, they are scrapped at a salvage value of R per unit, where R will be less than C. We now turn to the more complicated costing involved when the number of units scheduled do not produce the m good units required from the batch. We will assume that in any extra production run required, the generation of defectives is the same as before. Furthermore, the men now always finish one piece before starting another, so that exactly the required number of pieces is made, but the men concerned have to be paid for a full shift regardless of how many extra pieces are required. Thus, there will be a fixed cost T incurred if any additional units are required, and this cost is independent of the number of the additional units concerned. In addition, there will be the usual unit costs as before. Finally, S is the payment received per unit for the m units.

Suppose that $\Delta_{i(j)}$ is the incremental profit when the batch size is i, and j units are required to obtain m good units. Then $\Delta_{i(j)}$ is the difference between:

(*i*) the expected profit when $i+1$ units make up the production run and the number of units needed to obtain m good units is j, and

(*ii*) the expected profit when i units make up the production run and the number of units needed to obtain m good units is again j.

Consider now the scheduling of an extra unit, i.e. going from a basic production run of i units to one of $i+1$ units. Clearly i must, to be realistic, be greater than or equal to m. There are three separate cases to consider.

(*i*) The extra unit is not needed, i.e. $j<i+1$. We would then incur an extra cost of $C-R$ for the unit that must be scrapped, so the profit increases by $R-C$ which is negative. Hence:

$$\Delta_{i(j)}=(R-C).$$

(*ii*) The extra unit is just the one needed to complete the requirement of m good units, i.e. $j=i+1$. In this situation we save the cost T, i.e. the profit increases by T, and nothing else changes. Hence:

$$\Delta_{i(j)}=T.$$

(*iii*) The extra unit is still not enough to complete the m good units. Here overtime is still needed even when the extra unit is scheduled, i.e. $j>i+1$, and the profit is unchanged. The cost T is still incurred and there is no change on the number of defectives produced and scrapped. Hence:

$$\Delta_{i(j)}=0.$$

Now the expected incremental profit obtained by changing from a production run of i units, to one of $i+1$ units, will be equal to:

$$\sum_{j=m}^{\infty} \Delta_{i(j)} f(j). \tag{5.1}$$

Substituting the expressions obtained above we get:

$$\sum_{j=m}^{\infty} \Delta_{i(j)} f(j) = \sum_{j=m}^{i} (R-C) f(j) + T f(i+1) + \sum_{j=i+2}^{\infty} 0 \times f(j)$$
$$= (R-C)F(i) + T f(i+1) \tag{5.2}$$

where $F(i)= \sum_{j=m}^{i} f(j), f(j)$ being zero for j less than m.

Now if we label the expected profit when i units are scheduled for the production run as $\pi(i)$, then we have:

$$\pi(i+1)-\pi(i)= \sum_{j=m}^{\infty} \Delta_{i(j)} f(j)$$
$$= (R-C) F(i) + T f(i+1).$$

The function $\pi(i)$ is likely to be of the unimodal form illustrated in general terms by Fig. 5.2, i.e. it is likely to increase to a maximum with i and then

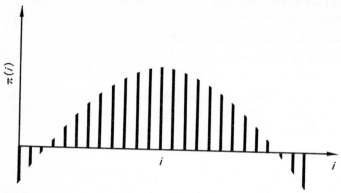

Fig. 5.2. Expected incremental profit function

decrease, thus having one maximum rather than having two or more maxima. The optimal number, i, to schedule is then the smallest value of i for which:

$$\pi(i+1) - \pi(i) \leqslant 0,$$

or

$$(R-C)F(i) + Tf(i+1) \leqslant 0,$$

or

$$Tf(i+1) \leqslant (C-R)F(i),$$

or

$$\frac{f(i+1)}{F(i)} \leqslant \frac{C-R}{T}. \tag{5.3}$$

That is the required value of i is the smallest i for which Eq. 5.3 holds; equally well, it can be shown to be the largest i for which:

$$\frac{f(i)}{F(i-1)} > \frac{C-R}{T}. \tag{5.4}$$

Either of these two equations will be sufficient to define the optimum value of i. Notice that the value of S, the selling price, does not enter the determination of the optimum production level. An example will illustrate the way in which the calculations proceed.

Example 5.4

A job shop has received an order to produce five special high-tolerance gears. These will be produced on automatic machines which require essentially no operator attention after the jigs and programmes for the machines have been set up. The raw material and production cost of each gear is £40 and, if a defective is turned out, its scrap value is only £15. If the number of pieces scheduled in the production run is insufficient, there will be an additional overtime manning cost of £200. The probability density function for x, the number of gears it is necessary to manufacture to produce five good gears, is:

$f(5) = 0.510$ $f(6) = 0.310$ $f(7) = 0.112$

$f(8) = 0.040$ $f(9) = 0.020$ $f(10) = 0.008$

What number of gears should be scheduled in the first instance? Here $C = 40$, $R = 15$, $T = 200$. Hence:

$$\frac{C-R}{T} = \frac{25}{200} = 0.125.$$

We need, using Eq. 5.3, to find the smallest value of i for which

$\phi = f(i+1)/F(i) \leqslant 0.125.$

From the data given we have:

$i = 5$, $F(5) = 0.510$, $f(6) = 0.310$, $\phi = 0.61$

$i = 6$, $F(6) = 0.820$, $f(7) = 0.112$, $\phi = 0.14$

$i = 7$, $F(7) = 0.932$, $f(8) = 0.040$, $\phi = 0.04$

As the last row has ϕ less than 0.125 for the first time, the condition is satisfied and we should schedule seven units for the run, i.e. two extra units are scheduled as a scrap allowance.

The reader is left as an exercise to apply this derivation of incremental analysis to the bakery problem described in Example 5.3.

5.6 Opportunity loss

The regret concept outlined earlier has a certain appeal, despite its apparently rather negative viewpoint. It ties in well with the economist's concept of the correct basis for decision, whereby actions are to be decided in the light of alternative future opportunities. For this reason, regrets are commonly called *opportunity losses*. If we use probabilities to weight the various opportunity losses corresponding to the possible outcomes from a given action, we can develop a further decision criterion, namely, to choose that course of action for which the expected opportunity loss (or *expected regret*) is a minimum.

We will now look at the relationship between the criteria of minimizing the expected opportunity loss, or maximizing the expected monetary value.

Suppose that, for action a_i and outcome r_j, the maximum pay-off is M_j. Then the regret, or opportunity loss, for the (action, outcome) combination (a_i, r_j) is:

$$L_{ij} = M_j - u_{ij} \tag{5.5}$$

The expected opportunity loss for action a_i is then:

$$\sum_{\text{all } j} L_{ij} f(r_j)$$

$$= \sum_{\text{all } j} (M_j - u_{ij}) f(r_j) = \sum_{\text{all } j} M_j f(r_j) - \sum_{\text{all } j} u_{ij} f(r_j)$$

$$= \pi_c - \pi(i). \tag{5.6}$$

where π_c is the expected profit under conditions of certainty, and $\pi(i)$ is the expected profit when action a_i is selected. Now a_k is the optimal action to take if $\pi(k)$ is the largest of the $\pi(i)$. From Eq. 5.6, however, if $\pi(k)$ is the largest of the $\pi(i)$ then the expected opportunity loss must be a minimum. Hence we have demonstrated that *the choice of optimal strategy is the same, whether we minimize the expected opportunity loss, or maximize the expected monetary value.* Note, however, that this conclusion holds only when the probabilities of the various outcomes are independent of the particular action selected.

It can be argued that, since the two approaches lead to identical decisions, there is no point in pursuing the concept of opportunity losses. This is not so, since opportunity losses represent profits foregone or losses incurred through lack of perfect information. This theme will be developed more formally in Chapters 10 and 11, where we consider the value of information in more detail, but meanwhile we will look at a comparison of expected opportunity loss and expected monetary value through an example.

Example 5.5

A firm selling through 20 000 industrial accounts is considering the addition of a new product to its range. Management is somewhat reluctant to make this proposed addition because the associated development costs are high, being estimated at £50 000 for full-scale development. Further, the management believes the proposed product to be a 'one-shot' product, having virtually no possibility of repeat sales to the same customer. Thus, its addition should not have any effects, either positive or negative, on the sales of existing lines.

The product would add nothing to existing overhead expenses (above the £50 000 development costs) and could be produced at a variable cost of £120 per unit. Variable selling expenses would be approximately £30 per unit. Because of the nature of the item, it can be produced to order and no finished stock need be held.

As a result of previous experience with similar products and interviews with company salesmen, the market research department believes the product could best be priced at £200. They have assigned the probability distribution shown in Table 5.7 to the proportion, h, of customers who will actually purchase the new product at this price. The problem facing management is to decide whether or not to undertake the development. (In this example we are only considering one product price. The analysis could be repeated for different product prices, when the probability distribution in Table 5.7 would change, and hence an optimum price found if it is decided to market the product.)

Table 5.7

Probability distribution for purchases of new product

Proportion purchasing (h)	Probability
0·02	0·1
0·04	0·3
0·06	0·3
0·08	0·2
0·10	0·1
	Total 1·0

A first step in the analysis of this problem is to calculate the economic breakeven value for h. This is a straightforward matter since, at the breakeven point, we must have revenue = costs, or:

$$200 \times \quad h \quad \times \quad 20\,000 = 50\,000 + \quad 150 \times h \times 20\,000$$

price   proportion   potential   fixed   variable costs of
        buying   customers   costs   producing and selling

giving $h = 0.05$. Hence 1000 out of the firm's 20 000 potential customers must buy the product if the firm is to break even.

If the true proportion of customers who would ultimately purchase the product is less than 0·05, then the total contribution to profit and overhead will not be sufficient to cover the fixed development costs that would be incurred if development went ahead. On the other hand, if h is greater than 0·05, an opportunity loss will be incurred if the product is not produced, as a result of the lost profit opportunity. These losses, which will be referred to as *conditional opportunity losses* (COL) are shown in Table 5.8. They are conditional in the sense that they depend upon the particular combination of action and outcome concerned. As an illustration of how these are obtained, consider the top lefthand cell in Table 5.8. If h is <0·05 and we develop, then we incur an opportunity loss that is equal to the net gain that

Table 5.8

Conditional opportunity losses

Action	Outcome	
	$h < 0 \cdot 05$	$h > 0 \cdot 05$
Develop	1 000 000 $(0 \cdot 05 - h)$	0
Don't develop	0	1 000 000 $(h - 0 \cdot 05)$

would have arisen by not developing (i.e. zero) minus the net gain achieved by developing. The latter is $-50\,000 + 50(h)(20\,000)$ and hence the opportunity loss is $50\,000 - 1\,000\,000h$, or $1\,000\,000(0 \cdot 05 - h)$. Similar considerations apply for the bottom righthand cell. Of course, if $h > 0 \cdot 05$, and the firm decides to produce, or if $h < 0 \cdot 05$, and the firm decides not to produce, a correct decision will have been made, and the firm will incur no opportunity loss. To calculate the COL for any act-event combination, we need only substitute the desired value of h in the appropriate expression in Table 5.8. This leads to the conditional opportunity loss figures given in Table 5.9.

Table 5.9

Conditional opportunity loss table

h	Develop	Don't develop
$0 \cdot 02$	30 000	0
$0 \cdot 04$	10 000	0
$0 \cdot 06$	0	10 000
$0 \cdot 08$	0	30 000
$0 \cdot 10$	0	50 000

If an immediate decision must be made as to whether or not to develop the product, we could proceed in a similar manner to that used in earlier examples. This requires us to calculate the *expected opportunity losses* (EOLs) of the two possible actions, using as weights the probabilities in Table 5.7. This procedure is carried out in Table 5.10 and the EOLs for the two possible actions are: develop 6000; and don't develop, 14 000. Hence, if no other information were available, we would choose to develop the product, since that action has the lower EOL. This is the same decision as would have been reached if the EMV or expected pay-offs for the two actions had been calculated, and the decision based on the action with the higher EMV. The calculations are shown in Table 5.11, the pay-off for developing the

Table 5.10

Analysis of decision by opportunity losses

		Outcome (*h*)					Expected opportunity loss
Action	*f*(*h*)	0·02 0·1	0·04 0·3	0·06 0·3	0·08 0·2	0·10 0·1	
Develop		30 000	10 000	0	0	0	6 000
Don't develop		0	0	10 000	30 000	50 000	14 000

(The figures in the body of Table 5.10 are the appropriate COLs.)

Table 5.11

Analysis of decision by expected monetary value

		Outcome (*h*)					Expected monetary value
Action	*f*(*h*)	0·02 0·1	0·04 0·3	0·06 0·3	0·08 0·2	0·10 0·1	
Develop		− 30 000	− 10 000	10 000	30 000	50 000	8000
Don't develop		0	0	0	0	0	0

(The figures in the body of Table 5.11 are the appropriate pay-offs)

product being $1\,000\,000(h - 0·05)$, whilst the pay-off is zero if the product is not developed.

5.7 Additional information

Because of the sizeable losses that could be incurred, an alert management might suggest either considering alternative prices or else obtaining additional information on the demand at the present price before coming to a decision. We consider here the latter suggestion, and set out an evaluation of the effect that such information has on the opportunity losses. Suppose that the firm's marketing research manager recommends an intensive survey of a random sample of customers to determine whether they would purchase the item in question. Since such a survey would be relatively expensive if definite commitments were to be obtained from all the customers concerned, the sampling is limited to twenty randomly selected customers. What rule do we now want to follow? Clearly we would like to specify a decision rule of the form: 'If more than *c* out of the twenty prospective purchasers buy the product in question, then go ahead with development; if *c* or less express an interest, do not develop the product.' The selection of the appropriate value of c should take into account both the opportunity losses for a wrong decision as well as the probability that various levels of h will occur.

The probability that use of a particular decision rule will lead to a wrong decision, for any given value of h, may be obtained directly from the binomial tables. Consider, for example, the case of the decision rule $n=20$, $c=0$. This rule states that if one or more of the prospective purchasers interviewed wishes to buy the product we will develop it, but not otherwise. The probability that this decision rule will lead to error, and even the nature of the error itself, depends upon the true value of h. Consider first the case where $h<0.05$ and take the particular value $h=0.02$. Then the probability that the rule will lead to an erroneous decision is given by the binomial probability:

$$P(x>c \mid n=20, \ h=0.02).$$

From the binomial tables in Appendix A, this value can be read off as 0.3324. If h were now taken as 0.04, the corresponding probability is 0.5580. If h is greater than 0.05, say 0.10, then the firm will make a profit through developing the product. The only way in which the decision rule could lead to the wrong decision (i.e. not to develop the product) is if the sample contains zero positive responses (since one or more positive responses will lead to the correct decision to develop). Thus, the probability that the rule will lead to an erroneous decision will be given by:

$$P(x=0 \mid n=20, \ h).$$

For $h=0.10$, the probability of zero favourable responses in the sample, and hence of an erroneous decision, is 0.1216. The various probabilities of wrong decisions are tabulated in column 3 of Table 5.12. Column 2 gives the conditional opportunity loss for a wrong decision of each value of h, taken from Table 5.9. Column 4 then gives the expected loss for each value of h in column 1. Column 5 gives the distribution of values of h, namely, $f(h)$ and the expected loss for the given value of h summed over all values of h. This is calculated in column 6 to give an EOL of 5281.

We can calculate the EOL for other decision rules in a similar manner. Keeping n fixed at 20 and taking $c=1$, a similar calculation to that shown in Table 5.12 leads to the EOL of 7790. This is higher than the EOL with $c=0$ and hence the latter is the preferable decision rule. General considerations show that, when $c=2$ or more, the EOL will be even higher and hence the rule with $c=0$ is the optimum. That is, if, in the sample of 20 potential customers, one or more give a favourable response, the development of the product should be undertaken. If not, development should not be undertaken.

When no sampling was carried out the EOL of the best decision was 6000. If a sample is taken the EOL depends, not unnaturally, on the decision rule that we adopt, since clearly a bad decision rule could be expected to lead to higher opportunity losses than a good decision rule. The best rule, however, categorized by $n=20$, $c=0$ leads to an EOL of 5281. This EOL is lower than

Table 5.12

Decision by opportunity loss after sample of 20

1	2	3	4	5	6
	COL for wrong decision	Probability of wrong decision, given h	Expected loss conditional on h 2×3		EOL for wrong decision 4×5
h				$f(h)$	
0·02	30 000	0·3324	9972	0·1	997
0·04	10 000	0·5580	5580	0·3	1674
0·06	10 000	0·2901	2901	0·3	870
0·08	30 000	0·1887	5661	0·2	1132
0·10	50 000	0·1216	6080	0·1	608
				Total	5281

the EOL for the best decision rule without any sample, and demonstrates that sample information properly used can only improve the quality of a decision; it cannot worsen it. Note that this is only true if the information is used in the best possible manner; it would not be true if a non–optimum decision rule were used in conjunction with the sample, e.g. if the rule $c = 2$ were used the EOL would be increased. Any reduction in EOL that is due to sampling must, of course, be offset against the cost of the sampling carried out. The value of the sample information, and the choice of the amount of sampling that it is desirable to carry out, will be explored in greater depth in Chapters 10 and 11.

5.8 Comparison of criteria

It will be useful to end this chapter by discussing the use of the various decision criteria on the sample example. For this purpose we will consider again Example 5.3 concerning the bakery. Table 5.13 repeats the basic data of Table 5.6 with some additions.

The figures in brackets in the main body of Table 5.13 are the regrets (or opportunity losses) for each action/outcome combination. The penultimate column gives the expected profit for each action, using the $f(r_j)$ as weights, and in brackets the expected regrets. The maximum expected profit is 107·5 for action a_4, and the minimum expected regret is 21·7, again for action a_4. Hence, the two criteria, as expected, lead to the choice of the same action. Notice, too, that the expected profit plus the expected regret is equal to 129·2 for each action.

Next we consider the maximin gain approach. The final column gives the minimum possible pay-off for each possible action. The maximum of these minima is -20, corresponding to action a_2. Hence, action a_2 is optimum from the maximin gain approach.

Table 5.13

Data table for baker's problem

Outcome		r_0	r_1	r_2	r_3	r_4	r_5	Expected profits (regrets)	Minimum profits (maximum regrets)
No. of cakes demanded		0	1	2	3	4	5		
$f(r_j)$		0·10	0·20	0·20	0·30	0·15	0·05		
Action	No. of cakes made								
a_0	0	0*	−40	−80	−120	−160	−200†	−94	−200
		(0)	(95)	(190)	(285)	(380)	(475)‡	(223·3)	(475)
a_1	1	−10	55*	15	−25	−65	−105†	−9·5	−105
		(10)	(0)	(95)	(190)	(285)	(380)‡	(138·7)	(380)
a_2	2	−20†	45	110*	70	30	−10	54	−20
		(20)	(10)	(0)	(95)	(190)	(285)‡	(75·3)	(285)
a_3	3	−30†	35	100	165*	125	85	96·5	−30
		(30)	(20)	(10)	(0)	(95)	(190)‡	(32·7)	(190)
a_4	4	−40†	25	90	155	220*	180	107·5	−40
		(40)	(30)	(20)	(10)	(0)	(95)‡	(21·7)	(95)
a_5	5	−50†	15	80	145	210	275*	102·7	−50
		(50)‡	(40)	(30)	(20)	(10)	(0)	(26·5)	(50)

* Denotes the best action (highest pay-off) for each outcome.
† Denotes the lowest pay-off for each action.
‡ Denotes the maximum regret for each action.

Finally, we can consider the minimax regret (or minimax opportunity loss) approach. The final column gives in brackets the maximum regret for each action. The minimum among these maximum regrets is 50, corresponding to action a_5. Summarizing, we have the following optimal decisions according to the criteria employed:

Expected monetary value
(or expected opportunity loss) a_4

Maximin gain a_2

Minimax regret a_5

Since the first of these criteria depends upon the relative weights given to the various outcomes, there is no particular reason why it should lead to the same optimal course of action as the other two criteria. To compare the optimal strategies derived from the other two criteria, it is necessary to realize that under maximin gain we have chosen a course of action whereby we must gain at least −20, and we cannot possibly fall below that level. We have, incidentally, at the same time given ourselves a maximum possible gain of 110. Under minimax regret, the possible pay-offs for action a_5 range from -50 to 275. However, the choice of action a_5 arises from the fact that, whatever the outcome, the pay-off can never be more than 50 below the pay-off that would have arisen from the best action for that outcome, and no other action could keep that maximum difference below 50 units. Hence, regret looks more firmly at loss opportunities, rather than minimum possible pay-offs.

Exercises on Chapter 5

(*Some additional binomial probabilities to help with certain of the exercises are given at the end of the chapter*)

1 Faced with a new market opportunity, management evaluated the profits of three courses of action against sales levels in the new market as shown in Table 5.14.

Table 5.14

		Action		
Sales	Probability of sales level	Operate as always	Expand current operation	Build new capacity
Under 30 000	0·1	20	−20	−40
30 000–50 000	0·5	30	40	0
Over 50 000	0·4	40	60	80

(Pay-off expressed in £'000s)

What action would management take if they based their choice of action on:

(*i*) The maximin profit concept?
(*ii*) The minimax regret concept?
(*iii*) The expected monetary value concept?

2 A company has the opportunity to computerize its records department and is considering three possible ways of doing this. A prime consideration is that existing personnel have job security under a union agreement. The costs of the three possible programmes for the changeover depend upon the attitude of the unions towards retraining, and have been estimated as shown in Table 5.15 (in £'000s).

(*i*) What strategy should be adopted under the minimax loss procedure?
(*ii*) What strategy should be adopted under the minimax regret procedure?
(*iii*) If the probabilities of the three attitudes are assessed by the personnel manager at 0·5, 0·3 and 0·2 respectively, irrespective of the programme adopted, what is the expected cost of each possible strategy and the strategy with the lowest expected cost?

Table 5.15

Programme	Attitude of the union		
	Antagonistic	Passive	Enthusiastic
General retraining	470	405	350
Selective retraining	460	400	355
Hire new employees	450	410	430

3 A card-shop owner is trying to decide how many boxes of an expensive Mother's Day card to stock. The cards carry a high profit margin and come in boxes of 20 cards; they cost £1·60 and retail for £2·70 per box. Each box unsold by Mother's Day can be sold afterwards for £1·20. Customers will not demand the special card if it is out of stock, as they look at the selection available and choose from it. The owner has, however, limited capital and does not like to invest in items that he will not sell because he could earn more by not tying up his capital in such a way. The owner feels that for each £1·60 invested in a box of these cards that are not subsequently sold in the season, he could have earned £0·40 profit by investing in other cards. He also estimates that the probability density function for the number of boxes of cards demanded will be:

$$f(0)=0·03 \qquad f(1)=0·04 \qquad f(2)=0·08 \qquad f(3)=0·15$$

$$f(4)=0·20 \qquad f(5)=0·20 \qquad f(6)=0·15 \qquad f(7)=0·05$$

$$f(8)=0·05 \qquad f(9)=0·03 \qquad f(10)=0·02$$

How many boxes should the owner stock at the beginning of the season if it is impossible to place reorders? (Ignore the possibility of the owner only selling part of a box of cards.)

4 A florist has to place his order with his supplier well in advance of Easter weekend. Boxes of flowers cost £1·00 each and retail for £2·50. In addition there is a transport cost of £0·25 per box, paid on all boxes purchased by the florist. Any boxes left over are a total loss. The florist does not think there is any loss in having a demand occur when he is out of stock. After due consideration, he decides that the probability density function for the demand x takes the following general form:

$$f(x)=k(x-2000) \quad 2000 \leqslant x \leqslant 2500$$

$$=k(3000-x) \quad 2500 \leqslant x \leqslant 3000$$

where the random variable x takes on the integer values 2000 to 3000 inclusive.

(*i*) Find the value of k.

(*ii*) Sketch the shape of the functions $f(x)$ and $F(x)$.

(*iii*) Determine the optimum number of boxes for the florist to order.

5 Some pieces of equipment are being constructed as part of a ship which has an estimated life of twenty years. The shipowners need to specify how many spares of a particular and very expensive part should be produced when the ship is being constructed. Each part costs £25 000 if produced simultaneously with the original parts in the ship, but £75 000 each if produced in isolation after the ship has been built. After a study of similar ships, the shipowner decides that no more than six of these spares should ever be needed, and he estimates the probabilities, $f(x)$, of the various numbers, x, of parts being required in the twenty-year period as:

$$f(0)=0.2 \qquad f(1)=0.3 \qquad f(2)=0.2 \qquad f(3)=0.1$$

$$f(4)=0.1 \qquad f(5)=0.06 \qquad f(6)=0.04$$

Any parts left over when the ship is finally scrapped will have an estimated salvage value of £1000 each.

How many spares should the shipowner order now if he uses expected monetary value as his criterion?

6 A distributor of Christmas tree lights is contemplating the purchase of a season's supply of 100 000 bulbs from a foreign manufacturer. The manufacturer claims that the new bulbs are 'at least as good' as the domestically produced brand the distributor has purchased in former years, which he knows from experience have about 2 per cent defective. However, the distributor has doubts concerning the quality of the foreign product, subjectively estimating the following probability distribution for the fraction defective:

Fraction defective	0·01	0·02	0·05
Probability	0·1	0·4	0·5

The cost of having to replace defective bulbs (including any cost due to loss of customer goodwill) is estimated at 50p per bulb. The foreign bulbs are 1p each cheaper to the distributor, but can be sold at the same price as the domestic bulbs.

(*i*) On the above information, would you recommend purchase of the foreign produced bulbs?

(*ii*) Suppose an independent testing laboratory will obtain and test a random sample of 50 of the foreign bulbs. How could the results from such a sample best be utilized?

(The distribution of fraction defective has been simplified to give just three possible levels of defectives.)

E

7 In your factory you have an old machine which performs a defined operation on a part you are manufacturing. The cost of labour plus material for the work performed by this machine comes to 46p per piece. You have an order for 50 000 parts. Before you produce them, you want to consider the possibility of buying a new machine for £8500 to replace the old machine, whose scrap value is £600. Because of increased speed, the new machine can produce parts at a unit cost of 30p.

With the old machine the proportion of defectives is known to be 0·05. Since the defective rate is a function of both the operator and the machine, the manufacturer cannot specify precisely the defective rate on the new machine. Based on his experience and yours, you arrive at the following probability distribution for the proportion defective:

p	0·05	0·07	0·09	0·11	0·13
$f(p)$	0·15	0·25	0·30	0·15	0·15

Assume that the defectives occur according to a binomial distribution and that the entire cost of the new machine would have to be allocated to the 50 000 parts.

   (*i*) If you have to make a decision without sampling, what should that decision be and what is the expected opportunity loss of the decision?

  (*ii*) The seller of the machine gives you the opportunity to take a random sample of 50 parts to determine the proportion defective by having your operator run a sample on a new machine owned by another manufacturer. The cost of a sample of 50 parts under these conditions is £20. Should you accept the offer and, if you do, what decision rule would you use based on the sample results?

8 The Ronics Corporation was a medium-size manufacturer of electromechanical components for the aerospace industry. It frequently developed components for its major customers and subsequently became the sole producer of such items.

In September 1971 it was trying to solve quality control difficulties it had encountered for some time with an item it had designed and was producing for the Gatson Aircraft Company. Ronics was Gatson's only supplier for this item, which sold at £240 per unit.

Gatson used the item as a component of a major subassembly of a missile guidance control system. If the subassembly failed a particular test, Gatson knew that the fault lay in the Ronics component. It was then necessary to strip it, regrind the mating surfaces of the Ronics component and reassemble. By the terms of the contract, there was a £130 penalty charge to Ronics whenever this occurred.

Ever since Ronics had begun producing this component for Gatson, it had paid this penalty charge on 30 per cent of the items produced and Ronics's quality control engineer was concerned since there seemed to be no improvement in the manufacturing process. Further, no means of identifying the faults before shipment had been found.

One of the engineers then suggested that the fault could be rectified if an additional grinding process were introduced at the end of the process at a cost of £30 per unit. The defective rate would then be negligible. At the same time, a new quality control device came on the market which, when applied to a number of known good and bad units, gave the proportions of positive and negative results shown in Table 5.16.

Table 5.16

Instrument reading	State of component	
	Good	Bad
Positive	0·75	0·20
Negative	0·25	0·80
Total	1·00	1·00

The cost of using the device is £8 per unit tested, and it is assumed that the nature of the quality control device is such that, for a particular component, the same result is obtained no matter how many times the component is tested.

(*i*) Should Ronics use the testing device assuming that, in their opinion, there is no loss of goodwill in shipping defective components to Gatson?

(*ii*) If loss of goodwill is a factor, how might it be taken into acount in making the decision as to whether to use the testing device?

Additional cumulative binomial probabilities for n = 50

x	p					
	0·01	0·02	0·07	0·09	0·11	0·13
1	0·3950	0·6358	0·9734	0·9910	0·9971	0·9991
2	0·0894	0·2642	0·8735	0·9468	0·9788	0·9920
3	0·0138	0·0784	0·6892	0·8395	0·9237	0·9661
4	0·0016	0·0178	0·4673	0·6697	0·8146	0·9042
5	0·0001	0·0032	0·2710	0·4723	0·6562	0·7956
6		0·0005	0·1350	0·2928	0·4760	0·6463
7		0·0001	0·0583	0·1596	0·3091	0·4789
8			0·0220	0·0768	0·1793	0·3217
9			0·0073	0·0328	0·0932	0·1955
10			0·0022	0·0125	0·0435	0·1074
11			0·0006	0·0043	0·0183	0·0535
12			0·0001	0·0013	0·0069	0·0242
13				0·0004	0·0024	0·0100
14				0·0001	0·0008	0·0037
15					0·0002	0·0013
16					0·0001	0·0004
17						0·0001

6 Decision trees

6.1 Introduction

The problems studied in the last chapter have been described by decision or pay-off tables, and the analysis has used this form of tabulation. Furthermore, the decisions have basically been single stage. With multistage decisions, it is rather more difficult, and sometimes confusing, to show all the alternatives in the form of a decision table or tables, and a different mode of presentation is commonly employed. This uses a *tree diagram*, the whole process of using such a diagram being referred to as a *decision tree analysis*. We will illustrate decision trees and their analysis with a number of examples of varying complexity. First, we will demonstrate the basic concept of a decision tree by putting one of the single-stage decision problems analysed in the previous chapter into this form. We will use EMV as the decision criterion throughout, as providing a rational, consistent and useful approach to decision-taking that is meaningful to an organization. Readers will recall that use of EMV and EOL lead to similar decisions. We will, however, occasionally digress to see how other criteria could affect the decisions being reached.

Example 6.1

This example uses the problem, discussed in Example 5.1, of Brown choosing between the purchase of either a single or a return ticket from London to Birmingham. The data given in the example are displayed as a decision tree in Fig. 6.1. The reasons for calling it a 'tree' diagram are self-evident. Note the alternating sequence of action-outcomes, starting from the left and moving across to the right. Each point where the branch forks into other

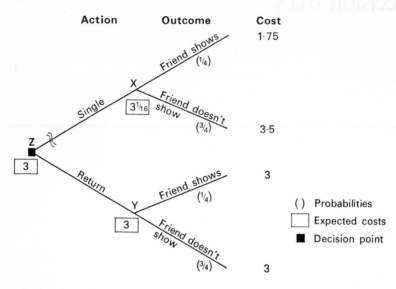

Fig. 6.1. Cost of travel

branches is called a *node*. Some nodes are decision or action nodes, indicated by a black square; others are outcome or event nodes, not specially marked. Under each branch which indicates an outcome is given, in brackets, the appropriate probability of that particular outcome. Here we assume w equals $\frac{1}{4}$. The total costs are given at the righthand side of each possible path through the tree. Thus, the top path assumes that Brown takes a single ticket and a friend shows up. Hence, Brown's total cost is £1·75. Then we compute the expected cost for each alternative action. These are entered in square boxes at the end of the branches representing actions, labelled X and Y. At the initial decision point Z, represented by a square, Brown will select that act for which the expected cost is a minimum. This would lead him to take the return ticket, at an expected cost of 3 units, and a double bar is placed on the diagram against the alternative of a single ticket that is thereby ruled out, to show the route that is favoured.

6.2 Multistage actions

A businessman looking at a problem often sees a vista of decisions spread over a long period of time and not just one immediate decision. There is thus a time sequence of decisions. Such a situation is particularly suitable to be represented by a tree diagram. For example, although an initial decision facing an oil company executive may involve the location of a new refinery, a later decision might involve whether he should increase its capacity or build another one. By generalizing our notions we can cope with this situation.

To see this, suppose that now we must select between two actions (call them a_1 and a_2). If we select a_1, then after two years the possible outcomes are b_1, b_2 and b_3. Suppose that outcome b_1 occurred. Then we are faced with a choice of, say, three new decisions labelled a_1', a_2', a_3' respectively, and each of these could lead to one of a number of possible outcomes. The process of choice of action followed by outcome could be repeated many times. A similar situation would arise had we selected action a_2 at the start, rather than action a_1. The whole array of possible sequences of actions and outcomes can be very conveniently represented by the branchlike diagram shown in Fig. 6.2, which is a more generalized form of decision tree. Again,

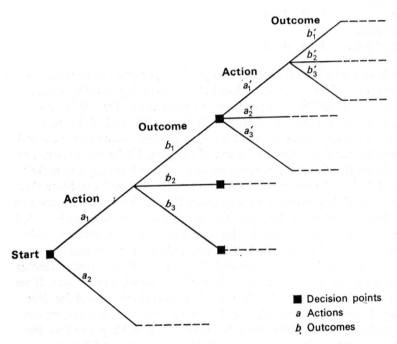

Fig. 6.2. Generalized decision tree

the small black squares represent decision nodes at which a conscious choice of action must be made. The outcomes which follow may not, but generally will, have a probabilistic element, for it is impossible now to predict precisely which outcome will occur.

The decision tree completely describes the sequence of decisions to be made, since it indicates for each node what actions or decisions face the decision-maker and the new decision situation resulting from any specified action/event combination that can occur.

The next example shows a four-stage decision problem, but with the rather special feature that all the relevant outcomes for each possible action are known. This kind of situation is sometimes described as decision-making under conditions of certainty. Afterwards we consider multistage decision-making under conditions of uncertainty, the main theme of this book.

Example 6.2

A paper mill unit uses 1 unit of pulp per quarter (the precise definition of a unit of pulp is unimportant for the purposes of this example). The storage capacity for pulp in the mill is 2 units of pulp. Pulp may be bought (in complete units only) at the following prices, the money units being arbitrary. The price depends upon the quarter of the year in which the purchase is made.

Quarter	1	2	3	4
Purchase price per unit of pulp	3	4	6	4

There is also a holding (or stock) charge of 0·5 per unit per quarter, the charge being based on the stock in hand at the beginning of each quarter. During a quarter, additions to stock can be made at any time. It is thus possible to leave the stock at capacity (if desired) at the end of the quarter. The mill has capacity stock stored (2 units) at the beginning of the year and must leave the same situation at the end of the year. Under these constraints, what is the most rational series of decisions for the mill manager to make?

Figure 6.3 gives the appropriate decision tree for this problem. Since there is only one possible outcome for each action, the tree has been telescoped so that the branch represents the alternative actions, and the outcome is circled at the end of the action branch. In this instance, there are thirteen possible action sequences that enable the mill to have pulp to function each quarter and leave a full supply at the year's end. Each of the thirteen routes denotes an action sequence that can be taken through the branches of the tree. If we denote a route by a four-digit code, such that (0121) is shorthand for 'Not buy', 'Buy 1 unit', 'Buy 2 units', 'Buy 1 unit' in successive quarters, we can quickly evaluate the net costs associated with each possible path of the tree. The net costs, the buying costs plus the holding costs, are as follows:

(1111)	21	(0121)	23
(1102)	$18\frac{1}{2}$	(0112)	21
(1021)	$22\frac{1}{2}$	(0103)	$18\frac{1}{2}$
(1012)	20	(0031)	$24\frac{1}{2}$
(1003)	$17\frac{1}{2}$	(0022)	22
(2011)	$21\frac{1}{2}$	(0013)	$19\frac{1}{2}$
(2002)	19		

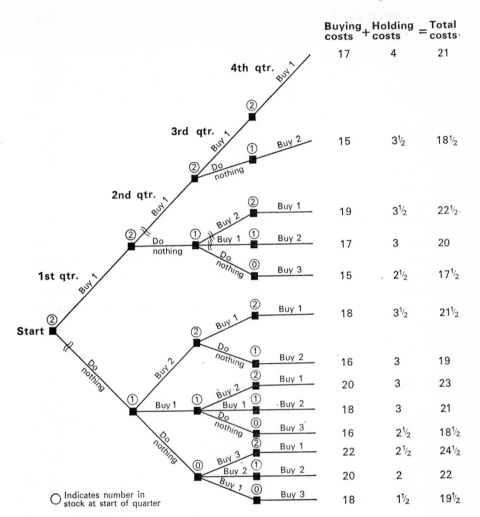

Buying costs	+	Holding costs	=	Total costs
17		4		21
15		3½		18½
19		3½		22½.
17		3		20
15		2½		17½
18		3½		21½
16		3		19
20		3		23
18		3		21
16		2½		18½
22		2½		24½
20		2		22
18		1½		19½

Fig. 6.3. Stockholding decision tree

Of the thirteen paths, that labelled (1003) has the lowest total net cost. Hence, the optimum strategy is to buy one unit in the first quarter and three units in the fourth quarter, but none in the other two quarters. This optimum path is marked off on the decision tree in the conventional manner. One other unusual feature occurs in this decision tree, namely, that the action in the fourth quarter is completely determined by the actions taken in the three preceding quarters. Hence, although it seems a four-stage decision problem, it is really only a three-stage problem.

The decision tree itself, of course, does not vary with changes in the different costs. The value of the various paths may however change and, in turn, change the optimum strategy. For example, suppose the stockholding cost is raised to the perhaps unlikely level of 2 per unit per quarter. (Unlikely, that is, relative to the initial cost of the pulp.) The previously optimum path of (1003) will now cost 25 units. All the other paths still cost more with the exception of (0013) which will now cost 24 units and becomes the optimum path, defining a new optimum strategy. Thus, the tree shows the logic of the decisions to be made, quite independently of the values placed on the various alternatives. Furthermore, once the alternatives have been drawn, we can, because each outcome is certain, evaluate each possible action combination, either by working forward from the beginning of the year or backward from its end. This will not be so in later examples where uncertain outcomes are involved.

6.3 Uncertainty considerations

We now move to situations where an element of uncertainty enters into the outcome that will follow a given action. It arises because the decision-maker does not have full knowledge or control of all the relevant outcomes of the available actions. The next example illustrates this difference and shows how to analyse the decision tree in such conditions, with the proviso that we are prepared to define the criterion to be used.

Example 6.3

On 1 May 1971, Mr G. K. Netford, the general manager of Wallace Controls Ltd, was told by his sales manager that if he would build a prototype of a special aircraft control component at Wallace's expense and submit it to an aircraft manufacturer, Ace Ltd, they might get an order for 1000 units. It would be placed on 30 June, either with Wallace or some other supplier, for delivery and payment in full on 30 September. Wallace would, of course, have to assure Ace that the production components would be of at least equal quality to the prototype. Ace are willing to pay £100 for each component, or £100 000 for the whole contract.

   This is the bare outline of the decision facing Mr Netford. Before proceeding, and certainly before deciding what to do now, he must consider three sets of information. The first is the possible methods of production, should the order be accepted, and the sequence of actions and outcomes that could possibly flow from such a decision. His production manager states that the prototype will necessarily have to use machined parts and, if the contract uses such parts, the units will certainly perform as well as the prototype units. Alternatively, it would be possible to substitute stampings for some of the machined parts in the unit. In this way, variable costs per unit can be lowered, but there will be an additional investment in dies, etc., and only after this investment has been made and the unit tested will it be possible to determine whether units with stamped parts can match the performance of the prototype.

Mr Netford is now in a position to draw a decision tree to show the various possibilities outlined above. The tree he draws at this stage is shown in Fig. 6.4. There are three decision points on the tree marked A, B and C

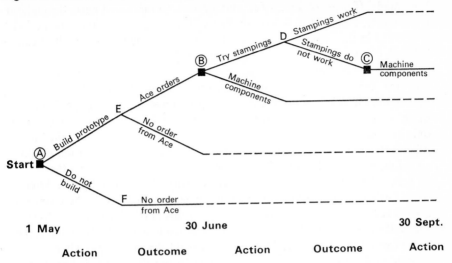

Start

1 May   30 June   30 Sept.

Action   Outcome   Action   Outcome   Action

Fig. 6.4. Wallace decision tree outline

respectively. At A (on 1 May) Mr Netford has to decide whether to build the prototype or not. At B, should he decide to build the prototype and should Ace subsequently place the order, he has to decide whether or not to try stampings. There is a third decision point C which in reality is an automatic decision in that, should the stampings fail, he must revert to machining the components to fulfil the contract. At this stage Mr Netford will look at the tree diagram and examine the timetable it presupposes, to ensure that the alternatives put down are real ones and can be handled within the time limits set for the contract. This could apply particularly to decision point C. If there were no time to revert to machined parts, should stampings fail, then the upper branches at decision point B must be all barred. Assuming that he is satisfied that the timetable permits the various alternatives shown, he can proceed to the second stage of analysis.

For this stage Mr Netford needs to put in the appropriate financial figures. Here consultations with several of his colleagues are essential. Design of the proposed unit would cost about £3000, and production of a single prototype, without production jigs, would cost about the same amount again. Assuming the order was subsequently received from Ace, the production manager estimates that a lot of 1000 units with machined parts would cost £10 000 for tooling, together with a variable cost of £70 per unit for materials, labour, etc. If stampings are substituted for some of the machined parts where this seems to be feasible, the variable production costs will be reduced to about £60 per unit, but the use of stampings will require an initial further investment of £5000 in dies and will only reduce the cost of other tooling by some £2000, thus implying a net additional fixed cost of £3000. It should be possible to tell if the stampings are successful once the £5000 expenditure on dies has been made. If it is not successful, and a return to machined parts throughout is necessary, the full £10 000 on tooling will be incurred. As the time period concerned in the project is so short, discounting of the money involved can be ignored. (In what follows the £ sign is omitted.)

Finally, Mr Netford looks into the relative likelihood of the possible outcomes for the various decisions concerned. Again, he consults his colleagues. He asks the production manager to assess the likely performance of units with certain stamped parts. As of now, the production manager can only say that stamped parts have succeeded in some designs, but failed in others. He confirms again that, if stampings should be tried and fail on this occasion, there will be plenty of time left to switch over and meet the 30 September deadline with units produced with all machined parts. After some further discussion, the production manager suggests that the chances are even that the stampings will be successful in this particular instance. Next, Mr Netford asks the sales manager to assess the likelihood of obtaining the order from Ace, should Wallace decide to build the prototype. After consultation with the design engineer, he feels that the chance is less than even, but above a third, and he ultimately puts it at $\frac{2}{5}$. This chance or probability, as in the similar situation for stampings versus machined parts, is a subjective probability. Wallace cannot know for sure whether they will or will not get the order, but, equally, because Mr Netford is unsure, he would not be prepared to leave it to the office boy to make the decision. It is quite natural for businessmen to give quantitative expression to their judgments in a situation like this, and to say, after due reflection and consideration both of precedents and of the constituent elements of the present situation: 'Everything considered, I'd guess that the chances we will get the order if we build a prototype are about two in five.'

Mr Netford is now in a position to put on his decision tree the appropriate costs, incomes and probabilities. The net income has been placed at the end of each possible tree path, as shown in Fig. 6.5. Thus, the first net cash flow is given by:

$$100\ 000 \underset{\substack{\text{Sales}\\\text{income}}}{} - \underset{\substack{6000\\\text{Prototype}\\\text{cost}}}{} - \underset{\substack{13\ 000\\\text{Stampings}\\\text{fixed cost}}}{} - \underset{\substack{1000 \times 60\\\text{Stampings}\\\text{variable cost}}}{} = 21\ 000$$

and the second net cash flow by:

$$100\ 000 \underset{\substack{\text{Sales}\\\text{income}}}{} - \underset{\substack{6000\\\text{Prototype}\\\text{cost}}}{} - \underset{\substack{15\ 000\\\text{Stampings}\\\text{and}\\\text{machinery}\\\text{fixed costs}}}{} - \underset{\substack{1000 \times 70\\\text{Machining}\\\text{variable cost}}}{} = 9000$$

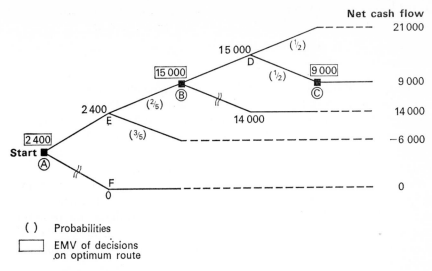

( )   Probabilities

☐   EMV of decisions
    ,on optimum route

Fig. 6.5. Wallace decision tree analysis

Similar calculations can be made for the other paths in the decision tree. Mr Netford is now in a position to analyse the tree, and he does this by working the tree backwards from the right to the left. This procedure is sometimes colloquially referred to as the *roll-back* procedure. It is necessary to follow this procedure since, in evaluating the various actions at some earlier decision point, we need to know the decisions that will be taken at later decision points, should we reach them. Only in that way do we know the values to be put on the alternative outcomes facing the earlier decisions. If we did not follow such a procedure, we would be forced to make the earlier decisions on some more arbitrary principle than would be the case for the later decisions.

The first decision point that we need to consider is, therefore, point B. The two alternatives here are:

Tool for stampings: expected monetary value

$$=\tfrac{1}{2}\times 21\,000+\tfrac{1}{2}\times 9000$$

$$=15\,000$$

Tool for machinings: expected monetary vaule

$$=14\,000.$$

Assuming that Mr Netford decides to use EMV as his guide to the best decision to make at each point on the decision tree, he should decide at point B to 'tool to stamp' since this decision has the higher EMV. The alternative decision 'Tool to machine' is therefore barred, and 15 000 is put as the EMV of point B on the tree diagram. The EMV at node point E, which is not a relevant decision point, can now be obtained as:

$\frac{2}{3} \times 15\,000\ +\frac{3}{5} \times (-6000)$ $= 2400$
Ace orders   Ace does not order

The figure of 2400 is entered as the EMV corresponding to point E.

Finally, Mr Netford has to consider decision point A. The EMV corresponding to the decision 'build prototype' is 2400, while that of the alternative decision to 'do nothing' is 0. Again, using the rule that Mr Netford should choose that decision which has the higher EMV, he should choose the action 'build prototype'. His overall EMV will be 2400.

Summarizing, the decisions that need to be made and implemented are in the reverse sequence of what has emerged from the analysis. The first decision in time is that he should build the prototype. If the prototype results in obtaining the order from Ace, Wallace will try stampings, and use them if they work. Should the stampings be unsatisfactory, then the order would go ahead with machined parts.

Two general comments must be made about this problem, which will apply to nearly all similar decision problems. First, EMV has guided the decision. But Mr Netford will not then receive the precise amount of money indicated by the EMV. Indeed, if he adopts the decision analysis just made, he will receive either -6000, 9000 or 21 000, according to which outcome of the decisions made emerges. If this method of assessing money values and probabilities were unbiased, then, over a series of similar problems and associated decisions, we would expect his total gain to approximate closely to the sum of the individual problems' EMVs. But, for any one decision, this agreement will not often be the case.

Second, the decisions reached depend upon the probabilities in the tree and the financial cost and income data involved at each stage. We have made the decision at point A and, by implication, the decisions at points B and C, should we reach these points on the tree, on the basis of the best information available to Mr Netford on 1 May. Now suppose that Mr Netford takes the optimal initial decision and decides to build the prototype, subsequently receiving the order from Ace on 30 June. By that date, his design engineer and production manager have learnt a lot more about the product and come along to Mr Netford saying that they would like to revise some of their earlier estimates. They now believe that the chance of stampings working is rather higher, say $\frac{3}{5}$ rather than $\frac{1}{2}$, but that the cost of the dies concerned will be 8000 rather than the previous figure of 5000. Should Mr Netford take this new information into account and reconsider his decision at point B?

The decisions and costs incurred prior to 30 June are effectively water under the bridge and cannot be changed in any way. If we make the decision on 30 June as originally suggested in the 1 May analysis, we ignore the extra information that has come to hand. This might be disastrous and would imply that once a multistage project was launched, no subsequent decision could be changed. But each decision point reached is effectively a new problem. If none of the information has changed from the earlier analysis, then the decision reached in that analysis still stands. But, should some or all of the information relevant to subsequent actions and outcomes have changed, the appropriate portion of the decision tree needs to be reworked. Hence, for the Wallace Company, Mr Netford should now make his decision at point B on the basis of the best information available to him at 30 June. Figure 6.6

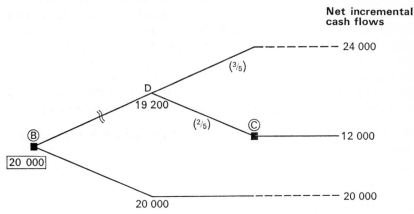

Fig. 6.6. Wallace revised decision tree

repeats the relevant part of the original decision tree, with the revised information incorporated in it. Notice that it is only necessary to consider the incremental cash flows from decision point B onwards. The 6000 already spent need not be considered from the point of view of making subsequent decisions. On computing the revised expected values, Mr Netford should now prefer to have machined parts, as the appropriate EMV is higher. At the same time we note that, having got the Ace order, Mr Netford now has a *certain* extra gain of 14 000, and prefers this to a gamble between extra gains of 18 000 and 6000.

6.4 Multibranch decision trees

The Wallace Company example had only two alternative decisions at the points where decisions had to be made. Many decision problems have more alternatives to consider at some, or all, of the decision nodes. We can still use the same criterion as before, namely, EMV, to choose between the alternatives, and we will again follow the previous principle of analysis of working through the tree from right to left, blocking off the branches that do not fall on the optimal decision path selected. The next example illustrates a situation which has more than two alternative decisions.

Example 6.4

The Nortraf Company has bought the rights to a new chemical product that is expected to revolutionize the improvement of grass lawns. It is estimated that the product will only have a life of five years from now, before it is overtaken by further new product developments in the same field. The general manager, Mr Cutler, is currently considering his best course of action.

The company, while anxious and able to manufacture and market the product now, realizes that it could probably significantly improve the product within a year if it carried out further research and development. This work would cost £200 000 but, in the considered opinion of the research manager, there would only be a 50 : 50 chance of success. If launching the product were delayed for a year, the product, in either the original or modified form, would then only have four effective years of life remaining.

The marketing manager has been asked to estimate the demand for the product and the likely profits that will accrue. He has done this by giving the following figures for yields and probabilities as he estimates them now:

(*i*) With the current product on sale, whenever the decision to market it is made:

Demand	Yield	Probability
High	£0·6m. p.a.	0·4
Low	£0·2m. p.a.	0·6

(*ii*) With an improved product on sale over each of the final four years:

Demand	Yield	Probability
High	£0·9m. p.a.	0·7
Low	£0·4m. p.a.	0·3

Yield is defined here as the net income from the product, excluding the costs of the research, if applicable, and the overhead costs of buildings, plant and equipment.

Once a given level of demand has been found to hold, demand will continue at that quantitative level throughout the period. The only exception is that if an improved product is brought in after one year to replace the original product already on the market, the demand, if already high, will remain high, while, if it is low, there is a 50 per cent chance that it will become high.

The production manager estimates that the overhead costs of building and installing the necessary plant and equipment are as follows:

(*i*) An initial plant for the present product—£0·2 million.
(*ii*) A new but upgraded plant in one year's time for the developed product—£0·3 million; this plant could not manufacture the original product;
(*iii*) A conversion operation from a plant suitable for the original product to one suitable for the developed product—£0·2 million.

In all three cases it is assumed, for simplicity, but a trifle optimistically, that a plant can be made available immediately the appropriate decision is made.

Mr Cutler has decided to base his decision on expected monetary values and to ignore any discounting of the sums involved. On the information given, what initial decision would Mr Cutler reach?

The basic decision tree is shown in Fig. 6.7(a) and two of the four paths, those labelled B and C, are shown in greater detail in Figs. 6.7(b) and 6.7(c). Note that initially the decision is from among four possibilities and, according to which decision is made, there may be other multiple choices to be made later. For each of the paths the income receivable has been placed at the end of the appropriate branch network, while the capital and research costs concerned have been placed against the particular portion of the branch network where they have been incurred, and will be deducted at the appropriate point in the analysis. All monetary quantities are expressed in £million throughout. This is a form of incremental analysis, and is a different procedure from that adopted in the previous example, but both procedures are equally acceptable and will lead to the same results. It is only necessary to ensure that the same procedure is used throughout any one analysis and convenience dictates the choice of approach. For more complex trees, the present approach is usually the more desirable.

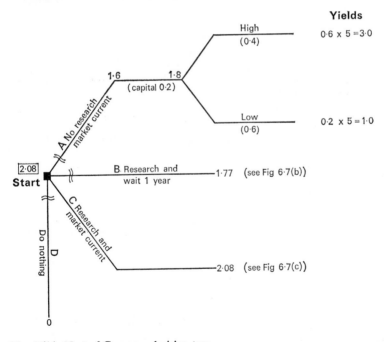

Fig. 6.7(a). Nostraf Company decision tree

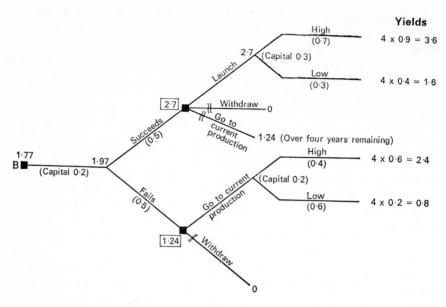

Fig. 6.7(b). Decision branch B

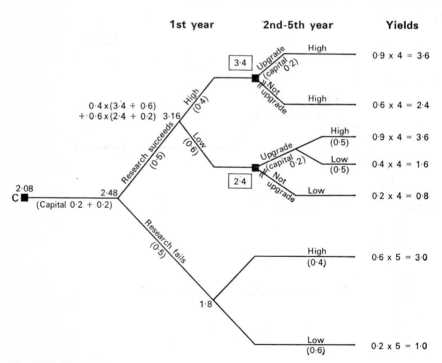

Fig. 6.7(c). Decision branch C

We will not go through the whole analysis, but will illustrate it by examining branch B shown in Fig. 6.7(b) in some detail. This branch presupposes that the research is done at a cost of 0·2 (first action) and the outcome is that the research either succeeds (probability $\frac{1}{2}$) or fails (probability $\frac{1}{2}$). If the research succeeds there are three new possible decisions: launch the improved product, produce the current product (for the four remaining years), or withdraw. If the revised product is launched, the corresponding EMV is computed as:

4	×	(0·7	× 0·9 +	0·3	× 0·4) −	0·3	=2·7
Number	Probability	Yield	Probability	Yield	Capital		
of	of high	p.a.	of low	p.a.			
years	demand		demand				

If the current product is produced and marketed, starting in year 2, the EMV is computed as:

4	×	(0·4	× 0·6 +	0·6	× 0·2) −	0·2	=1·24
Number	Probability	Yield	Probability	Yield	Capital		
of	of high	p.a.	of low	p.a.			
years	demand		demand				

If the company decides to withdraw, the EMV is zero. Notice that these three EMVs have all been calculated as at the moment the research is done, so that the cost of the research itself is not included. The highest EMV is the first of these, namely, 2·7, and this implies launching the new product.

If the research fails, then the two alternatives are to go into production with the current product, or to withdraw. For the former, the EMV has already been computed as 1·24, while for the latter it is zero. Hence, in this eventuality, the company would decide to go ahead with production of the current product. This is shown against the lower decision point in Fig. 6.7(b). Now the estimated probabilities of the research succeeding or failing are both $\frac{1}{2}$. Hence, the overall EMV for branch B of the tree is:

$\frac{1}{2}$×2·7	+ $\frac{1}{2}$×1·24 −	0·2	=1·77
Research	Research	Research	
succeeds	fails	costs	

Proceeding in the same manner, we find that the EMVs for the four alternatives at the initial decision point are:

A   No research, market current product   1·6

B   Research, wait 1 year before any marketing   1·77

C   Research, meanwhile market current product   2·08

D   Do nothing   0

Hence, branch C has the highest EMV, implying that Nortraf should go ahead with the research, but meanwhile market the current product. On current information the plant is upgraded to produce the new product if the research succeeds but, if it fails, the current product is continued.

Again, we should point out that, if the research is done and the results are available after one year, then the decision affecting the last four years should be reappraised in the light of the relevant information available at that time. The decision implied by the original analysis for that particular eventuality may need to be modified.

If, instead of EMV, we use the maximin gain approach, we need to establish first the minimum possible gain for each of the four possible initial decisions. These minima can be established from the appropriate portions of the tree as follows:

A   0·8
B   0·6   (When research fails, go to
          current production and demand
          turns out to be low.)
C   1·0   (When research succeeds, low
          initial demand, upgraded plant,
          low subsequent demand.)
D   0

Of these four quantities, C is the highest and hence this is, once again, the optimum initial decision. The reader is left, as an exercise, to consider the application of the notion of regrets to the problem.

6.5 Effect of discounting

It will be recalled that Mr Cutler decided to ignore discounting of the sums involved in the foregoing analysis. This was done in the main to simplify the arithmetical procedures and to highlight the form of analysis, which does not depend upon discounting. Yet, it is clear that discounting could affect the initial decision in that the timing of the various income and expenditure items differs for the various possible decisions. To bring in discounting, we need to evaluate the initial EMV for each of the possible initial decisions, allowing for the timing of the various items. Mr Cutler will then select that initial decision which has the highest discounted EMV.

To illustrate the method of computation, we will consider branch B again, assuming an interest rate of 7 per cent, and also assuming that all costs are incurred at the beginning of the year concerned, but that the yield is obtained at the end of the appropriate year. We first note that the discounted value of 1 monetary unit at 7 per cent for various years ahead is as follows:

1 year 0·935   2 years 0·873   3 years 0·816

4 years 0·763   5 years 0·713

We now go back to the situation at the end of the first year at the point where the research succeeds as outlined on page 135. The discounted EMV for launching the revised product is:

$$0·7 \times 0·9 \underset{\text{high demand}}{(0·935 + 0·873 + 0·816 \times 0·763)} +$$

$$+ 0·3 \times 0·4 \underset{\text{low demand}}{(0·935 + 0·873 + 0·816 + 0·763)} - \underset{\text{capital}}{0·3} = 2·24.$$

This is, of course, a rather lower figure than the 2·7 we had before, when we ignored discounting and effectively assumed an interest rate of zero. It is clear at this stage that the decision to launch will still have the highest EMV.

If the research fails, the discounted EMV for going to production with the current product will be:

$$0·4 \times 0·6 \ (0·935 + 0·873 + 0·816 + 0·763) +$$

$$+ 0·6 \times 0·2 \ (0·935 + 0·873 + 0·816 + 0·763) - 0·2 = 1·02.$$

Hence, the optimum decision at that stage is to go into current production. The overall discounted EMV for branch B at the start of the first year is therefore:

$$0·5 \times 2·24 \times 0·935 + 0·5 \times 1·02 \times 0·935 - 0·2 = 1·32,$$

as the yields have to be discounted for one further year, but the research costs are incurred immediately. This figure of 1·32 should be compared with the EMV of 1·77 obtained when discounting was ignored and the interest rate effectively taken as zero.

The reader is left to recompute for himself the discounted EMVs corresponding to the other three branches of initial decisions. The results are shown in Table 6.1, alongside the EMVs found earlier for a zero interest rate. As is to be expected, the EMVs are lower for a 7 per cent interest rate than for a zero interest rate (decision D is a rather special case). The order of preference still remains the same as before, but there is numerically rather less between the choices than before, and choices A and B are virtually indistinguishable. Although, in this particular instance, the initial choice remains unchanged, this will not universally be the position. Moreover, the precise ordering of the alternatives may depend upon the interest rate assumed in the computations. A higher interest rate favours paths in the decision tree where expenditure is delayed *vis-à-vis* the receipt of income, and the timing of the various items of income and expenditure becomes of greater importance the higher the interest rate assumed.

Table 6.1

Comparison of EMVs

	EMV	
Decision branch	Zero interest rate	7% interest rate
A	1·60	1·28
B	1·77	1·32
C	2·08	1·57
D	0	0

It is outside the scope of this book to discuss the detailed implications of tax on the choice of interest rate to be used in the analysis. It is, however, usual in computations such as these to use a net rate of interest. Any special allowances, such as investment grants, should be brought into account bearing in mind the likely moment of time when they will be paid, which is often some time after the related expenditure has been incurred.

6.6 A multistrategy game

The final example that will be examined in detail in this chapter is of a rather different kind, in that it involves a sequence of decisions that could, in theory at any rate, go on for ever. The example also involves what may appear at first sight to be an extremely artificial game situation. It will become apparent at the end of the analysis, however, that there are some interesting analogies (that must not be stretched too far) between the rather eighteenth century flavour of the problem and certain facets of modern business competition, or even of power problems in international politics.

Example 6.5

Black, Green and White agree to fight a pistol duel under the following somewhat unusual conditions. After drawing lots to decide who is to fire first, second and third, they take their places at the corner, of an equilateral triangle. It is agreed that they will fire single shots in turn, and continue in the same cyclic order until two of them are dead. At each turn the man who is firing may aim wherever he pleases. All three duellists know that Black always hits (and kills) his target, Green is 80 per cent accurate (in terms of killing) and White is 50 per cent accurate (in terms of killing). Each duellist will adopt the best strategy for his own survival, and it is assumed that no one is killed by a wild shot not intended for him. What is the best strategy for each duellist to adopt, and what are their respective probabilities of survival if these strategies are followed?

Before tackling the complete problem as posed with three duellists, it is worth considering a similar but reduced problem, but with two duellists only. The three-duellist problem must, sooner or later, reduce to a two-duellist problem and hence it is worth analysing the simpler problem first.

Suppose we call the two duellists A and B, with probabilities p_1 and p_2 respectively of hitting their targets, and suppose that it is A's turn to fire first. A can shoot at B or, alternatively, fire in the air. The latter strategy is obviously the poorer, since B then has the opportunity to fire at A, and only if he misses is A back in the running for survival. Hence his overall chance of survival is lowered and the better alternative must be for him to aim at B. A similar argument holds for B, if and when it comes to his turn to fire. Suppose we denote by A' a successful shot by A, and by $\bar{A}$ a losing shot by A; similarly for B. Then if A is to win (i.e. survive) one of the following sequences must occur:

A'

$\bar{A}\bar{B}A'$

$\bar{A}\bar{B}\bar{A}\bar{B}A'$

$\bar{A}\bar{B}\bar{A}\bar{B}\bar{A}\bar{B}A'$

$\ldots$, etc.

Assuming that the results of the shots fired are independent of each other, the probabilities of these sequences, by using the multiplication rule for probabilities, are:

p_1

$(1-p_1)(1-p_2)p_1$

$(1-p_1)(1-p_2)(1-p_1)(1-p_2)p_1$

$(1-p_1)(1-p_2)(1-p_1)(1-p_2)(1-p_1)(1-p_2)p_1$, etc.

and the overall probability of A surviving is the sum of these probabilities, or:

$$p_1[1+(1-p_1)(1-p_2)+(1-p_1)^2(1-p_2)^2+(1-p_1)^3(1-p_2)^3+\ldots].$$

The portion in the square brackets is a geometric series with common ratio of $(1-p_1)(1-p_2)$, and, hence, the required sum is:

$$p_1\left[\frac{1}{1-(1-p_1)(1-p_2)}\right] \quad \text{or} \quad \frac{p_1}{p_1+p_2-p_1p_2}. \tag{6.1a}$$

Since either A or B must survive, the probability of B's survival must equal unity minus the probability of A's survival, or:

$$1-\frac{p_1}{p_1+p_2-p_1p_2}=\frac{(1-p_1)p_2}{p_1+p_2-p_1p_2} \tag{6.1b}$$

Let us now return to the problem of the three duellists, and consider the position of White, the poorest shot, if and when it comes to his turn and all three duellists are still alive. If he aims at either Black or Green and scores a hit, then the other duellist left will open a two-man duel with White. To illustrate this situation we calculate, from Eqs. 6.1a and 6.1b above, White's chances of survival in a two-man duel with either of the others if he fires first or, alternatively, if he fires second. These chances, with the duellist who fires first *in italics,* are:

Black v. White 0;

Green v. White $\frac{1}{9}$;

White v. Black $\frac{1}{2}$;

White v. Green $\frac{5}{9}$.

Hence it is clear that it is to White's advantage to fire first when the duel is reduced to two men. Now if, in the three-duellist situation, White kills the other man, he will fire second, whereas if Black or Green kills the third man White must fire first. Thus White should, if there are still three duellists when it comes to his turn, fire into the air. If Black is to fire first when there are three duellists, he will clearly aim at Green, since Green has the best chance of killing Black. Similarly, if Green fires first, he will aim at Black, since Black will kill Green when his turn to fire arrives.

We are now in a position to draw an appropriate decision tree, which is shown in Fig. 6.8, together with the appropriate probabilities. For reasons given above, White can be omitted from the initial branching as he will shoot in the air at this stage. Sooner or later the duel reduces to two men as shown, and the respective probabilities of survival, from Eqs. 6.1a and 6.1b, are shown in brackets on the righthand side. We can now compute the respective overall probabilities of survival as follows:

Black $0 \cdot 5 \times \frac{1}{2} + 0 \cdot 5 \times 0 \cdot 2 \times \frac{1}{2} = \frac{3}{10}$ (or $0 \cdot 3$)
   (top   (bottom
   branch)   branch)

Green $0 \cdot 5 \times 0 \cdot 8 \times \frac{4}{9} = \frac{8}{45}$ (or $0 \cdot 178$)
   (middle
   branch)

White $0 \cdot 5 \times \frac{1}{2} + 0 \cdot 5 \times 0 \cdot 8 \times \frac{5}{9} + 0 \cdot 5 \times 0 \cdot 2 \times \frac{1}{2} = \frac{47}{90}$ (or $0 \cdot 522$)
   (top)   (middle   (bottom
   branch) branch)   branch)

These three probabilities add to unity, as they should do, since from the rules of the duel one and only one of the three duellists will survive. The numerical results are interesting, in that Black's position, which looked

Initial target   **Initial outcome**   **Two-duellist situation**

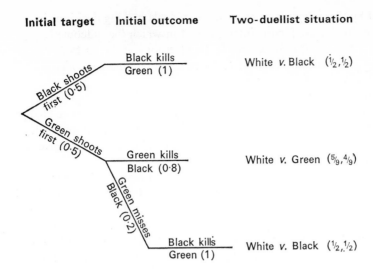

Black kills
Green (1)   White *v.* Black   (½,½)

Black shoots
first (0·5)

Green shoots
first (0·5)

Green kills
Black (0·8)   White *v.* Green   (⁵/₉,⁴/₉)

Green misses
Black (0·2)

Black kills
Green (1)   White *v.* Black   (½,½)

(The two-duellist situation that is reached is given with
the first-named as the first to fire, and the respective
survival probabilities of the two-person duel in brackets.)

Fig. 6.8. The three-duellist problem

virtually impregnable at a first glance, is not really so good, his overall
chance of survival being only 0·3. Poor White, for whom we all felt some
sympathy at first sight, actually has the best overall chance of survival at
0·5222.

The moral to be drawn from the foregoing example seems to be that, if the
weakest competitor can arrange matters to let the two stronger competitors
exhaust themselves first, he has a very good chance of being the eventual
winner. This may seem a self-evident dictum but evidence suggests that in
practice, businesses and nations do not always behave as logically as a
knowledge of probability might indicate, although there are a number of
examples from politics which would seem to bear out that this analysis is
well understood.

The reader is, however, left to prove for himself that even if 'Fifty : fifty'
White decides, against his own apparent best interest, to blaze away at the
opponent he believes to be the more dangerous, his chance of survival is still
0·447, while Black's chance is down to 0·242 and Green's chances rise to
0·311. Dead-eyed shot Black is again bottom as regards his chances of
survival. The moral for businesses or nations that regard themselves in
strong positions seems to be a rather disturbing one.

The foregoing example is an illustration of a competitive situation or, as it
is sometimes termed, a competitive game. In general such situations are

characterized by there being two or more individuals making decisions in situations that involve conflicting interests, and in which the outcome is controlled to a greater or lesser extent by the decisions of the parties involved. Many conflict situations of this type are found in economic, business, social, political or military problems.

Such situations commonly involve elements of chance, as for example the weather during a military attack, or a competitor's reaction to a price change. The theory of games assumes that, in all these competitive situations, each opponent is going to act in a rational manner and will attempt to resolve the conflict of interests in his favour.

The approach to competitive problems of this kind developed by the well-known economist, von Neumann, utilizes the minimax principle outlined earlier. This approach has been developed further and, whilst the fascinating subject of games is not taken further in this book, interested readers are referred to J. D. Williams *The Compleat Strategyst* (McGraw-Hill, 1954) or *Fundamentals in Operations Research* by R. L. Ackoff and M. W. Sasieni, Chapter 13 (Wiley, 1968).

6.7 Summary of procedure

There are four basic elements relevant to any decision problem, namely:

- (*i*) What are the options open? (Actions.)
- (*ii*) What are the possible outcomes? (Events and pay-offs.)
- (*iii*) What are the relevant uncertainties? (Probabilities.)
- (*iv*) What is the decision-maker's basis of choice? (Criteria.)

All these elements can be represented on a decision tree and taken into account in its analysis. This is not to suggest, however, that putting a decision problem in such a form is necessarily straightforward. The irrelevant factors of a situation must be stripped away so as to display the basic anatomy of the decision problem in manageable form. It is not an easy task to identify the viable courses of action and the basic sources of uncertainty, and show how these interact in sequential order. The numerical figures for pay-offs, costs and probabilities will rarely be available in a clear-cut manner, and much work may be necessary to obtain appropriate figures.

When the tree, with relevant numerical data, has been constructed, the analysis can proceed. The decision tree gives, in chronological order, those moves that the decision-maker can choose and those which are governed, in part or in whole, by chance. The analysis proceeds by going out to the tips of the tree and working backwards by successive use of two procedures at each decision point or node:

- (*i*) A calculation of the expected monetary value for each possible decision path.

(*ii*) A choice procedure that selects the path yielding the maximum expected monetary value.

This process is carried out working from the tips of the tree back to the starting point. It is sometimes referred to as the *averaging out and folding back* procedure or the *roll-back* procedure.

   One of the great attractions of the decision tree approach is that once the inputs have been specified in such a way that the tree can be drawn and appropriately quantified, the optimum solution can be computed on a routine basis. The analyst does not need to keep in his head all the considerations that should be taken into account. Indeed, it is possible for different people to evaluate the various items, although the person making the overall decision must accept all the individual evaluations. This enables contentious elements in the analysis to be lifted out, and revised assessments substituted for these elements without having to reconsider every other element in the tree. Decision analysis is a powerful aid to consistent and logical decision-making in complex situations.

6.8 Incorporation of further data

In all the examples that have been discussed so far in this chapter, the various actions were followed by one of a number of possible outcomes. Subsequent decisions then rested upon the probabilities currently assigned to the outcomes of further decisions. Sometimes, however, we may be able to purchase information such as market research data, that would assist us to reassess the various probabilities that we have previously placed on the different outcomes. Such data would have to be paid for, which implies that it is necessary to assess the worth of the information, before it is decided whether or not to purchase it.

Example 6.6
A decision is to be made whether to leave a sum of £100 000 on deposit in a bank for three months, or to invest it in a particular block of stock market equity shares. The investor has made his own probabilistic assessment of the chances of a rise or fall in the equity price, but he can also obtain for a fee the services of a recognized and well-known investment analyst. For simplicity of illustration we will assume that the shares can only rise or fall by 20 per cent in the timespan concerned. While his advice will be either to buy the shares or not to buy them, the possible outcomes of following his advice can only be described in probabilistic terms. We would expect that his chances of spotting winners or losers is rather better than our own unaided efforts and, hence, the investor has to decide first of all whether or not to buy the advice and, second, whether or not to invest (either with or without the advice). The decision tree for this problem is shown in Fig. 6.9, where a_1, a_2, a_3 represent the initial decision to consult the analyst, or to buy the

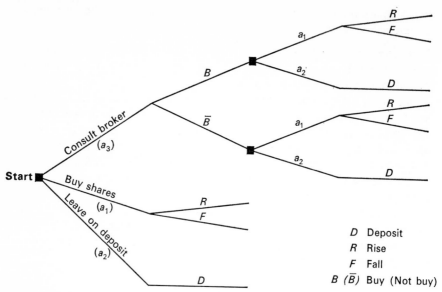

Fig. 6.9. Investment of funds

shares, or to leave the money on deposit respectively. If the analyst is consulted, B and $\bar{B}$ represent his advice to buy or not to buy. The outcome if the money is put on deposit (indicated by D) is certain, while if the shares are bought they can either rise, denoted by R, or fall, denoted by F.

Looking at this tree, we can pursue a very partial analysis without further information, provided we assume that we would always follow the analyst's recommendation; that if we purchased the analyst's advice and that it was not to buy, then we do not buy, otherwise it would hardly be worth-while paying for the advice in the first place. Similarly for advice to buy. But we cannot really go any further than this. The probabilities that we are willing at the start to put on the R and F branches, following decision a_2 at the start, may be changed if we decide to buy the analyst's advice and, hence, in deciding between actions a_2 and a_3 on an EMV basis, we may have different probabilities for R and F according to whether we are on paths $a_1 \rightarrow B \rightarrow a_2$, or a_2 by itself.

What we need to have now is some method whereby we can revise the probabilities that we originally placed upon the events 'equity appreciates' or 'equity depreciates' in the light of the additional information from the investment analyst, the latter information being also of a probabilistic nature. This problem will be tackled in the next chapter and a method developed for the revision of probabilities in such situations. A revised form of this particular example will then be re-examined in a futher discussion of decision trees in Chapter 8, when we will have some additional methods of analysis at our disposal.

Exercises on Chapter 6

1 Mr Stanley is trying to decide whether to travel to Rome from London to negotiate the sale of a shipment of china novelties. He holds the novelties in stock and is fairly confident, but by no means sure, that if he makes the trip he will sell the novelties at a price that will give him a profit of £3000. He puts the probability of obtaining the order at 0·6. If he does not make the trip, he will certainly not get the order.

If the novelties are not sold in Rome, there is a United Kingdom customer who will certainly buy them at a price that leaves him a profit of £1500, and his offer will be open at least until Mr Stanley returns from Rome. Mr Stanley estimates the expenses of the trip to Rome at £250. He is, however, concerned that his absence, even for only three days, may lead to production inefficiencies in his factory. These could cause him to miss the deadline on another contract, with the consequence that a late penalty of £1000 will be invoked. Mr Stanley assesses the probability of missing the deadline under these circumstances at 0·4. Furthermore, he believes that in his absence there will be a lower standard of housekeeping in the factory, and the raw material and labour costs on the other contract will rise by about £200 above the budgeted figure.

Draw an appropriate decision tree for Mr Stanley's problem and, using EMV as the appropriate criterion for decision, find the appropriate initial decision.

2 An oil wildcatter is trying to decide whether or not to buy the rights on a piece of land and drill. The well that he sinks may either be dry (which is bad), or wet (so-so), or soaking (good). Before making a final decision, he can have a seismic survey carried out at a fee. This survey records one of three results: negative, neutral or positive. These three results are roughly, but not precisely, linked to the three types of well.

Draw a decision tree for the decisions which face the oil wildcatter.

3 A businessman has just been asked to attend an important meeting in winter in Scandinavia at a town on the other side of a mountain range. He can travel to the town from his hotel either by train or by his car. If he travels by train he expects to be on time. He may be late at the meeting, but he will certainly not arrive so late as to miss the whole meeting. If he travels by car, he may find that the mountain pass over which he has to travel is closed. If it is closed and he returns to his hotel he will then have missed his train and cannot catch another train to arrive in time for the meeting. If the pass is open, there is no guarantee that the road conditions will be good. If good, he should get to the meeting on time. If bad, there is not only the high possibility of arriving too late for the meeting, but also of an accident occurring to himself.

Draw a decision tree for this problem. Discuss the difficulties regarding data that would be associated with the analysis of the tree in order to reach a decision as to whether to go by train or car.

4 The PQR Company has received an order from the LMN Company for a batch of a certain chemical, but PQR's management is uncertain whether or not to accept the order. The chemical is so unstable that the reaction used to produce it may get out of control and cause an explosion, completely destroying the production facilities. Even if no explosion occurs, the finished batch of chemical may fail to meet the specification and have to be scrapped.

If the order is accepted, the required labour and raw material will cost £10 000 for the ordered quantity of chemical, all of which will be lost if an explosion occurs or the product is unsatisfactory. If a satisfactory product is delivered, LMN will pay £25 000. If PQR accept the order, but fail to deliver a satisfactory product (or any product) there is a penalty of £5000. Furthermore, while there would be time to repeat the manufacturing process once again if the product were found to be unsatisfactory, this could not be done if an explosion had occurred. The damage done to the plant by an explosion would cost £40 000 to repair.

(*i*) Draw an appropriate decision tree, and value the various alternative paths on the tree.

(*ii*) The management of PQR assess the risk of an explosion at their plant at 0·01 each time a batch of this chemical is made. Suppose that the risk of a batch produced being unsatisfactory is α. For what values of α should PQR accept the order?

5 The Dissolving Chemical Company has to decide whether to build a small or large plant to manufacture a new product that will have an expected market life of ten years. The decision hinges partly on the size of the market the company can obtain for the product.

Demand may possibly be high during the first two years but, if many of the initial users find the product unsatisfactory, the demand could then fall to a low level thereafter. High initial demand might alternatively indicate the possibility of a sustained high-volume market for the remaining eight years. If the demand is initially high and remains so, and the company finds itself with insufficient capacity within the first two years, competitive products will certainly be introduced by other manufacturers.

If the company initially builds a big plant, it must live with it for the whole ten years, whatever the size of the market demand. If it builds a small plant, there is the option of expanding the plant in two years' time, an option that it would only consider taking up if demand were high during the introductory period. If a small plant is built initially and demand is low during the introductory period, the company will maintain operations in the small plant and make a good profit on the low-volume throughput.

The manager is uncertain as to the action he should take. The company grew rapidly during the middle 1960s, keeping pace with the chemical industry generally. The new product, if the market turns out to be large, offers the company a chance to move into a period of extremely profitable growth. The development department, particularly the development project engineer, is anxious to build the large-scale plant in order to exploit the first major product development the department has had in some years.

The chairman, a principal stockholder, is wary of the possibility of having a large amount of plant capacity, and, hence, capital, lying idle. He currently favours a smaller initial plant commitment, but recognizes that possible later expansion to meet high-volume demand would, overall, require more investment and be less efficient to operate. The chairman also recognizes that, unless the company moves promptly to fill the demand which develops, once the product is on the market, competitors will be tempted to move in with equivalent products.

Various items of information have been obtained, or estimated, by the appropriate managers within the company. This information is summarized as follows:

(*i*) *Marketing information.* The marketing manager suggests a 60 per cent chance of a large market in the long run and a 40 per cent chance of a low demand, developing initially as follows:

Initially high, sustained high	60 per cent	
Initially high, long-term low	10 per cent	Low 40 per cent
Initially low, continuing low	30 per cent	
Initially low, subsequently high	0 per cent	

(*ii*) *Annual income.* The management accounting section have put forward the following financial estimates:

(*a*) A large plant with high market volume would yield £1 million annually in cash flow (for ten years).

(*b*) A large plant with low market volume would yield only £0·1 million annually because of high fixed costs and inefficiencies.

(*c*) A small plant with low market demand would be economical and would yield annual cash income of £0·4 million per annum.

(*d*) A small plant, during an initial period of high demand, would yield £0·45 million per annum, but this would drop to £0·25 million per annum in the long run if high demand continued, because of competition from other manufacturers.

(*e*) If an initial small plant were expanded after two years to meet sustained high demand, it would yield £0·7 million annually for the remaining eight years, and so would be less efficient than a large plant built initially.

(*f*) If the small plant were expanded after two years, but high demand were not sustained, the estimated annual cash flow for the remaining eight years would be £0·05 million.

(*iii*) *Capital costs*. Estimates obtained from construction companies indicate that a large plant would cost £3 million to build and put into operation, a small plant would cost £1·3 million initially and an additional £2·2 million if expanded after two years. (Ignore any delays in construction of plant.)

Use the information given to draw an appropriate decision tree for this problem. Using EMV as the appropriate criterion for decision, find the appropriate initial decision that the company should make. Ignore any discounting of the cash flows.

6 Repeat the analysis of the problem in Exercise 5 above, assuming an interest rate of 10 per cent per annum. Is the initial decision reached the same as before?

7 A complex airborne navigating system incorporates a subassembly which unrolls a map of the flight plan synchronously with the movement of the aeroplane. This subassembly is bought on very good terms from a subcontractor, but is not always in perfect adjustment on delivery. The subassemblies can be readjusted on delivery to guarantee accuracy at a cost of £50 per subassembly. It is not, however, possible to distinguish visually those assemblies that need adjustment.

Alternatively, the subassemblies can each be tested electronically to see if they need adjustment at a cost of £12 per subassembly tested. Past experience shows that about 40 per cent of those supplied are defective; the probability of the test indicating a bad adjustment when the subassembly is faulty is 0·7, while the probability that the test indicates a good adjustment when the subassembly is properly adjusted is 0·8. If the adjustment is not made and the subassembly is found to be faulty when the system has its final check, the cost of subsequent rectification will be £150.

Draw up an appropriate decision tree to show the alternatives open to the purchaser and use it to determine his appropriate course of action.

8 A German jeweller owns a set of four rough gems that can be sold immediately for DM 1250 per gem. Alternatively, the four rough gems can be subjected to an expensive cutting and polishing process, one after the other, at a cost of DM 2000 per gem handled. Sets of cut and polished gems are highly priced, the price depending very critically on the number in the set and is as shown in Table 6.2.

Table 6.2

Selling prices of gem sets

Number of gems in set	1	2	3	4
Total selling price (DM)	2500	7500	15000	25000

Unfortunately, the cutting process is far from foolproof, and there is a probability of 0·25 that a gem will be ruined and made valueless. A decision can be made at any point in processing the set to sell any cut gems already produced as a set and any remaining unprocessed gems at the original price of DM 1250 per gem.

Formulate, on the basis of expected monetary value, the optimal strategy for the jeweller to follow. (Ignore any taxation considerations.)

9 A client asks an estate agent to sell three properties (A, B and C) for him and agrees to pay him a 5 per cent commission on each sale. He specifies certain conditions. The estate agent must sell A first, and this he must do within 60 days. If, and when, A is sold the agent receives his 5 per cent commission on that sale. He can then either back out at this stage or nominate and try to sell one of the two remaining properties within 60 days. If he does not succeed in selling the nominated property in that period, he is not given the opportunity to sell the other. If he does sell it in the period, he is given the opportunity to sell the third property on the same conditions. Table 6.3 summarizes the prices, selling costs (incurred whenever a sale is attempted) and the estate agent's estimated probabilities of making a sale:

Table 6.3

Data for property sales

Property	Price of property	Selling costs	Probability of sale
A	£12 500	£400	0·7
B	£25 000	£225	0·6
C	£50 000	£450	0·5

(*i*) Draw an appropriate decision tree for the estate agent.
(*ii*) What is the estate agent's best strategy under an EMV approach?

7 The revision of probabilities

7.1 The modification of decisions

So far probability theory has been used to derive some basic rules, whereby the probability of the happening of some compound event or a sequence of events can be derived from the probabilities of other basic events. The assumption has been that, using what are termed *prior* probabilities, the required probabilities of these more complex happenings can be computed.

The natural reaction of anyone faced with making a decision when there is uncertainty present in the form of the prior probabilities of various alternative outcomes, is to try to remove the uncertainty by finding out what is the true state of affairs. Knowledge is, in general, assumed to be beneficial to the making of a decision. Complete knowledge is certainly a way out of all difficulties, provided we are clear as to the criteria we would use for decisions, but it is rarely practicable where decisions involve some consideration of the future. Thus a Stock Exchange investor trying to decide whether or not to invest in a particular stock would not know for certain whether the stock was going to appreciate or not. Again, cost may be a powerful deterrent to the removal of uncertainty; it may just be too expensive to find out the complete truth. An engineer designing a plant will not often be able to build a trial plant, but may think it useful to build a prototype to resolve some of the uncertainties in the design problem. A prototype may, however, in itself sometimes cost so much that it is better to build the plant in a fairly flexible manner and learn from experience the form of any modifications that are needed.

Thus while it is usually a good thing to seek the removal of all uncertainty from a problem, it is commonly not a practicable aim. There is very often, however, a partial solution available to us in that, while it may not be possible to remove all the uncertainty, it is sometimes feasible to reduce it by obtaining some relevant information. Thus, the investor may consult his stockbroker, who is presumably more knowledgeable than the investor, as to expectations concerning the particular stock in question. The engineer, thwarted of his prototype, may obtain some information from calculations of the likely behaviour of the system or from visits of inspection to similar plants. In these situations we will still not be able to determine the true situation, but at least in general we will be more knowledgeable than we would have been without the information. If we combine this extra information with the prior probabilities to form revised probabilities, the latter are then referred to as *posterior* probabilities, and provide us with a revised basis on which to make our decision.

7.2 Posterior probabilities

Assume now that we have available to us the prior probabilities of certain alternative outcomes. Some experiment has been performed, or sample investigation carried out, and the resultant information is known to us. What are now the posterior probabilities corresponding to the original prior probabilities of the various outcomes? A simple illustration will help to make the position clear.

First, we will accept that twins are of two types, identical (I) and non-identical (N), and that in the population as a whole there are 50 per cent of each type. Second, suppose that identical twins are always of the same sex, with a 50 per cent chance of each sex occurring, while for non-identical twins the sex of each child has an independent 50 : 50 chance of being male or female. The mix that would result from these suppositions is shown pictorially in Fig. 7.1. For example, the prior probability that a pair of twins chosen at random are both girls is given by the area ACHJKGA, or $\frac{1}{2} \times \frac{1}{2} + \frac{1}{2} \times \frac{1}{4} = \frac{3}{8}$. Again, the chance that a randomly chosen pair of twins are identical is given by the area AFLE, or $\frac{1}{2}$. Such probabilities are referred to as *prior* probabilities. Thus, the prior probability that a pair of randomly chosen twins are identical is $\frac{1}{2}$.

Let us now imagine that, having selected a pair of twins at random from the population, you are given the additional information that both of the twins are known to be girls. What is now the revised (or posterior) probability that the pair of twins is an identical pair? It is unlikely that you would still assign equal probabilities to the twins being identical or non-identical, since more identical sets of twins have two girls than do non-identical sets of twins. The argument, therefore, proceeds as follows:

Of all the twins in the population, the proportions that were both girls can be categorized into subsets as follows:

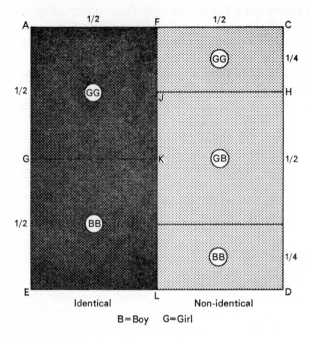

Fig. 7.1. Composition of twin population

Both girls and non-identical	Area FCHJ	$\frac{1}{2} \times \frac{1}{4} = \frac{1}{8}$
Both girls and identical	Area AFKG	$\frac{1}{2} \times \frac{1}{2} = \frac{1}{4}$
Both girls and either non-identical or identical	Area ACHJKG	$\frac{1}{2} \times \frac{1}{4} + \frac{1}{2} \times \frac{1}{2} = \frac{3}{8}$

Hence, the probability that the twins were identical, given that we know they are both girls, is the ratio of the two areas AFKG and ACHJKG shown in Fig. 7.1, or $\frac{1}{4}/\frac{3}{8} = \frac{2}{3}$.

The calculations can also be laid out in tabular form as shown in Table 7.1. The outcomes on which interest is concentrated, namely identical or non-identical, are listed in column 1, and their original prior probabilities are given in column 2. The prior probabilities in this column sum to unity, indicating that the events in column 1 are mutually exclusive and the only possible. Column 3 shows, first, the probability of two girls, given that they were identical twins, and, second, the corresponding probability given that they were non-identical twins. The values can be taken directly in this instance from Fig. 7.1. These probabilities are denoted later by the symbols $P(G|I)$ and $P(G|N)$ respectively, i.e. the probability of two girls given that the twins are known to be identical, etc.

Table 7.1

Calculation of posterior probabilities

Event of interest	Prior probabilities		Revised probabilities	
	Probability of event in (1)	Probability of two girls, in (1)	Joint probability of two girls and event in (1)	Probability of event in (1) given two girls
(1)	(2)	(3)	$(4)=(2)\times(3)$	$(5)=(4)\div\Sigma\,(4)$
Identical	$\frac{1}{2}$	$\frac{1}{2}$	$\frac{1}{4}$	$\frac{2}{3}$
Non-identical	$\frac{1}{2}$	$\frac{1}{4}$	$\frac{1}{8}$	$\frac{1}{3}$
Totals	1	$\frac{3}{4}$	$\frac{3}{8}$	1

The theory of probability outlined in Chapter 2 is now used to compute revised probabilities from the two sets of basic probabilities, given in columns 2 and 3, the work being shown in the last two columns of the table. First, the multiplication rule (Section 2.5, Rule 3, page 20) is used to compute the joint probabilities of 'two girls and identical' and 'two girls and non-identical', shown in column 4. The addition rule (Section 2.4, Rule 2, page 19) is used to sum column 4 to give the prior marginal probability of two girls; this is the $\frac{3}{8}$ total of the joint probabilities given at the foot of column (4). Finally, column 5 uses the definition of conditional probability to compute the revised or posterior probabilities as the ratio of the appropriate probability in column 4 to the total of column 4. The two posterior probabilities sum to unity. (Readers should note that the probabilities in column 3 do not necessarily sum to unity and the total has no particular significance in the present context.)

7.3 Bayes' theorem

Returning to the previous illustration, the logic in Table 7.1 can now be expressed more compactly by the use of algebraic notation. First, from the multiplication rule (Rule 3, page 20) we have:

$$P(G\cap I)=P(I)\,P(G|I)$$
(both G and I),

and

$$P(G\cap N)=P(N)\,P(G|N)$$
(both G and N).

Since the events $(G\cap I)$ and $(G\cap N)$ are mutually exclusive and only possible if the outcome of selecting a pair of twins is to have two girls, it follows that:

$$P(G)=P(G \cap I)+P(G \cap N)$$

from Rule 2 (page 19) for total probability.
  Hence, we have

$$P(G)=P(I) P(G|I)+P(N) P(G|N).$$

  Finally, Rule 3 gives:

$$P(I \cap G)=P(G) P(I|G)$$

or

$$P(I|G)=\frac{P(I \cap G)}{P(G)}=\frac{P(I) P(G|I)}{P(I) P(G|I)+P(N) P(G|N)}.$$

This expression is known as *Bayes' theorem*, named after the Methodist clergyman Thomas Bayes (1702–61) who first formulated it, but it is really little more than an extension of the definition of conditional probability in Chapter 2. In the present instance only two events are concerned, but the result can be straightforwardly generalized to r events to give the usual form in which Bayes' theorem is stated as follows: if E_i ($i=1, 2, \ldots r$) are r mutually exclusive and only possible results, such that an event F can occur only if one of these r events happens, then the probability that E_j happens when F is known to have happened is:

$$P(E_j|F)=P(E_j) P(F|E_j) \Big/ \sum_{i=1}^{r} P(E_i) P(F|E_i). \tag{7.1}$$

Four examples, of differing complexity, of the application of this theorem will now be given.

Example 7.1

A dealer has purchased a batch of machine parts from a manufacturer. He knows that the parts are produced by either machine A or machine B, but he does not know which machine has manufactured the particular batch he has purchased. From past experience he believes that if machine A produced the parts 15 per cent will be defective, while if machine B produced them 25 per cent will be defective. The manufacturer has reported to him that 60 per cent of batches come from machine A and 40 per cent from machine B. If the dealer selects a random sample of three parts from the batch and finds none defective, what is the (posterior) probability that the batch was produced by machine A?

  Here, let E_1 and E_2 represent manufacture on each of the two machines and F the event that, with a random sample of three parts, no defectives are found. From the data given, the following probabilities can be directly written down:

(*i*) The prior probabilities that the two particular machines would give rise to the batch purchased:

$$P(E_1) = 0.6, \quad P(E_2) = 0.4.$$

(*ii*) The probabilities, for each machine in turn, that if a random sample of three items is drawn from a batch produced by that machine, none will be found defective.

$$P(F|E_1) = (1-0.15)^3 = 0.85^3,$$

$$P(F|E_2) = (1-0.25)^3 = 0.75^3.$$

Hence:

$$P(E_1|F) = \frac{P(E_1)\,P(F|E_1)}{P(E_1)\,P(F|E_1) + P(E_2)\,P(F|E_2)}$$

$$= \frac{0.6 \times 0.85^3}{0.6 \times 0.85^3 + 0.4 \times 0.75^3}$$

$$= 0.686.$$

Note that the bringing in of the sample information has lifted the initial *prior* probability for machine A of 0.6 to a *posterior* probability of 0.686. This is clearly in the right direction, since the sample result is more suggestive of machine A than of machine B.

The reader is left to verify that the posterior probability that the batch was produced by machine B is 0.314 and hence that the two posterior probabilities sum to unity.

Example 7.2

A bookclub sells paperback reprints of hardback scientific books by mail order to its registered members only. The bookclub has been offered the paperback rights to a hardback book, *Analogue Business Controls* (*ABC*), and will make a profit provided that it sells copies at the normal bookclub price to more than 4000 of its 100 000 members. Past experience suggests that (in a simplified form) the sales of this kind of book are likely to fall into one of three categories with the stated prior probabilities as shown in Table 7.2.

Table 7.2

Bookclub selling probabilities

Category (event)		Proportion of members purchasing (p_i)	Prior probability
Low sales	E_1	0.01	0.04
Medium sales	E_2	0.03	0.30
High sales	E_3	0.05	0.66

Event E_3 would lead to financial success, while events E_1 and E_2 would lead to a financial loss. The publisher, not entirely satisfied with his *prior* chance of 0·66 of financial success, decides to test the market. He does this by sending out an advance card to 100 of his members, randomly selected from his membership list, asking them if they wish to place an order for the book. (Any orders received can be met, even if the publisher does not go ahead with the paperback edition, by supplying hardback copies at a small loss.) Of the 100 cards sent out, 6 result in an order being placed for *ABC*. What is now the revised posterior probability of E_3 (the only financially rewarding event)?

Clearly, we cannot just rule out E_1 and E_2 on the grounds that the observed result is most consistent with E_3, since there is still some finite chance that it could have arisen from an E_1 or E_2 situation. But it will, nevertheless, affect the prior probabilities originally established.

Here the prior probabilities are: $P(E_1)=0·04$, $P(E_2)=0·30$, $P(E_3)=0·66$. These three sum to unity.

The probabilities of obtaining the sample information for each of the three events are:

$$P(F|E_1) = \binom{100}{6} (0·01)^6 (0·99)^{94}, \quad \text{since} \quad p_1 = 0·01;$$

$$P(F|E_2) = \binom{100}{6} (0·03)^6 (0·97)^{94}, \quad \text{since} \quad p_2 = 0·03;$$

$$P(F|E_3) = \binom{100}{6} (0·05)^6 (0·95)^{94}, \quad \text{since} \quad p_3 = 0·05.$$

Hence,

$$P(E_3|F) = \frac{P(E_3)\,P(F|E_3)}{P(E_1)\,P(F|E_1) + P(E_2)\,P(F|E_2) + P(E_3)\,P(F|E_3)}$$

$$= \frac{0·66 \binom{100}{6} (0·05)^6 (0·95)^{94}}{0·04 \binom{100}{6} (0·01)^6 (0·99)^{94} + 0·30 \binom{100}{6} (0·03)^6 (0·97)^{94} + 0·66 \binom{100}{6} (0·05)^6 (0·95)^{94}}$$

$$= 0·868.$$

This is considerably higher than the original *prior* probability of 0·66, and might well incline the publisher more firmly in favour of undertaking the paperback venture. By a similar calculation we find that $P(E_1|F)=0·000$ (to three decimal places) and $P(E_2|F)=0·132$. These three posterior probabilities sum to unity.

It is worth our while to explore this example a little further, to illustrate the value of yet further information in terms of the effect it would have on the posterior probabilities. Suppose that the publisher had sent out 200 cards and 12 came back placing an order for *ABC*. The percentage of successful response is the same as before, namely 6 per cent, but the number of members sampled is double, at 200 in place of 100. How would this sample investigation have affected the posterior probabilities? We can carry out the same calculations as before, using the same prior probabilities, only in this instance the probabilities $P(F|E_i)$ will represent the probability that in a sample of 200 members, each of whom has a probability p_i of ordering, there are exactly 12 orders. Calculation gives:

$P(F|E_1)=0.0000;$

$P(F|E_2)=0.0113;$

$P(F|E_3)=0.0948.$

and then, using Bayes' theorem again, the corresponding posterior probabilities are:

$P(E_1|F)=0.000;$

$P(E_2|F)=0.051;$

$P(E_3|F)=0.949.$

Thus, the posterior probability of E_3, the profitable category, has risen still further. This is surely to be expected, since there is now even more sample information pointing to the veracity of E_3. Indeed, as the amount of sample information available grows, the prior probabilities become of less and less importance and the sample information becomes dominant. (Readers should note that in calculating the probabilities required in this example, sufficient accuracy will be obtained by approximating to the binomial probabilities with a Poisson distribution with parameter $100\,p_i$ or $200\,p_i$ respectively.)

† *Example 7.3*

The market for a product can be one of high demand (*H*), medium demand (*M*) or low demand (*L*). Marketing estimates indicate that the chances of these three outcomes are 0.60, 0.10 and 0.30 respectively. A decision has to be made as to whether to enter the market with the product. Before making a decision, however, the possibility of a sizeable pay-off from good research needs investigation, in that it should reduce the likelihood of making a mistake. The research, however, does not give a unique indication of the state of market demand, but merely a positive or negative indication. Management estimates that:

(*i*) If the market is actually of high demand, *H*, the chance that the research will give a positive indication is 0.70.

(*ii*) If the market is actually of medium demand, M, the chance that the research gives a positive indication is 0·50.

(*iii*) If the market is actually of low demand, L, the chance that the research gives a positive indication is 0·05.

Thus, the research provides an indication of what the market is like, but not an infallible indication. Is the research worth while? As a first step to answering this question, we need to assess the posterior probabilities on the basis of the sample information from the research. First, we consider the case when the research is positive. What are the revised posterior chances of H, M and L?

Let $P(H)$ indicate the prior probability of high demand, $P(H|F)$, the probability of high demand when the research findings were positive, $P(N|H)$ the probability of finding negative research results when there was in reality high demand, etc. Then Bayes' theorem states that:

$$P(H|F) = \frac{P(F|H)\,P(H)}{P(F|H)\,P(H) + P(F|M)\,P(M) + P(F|L)\,P(L)}$$

$$= \frac{0·7 \times 0·6}{0·7 \times 0·6 + 0·5 \times 0·1 + 0·05 \times 0·30}$$

$$= \frac{0·42}{0·485} = 0·87;$$

$$P(M|F) = \frac{P(F|M)\,P(M)}{P(F|H)\,P(H) + P(F|M)\,P(M) + P(F|L)\,P(L)}$$

$$= \frac{0·5 \times 0·1}{0·485} = 0·10;$$

$$P(L|F) = \frac{P(F|L)\,P(L)}{P(F|H)\,P(H) + P(F|M)\,P(M) + P(F|L)\,P(L)}$$

$$= \frac{0·015}{0·485} = 0·03.$$

These three probabilities sum to unity, as they must. Note that the denominator remains the same in each expression, namely, the sum of the conditional probabilities concerned, and it is only the numerator which changes.

The consequence of positive research information is that the prior probability for H of 0·60 has been adjusted to a posterior probability of 0·87. This increase has been at the expense of M and L which have much lower posterior probabilities.

We must now consider the effect on the prior probabilities of carrying out the research and getting a negative result. Then we have:

$$P(H|N) = \frac{P(N|H)\,P(H)}{P(N|H)\,P(H)+P(N|M)\,P(M)+P(N|L)\,P(L)}$$

$$= \frac{0\cdot3\times0\cdot6}{0\cdot3\times0\cdot6+0\cdot5\times0\cdot1+0\cdot95\times0\cdot3}$$

$$= \frac{0\cdot18}{0\cdot515} = 0\cdot35.$$

Similarly $P(M|N)=0\cdot10$ and $P(L|N)=0\cdot55$. Hence, in this situation there is, not unnaturally, a big decrease in the probability of H, with a corresponding increase in the probability of L, the probability of M again remaining unchanged. The results obtained are summarized in Table 7.3. They indicate that carrying out the research enables a rather finer discrimination between market demands to be made. Thus, suppose H is the only demand level that is profitable. Then, if the research is carried out and found positive, there is only a $0\cdot13$ chance of being wrong if the market is entered. If the results are negative, entering the market becomes even more risky than before and a decision to enter might not be thought worth while unless further acceptable information was obtained.

Table 7.3

Summary of market probabilities

Market demand	Prior probabilities	Posterior probabilities after research	
		Positive findings	Negative findings
H	0·60	0·87	0·35
M	0·10	0·10	0·10
L	0·30	0·03	0·55

† *Example* 7.4

A diagnostic test for flaws in metal bars is being applied to individual metal bars draw from a large batch of manufactured bars. The overall incidence of bars with flaws is known, from experience of similar batches, to be about 5 per cent. A test has been devised to detect the flaws, based on an X-ray procedure which can be applied to each individual bar, but the procedure is not entirely accurate. It has been established that there is a 90 per cent chance that a bar with a flaw gives a positive indication from the test. Furthermore, there is a 90 per cent chance that, if the bar does not have a flaw, the indication will be negative.

(*i*) What is the probability that, if the indication is positive, the bar concerned has a flaw?

(*ii*) What would be the revised chance if the bar were put through two separate and independent X-ray tests and both tests give positive indications?

Let A denote the event that the bar concerned has a flaw, and B denote the event that a single test undertaken gives a positive indication. $\bar{A}$ and $\bar{B}$ denote the converse events. Then:

$$P(A)=0.05 \qquad P(\bar{A})=0.95$$

$$P(B|A)=0.9 \qquad P(\bar{B}|\bar{A})=0.9$$

Now (*i*) requires the value of $P(A|B)$ for which Bayes' theorem gives the appropriate expanded expression as:

$$P(A|B)=\frac{P(A)\,P(B|A)}{P(A)\,P(B|A)+P(\bar{A})\,P(B|\bar{A})}$$

$$=\frac{0.05\times0.9}{0.05\times0.9+0.95\times0.1}=0.32.$$

(Note that $P(\bar{B}|\bar{A})+P(B|\bar{A})=1$ and hence $P(B|\bar{A})=1-0.9=0.1$.)

Thus $P(A|B)=0.32$, a result which is surprisingly low at first sight. It apparently indicates that only one-third of the bars tested, which give positive indications, do, in reality, have flaws. Nevertheless, what it really highlights is the need for good diagnostic tests, in situations where few of the individuals have the characteristic being sought.

Under (*ii*) we need first the probabilities that two tests both separately give positive indications in each of the two instances where the bar does, or does not, have a flaw. Let C denote the event 'two successive tests on the same bar positive'. Then:

$$P(C|A)=(0.9)^2=0.81,$$

$$P(C|\bar{A})=(0.1)^2=0.01.$$

From Bayes' theorem, the posterior probability that the bar has a flaw after two positive tests is then:

$$P(A|C)=\frac{P(A)\,P(C|A)}{P(A)\,P(C|A)+P(\bar{A})\,P(C|\bar{A})}$$

$$=\frac{0.05\times0.81}{0.05\times0.81+0.95\times0.01}=0.81.$$

The probability of a correct diagnosis has thus been very considerably enhanced by using the pair of tests instead of a single result, and only accepting that the bar has a flaw if both tests give positive indications.

7.4 The processing of information

The examples given in Section 7.3 illustrate the way in which Bayes' theorem quantifies what we learn (or possibly ought to learn) from information made available to us. It shows how our original beliefs, in terms of prior probabilities, can and should be modified by information which can be described in objective probabilistic terms to give new beliefs expressed in terms of posterior probabilities. It cannot, of course, describe all forms of learning, for example, learning which leads to the acquisition of particular manual skills. However, it can be looked upon as a way of sequential data-processing that combines information as it becomes available so as to rationalize the taking of decisions. The next example, deliberately simplified for purposes of discussion, will be used to illustrate this approach.

Example 7.5

A patient visits his doctor and, from talking with the patient, before any detailed examination has been carried out, the doctor believes that he could be suffering from one of three diseases: $D_i(i=1, 2, 3)$ with prior probabilities 0·5, 0·4 and 0·1 respectively. Thus, diseases D_1 and D_2 are relatively common on the symptoms described, but disease D_3 not so common. Disease D_1, on the face of things, appears to be the most likely. The patient is then given a detailed clinical examination, and, as a consequence, a certain symptom S is noted. Past experience shows that the probabilities of a patient having symptom S, given that he has each of the diseases concerned, is as follows:

$$P(S|D_1)=0·1; \quad P(S|D_2)=0·3; \quad P(S|D_3)=0·8.$$

In other words, the observed symptom S occurs only rarely with D_1, but is very common with D_3, disease D_2 being intermediate. Thus, as is commonly the case, the symptom is not unique to a particular disease. What are the posterior probabilities of the three diseases?

Here we need first to form the products:

$$P(D_1)\,P(S|D_1)=0·5\times0·1=0·05;$$

$$P(D_2)\,P(S|D_2)=0·4\times0·3=0·12;$$

$$P(D_3)\,P(S|D_3)=0·1\times0·8=0·08.$$

The total of the three probabilities is

$\sum_{i=1}^{3} P(D_i)\,P(S|D_i)=0·25$, leading to the posterior probabilities:

$$P(D_1|S)=0·05/0·25=0·20$$

$$P(D_2|S)=0·12/0·25=0·48$$

$$P(D_3|S)=0·08/0·25=0·32$$

These three posterior probabilities add to 1·00. Comparing them with the original prior probabilities, we see that the effect of including the information contained in the symptom is that the intermediate disease D_2 is now the most probable. The disease D_1, that originally was most suspected, has dropped to bottom place and the disease with the outside chance is now much more likely than before.

This example gives us a powerful glimpse into the way diagnoses may well be handled in the future in many fields besides medicine. In the example just discussed we have put into a formal approach what a doctor will do, even though he has never heard of Bayes' theorem. His prior beliefs will be coloured by where he is working—the prior probability of a patient having beri-beri would be different in England from Tanzania. Hence, in England, the doctor would not diagnose beri-beri unless the symptoms were very emphatic indeed.

Furthermore, the doctor need not consider just one test or symptom. He can look at a whole battery of tests and the information from each of these needs to be combined in some form. What might happen in the future is that the doctor would have a console on his desk connected to a computer; he would then type on the console the pieces of independent diagnostic information $S, T, U \ldots$ as he noted them. The computer would be programmed with the relevant prior probabilities, relevant to both the locality concerned, current epidemics and individual patient knowledge. It would then use Bayes' theorem to form posterior probabilities and give a diagnosis of the disease. The prior probabilities $P(D_i)$ would be stored and updated at intervals in the computer, as would be the information probabilities $P(S|D_i)$, $P(T|D_i)$, etc. The latter would be taken from the whole of medical experience.

Such a system would have not only the advantage of objectivity in combining information, but also the merit of using the whole of medical experience and not just that of the doctor concerned. The computer could store and retrieve much more information than the doctor could by himself. Looked at as a tool to help the doctor, and not as a substitute for him, the concept is potentially very valuable. It takes a further step forward along a path of analytical development of diagnosis that is continually being explored by medical workers.

7.5 Continuous variables

So far we have only dealt with posterior probabilities relating to situations for which discrete random variables are suitable. The methods derived above can, however, be readily extended to deal with situations for which continuous random variables are appropriate in a similar manner. To illustrate the procedure consider two examples which are discussed in some detail.

†*Example 7.6*

The prior distribution of the failure frequency rate (the total number of failures expected per unit time interval) among a very large group of semi-automatic machines in a factory, is believed to be exponential, with a mean of 1. Put formally, this implies that if λ is the random variable denoting the mean number of failures per unit time, then

$$p(\lambda) = e^{-\lambda} \quad \text{for} \quad 0 \leqslant \lambda \leqslant \infty \tag{7.2}$$

The group of machines is observed and, in a period of unit time, the machines have r failures among them. With this information, what is the posterior probability distribution of the failure rate λ? (It is assumed that no machine will have more than one failure in the time interval concerned.)

The probability of precisely r failures occurring in unit time, given the appropriate value of λ, is obtained from the Poisson distribution shown in Expression 3.12 (page 57) as

$$P(r|\lambda) = \frac{\lambda^r e^{-\lambda}}{r!} \quad r = 0, 1, 2 \dots$$

This arises because we can imagine unit time divided up into a large number n of equal intervals, in each of which the probability of a breakdown occurring is λ/n. The expected number of breakdowns in the unit time interval is then $n \times \lambda/n$ or λ, and we have the conditions applicable for the Poisson approximation to the binomial distribution to hold. By analogy with the previous definition of Bayes' theorem for discrete random variables the posterior distribution for λ is given by:

$$p(\lambda|r) = \frac{p(\lambda) P(r|\lambda)}{\int_\lambda p(\lambda) P(r|\lambda) d\lambda} \tag{7.3}$$

The integral sign in the denominator has replaced the summation sign in Bayes' theorem as it was previously displayed in Expression 7.1. Substituting the appropriate expressions we have, in this particular instance, the posterior probability:

$$p(\lambda|r) = \frac{e^{-\lambda} \dfrac{\lambda^r e^{-\lambda}}{r!}}{\dfrac{1}{r!} \displaystyle\int_0^\infty e^{-2\lambda} \lambda^r d\lambda}$$

$$= e^{-2\lambda} \lambda^r \Big/ \int_0^\infty e^{-2\lambda} \lambda^r d\lambda$$

which, on integrating the denominator successively by parts, reduces to the expression:

$$2^{r+1} e^{-2\lambda} \lambda^r / r! \tag{7.4}$$

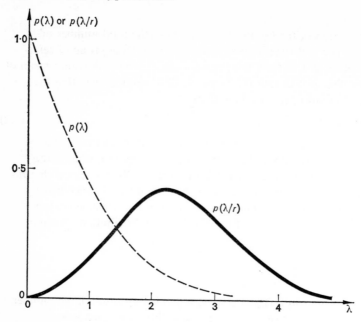

Fig. 7.2. Prior and posterior distributions

Figure 7.2 illustrates the differences in shape between the prior distribution in Expression 7.2 and the revised posterior distribution in Expression 7.4 for the particular situation when $r=4$. Notice how the distribution has been 'pushed to the right'. This is to be anticipated, since the sample information has given an observed number of breakdowns rather above expectation, i.e. r has been greater than would have been originally forecast with a mean of 1. Had r been zero, for instance, the changes in the posterior distribution would have been in the opposite direction, calculations showing that

$$p(\lambda|r=0)=2\ e^{-2\lambda}.$$

This is a rather more J-shaped exponential distribution than the form of the original prior exponential distribution.

Example 7.7

The number of accidents, x, experienced by a bus driver in a unit length of time (e.g. one year) is assumed to be represented by a Poisson variable with parameter λ. Hence:

$$P(x|\lambda)=\frac{\lambda^x\ e^{-\lambda}}{x!}\quad\text{for } x=0, 1, 2\ldots.$$

It is further assumed that λ varies from driver to driver with a distribution that is described by the equation

$$p(\lambda)=\frac{\lambda^k e^{-\lambda}}{k!} \quad \lambda>0, \, k \geqslant 0. \tag{7.5}$$

Note that the distribution of x is discrete, while for λ it is continuous.

A man, selected at random, has exactly x accidents in a period of unit time. Suppose that the number of accidents that the man has in the succeeding period of unit time is denoted by y. First, assuming statistical independence between the accidents occurring in the two periods, what is $p(y|x)$, i.e. the probability distribution of y (the number of accidents in the second period) given the number of accidents, x, which occurred in the first period?

Second, what is the expected value of y in terms of x and k, the two parameters involved?

First, we write down an expression for the posterior distribution of λ, given the observed value of x, i.e. $p(\lambda|x)$. This will be:

$$p(\lambda|x)=p(\lambda)\,P(x|\lambda)\Big/\int_0^\infty p(\lambda)\,P(x|\lambda)\,d\lambda.$$

Substituting the appropriate values for $p(\lambda)$ and $P(x|\lambda)$, this gives:

$$p(\lambda|x)=\frac{\lambda^x e^{-\lambda}}{x!}\cdot\frac{\lambda^k e^{-\lambda}}{k!}\Big/\int_0^\infty \frac{\lambda^x e^{-\lambda}}{x!}\cdot\frac{\lambda^k e^{-\lambda}}{k!}\,d\lambda$$

which, on simplification and integration of the denominator by parts, gives:

$$p(\lambda|x)=2^{x+k+1}\lambda^{x+k}\,e^{-2\lambda}/(k+r)! \tag{7.6}$$

Next, we will write down an expression for the probability distribution of y, given the information regarding x. First, we write down an expression for

$$p(y,\,\lambda|x)=P(y|\lambda)\,p(\lambda|x).$$

This expression then has to be summed (or integrated in this instance) over all values of λ in order to provide us with the probability we require. Hence:

$$p(y|x)=\int_0^\infty P(y|\lambda)\,p(\lambda|x)\,d\lambda$$

Substituting the appropriate values this gives:

$$p(y|x)=\int_0^\infty \frac{\lambda^y e^{-\lambda}}{y!}\cdot\frac{2^{x+k+1}\lambda^{x+k}\,e^{-2\lambda}}{(x+k)!}\,d\lambda$$

which reduces, after evaluating the integral by parts and a good deal of algebraic manipulation, to give:

$$p(y|x)=\frac{2^{x+k+1}(x+y+k)!}{y!\,(x+k)!\,3^{x+y+k+1}} \quad \text{for } y=0,\,1,\,2,\,\ldots \tag{7.7}$$

This expression does not appear particularly inviting, and it is not obvious what shape the distribution takes. If the successive terms are labelled p_0, p_1, p_2, etc., it can readily be seen that:

$$p_1 = \frac{x+k+1}{3} p_0$$

$$p_2 = \frac{x+k+2}{6} p_1$$

$$p_3 = \frac{x+k+3}{18} p_2, \text{ etc.}$$

Hence, if $x+k+1 < 3$, the terms are successively smaller, while if $x+k+1 > 3$, the terms rise to a maximum and then fall away. Incidentally, the sum of probabilities, i.e. $\sum p_i$ over all i from 0 to infinity, is 1 as it must be for a probability distribution.

A result of more general interest arises from considering the expectation of y, assuming the values of x and k are given. The expression to be evaluated is:

$$E(y|x, k) = \sum_{\text{all } y} y \, p(y|x), \quad \text{as } k \text{ was assumed fixed in evaluating } p(y|x),$$

$$= \sum_{\text{all } y} \frac{2^{x+k+1}(x+y+k)!}{(y-1)! \, (x+k)! \, 3^{x+y+k+1}}$$

$$= \frac{2^{x+k+1}}{3^{x+k+1}} \left(\frac{x+k+1}{3} \right) \left[1 + \frac{(x+k+2)}{3.1!} + \frac{(x+k+2)(x+k+3)}{3^2.2!} + \cdots \right]$$

$$= \frac{2^{x+k+1}}{3^{x+k+1}} \left(\frac{x+k+1}{3} \right) \left(1 - \frac{1}{3} \right)^{-(x+k+2)}$$

as the expansion is that of a binomial series with negative exponent,

$$= \tfrac{1}{2}(x+k+1). \tag{7.8}$$

This last result, a surprisingly simple one, is extremely interesting in that it demonstrates a linear relationship between the expected value of y and the assumed known value of x. Hence, we could predict the number of accidents to be expected in a second period from a group of drivers whom we have observed in a first period as each having had x accidents. Alternatively, we could use data in two non-overlapping periods to help us to estimate k, the original parameter in the assumed prior distribution for λ, the distribution of accident rates from person to person. Results such as these have been used in a number of studies directed at the detection of accident proneness among groups of industrial workers such as drivers or machine operators.

7.6 Normal prior distribution

A great deal of statistical analysis is based on the assumption of a normal prior distribution, and we must now give some detailed attention to the results that follow from this particular assumption. We will leave on one side for the moment the question as to the appropriateness of the normal prior distribution for particular circumstances, or how greatly any such assumption is sensitive to subsequent results.

To fix ideas, let us suppose that a company has developed a new product, but hesitates to put it into production because average sales volume ($\bar{\mu}$) per sales outlet may not be sufficient to cover the cost of tooling up for production, let alone to allow for any net profit. Management has made some prior assessment of the likely sales volume that will be achieved. The executive concerned decides, however, to carry out some market research as well by taking a sample of potential outlets and measuring in detail, through market research techniques, their likely demand. The final decision as to whether or not to go into production will now turn partly on the prior evidence of sales volume that was based on marketing judgment, but also on the additional evidence obtained from the sample.

Suppose that the executive making the decision puts the prior information concerning likely sales volume in the form of a probability distribution of guesses, say, normal with mean μ_0 and standard deviation σ_0. This would imply that he is guessing that there is a 50 per cent chance that the sales volume will exceed μ_0, a 16 per cent chance that it will exceed $\mu_0 + \sigma_0$, a 68 per cent chance that it will lie between $\mu_0 \pm \sigma_0$, etc. (These percentages, and other similar ones, can be obtained from a study of the values for the normal distribution function given in Appendix B.) The sample is then taken, and it is assumed that we now wish to revise the distribution of $\bar{\mu}$ to take account of the new evidence of the sample. This extra evidence is in the form of an observed sample mean $\bar{x}$ which is assumed to be itself normal, with a mean $\bar{\mu}$ and standard deviation σ_1. Bayes' theorem can be used to derive the appropriate posterior distribution. (It is not essential to follow the method of derivation of Eqs. 7.9a and 7.9b outlined here.) Using the theorem, the posterior distribution of $\bar{\mu}$, the average sales volume, will be:

$$p(\bar{\mu}) = \theta/\phi \quad \text{where}$$

$$\theta = p(\bar{\mu}) \, p(\bar{x}|\bar{\mu})$$

$$= \frac{1}{2\pi\sigma_0\sigma_1} \exp -\tfrac{1}{2} \left\{ \left(\frac{\bar{x}-\bar{\mu}}{\sigma_1}\right)^2 + \left(\frac{\bar{\mu}-\mu_0}{\sigma_0}\right)^2 \right\}$$

and

$$\phi = \int p(\bar{\mu}) \, p(\bar{x}|\bar{\mu}) \, d\bar{\mu}$$

$$= \int \theta \, d\mu$$

The exponent in θ can be rearranged to give:

$$-\frac{1}{2\left(\frac{1}{\sigma_0^2}+\frac{1}{\sigma_1^2}\right)}\left\{\left(\bar{\mu}-\frac{\frac{\bar{x}}{\sigma_1^2}+\frac{\mu_0}{\sigma_0^2}}{\frac{1}{\sigma_0^2}+\frac{1}{\sigma_1^2}}\right)^2+\frac{\bar{x}^2\sigma_0^2+\mu_0^2\sigma_1^2}{\sigma_0^2+\sigma_1^2}-\left(\frac{\bar{x}\sigma_0^2+\mu_0\sigma_1^2}{\sigma_0^2+\sigma_1^2}\right)^2\right\}$$

The second and third terms in { } will cancel in numerator and denominator of θ/ϕ leaving us, after some further simplification, with the expression

$$p(\bar{\mu}|\bar{x})=\frac{1}{\sqrt{2\pi}\sqrt{\frac{\sigma_0^2\sigma_1^2}{\sigma_0^2+\sigma_1^2}}}\exp\left\{-\frac{\sigma_0^2+\sigma_1^2}{2\sigma_0^2\sigma_1^2}\left(\bar{\mu}-\frac{\mu_0\sigma_1^2+\bar{x}\sigma_0^2}{\sigma_1^2+\sigma_0^2}\right)^2\right\}$$

Hence $p(\bar{\mu}|\bar{x})$ is normal with

$$\text{mean}=\frac{\mu_0\sigma_1^2+\bar{x}\sigma_0^2}{\sigma_1^2+\sigma_0^2}$$

or

$$\left(\frac{\mu_0/\sigma_0^2+\bar{x}/\sigma_1^2}{1/\sigma_0^2+1/\sigma_1^2}\right) \tag{7.9a}$$

together with

$$\text{standard deviation}=\sqrt{\left(\frac{\sigma_0^2\sigma_1^2}{\sigma_0^2+\sigma_1^2}\right)}$$

or

$$\frac{1}{\text{standard deviation}}=\sqrt{\left(\frac{1}{\sigma_0^2}+\frac{1}{\sigma_1^2}\right)} \tag{7.9b}$$

Notice first of all that the posterior distribution is itself normal, like the original prior distribution for $\bar{\mu}$, only with a new mean and standard deviation. Second, note that the posterior mean itself is a weighted average of the prior mean and the sample mean, the weights being the reciprocals of the variances of the two distributions. The revised variance (being the square of the standard deviation) is a form of average that is sometimes referred to as a harmonic average.

Example 7.8

Let us now pursue the foregoing discussion further by using some numerical values in the particular example concerned. Suppose that the executive assesses his probability distribution for $\bar{\mu}$ as being normal with

$$\mu_0=18 \quad \text{and} \quad \sigma_0=3{\cdot}0$$

A random sample of 100 outlets from an estimated population of 20 000 outlets gives the sample information $\bar{x}=15$ and $s=12$.

Since the sampling fraction is extremely small ($100/20\,000 = 0\cdot005$), any error caused by assuming the population to be infinite will be negligible and

$$\sigma_1 = \frac{12}{\sqrt{100}} = 1\cdot2.$$

(Analogy with the hypergeometric distribution discussed in Section 3.8, page 59, suggests that the finite sampling correction would be of the order of $\sqrt{0\cdot995}$, which could only affect the third decimal place in σ_1.) Hence, from Eqs. 7.9a and 7.9b, the posterior distribution of $\bar{\mu}$ is normal with parameters

mean
$$= \frac{18/3\cdot0^2 + 15/1\cdot2^2}{1/3\cdot0^2 + 1/1\cdot2^2} = 15\cdot4$$

and

standard deviation $= \sqrt{\dfrac{(3\cdot0)^2(1\cdot2)^2}{3\cdot0^2 + 1\cdot2^2}} = 1\cdot113$

The striking thing that emerges from this example is the way in which the evidence supplied by the sample has virtually overwhelmed the executive's original beliefs about the sales of the new product. The posterior mean is close to the sample mean and the standard deviation of the posterior distribution for $\bar{\mu}$ is very much smaller than that of the prior.

It is worth pursuing the weight given to the sample information further. Suppose, alternatively, that the executive had decided that the prior information was totally negligible, in comparison with the information obtained from 100 actual observations on the population whose mean was in question, and could be ignored. Then he would have used the sample information as it stood, namely:

$$E(\bar{\mu}) = 15$$

$$\sigma_1(\bar{\mu}) = 1\cdot2.$$

which is not so very different from the posterior distribution actually obtained. As an intermediate situation, suppose that the sample information had provided the same $\bar{x}$ and s, but based on a sample of 25 rather than 100. Then we find from Eqs. 7.9a and 7.9b that $E(\bar{\mu}) = 16\cdot1$ and $\sigma_1(\bar{\mu}) = 1\cdot87$, showing that the prior distribution is exerting rather more influence in this situation, where there is a smaller sample size. Hence, there is a slow but steady change in the influence that the prior distribution has on the posterior distribution as more sample information becomes available.

Example 7.9

You have just purchased a small company, among whose balance sheet assets is the sum of £140 000 due from debtors. You are sceptical about your ability to collect these accounts, which represent balances owing to the company by 900 different customers, many of the accounts being long overdue. You are considering selling the accounts to a debt collector who takes full responsibility for collection, as well as the risk of non-collection. The collector offers you the sum of £70 000 (or 50 per cent of book value) for the accounts.

You estimate that it would cost you about £25 per customer in collection expenses to collect the debts yourself. Furthermore, because of the low credit ratings of many of the customers and the large number of accounts in dispute by the customers, there is some uncertainty about how much could be collected. You estimate after a careful study of the books that it should average about £125 per customer before collection expenses, but accept that there is a 20 per cent chance that the average could be £85 or lower. Before making a decision as to whether to sell the debts or not, your accountant suggests trying to collect the outstanding debts from a random sample of accounts. Ten accounts are selected, giving yields (i.e. gross amount collected less collection expenses) that have a mean recovery of £90 and a standard deviation of £40. On the basis of this information, what is the posterior distribution of the net collection per account? Would you consider that the debts should be sold to the debt collector on the terms proposed?

The sampling fraction is again extremely small, namely, 10/900 or 0·01, so that any error caused by assuming the population to be infinite will be negligible. Using the same notation as before, we have:

$$\sigma_1 = \frac{40}{\sqrt{10}} = 12 \cdot 63.$$

Next, we estimate σ_0. Since 20 per cent of the prior distribution is estimated to be below 85, we must have:

$$\frac{85 - 125}{\sigma_0} = -0 \cdot 84,$$

where $-0 \cdot 84$ is taken from the normal distribution tables. Hence, $\sigma = 48$. The prior mean, $\bar{\mu}_0$, is 100 and the sample mean, $\bar{x}$, is 90, in each instance, allowing for the cost of collection. Hence, from Eqs. 7.9a and 7.9b, the posterior distribution of $\bar{\mu}$ is normal with parameters

$$\text{mean} = \frac{100 \times 12 \cdot 63^2 + 90 \times 48^2}{12 \cdot 63^2 + 48^2} = £90 \cdot 7,$$

together with

$$\text{standard deviation} = \sqrt{\left(\frac{48^2 \times 12 \cdot 63^2}{48^2 + 12 \cdot 63^2} \right)} = £12 \cdot 4.$$

These results answer the first question, indicating a posterior distribution that is close to that indicated by the sample mean. For the second part of the question we note that, from the posterior distribution, the estimated expected net revenue from collecting the debts yourself is

$$900 \times 90 \cdot 7 = £81\ 630.$$

This is in excess of the sum of £70 000 offered by the debt collector. Hence, on straight expected gain, you would decide to collect the debts yourself. However, it is worth looking at the chance your collection might fall below £70 000. To estimate this probability, we calculate first the mean net collection per customer to raise £70 000 precisely. This is 70 000/900 = £77·8 per customer. We next calculate the unit normal variable corresponding to this average figure of 77·8. This is given by:

$$x = \frac{77·8 - 90·7}{12·4} = -1·04.$$

From Appendix B we find that $F_N(x) = 0·149$. Hence, there is a probability of approximately 0·15 that, if we decide to collect the accounts ourselves, the net amount raised will be less than the amount obtainable by selling the accounts outright. The average shortfall, though, in such a contingency is not very great and you would therefore probably feel justified in collecting the debts for yourself.

7.7 Effect of prior distribution

The preceding examples suggest that, provided a reasonable amount of sample information is available, the precise numerical values assumed for the parameters of the prior distribution have little effect on the corresponding parameters of the posterior distribution. It is worth considering as well whether the shape assumed for the prior distribution is a critical factor or not in determining the posterior distribution. To do this, two extremely contrasting prior distributions for the mean μ are considered:

(*i*) Normal, mean 3 and standard deviation 1.
(*ii*) Exponential, mean 3 and standard deviation 1, with the extra proviso that $p(\mu) = 0$ for all μ less than 2; i.e. $p(\mu) = e^{-(\mu-2)}$ for $\mu \geqslant 2$.

The exponential distribution is about as violently non-normal as any smooth distribution can be; it is J-shaped rather than symmetrical and zero probability is assigned to all values of μ below 2. The shapes of these two distributions are shown in Fig. 7.3. Figures 7.4 and 7.5 show the resultant posterior distributions for samples of size 4 (Fig. 7.4) and size 25 (Fig. 7.5) when the observed sample mean is 3 and it is assumed that var $\bar{x} = 1/n$, where n is the sample size and the standard deviation of x is 1. (The derivation of the posterior distribution for case (*ii*) is not given here.) The means of the various posterior distributions must clearly be 3 in each case, as prior and sample information means coincide. The variances of the posterior distributions are, however, rather different from those of the prior distributions, and it is therefore revealing to see what effect the two different prior distributions have on the posterior distributions. While with a sample of size 4, there is still some difference between the two posterior distributions, the differences have

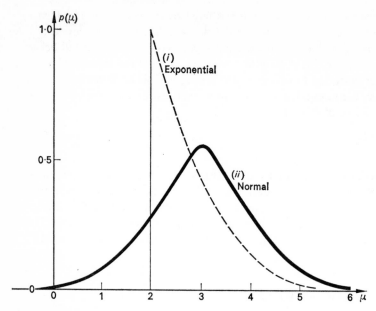

Fig. 7.3. Normal and exponential priors

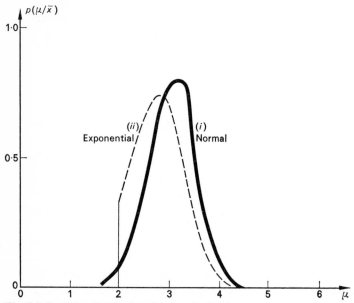

Fig. 7.4. Posterior distributions for sample size 4

become pretty well negligible by the time a sample of size 25 has been reached. Although this illustration is only a special case, the general nature of the conclusion, that increasing sample information eradicates differences in

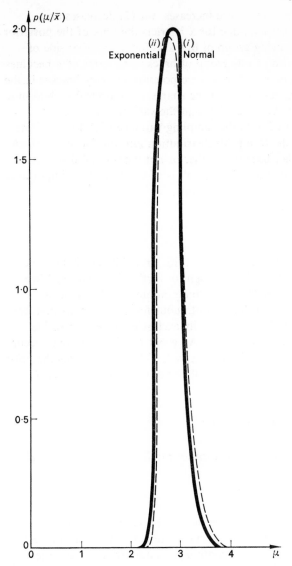

Fig. 7.5. Posterior distributions for sample size 25

the shape of the posterior distribution, can be shown to hold for any prior distribution that is reasonably smooth in the vicinity of the observed sample mean $\bar{x}$.

In general terms, it is possible to argue that the posterior probability that μ lies within any small interval or 'bracket' is roughly proportional to both the prior probability of that bracket and the probability density of the observed value of $\bar{x}$. As the sample size increases, var $(\bar{x})$ decreases and, therefore, the probability density value for $\bar{x}$ restricts the bulk of the posterior probability to an ever narrowing group of brackets for μ on either side of $\bar{x}$. Ultimately, the total width of this group of brackets in terms of μ becomes so small that the prior probability for μ corresponding to every bracket in the group is virtually the same, regardless of the shape of the prior distribution as a whole. Hence it is reasonable, provided that the variance of the prior distribution is large compared with the sampling variance of $\bar{x}$, to substitute the mean and variance of the true prior distribution into the formulae which apply to a normal prior distribution, whether or not the normal distribution precisely fits the prior information. This result is of great practical importance in deducing appropriate posterior distributions.

7.8 Summary

This chapter has shown the way in which prior probabilities about some random variable x may be revised in the light of further information. Two cases have been considered, the first when the random variable x has a discrete form, the second when it has a continuous form. Under the first, we assume there to be E_j $(j=1, 2 \ldots r)$ mutually exclusive and only possible values for the random variable concerned. An event F, which can only occur if one of the E_j values is true, has been observed. If $P(E_j)$ represents the prior probabilities of the E_j, and $P(F|E_j)$ the probability that F occurs given E_j is true, then:

$$P(E_j|F) = P(E_j) \, P(F|E_j) \bigg/ \sum_{j=1}^{r} P(E_j) \, P(F|E_j).$$

For the second case of a continuous form of random variable, we have:

$$p(x|F) = p(x) \, p(F|x) \bigg/ \int_x p(x) \, p(F|x) \, dx,$$

with the same notation as before. Notice that in this case the extra information F may either be of a discrete nature (e.g. the number of sales made in a sample of 25 calls) or of a continuous nature (e.g. the average value of sales made in 25 calls).

Exercises on Chapter 7

1 A fair coin is tossed unseen by a friend. If it falls heads, a ball is drawn from urn 1: if tails, from urn 2. Urn 1 contains three red balls and one white ball, while urn 2 contains one red ball and three white balls. You are told that the ball drawn is red. What are the posterior probabilities of the two urns?

2 In the experience of a certain insurance company, customers who have sufficient funds in their bank postdate a cheque by mistake once in 1000 times, while customers who write cheques on insufficient funds invariably postdate them. The latter group constitutes 1 per cent of the total cheques received by the insurance company. A company receives a postdated cheque from a policy-holder. What is the probability that the customer has insufficient funds?

3 Erewhon is inhabited by two tribes in equal numbers: the Idogoes, who always tell the truth, and the Edibads, who tell the truth with probability $\frac{1}{2}$, the answers given to different questions being statistically independent. A traveller, being lost and encountering an inhabitant of unknown tribe at noon, asks the questions 'Is it day or night?' and 'In which direction is the nearest town?' If the answer to the first question is 'day', what is then the probability that the next answer will be correct?

4 A dealer wishes to buy a batch of machine parts from a surplus warehouse. He knows that the parts are produced by either company A or company B, but he cannot tell which they come from by inspection. From past experience he knows that if company A produced the parts, 25 per cent will be defective, and that if company B produced them, 50 per cent will be defective. The surplus dealer informs him that 70 per cent of his batches come from company A and 30 per cent from company B. If the parts dealer selects a random sample of 4 parts from the batch he is proposing to purchase and finds one defective among them, what is the posterior probability that the batch was produced by company A?

5 Look again at Problems 2.3 and 2.4 on page 12. You are now in a position to work out numerical answers for the problems posed and compare them with your earlier estimates. Most readers will find that they have considerably underestimated the probabilities concerned and are surprised at the true figures.

6 An insurance company classifies drivers as class A (good risks), class B (medium risks) and class C (poor risks). The company believes that class A risks constitute 30 per cent of the drivers who apply for insurance, class B 50 per cent and class C 20 per cent. The probability that a class A driver has an accident in any 12-month period is 0·01; for a class B driver the probability is 0·03; and for a class C driver it is 0·10. Assume that the probability of more than one accident in a year is negligible.

(*i*) Mr Jones takes out an insurance policy and within 12 months he has an accident. What is the probability that he is a class C risk?

(*ii*) If a policyholder goes five years without an accident, and we assume years to be statistically independent, what is the probability that he belongs to class A?

7 The Great European Hotel Association is about to poll its members whether or not the association should accept a certain credit card. The secretary of the association attaches the probabilities shown in Table 7.4 to various percentages of members in favour.

Table 7.4

Probabilities in favour of credit cards

Percentage of member hotels in favour	Prior probability of exactly that percentage in favour
30	0·10
40	0·30
50	0·40
60	0·20

(*i*) On this information only, would you, as secretary, expect a vote for the credit card to be carried?

(*ii*) Suppose a random sample of 15 hotels were drawn and 8 were in favour and 7 opposed. What probabilities would you now assign to the various percentage of hotels in favour?

(*iii*) After the sample in (*ii*) has been taken, what is the expected proportion of hotels in favour.

8 Mr Windsor, the owner of a small airline, is offered the two planes of a foreign line that is going out of business. The condition of the two planes, i.e. whether or not they require a major overhaul, is a key determinant of the pay-off that Mr Windsor will receive if he accepts the offer. Mr Windsor has no reliable information on the condition of the two planes, but is able to assign the prior probabilities shown in Table 7.5 on the basis of judgment and experience.

Table 7.5

Aeroplanes requiring overhaul

No. of planes requiring major overhaul	Prior probability
0	0·40
1	0·20
2	0·40

Mr Windsor arbitrarily decides to have one of the two planes inspected and picks one at random. The inspection shows that it is in good operating condition and does not require major reconditioning. Revise Mr Windsor's prior probabilities on the basis of this sample information.

9 A large and well-established international mining company is investigating the possibility of purchasing a piece of land in Africa and developing a new mine on it. The mine is estimated to contain 5 million tons of ore. It will cost £1 million to purchase the land and develop the mine, while the variable costs of mining and processing are £25 per ton of ore. The selling price of the metal recovered from the ore is 12p per pound. It is assumed that all the metal in the ore is recoverable and that there are no other by-products of value.

On the basis of past experience and preliminary site-testing, management estimates that the average percentage of metal in the ore is 11, and that it is reasonable to assume a normal prior distribution for the average percentage with a 50 : 50 chance that the percentage falls within the band 11 ± 1.

To assist him in making the decision as to whether to purchase, the manager decides to drill 25 test cores in a random pattern in the mine area to check the ore quality. When this is done, it is found that the average content of metal from the 25 cores is 8·5 per cent with a standard deviation among the 25 cores of 2·5 per cent metal.

Should the manager decide to buy the mine or not? If there is any further information you would require before making a decision, state what it is and how you would use it. (Ignore discounting of the cash flows concerned and assume there is no charge for the 25 test cores.)

10 A purchaser of a large batch of corrugated boxes believes that the average strength, measured in pounds per perimeter inch (ppi) is equally likely to lie anywhere between 10 and 12, but not outside this range. He selects a random sample of 16 boxes from the batch and measures their strength. The average strength of the sample is 11·5 and the standard deviation of strength within the sample is 1·5 (ppi).

  (*i*) Find an expression (but do not attempt to simplify it) for the posterior distribution of the mean batch strength, and plot the posterior distribution graphically.
 (*ii*) What difference would it have made to the posterior distribution if the prior distribution had been assumed to be normal with mean 11 and standard deviation $\frac{1}{3}$ (ppi)?

11 A simplified version of the way a law relating to drunken driving operates in a number of countries is as follows. A motorist can be stopped by a policeman and asked to take a breath test. If this is negative, no further action ensues. If the test is positive the motorist is taken to a police station where a second test based on a blood test is given. If this second test is negative the motorist is released, if positive the motorist is automatically charged and convicted of drunken driving.

The two tests concerned are not entirely precise in their operation and their accuracy has been investigated with a large scale controlled trial on a probabilistic basis with the results shown in Table 7.6.

Table 7.6

Probabilities of test results

| Test | Motorists true state | | Test result |
	Drunk	Sober	
First test	$\left.\begin{array}{l}0\cdot8\\0\cdot2\end{array}\right\}1\cdot0$	$\left.\begin{array}{l}0\cdot2\\0\cdot8\end{array}\right\}1\cdot0$	+ −
Second test	$\left.\begin{array}{l}0\cdot9\\0\cdot1\end{array}\right\}1\cdot0$	$\left.\begin{array}{l}0\cdot05\\0\cdot95\end{array}\right\}1\cdot0$	+ −

(*i*) What is the probability that a motorist stopped who is, in reality, drunk will be convicted under this law? Conversely, what is the probability that a stopped motorist who is, in reality, sober will be convicted?

(*ii*) Past information suggests that the proportion, P, of those stopped for the first test who are in reality drunk is 0·6. A motorist is stopped for testing and subsequently convicted. What is the probability that he was actually drunk? What is the probability that he was sober? Comment on how the latter probability varies with changes in P.

8 Decision trees with revised probabilities

8.1 Introduction

In Chapter 5 we discussed, through single-stage decision examples, a number of possible decision criteria, and dwelt in particular upon the use of expected monetary value as an appropriate criterion for choice between alternative courses of action. In Chapter 6 we considered some multistage decision problems showing how, in these circumstances, the pay-off table or matrix could be replaced by the decision tree, and the latter could then be analysed on the fold-back or roll-back principle. This principle was again combined with the use of EMV as a consistent criterion of choice throughout, starting with the later decisions first, and folding back the tree until ultimately the optimum initial decision is made. In all the examples given in those chapters it was assumed that the information available at the present moment of decision was all that could be obtained. No further information would subsequently become available, nor could any further information be bought at the outset at some cost to be defined. Obviously, in many situations, extra information can be bought before the initial decision is made. In Chapter 7 we considered in some detail how extra information obtained of a probabilistic nature could be combined with the original, or prior, probabilities of various outcomes to give the revised or posterior probabilities of these same outcomes. In the present chapter we are going to look at a number of examples where there is both a multistage decision process as discussed in Chapter 6, and also the possibility of obtaining extra information (at a price) that could modify the original prior probabilities of the various outcomes. No new principles or concepts are involved, but it is again necessary to use a systematic manner of approach to the analysis of such problems and this is illustrated in the four examples that are discussed in detail in this chapter.

Example 8.1

A metal broker has an option to buy a bulk shipment of 1000 tons of copper ore from an African government at £400 per ton, a price that is well below the world price of approximately £550 per ton. The broker believes that he can obtain £525 per ton for this ore, but he is also a trifle worried as to whether he will obtain the requisite import licence for the copper. Should he contract to buy the copper and subsequently fail to obtain the licence, the contract could be annulled at a penalty to the broker of £40 per ton. The broker estimates, from experience of related contracts, that his chance of getting the licence is 0·6. He realizes that he could delay his decision on the option while he gathers some additional information. The first way this could be done is to apply for government permission before he actually commits himself to purchasing the ore. However, he fears that by the time he gets an answer, the option may no longer be available to him. On reflection, the broker thinks that the chance that the option will still be open by the time he finds out the government's answer is 0·5. A second way in which he could gather further information is to consult an expert, who offers, for a fee of £5000, to sound out in depth, through his various contacts, the government position on importing copper from the particular African country concerned. The consultant is by no means infallible, but he has acted as a go-between on a number of deals of this kind and has a reasonable record in these matters. The consultant will provide a report that is either favourable or unfavourable as regards obtaining approval and the broker summarizes his views of the consultants reliability as shown in Table 8.1. This table is read horizontally. Thus, should the government be going to give approval, there is a 0·9 chance that the consultant reports favourably and only a 0·1 chance that he reports unfavourably. Conversely, if the government is not going to give its approval, there is a 0·2 chance that the consultant reports favourably and a 0·8 chance that he reports unfavourably. Any delay through using the consultant will not,

Table 8.1

The consultant's reliability

	Consultant's report		
Government outcome	Favourable (*F*)	Not favourable (*F̄*)	Total
Approval (*A*)	0·9	0·1	1·0
Non-approval (*Ā*)	0·2	0·8	1·0

in the broker's opinion, lead to any risk of the option being removed before receiving the consultant's report. The problem that now faces the broker is: what should be his immediate decision?

The various alternatives are shown in Fig. 8.1, with the decision points marked with bold squares as usual, and the various actions and outcomes labelled as indicated. Figure 8.2 gives the consequential net cash flows for each branch of the tree. Thus, the net yield for the sequence 'Use consultant' —'Favourable report'—'Buy'—'Approved' is $1000 \times (525 - 400) - 5000$ or 120 000. For the sequence 'Use consultant'—'Non-favourable report'—'Buy' —'Not approved' it is $1000 \times (-40) - 5000$ or $-45\,000$. Similarly for the other branch networks. All monetary quantities given on the tree are expressed in £'000s and the £ symbol is dropped when it does not cause confusion. There are four key decision points, labelled W, X, Y and Z respectively. There is also a fifth decision point labelled V, but the decision here, namely, to buy, is self-evident without formal analysis.

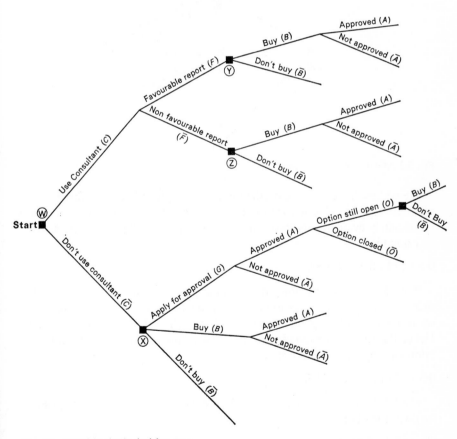

Fig. 8.1. Metal broker's decision tree

G

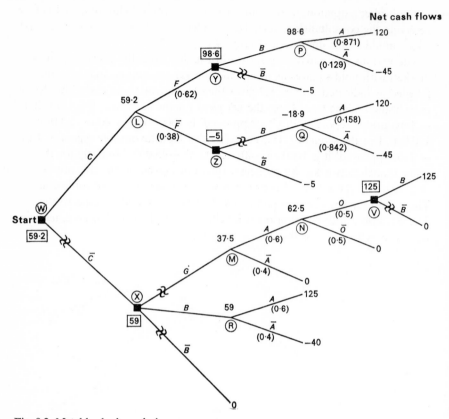

Fig. 8.2. Metal broker's analysis

We will evaluate point X on the lower branch first. There are three alternatives here, of which $\bar{B}$ (do not purchase option, withdraw from deal) is immediately evaluated as zero. The EMV for decision B (sign contract to buy now) is:

$0.6 \times 125 - 0.4 \times 40 = 59.$

For decision G (apply for government approval before signing contract) there are two stages. If governmental approval is given and the option is still open, the decision at point V will be to buy with an EMV, at point V, of 125. Hence the EMV corresponding to point N on the tree (i.e. government approval applied for and obtained) is:

$0.5 \times 125 + 0.5 \times 0 = 62.5.$

The EMV corresponding to point M (i.e. government approval applied for) will then be:

$0.6 \times 62.5 + 0.4 \times 0 = 37.5.$

Hence, the optimum decision at point X is to buy now without waiting for government approval and the appropriate EMV is 59. This is entered on Fig. 8.2.

We will now consider the upper part of the decision tree and, in particular, the decision at point Y. If the broker has reached decision point Y, it implies that he decided to have a report from the consultant and that the report he received was favourable. We now need to evaluate the probabilities to be placed upon the subsequent outcomes 'government approval', A, and 'government non-approval', $\bar{A}$, should he decide to sign the contract in the light of the consultant's information. For this we need to use Bayes' theorem. From this theorem we have:

$$P(A|F) = \frac{P(A)\,P(F|A)}{P(A)\,P(F|A) + P(\bar{A})\,P(F|\bar{A})}$$

Now, from the data given:

$P(A) = 0.6$ $P(F|A) = 0.9$ $P(F|\bar{A}) = 0.2$

$P(\bar{A}) = 0.4$ $P(\bar{F}|A) = 0.1$ $P(\bar{F}|\bar{A}) = 0.8$

and these are the quantities required for insertion in the Bayes' expression for $P(A|F)$. Hence:

$$P(A|F) = \frac{0.6 \times 0.9}{0.6 \times 0.9 + 0.4 \times 0.2} = 0.871,$$

and, similarly, $P(\bar{A}|F) = 0.129$, so that:

$$P(A|F) + P(\bar{A}|F) = 1.000.$$

We can now evaluate the decision B (contract to buy) and $\bar{B}$ (do not contract to buy) at point Y. For decision B we have:

$$\text{EMV} = 0.871 \times 120 - 0.129 \times 45$$

$$= 98.6.$$

For decision $\bar{B}$ the value is $\text{EMV} = -5$. Hence, the optimum decision at point Y is, not surprisingly, to go ahead with the contract to buy and the appropriate EMV is then 98.6.

We can now evaluate, in a similar fashion the decision at point Z. We find from Bayes' theorem that:

$$P(A|\bar{F}) = \frac{P(A)\,P(\bar{F}|A)}{P(A)\,P(\bar{F}|A) + P(\bar{A})\,P(\bar{F}|\bar{A})}$$

$$= \frac{0.6 \times 0.1}{0.6 \times 0.1 + 0.4 \times 0.8} = 0.158$$

and similarly $P(\bar{A}|\bar{F}) = 0.842$, giving: $P(A|\bar{F}) + P(\bar{A}|\bar{F}) = 1.000$.

Hence the appropriate EMVs for the decision of whether to contract to buy or not are:

$$\text{EMV } (B) = 0{\cdot}158 \times 120 - 0{\cdot}842 \times 45$$

$$= -18{\cdot}9,$$

while

$$\text{EMV } (\bar{B}) = -5.$$

The decision $\bar{B}$, not to contract to buy, has the higher EMV and hence is, again not surprisingly, the better decision to make. This result is now entered on Fig. 8.2. The next step is to compute for the decision tree the probabilities corresponding to the two branches F and $\bar{F}$, so that the two EMVs for points Y and Z can be appropriately weighted to get an overall EMV at point L for the decision to call in the consultant.

The original prior probabilities given to the two outcomes A and $\bar{A}$ by the broker were 0·6 and 0·4 respectively. Hence, the probability that the consultant, if called in, will give a favourable (F) reply is:

$$P(F) = P(A)\,P(F|A) + P(\bar{A})\,P(F|\bar{A})$$

$$= 0{\cdot}6 \times 0{\cdot}9 + 0{\cdot}4 \times 0{\cdot}2 = 0{\cdot}62,$$

and, similarly:

$$P(\bar{F}) = P(A)\,P(\bar{F}|A) + P(\bar{A})\,P(\bar{F}|\bar{A})$$

$$= 0{\cdot}6 \times 0{\cdot}1 + 0{\cdot}4 \times 0{\cdot}8 = 0{\cdot}38.$$

These two probabilities add to unity as they must do. The EMV for the decision to hire the consultant is thus:

$P(F) \times \text{EMV}$ for optimum decision at point $\text{Y} + P(\bar{F}) \times \text{EMV}$ for optimum decision at point X

or $0{\cdot}62 \times 98{\cdot}6 - 0{\cdot}38 \times 5 = 59{\cdot}2.$

Hence, the initial choice is now between:

> Hire consultant   EMV $= 59{\cdot}2.$

Don't hire consultant   EMV $= 59.$

On the basis of choosing that decision which has the higher EMV, the broker should hire the consultant, giving himself an overall EMV of 59·2.

Notice that the two EMVs for the initial decision are extremely close, with a difference of 0·2 only. If the consultant proposed to charge 6, then the EMV for the decision 'hire consultant' would fall to 58·2, and the optimum initial decision would change to 'contract to buy'. Indeed, one could say from this analysis that the maximum amount that it is worth paying for the consultant's advice is 5·2 because at that level the EMVs of the two decisions 'hire consultant' and 'don't hire consultant' become equal, and our decision-maker (the broker) should, on the basis of EMV, become indifferent between the two decisions.

Finally, as shown in Table 8.2, it is instructive to put down for the two initial decisions the possible net cash flows that can occur and the probabilities associated with each, assuming that we select the optimum actions subsequent to the initial decision. These results are instructive since they show that, although the decision to hire the consultant is only marginally better on an EMV basis than the alternative decision not to hire him, calling in the consultant has an added merit. This arises because the probability of a

Table 8.2

The probabilities of gains and losses

Decision	Possible cash flows	Probability
Hire consultant	(*i*) 120	$0·62 \times 0·871 = 0·54$ ⎫
	(*ii*) −45	$0·62 \times 0·129 = 0·08$ ⎬ 1·00
	(*iii*) −5	0·38 ⎭
Don't hire consultant	(*iv*) 125	0·6 ⎫
	(*v*) −40	0·4 ⎬ 1·00

large loss is very considerably reduced, there being a loss of 45 with a probability of only 0·08, compared with a loss of 40 with the much higher probability of 0·4 should the broker contract to buy right from the start without calling in the consultant. On a strict minimax approach, the broker would do nothing. But if that option were eliminated he would contract to buy without hiring the consultant, as the maximum possible loss is only 40 compared with 45 for the situation when he hires the consultant.

Example 8.2

Our next example concerns a problem situation that has already been described in Exercise 2 of Chapter 6 on page 145, and is commonly referred to as the oil wildcatter's decision problem. The basis of the problem is that an oil wildcatter must decide whether or not to drill for oil at a given site before his option on the site expires. He is uncertain about many things: the cost of drilling, the extent of the oil deposits at the site, the cost of raising the oil if there is any, and so forth. He has available the objective records of similar and not quite so similar drillings in the same area, and he has already discussed the features peculiar to this particular option with his geologist, his geophysicist and his land agent. He could gain further relevant information (but still not necessarily perfect information) about the underlying geophysical structure at this particular site by arranging for seismic soundings to be taken. Such information, however, is quite costly and not of a stratigraphical nature (i.e. it does not indicate the kind of rock, sandstone, limestone, etc.). Only drilling can determine this, and the wildcatter has to decide whether or not to purchase this information before he makes his basic decision whether or not to drill.

To put the problem in a more formal framework, let us suppose that any well sunk can be either dry (w_1) or wet (w_2) or soaking (w_3). The former is bad and would lead to a net loss of £100 000. Outcome w_2 is so-so and would give a net profit of £100 000, while outcome w_3 is very good and would lead to a net profit of £500 000. Net profit or loss here is the difference between sales revenue and all costs of production, including the sinking of the well. After appropriate discussions, but without taking any seismic soundings, the oil wildcatter estimates that the probabilities of the three possible outcomes are 0·5 for w_1, 0·25 for w_2 and 0·25 for w_3. The seismic soundings, which could help him to determine more precisely the nature of the underlying geological structure, would cost £30 000. They will give a result in the form of a good or not so good indication. A good indication (G) is linked to the presence of oil (i.e. to outcomes w_2 and w_3), while a not so good indication ($\bar{G}$) is linked to the absence of oil (i.e. to outcome w_1). However, these are not precise deterministic relationships, but probabilistic ones. Past experience of seismic soundings, in this and other areas, shows that the probabilities given in Table 8.3 are a reasonable summary of the relationship between the results of seismic soundings and subsequent drilled well results.

Table 8.3

Seismic results

Drilled well	Seismic sounding		Total
	G	$\bar{G}$	
w_1 dry	0·2	0·8	1·0
w_2 wet	0·6	0·4	1·0
w_3 soaking	0·8	0·2	1·0

Thus, if a drilled well at a site were wet (w_2), then a seismic survey carried out at the site would have a probability of 0·6 of giving a positive result and a probability of 0·4 of giving a negative result. Similarly, the corresponding probabilities are given for the other two possible drilling outcomes. We note that the seismic sounding results are very much linked to the drilling outcomes, and that such sounding do discriminate, albeit not precisely, between good and bad situations. The whole situation and the alternatives

open to the oil wildcatter are summarized in the decision tree shown in
Fig. 8.3.

We can now proceed to the analysis, the details of which are displayed in
Fig. 8.4. The first thing we do is to place against each possible branch of the
tree the total pay-off or net gain. This is done on the righthand side in
Fig. 8.4. All net gains are expressed in £'000s and the £ symbol is dropped
whenever it cannot cause confusion. There are four decision points, which
have been labelled W, X, Y and Z.

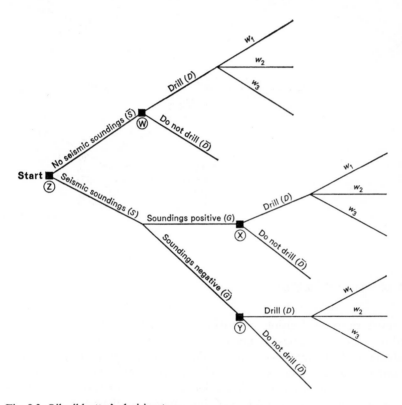

Fig. 8.3. Oil wildcatter's decision tree

We will analyse first of all the upper portion of the decision tree, namely
the decision not to take seismic soundings. The EMV at decision point W for
the decision 'drill' will be:

$$0.5 \times (-100) + 0.25 \times 100 + 0.25 \times 500 = 100.$$

The EMV for the decision not to drill is clearly zero. Hence, the decision at
point W will be to drill (D), since this has the higher EMV. The value of 100
is accordingly inserted on the decision tree at point W and branch $\bar{D}$ is barred.

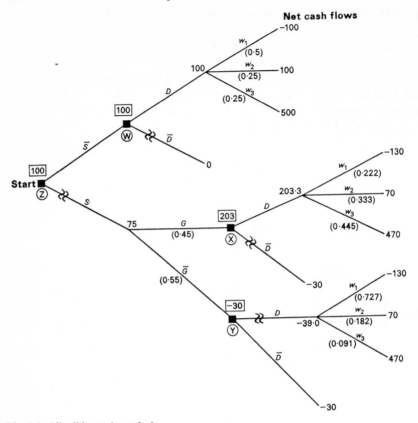

Fig. 8.4. Oil wildcatter's analysis

We next turn to the decision at decision point X. This point is only reached if seismic soundings are taken and they give a positive response (*G*). To evaluate the EMV for a decision to drill, we need the posterior probabilities of the three possible outcomes w_1, w_2 and w_3, given both the original prior probabilities and the seismic sounding evidence of a good response. From the data given earlier, we have the following information on the prior probabilities of the three outcomes—

$$P(w_1)=0.5; \quad P(w_2)=0.25; \quad P(w_3)=0.25.$$

Conditional probabilities of the seismic sounding outcomes, given the drilling outcome:

$P(G|w_1)=0.2 \qquad P(\bar{G}|w_1)=0.8$

$P(G|w_2)=0.6 \qquad P(\bar{G}|w_2)=0.4$

$P(G|w_3)=0.8 \qquad P(\bar{G}|w_3)=0.2$

Using Bayes' theorem, we have:

$$P(w_1|G) = \frac{P(w_1)\,P(G|w_1)}{P(w_1)\,P(G|w_1) + P(w_2)\,P(G|w_2) + P(w_3)\,P(G|w_3)}$$

$$= \frac{0.5 \times 0.2}{0.5 \times 0.2 + 0.25 \times 0.6 + 0.25 \times 0.8}$$

$$= \frac{0.10}{0.10 + 0.15 + 0.20} = \frac{2}{9}.$$

Similarly,

$$P(w_2|G) = \frac{0.15}{0.45} = \frac{3}{9},$$

and

$$P(w_3|G) = \frac{0.20}{0.45} = \frac{4}{9}.$$

These three probabilities add up to unity, and are now entered on the appropriate branches of the decision tree. The EMV for the decision to drill at decision point X is now given by:

$$\tfrac{2}{9} \times (-130) + \tfrac{3}{9} \times 70 + \tfrac{4}{9} \times 470 = 203 \cdot 3.$$

The decision not to drill ($\bar{D}$) has an EMV of -30, and so the better decision, on an EMV basis, is to drill. The EMV of 203·3 is now entered at point X and the decision $\bar{D}$ is barred.

At decision point Y a similar reasoning can be followed. Here the result of the seismic sounding has been a not so good response. Using the same basic probabilities given above, Bayes' theorem can again be used to give the appropriate posterior probabilities.

Thus we have:

$$P(w_1|\bar{G}) = \frac{P(w_1)\,P(\bar{G}|w_1)}{P(w_1)\,P(\bar{G}|w_1) + P(w_2)\,P(\bar{G}|w_2) + P(w_3)\,P(\bar{G}|w_3)}$$

$$= \frac{0.5 \times 0.8}{0.5 \times 0.8 + 0.25 \times 0.4 + 0.25 \times 0.2} = 0 \cdot 727.$$

Similarly,

$$P(w_2|\bar{G}) = 0 \cdot 182 \qquad P(w_3|\bar{G}) = 0 \cdot 091,$$

and the three probabilities again add up to unity as they should.

Hence, the EMV for the decision to drill at decision point Y is:

$$0 \cdot 727 \times (-130) + 0 \cdot 182 \times 70 + 0 \cdot 091 \times 470 = -39 \cdot 0.$$

Comparison of this EMV with that of the decision not to drill shows the latter to be the better, as the EMV of the latter is only -30 in comparison with -39. Hence, we insert -30 at point Y and bar the decision to drill (D).

The next step is to combine the two branches, G and $\bar{G}$, weighting them according to the prior probabilities of obtaining G or $\bar{G}$ results, should we decide to take seismic soundings. These probabilities can be computed as follows:

$$P(G)=P(w_1)\,P(G|w_1)+P(w_2)\,P(G|w_2)+P(w_3)\,P(G|w_3)$$

$$=0\cdot5\times0\cdot2+0\cdot25\times0\cdot6+0\cdot25\times0\cdot8$$

$$=0\cdot45.$$

Hence $P(\bar{G})$ is equal to $1-0\cdot45$ or $0\cdot55$, although this result could be calculated from the basic data in precisely the same manner as was done for $P(G)$. These probabilities are entered on the decision tree. The combined EMV for the decision to take seismic soundings can now be evaluated as:

$$0\cdot45\times203\cdot3+0\cdot55\times(-30)=74\cdot985.$$

We can now, finally, look at the starting position denoted as decision point Z. The EMV for the decision to have a seismic sounding (S) is 75, while that for the decision not to have a seismic sounding ($\bar{S}$) is 100. The latter is the higher EMV, and, hence, the oil wildcatter should go ahead without a survey and drill: his EMV thereby will be 100.

The seismic survey, on these data, would have to be reduced in cost to 5 if it were to become a viable proposition on an EMV decision basis. It is, however, worth pointing out once again that the probabilities of a loss (any loss) under the two initial decisions are very different. Under the decision to take the seismic survey, the probabilities of losses are as follows:

Loss of 130   Probability $0\cdot45\times\frac{2}{9}$ or $0\cdot1$.

Loss of 30   Probability $0\cdot55$.

Under the decision to drill straight away without a seismic survey at all, the probability is:

Loss of 100   Probability $0\cdot5$.

Hence, if a loss of 100 or more is serious to the oil wildcatter, but losses of less than that amount are not so serious, the decision to drill straight away carries with it certain important implications and the wildcatter might prefer to take the survey. If any form of loss is of importance to the oil wildcatter, then the two decisions do not differ very materially in this respect.

8.2 Choice of level of information

The two examples discussed so far in this chapter have incorporated as one possible initial decision the purchasing of additional information of a fixed quantity and defined quality at a predetermined price. In some instances, not only the question of purchasing further information is open to the decision-maker but also, if he decides to obtain information, he can choose the amount he purchases. The next two examples involve situations where such a double choice exists. In Example 8.3 the information, if purchased, gives a definite or deterministic indication, while in Example 8.4 the information is still of a probabilistic form.

Example 8.3

The Setaw Excavation Company is offered a contract to excavate sites for three experimental radar towers to be erected at widely spread sites on a Mediterranean island. If Setaw accepts the contract, his firm will receive £22 500 for the job. The manager, Mr Andrews, estimates that it will cost his firm £6000 to excavate each site where no rock layer is encountered in the work of laying the foundations for the towers, and £8500 to excavate on a site where a rock layer is encountered. The pay-off, if Mr Andrews rejects the contract, is zero and he knows that, should he turn down the offer, another firm which has already quoted £22 500 will get the contract.

Mr Andrews cannot predict with absolute certainty whether a rock layer will be encountered in any of the three sites, but is able to assign the prior probabilities given in Table 8.4 on the basis of extensive experience in the general region of the excavation sites.

Table 8.4

Prior probabilities of rock layers

Number of sites containing rock layer	Prior probability
0 out of 3	0·20
1 out of 3	0·36
2 out of 3	0·24
All 3	0·20

Before signing the contract, Setaw have time to carry out a pilot drill at one or more, of the three sites at a cost of £250 per site drilled. The cost has to be borne by Setaw, and the drilling determines precisely whether or not a rock layer will be encountered. This work will be carried out by bringing in a specialist sub-contractor and Setaw must decide at the outset whether they will carry out any pilot drilling and, if so, at how many sites. They cannot commission the pilot drilling on a sequential basis. The sites for pilot drilling would be selected on a random basis.

What is the optimum amount of pilot drilling that Setaw should carry out? For this optimum amount of experimental drilling, what is Setaw's expected pay-off, net of all costs?

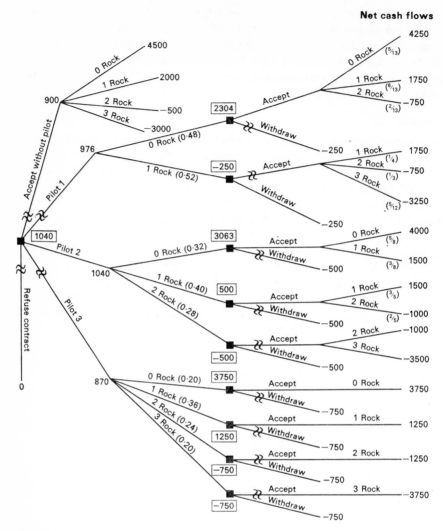

Fig. 8.5. Setaw decision tree

The basic decision tree is straightforward, being shown in Fig. 8.5. The net pay-off for each branch, including the pilot drilling costs, is given at the end of the appropriate branch. Once again, we can analyse the tree systematically on the roll-back principle. Clearly, the EMV for the initial decision 'refuse contract' is zero. For the initial decision 'accept contract with no pilot drilling', the EMV is given by:

$$0 \cdot 20 \times 4500 + 0 \cdot 36 \times 2000 + 0 \cdot 24 \times (-500) + 0 \cdot 20 \times (-3000) = 900.$$

Hence, it is better to accept the contract without pilot drilling than to refuse it outright, and the latter decision can straight away be barred on the decision tree.

We will next consider the decision corresponding to 'carry out pilot drillings on two of the sites'. There are three possible outcomes to this pilot drilling. Either 0, 1 or 2 of the sites selected show rock, and we take these three cases in turn.

(*i*) *Drillings show neither site with rock*

Table 8.5

Probabilities for neither site with rock

(1) Sites with rock	(2) Prior probability	(3) Probability of no. of sample sites with rock	(4) Joint probability $(2) \times (3)$	(5) Posterior probability $(4)/\Sigma\,(4)$	(6) Net pay-off
0	0·20	1	0·20	$\frac{5}{8}$	4000
1	0·36	$\frac{1}{3}$	0·12	$\frac{3}{8}$	1500
2	0·24	0	0	0	−1000
3	0·20	0	0	0	−3500
			Total 0·32	1	

Table 8.5 gives the basic calculations required in this situation. Column (3) may need a little explanation. If none of the three sites have rock and two sites are chosen at random, the probability that of these two sites, neither site has rock, is clearly 1. Suppose that one site (A) has rock and two (B and C) do not and, again, two sites are chosen at random. There are three possible pairs of sites (AB, AC, BC) and only BC has both without rock. Hence, the probability that both are without rock is $\frac{1}{3}$. If two or three sites have rock, then it is impossible to select two sites without rock; the appropriate probability is therefore zero.

Using columns (5) and (6) we have:

EMV (accept contract)$= \frac{5}{8} \times 4000 + \frac{3}{8} \times 1500$

$$= 24\,500/8 = 3063.$$

The EMV of the alternative decision to refuse the contract is -500. Hence, the optimum decision in this instance will be to accept the contract.

(*ii*) *Drillings show one site with rock and one site without rock*
Table 8.6 gives the basic calculations required in this situation. From columns (5) and (6) we have:

EMV (accept contract)$=0·6 \times 1500 + 0·4 \times (-1000)$

$$= 500.$$

Table 8.6

Probabilities for one site only with rock

(1) Sites with rock	(2) Prior probability	(3) Probability of no. of sample sites with rock	(4) Joint probability $(2) \times (3)$	(5) Posterior probability $(4)/\Sigma\,(4)$	(6) Net pay-off
0	0·20	0	0	0	4000
1	0·36	$\frac{2}{3}$	0·24	0·6	1500
2	0·24	$\frac{2}{3}$	0·16	0·4	−1000
3	0·20	0	0	0	−3500
			Total 0·40	1·0	

The EMV of the alternative decision to reject the contract is the same as before, namely, − 500. Hence, the optimum decision in this instance is again to accept the contract, giving an EMV of 500.

(iii) Drillings show both sites with rock

Here we can short-circuit some of the calculations. Since two pilot drillings show rock, this implies that either two or three of the sites must have a rock layer. Since the expected gain from drilling if there are two sites with rock is negative, and the same is true of three sites with rock, it is clearly not worth while to accept the contract in this instance since the expected further net gain, above the costs already incurred in such an eventuality, must be negative. Hence, the contract would be refused and the overall EMV is − 500, the cost of the pilot drilling. Note that, in putting forward this argument, it is the gains or losses after the pilot drilling has been carried out (and paid for) that matter. The overall EMVs for the three branches concerned are all negative (including the decision to withdraw). The judgment at this decision point is to find the branch which gives rise to the highest additional EMV, which is then added to the negative gain (cost) already incurred. To accept at this stage is to add a negative EMV, to withdraw is to add zero. Thus, the latter is taken as the optimum decision, even though the overall EMV on the tree for the branch is given as negative. The incremental EMV is zero, not negative and it is this that matters.

We must now put together the three possible outcomes that arise when pilot drillings are carried out at two sites to give an overall EMV for this particular branch of the tree. If there are zero rock layers in the two pilot drillings, then there can be either zero rock layers at the three sites (giving a probability of 1 that the two pilot drillings show zero rock layers) or there can be one rock layer among the three sites (giving a probability of $\frac{1}{3}$ that the two pilot drillings show zero rock layers). Hence, the prior probability of getting zero rock layers in the two pilot drillings is $0.20 \times 1 + 0.36 \times \frac{1}{3} = 0.32$. Similarly, the prior probability of getting exactly one rock layer in the two pilot drillings is $0.36 \times \frac{2}{3} + 0.24 \times \frac{2}{3} = 0.40$, and the prior probability of both showing rock layers is $1 - 0.32 - 0.40 = 0.28$. Hence, the overall EMV for the initial decision to carry out pilot drilling at two of the three sites is:

$$0.32 \times 3063 + 0.40 \times 500 + 0.28 \times (-500) = 1040.$$

(iv) Pilot drilling at one site
The reader is now left to evaluate the EMVs corresponding to the other two branches, namely, 'carry out one pilot drilling' or 'carry out three pilot drillings'. The key intermediate results that should be obtained for pilot drilling at one site are given in Table 8.7.

Table 8.7

Pilot drilling at one site

No. of sites with rock	Posterior probabilities	
	Sample site shows no rock	Sample site shows rock
0	$\frac{5}{13}$	0
1	$\frac{6}{13}$	$\frac{3}{12}$
2	$\frac{2}{13}$	$\frac{4}{12}$
3	0	$\frac{5}{12}$

From consideration of the EMVs, the contract is accepted if the pilot shows no rock, refused if the pilot does show rock. The former decision has an EMV of 2304 and the latter an EMV of -250. The prior probability that the pilot drilling shows one site with rock is 0.52, and that it shows no site with rock is 0.48.

(v) Pilot drilling at three sites
Here, the pilot drilling will show quite explicitly in a deterministic fashion the number of sites in the whole contract that have rock. Thus, Setaw would accept the contract, having carried out pilot drillings at all three sites, if zero or one sites were found without rock layers, but would otherwise reject the contract. The prior probabilities that the pilot drilling shows either zero or one of the sites to have rock are 0.2 and 0.36 respectively.

The EMVs for all the initial decisions are given in Fig. 8.5 and the highest EMV, although not by much, occurs for the decision to have pilot drilling at two sites only. This has an EMV of 1040. It should be noted that, following this decision, the lowest possible pay-off is -1000. Had the decision been taken to accept without a pilot, not only is the EMV lower at 900, but the lowest possible pay-off is now −3000.

It will be noticed that in each of the three possible levels of pilot drilling, the subsequent decision as to whether to drill or not varies according to the outcome of the pilot drillings and is not always the same at any given level of pilot drilling. A moment's reflection will show that, if this were not so, it would be useless to carry out that level of pilot drilling at all since, whatever the result, the subsequent action would be the same. Hence, if pilot information is to be worth purchasing, it must be such that it could, in some but not necessarily all of the possible outcomes alter the decision that would have been made without obtaining the pilot information in the first instance.

Example 8.4*

The marketing manager for a consumer firm is concerned with the sales appeal of the firm's present label for one of its products. Marketing research indicates that supermarket consumers find little eye appeal in the drab, somewhat cluttered appearance of the label. The firm has hired a design artist who has produced some prototype labels, all of which have been evaluated by the firm's marketing executives. One label design has consistently come out on top in all preference tests which have been conducted among these executives. Nevertheless, the marketing manager is still in some doubt as to whether the new label would have an appreciable benefit on sales. He accordingly decides to make a more exhaustive quantitative analysis of the consequences of a decision to switch to the new label.

First, he considers the costs associated with converting his firm's machinery, inventory, point of purchase displays, etc., to the new label, and estimates that an out of pocket, once and for all, cost of £250 000 would be involved. If the new label were really superior to the old, the marketing manager estimates that the present value of all net cash flows related to increased sales generated over the next three years by the more attractive label will be £400 000. (For purposes of simplicity the analysis is kept to a three-year planning horizon only.) But, based on his prior experience and the discussions he has held with his colleagues, he is willing to assign only a 0·5 probability to the outcome 'new label superior to old'. Rather than make his decision on these data alone, however, he could delay it and obtain further market research information. Again, the market research can be done in various ways. After discussions the manager confines his attention to three possible forms, the cost and reliability varying from one form to another. The possible forms of market research are:

Market research type M_1 A 'perfect' survey at a cost of £150 000.

Market research type M_2 A survey that is 80 per cent reliable at a cost of £50 000.

* This example is partially based on a problem discussed by P. E. Green and R. E. Frank in *Applied Statistics*, November 1966, p. 173.

Market research type M₃   A survey that is in two stages. The first stage is
70 per cent reliable, but the survey can be taken to
the second stage when the reliability increases to
80 per cent. Cost of the first stage sample is
£35 000 and the second stage, if needed, costs an
extra £40 000.

The appropriate decision tree can now be drawn to show the various
alternatives open to the marketing manager and is given in Fig. 8.6(a) and

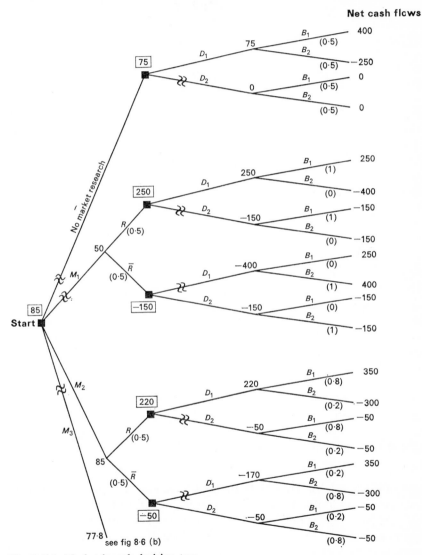

Fig. 8.6(a). Market launch decision tree

(b). The decision to change to the new label is denoted by D_1 and to keep the old by D_2. The outcome 'new label superior to old' is denoted by B_1 and the outcome 'new label not superior to old' by B_2. The information from the market research surveys is shown as either positive (R) or negative ($\bar{R}$) in

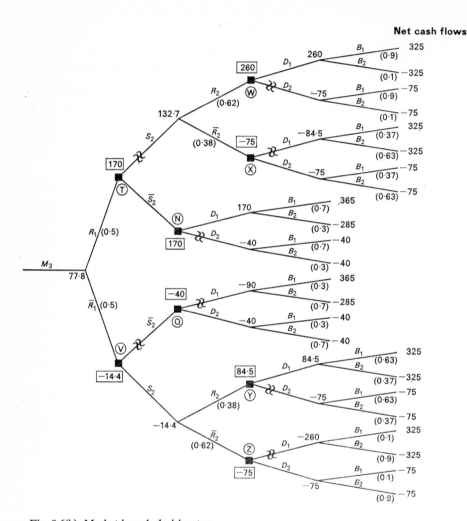

Fig. 8.6(b). Market launch decision tree

favour of the new label. Subscripts are used to denote the two-part sampling for market research of type M_3. All monetary quantities are inserted as £'000s and the £ sign is omitted where there is no likelihood of confusion. The net cash flows at the end of each branch include the costs of the surveys, where relevant.

We can evaluate the top branch relating to the decision 'No market research' very straightforwardly:

EMV $(D_1)=0.5\times400+0.5\times(-250)=75$.

EMV $(D_2)=0$.

Hence, decision D_1 is the better decision to take and this is entered on the tree, decision D_2 being barred for this particular branch.

We will next tackle the branch labelled M_1. Here we have the possibility of a perfectly reliable survey, which implies that the survey would disclose without error which outcome B_1 or B_2, is the 'true state' of nature. Hence, the conditional probabilities are:

$P(B_1|R)=1$; $P(B_2|R)=0$;

$P(B_1|\bar{R})=0$; $P(B_2|\bar{R})=1$.

Thus, given that the information is positive (R), the EMVs are:

EMV $(D_1)=250$;   EMV $(D_2)=-400$.

Hence, D_1 is the better decision in these circumstances. If the information is negative $(\bar{R})$ we have:

EMV $(D_1)=-400$;   EMV $(D_2)=-150$.

Hence D_2 is now the better decision. The two possible market research outcomes must now be combined by weighting the optimum decision EMVs for each market research outcome by the prior probability of each of them and by summarizing. These probabilities are clearly both 0·5 and, hence, the overall EMV for the initial decision to undertake market research of type M_1 is: $0.5\times250+0.5\times(-150)=50$.

The next branch which will be tackled is that relating to the initial decision to undertake market research of type M_3. Here we indicate in Fig. 8.6(b) the first survey results by R_1 and $\bar{R}_1$, and the second survey results, if taken, by R_2 and $\bar{R}_2$. The decision to take the second survey is indicated by S_2, while the decision not to take it is indicated by $\bar{S}_2$. The key decision points are labelled N, Q, T, V, W, X, Y and Z. We must now interpret formally the original statements made concerning the reliability of the surveys. For the first survey we take the statement to imply that:

$P(R_1|B_1)=0.7$; $P(\bar{R}_1|B_1)=0.3$;

$P(R_1|B_2)=0.3$; $P(\bar{R}_1|B_2)=0.7$.

Hence we have $P(B_1|R_1)=0.7$ and $P(B_2|R_1)=0.3$ since both $P(B_1)$ and $P(B_2)$ are equal to 0·5.

Assuming that we decide not to take the further part of the survey, the EMVs for the two alternative decisions D_1 and D_2 will depend upon whether the initial survey is positive (R_1) or negative $(\bar{R}_1)$ and will be as follows:

For R_1 (and $\bar{S}_2$)

$$\text{EMV } (D_1) = 0 \cdot 7 \times 365 + 0 \cdot 3 \times (-285)$$

$$= 170.$$

$$\text{EMV } (D_2) = 0 \cdot 7 \times (-40) + 0 \cdot 3 \times (-40)$$

$$= -40.$$

Hence, the decision at decision point N in this instance would be to accept the new label (D_1), giving an EMV of 170. When the initial survey results are negative $(\bar{R}_1)$ we have:

For $\bar{R}_1$ (and $\bar{S}_2$)

$$\text{EMV } (D_1) = 0 \cdot 3 \times 365 + 0 \cdot 7 \times (-285)$$

$$= -90.$$

$$\text{EMV } (D_2) = -40.$$

Hence, the decision at decision point Q in this instance would be not to accept the new label (D_2), giving an EMV of -40.

These two results can be entered on the decision tree and the non-optimum routes barred.

Next we need to consider the consequences of deciding to take the second survey. Initially we consider the situation where both parts of the survey give positive results. The information given earlier concerning the accuracy of results in the second part of the survey can be summarized as follows:

$$P(R_2|B_1) = 0 \cdot 8; \qquad P(\bar{R}_2|B_1) = 0 \cdot 2;$$

$$P(R_2|B_2) = 0 \cdot 2; \qquad P(\bar{R}_2|B_2) = 0 \cdot 8.$$

The probabilities associated with B_1 and B_2 can now be found from Bayes' theorem:

$$P(B_1|R_1, R_2) = \frac{P(B_1)\,P(R_1|B_1)\,P(R_2|B_1)}{P(B_1)\,P(R_1|B_1)\,P(R_2|B_1) + P(B_2)\,P(R_1|B_2)\,P(R_2|B_2)}$$

$$= \frac{0 \cdot 5 \times 0 \cdot 7 \times 0 \cdot 8}{0 \cdot 5 \times 0 \cdot 7 \times 0 \cdot 8 + 0 \cdot 5 \times 0 \cdot 3 \times 0 \cdot 2}$$

$$= 0 \cdot 90.$$

Similarly,

$$P(B_2|R_1, R_2) = \frac{P(B_2)\,P(R_1|B_2)\,P(R_2|B_2)}{P(B_1)\,P(R_1|B_1)\,P(R_2|B_1) + P(B_2)\,P(R_1|B_2)\,P(R_2|B_2)}$$

$$= \frac{0 \cdot 5 \times 0 \cdot 3 \times 0 \cdot 2}{0 \cdot 5 \times 0 \cdot 7 \times 0 \cdot 8 + 0 \cdot 5 \times 0 \cdot 3 \times 0 \cdot 2}$$

$$= 0 \cdot 10.$$

By similar calculations we can obtain the appropriate probabilities for the other three possible combinations of survey results as follows:

$\bar{R}_1$ with R_2 $\begin{cases} P(B_1|\bar{R}_1, R_2)=0\cdot63 \\ P(B_2|\bar{R}_1, R_2)=0\cdot37. \end{cases}$

R_1 with $\bar{R}_2$ $\begin{cases} P(B_1|R_1, \bar{R}_2)=0\cdot37 \\ P(B_2|R_1, \bar{R}_2)=0\cdot63. \end{cases}$

$\bar{R}_1$ with $\bar{R}_2$ $\begin{cases} P(B_1|\bar{R}_1, \bar{R}_2)=0\cdot10 \\ P(B_2|\bar{R}_1, \bar{R}_2)=0\cdot90. \end{cases}$

We can now evaluate the EMVs associated with the point marked W. These will be:

EMV $(D_1)=0\cdot9\times325+0\cdot1\times(-325)=260.$

EMV $(D_2)=0\cdot9\times(-75)+0\cdot1\times(-75)=-75.$

Hence, the best decision at point W will be D_1 with an EMV of 260.

At point X the EMVs will be:

EMV $(D_1)=0\cdot37\times325+0\cdot63\times(-325)=-84\cdot5.$

EMV $(D_2)=0\cdot37\times(-75)+0\cdot63\times(-75)=-75.$

Hence, the best decision at point X will be D_2 with an EMV of -75.

At point Y, the EMVs will be:

EMV $(D_1)=0\cdot63\times325+0\cdot37\times(-325)=84\cdot5.$

EMV $(D_2)=0\cdot63\times(-75)+0\cdot37\times(-75)=-75.$

Hence, the optimum decision at point Y will be D_1 with an EMV of 84·5.

Finally, at point Z, we have:

EMV $(D_1)=0\cdot1\times325+0\cdot9\times(-325)=-260.$

EMV $(D_2)=0\cdot1\times(-75)+0\cdot9\times(-75)=-75.$

Hence the optimum decision at point Z will be D_2, not to change, with an EMV of -75.

We can now merge the decisions at points W and X, in that the probability of R_2 occurring on that branch is:

$P(R_2|R_1)=P(R_1R_2)/P(R_1)$

$$=\frac{P(R_1, R_2B_1)\,P(B_1)+P(R_1, R_2B_2)\,P(B_2)}{P(R_1B_1)\,P(B_1)+P(R_1B_2)\,P(B_2)}$$

or

$$\frac{0\cdot7\times0\cdot8+0\cdot3\times0\cdot2}{0\cdot7+0\cdot3}=0\cdot62.$$

Similarly, the probability of $\bar{R}_2$ occurring on that branch is:

$$P(\bar{R}_2|R_1) = \frac{P(R_1, R_2|B_1)\, P(B_1) + P(R_1, R_2 B_2)\, P(B_2)}{P(R_1|B_1)\, P(B_1) + P(R_1 B_2)\, P(B_2)}$$

or

$$\frac{0\cdot7 \times 0\cdot2 + 0\cdot3 \times 0\cdot8}{0\cdot7 + 0\cdot3} = 0\cdot38.$$

This gives an overall EMV for this upper branch of:

$$0\cdot62 \times 260 + 0\cdot38 \times (-75) = 132\cdot7.$$

Hence the optimum decision at point T will be not to take the second survey, as the EMV of 170 for $\bar{S}_2$, is higher than the EMV of 132·7 for S_2. In a similar way we can merge the decisions at points Y and Z. A computation, analogous to that just made, gives the probabilities of R_2 and $\bar{R}_2$ on this branch as 0·38 and 0·62 respectively. This gives an overall EMV for this branch of:

$$0\cdot38 \times 84\cdot5 + 0\cdot62 \times (-75) = -14\cdot39.$$

Hence, the optimum decision at point V is to carry out the second survey, when the overall EMV will be $-14\cdot4$, in preference to not carrying it out when the EMV is -40. Note that this EMV is negative, but it is still worth taking the second survey, as we would already have expended 35 on the first survey and we would, therefore, have a positive expectation of $35 - 14\cdot4$ or 20·6 in going on to the next stage.

The final step in the evaluation of the M_3 branch of the overall tree is to combine the EMVs at the two decision points T and V. Since the prior probability of result R_1 is $0\cdot5 \times 0\cdot7 + 0\cdot5 \times 0\cdot3 = 0\cdot5$, and similarly for $\bar{R}_1$, we have an overall EMV for decision M_3 of:

$$0\cdot5 \times 170 + 0\cdot5 \times (-14\cdot4) = 77\cdot8.$$

The reader is now left to carry through the similar, but somewhat less protracted, calculations appropriate for initial decision M_2. The key figures obtained are shown in Fig. 8.6(a) and the overall EMV obtained is 85. From Fig. 8.6(a) the highest EMV of 85 corresponds to decision M_2, and hence this, under the EMV principle, is the optimal initial decision. Under this decision, a market research survey of 80 per cent reliability is taken and, if the survey is favourable, the change is made, but not otherwise. Of course, if, by the time the survey has been carried out, extra information concerning markets or costs has come to hand, this must be included in the assessment made at that stage,

8.3 Summary of procedure

In this chapter we have been concerned with the use of posterior probability concepts to examine the value of differing quantities of information in order to reach optimal decisions. We have not introduced any new principles or procedures. The basic steps necessary for the analysis of such a problem are:

(*i*) A decision tree is drawn to display the alternative actions and outcomes, including the purchase of various levels of information (if relevant).

(*ii*) The net cash flows are calculated and placed on the extremities of the appropriate branches.

(*iii*) The relevant probabilities are placed on the tree, using Bayes' theorem to convert prior probabilities to posterior probabilities when sample information is being obtained.

(*iv*) The tree is analysed on the roll-back principle, working from the extremities back to the main trunk.

(*v*) Expected monetary value is used as a means of deciding between alternative decisions at each node or decision point.

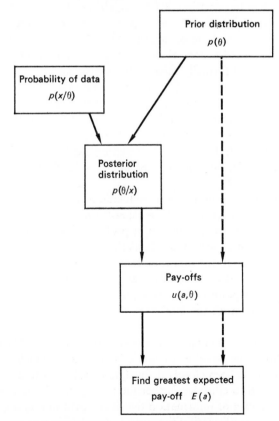

Fig. 8.7. Schematic form of Bayesian analysis

Using this approach, complex problems can be broken down into a number of simpler problems, each of which can be analysed through such an approach. At each node on the appropriate decision tree, the choice between alternatives is made following the expected monetary value principle. This is illustrated in schematic form in Fig. 8.7, where θ refers to the outcome, u the associated pay-offs, x the extra information made available and a the possible actions. The dotted line indicates the principle followed if no extra information is available from which to form posterior probabilities—which was the situation for the problems discussed in Chapter 5. The unbroken lines indicate the procedure to be followed when extra information is available as in this chapter to be incorporated with the prior probabilities in the decision analysis.

8.4 Discussion

This chapter has considered examples in which the optimal policy for a series of sequential decisions has been found by considering the final decision first and working backwards to the initial decision. To do so, all the circumstances in which the last decision might be made had to be envisaged. It is not necessary to consider how each outcome arises, or what previous decisions were, and this enables the decisions to be considered one at a time. The structure of analysis adopted is formally referred to as dynamic programming, and whilst many problems of this form can be tackled by dynamic programming this is not universally the case. For example, it is necessary to assume that the payoffs from each decision are additive, and that no matter how an outcome arose, the consequences for the future are the same. Readers interested in pursuing this line are referred to text books on dynamic programming, for example, *Dynamic Programming* by K. Williams (Longmans, 1970).

The methods, and examples used to illustrate these methods, in the last four chapters of this book have all needed to make extensive use of probabilistic data. This has involved the estimation of probabilities, and their interpretation, in ways that are not as neat and tidy as the way in which probability was conceived and used in the first four chapters of this book. Chapter 9 is therefore devoted to a discussion of the assessment of probabilities, and is placed at this point in the development of the material since the reader is by now familiar with the kind of problem whose analysis concerns us.

Some of the examples in the present chapter have involved the possibility of purchasing sample information. The possible amount of information which may be purchased has in each case been closely defined, and restricted to a very few possible levels. We need to consider further the more general question of deciding upon the optimum level of information that it is worth purchasing when there is a considerable range of possibilities open to the decision-maker. This problem will be discussed, and appropriate methods developed, in Chapters 10 and 11. Chapter 10 deals with situations where the information obtained from each unit examined is of a yes/no variety (e.g. when individual items of a batch of electronic components being considered for purchase are examined, they either are or are not defective). Chapter 11 deals with situations where the information obtained from each item examined is of a continuous nature (e.g. electronic components being tested by examining their length of life before failure).

So far in this book we have also made the tacit assumption that the attractiveness of various alternative results is directly reflected in the monetary pay-off associated with each of these alternatives. By such means, gains and losses can be satisfactorily measured in terms of money. Two problems arise here: first, it is sometimes difficult to attach such a monetary scale to many outcomes. For example, somebody's arrival at a business meeting on time, to quote Exercise 6.3, is not something to which we can readily attach a monetary pay-off. Hence, we are necessarily restricted in the range of problems for which we may directly use our means of analysis.

Second, we are inherently assuming that the decision-maker's attitude towards the gain or loss of money is linear. By this we mean, for example, that his attitude towards acquiring or losing an extra £5000 when he already possesses £25 000 capital is precisely the same as his attitude would be should his capital only be £2500. Although such an attitude might well be true of two business firms, one with a capital of £10 million and the other with a capital of, say, £12 million, each concerned with a project that could gain or lose them £50 000, it is demonstrably not true in many other real life situations.

These difficulties can be surmounted by using, in place of money, a numerical scale of *utility*. This is a number associated with an outcome which measures the attractiveness of that outcome; the higher the utility the more desirable is the outcome, and an outcome with higher utility will be preferred to one with lower utility. Once utility has been established for the possible outcomes, the analysis may proceed as before on the basis of expected utility rather than expected monetary value. This concept is discussed in more detail in Chapter 12.

Exercises on Chapter 8

1 M. Borel, the owner of a French cargo shipping line, is offered two ships of a European line that is going out of business, in exchange for an ongoing interest in M. Borel's line. M. Borel proposes either to accept the European line's offer or to reject it outright. The condition of the two ships (i.e. whether or not they require a major overhaul) is a key determinant of the pay-off that M. Borel will receive if he accepts the offer. If he rejects the offer, his pay-off is zero in any case.

M. Borel decides to base his decisions on an EMV approach. He has no precise information on the condition of the two ships, but is able to assign the prior probabilities shown in Table 8.8 as to the conditions of the ships as a set on the basis of judgment and experience. (He does not attempt to apply probabilities to the individual ships.) Also shown are M. Borel's specific estimates of the total discounted pay-offs that he would receive if he accepts the offer under the different possible outcomes (in millions of New Francs).

Table 8.8

Foreign line ship data

No. of ships requiring major overhaul	Prior probability	Pay-off if accepted
0	0·30	60
1	0·10	10
2	0·60	−40

(*i*) Suppose M. Borel must make his decision between accepting and rejecting the offer without obtaining further information on the condition of the two ships. Which decision should he make?

(*ii*) M. Borel has the option of having one or both ships taken to a reliable inspection station in a second foreign country before he makes his decision. The cost (to be paid by M. Borel) is 0·6 million NF per ship so inspected. What is M. Borel's best strategy? Give the number of ships he should inspect (i.e. 0, 1 or 2) together with the action he should take in each eventuality (e.g. inspect two, one fails and he accepts the offer, etc.) and the EMV of following your proposed strategy.

(*iii*) Are there conditions under which M. Borel might not be willing to take the action proposed under (*ii*)?

2 A manufacturer's agent receives, periodically, railway shipments of four large machines from one of the firms he represents. The machines have to be moved from the railway siding on arrival and installed in good working order in the customers' plants. The representative must either accept or reject the shipment on arrival at the siding. If the agent accepts responsibility he receives a fee of £400 from the manufacturer but must then reset, at his own cost, any machines that may have been jarred out of alignment while being shipped. The cost of resetting each machine found to be out of alignment is about £150. If the agent rejects responsibility for a given shipment, he receives no fee but is reimbursed by the manufacturer for any direct costs incurred in resetting of damaged machines in that shipment. Transport costs are paid by the purchaser and do not concern the agent.

The agent has collected extensive data on the number of machines that have had to be reset in past shipments of similar machines. The relevant frequency distribution that he has compiled from this information is as follows:

No. of damaged machines	0	1	2	3	4
Relative frequency	0·4	0·2	0·1	0·1	0·2

Time just permits the agent to examine two of the machines in the shipment before making his final decision, should he desire to do so. This would cost him £50 in time and labour, but he would be able to determine precisely for the two machines examined whether they did or did not need resetting. The machines to be examined would be chosen at random. What is the agent's optimal strategy, assuming that he uses EMV as his decision criterion?

3* A company sells welding supplies to industrial customers and maintains an extensive distribution network throughout the United States with its 250 salesmen. The company has been in existence for about 25 years and sells only the most traditional types of welding supplies. In recent years a fairly new welding method, Tungsten inert gas welding (TIG) has been making some inroads into the sales of this company. There is, however, still a vast untapped market of potential customers estimated to be equivalent to at least 100 000 units.

Recently, the company has been given an opportunity to market a new inexpensive and very flexible TIG torch which could be used as an adaptor for a traditional arc welder. The marketing of this product would involve a fixed investment of approximately $50 000, consisting mostly of sales literature and advertising. Net profit, that is the sales price less the manufacturer's royalties and salesmen's commissions, was conservatively estimated to be $25 per sale. The management of the company has to decide whether or not to market the product.

The product planning committee has met in emergency session and agreed that an appropriate prior distribution for π, the proportion of the potential market who would buy the torch, was given by an exponential distribution with a mean of 0·025, i.e. $p(\pi) = 40e^{-40\pi}$.

There is just time to carry out a small test marketing of the product. This could be done by selecting a simple random sample of 100 potential customers at a cost of $4000, including the purchase of the torches likely to be sold on such a test marketing.

What should be the company's choice of initial strategy—accept the offer, carry out a test market, or reject the offer? If you recommend a test market, state the decision rule for acceptance or rejection of the offer that would be followed. (Note that the suggested prior distribution actually allows π to be greater than 1, but the probability of such a value is effectively zero.)

* Based in part on a problem discussed by L. Harris in *Applied Statistics*, 1968, Vol. 17, page 39.

4 This example concerns a special kind of fruit machine called a *two-armed bandit*. A one-armed bandit is essentially a machine with one arm which, on being pulled, can either result in a win of 10p (5p after deducting the stake money of 5p) or a loss of your 5p stake money. On each pull of the handle there is a fixed chance of success, and successive pulls do not influence one another (although they may influence your beliefs about the fixed chance of success). A two-armed bandit is a similar machine, but with two arms, the participant selecting which arm to pull. The arms have nothing to do with each other and the chances of winning are not necessarily the same for both arms. Assuming that you have decided to enter and put up the stake of 5p, the problem with a two-armed bandit is which arm to pull.

Suppose that you have good knowledge of the righthand arm, and believe the chance of success using it is 0·5. For the lefthand arm you are not so sure, as you have only been able to witness a few trials. You summarize your views by saying that you think there is either a 0·3 chance of success or a 0·7 chance of success at a single pull, and the prior weights you would attach are 0·6 and 0·4 respectively. Thus, if a series of pulls were envisaged, it might be worth trying a few goes at the lefthand arm, even though it is probably worse than the other arm, simply because one knows little about it. In the same way, a motorist might try a strange route, even if it does not appear at first sight to be very promising, simply because his knowledge of it is vague and that it might, after all, be good.

Investigate the gambler's best strategy, using EMV as his decision criterion, for two pulls only of the two-armed bandit.

5* In early March 1970, Mr Sparrow, the president and sole owner of the Sparrow Drilling Company, was about to reach a final decision concerning a lease that Sparrow held on a plot of land in an oil-bearing region in Central Kansas. The lease gave the lessee (Sparrow) the right to drill for oil at any time up to a final date of 31 March 1972; the right would automatically lapse if drilling had not begun by that date. If drilling began before the final date, it could be continued until either oil was struck or the driller decided to give up; if oil were struck, the lessee was obliged to pay the lessor (the owner of the land) royalties equal to one-sixth of the gross revenues received from all oil raised.

The Sparrow Drilling Company had been founded in 1964 by Mr Sparrow, until then operations vice-president of a large petroleum company, in an effort to 'make money for myself instead of for others'. Until 1969 the company's business had consisted entirely of drilling exploratory wells for the major oil producers, but in that year Sparrow decided to try exploratory drilling on Sparrow's own account. A large bank loan payable in instalments over three years had been obtained to finance the drilling, with Sparrow's

---

* Based in part on a problem described in the case of the Acme Drilling Company, Harvard Business School.

drilling rigs being pledged as security. Leases had been negotiated for drilling rights on five widely scattered sites in 1969, and drilling had taken place on four of the sites, leaving Central Kansas untouched by the spring of 1970. All these holes had turned out to be dry, and unexpected delays in redeploying Sparrow's four drilling rigs from these private ventures back to paid work for the major oil producers had put Sparrow in a precarious financial position in the spring of 1970. Working capital had been reduced practically to zero, and Sparrow had been compelled to obtain the bank's consent to a delay in the first scheduled payment on the instalment loan.

From April 1970 to March 1972, Sparrow's four rigs had been kept busy more than 90 per cent of the time drilling exploratory wells on a contract basis; profits on these contract operations had been sufficient to permit Sparrow not only to meet all payments on the bank loan as they fell due, but also to build its working capital back to about $80 000. Drilling contracts already in hand were expected, in the absence of bad luck, to generate the funds needed to make the last $100 000 loan payment when it fell due in November 1973.

In these circumstances Sparrow was financially able in March 1972 to drill the last of its five sites. Although it was true that drilling a dry hole would again put Sparrow in a difficult financial position, success would mean that, for the first time since Sparrow was founded, it would be in the pleasant situation of having a really substantial amount of cash in the bank. Mr Sparrow had already decided that, if he did drill and strike oil, he would sell the site immediately to a major company rather than tie up his capital in lifting the oil himself and thus risk very serious embarrassment should his drilling contracts not yield enough cash to pay off the bank loan. The sale would be very straightforward from Sparrow's point of view, since the buyer would be responsible for all costs incurred in 'completing' the well and for the payments to the lessor called for under the lease. Sparrow would receive a single, immediate cash payment proportional to the ultimate recoverable reserves as estimated immediately after oil was struck. At the going prices for new wells in this region, the payment would yield Sparrow $1·50 per barrel net after taxes.

Sparrow did not propose to carry out the drilling with his own rigs, however, since these were completely tied up in contract work for several months ahead. Accordingly, Mr Sparrow had asked his treasurer, Mr Russell, to obtain bids for the drilling, from other contract drillers who had rigs in the vicinity of the plot on which Sparrow held the drilling lease. In seeking these bids Sparrow had asked bidders to quote a single total price for drilling until either oil was struck, or a depth of 6000 feet was reached (at which point the well would be abandoned), whichever occurred first. This was not the usual form of contract, which specified a fixed price per foot and left the person paying for the drilling free to stop at any depth he chose. Mr Sparrow had, however, decided after consultation with his geologist,

Mr Heffern, that the unusual form of contract would almost certainly be advantageous to Sparrow under the special circumstances of this particular case. Experience with wells that had been drilled in the general area surrounding Sparrow's site, together with knowledge of the geological formations in this area, had convinced Mr Heffern that if there was any oil at all under the site, it almost certainly lay somewhere between 5500 and 6000 feet below the surface. Under the usual system of pricing by the foot, drilling contractors usually quoted a price high enough to cover their fixed costs—particularly the cost of bringing the rig to the site—even if the drilling were to stop at a depth of 2000 or 3000 feet. Mr Sparrow believed that by guaranteeing, in effect, payment for 6000 feet he would almost certainly get a lower effective price per foot, even if oil was actually struck at a depth of only 5000 feet.

Mr Sparrow's reasoning was confirmed when the bids came in, several of them corresponding to per-foot prices appreciably less than those usually quoted in this area of the country. The most favourable bid was from Klimm Drillers, Inc, who made their price contingent on the depth at which a lime-shale formation was encountered. If such a formation was not encountered, or was encountered at a depth greater than 4000 feet, the net cost to Sparrow after adjustment for tax effects would be only $64 000. If a lime-shale formation was encountered above 4000 feet, the net cost after taxes would be $72 000. This offer was only open, however, for two weeks, since the reason Klimm was able to bid so low was that they currently had a rig in the immediate vicinity of the Sparrow plot. Since even the $72 000 cost was lower than that proposed by any other bidder, Mr Sparrow felt that he should reach some definite decision immediately.

The indefiniteness about drilling costs that resulted from uncertainty about the depth at which a lime-shale formation would be encountered bothered Mr Sparrow very little in thinking about his decision problem, but this same uncertainty about the lime-shale formation also entered the problem in two other, much more important, ways. The lime-shale formation in the general region of the plot leased by Sparrow was known with near certainty to lie nearly horizontally at a depth of about 5000 feet except where it rose abruptly to a depth of about 2500 feet in so-called 'flat domes', and both the chances of finding oil at all, and the amount of these reserves if oil was found, depended on whether the well penetrated one of these domes. Mr Heffern told Mr Sparrow that, considering both the general geology of the region and the available information concerning other wells drilled in the region, he thought there was about one chance in three of finding oil beneath a dome, but only about one chance in ten elsewhere; as to the size of the reserves in case oil was struck, he thought the most probable figure was 600 000 barrels, if the oil was found under a dome, but only 400 000 barrels if it was found elsewhere.

When Mr Sparrow questioned Mr Heffern concerning the chances that a dome would actually be found beneath the Sparrow site, Mr Heffern replied that, on the basis of the same kind of evidence that underlay his other opinions, the chances were about two in five; but on this point much better evidence could be obtained by having a seismic sounding made. Seismic soundings indicated the depth of the lime-shale formation and hence could be used to predict the existence or non-existence of a dome. A sounding would cost Sparrow only $10 000 net after tax and could be made within a week or ten days, the time being required to engage a specialist in seismic work and get his crew and apparatus to the site.

The idea of a seismic sounding appealed to Mr Sparrow as a relatively inexpensive way of reducing the risk of drilling a dry hole, the loss on which would again virtually wipe out Sparrow's working capital. He was, however, far from certain that it reduced the risk enough, since even if a sounding revealed the presence of a dome, the chances of drilling a dry hole would still be higher than 50 per cent.

Mr Sparrow called a meeting with Mr Russell and Mr Heffern to discuss their course of action. Just as the meeting opened, a telephone call was received from Klimm Drillers who said that their contract prices were incorrect; they should be $100 000 if a lime-shale formation was not encountered or was encountered at a depth greater than 4000 feet; $108 000 otherwise.

The meeting started to discuss the effect of this change in costs, when Mr Heffern pointed out that the assumption that a seismic sounding would tell for sure whether or not there was a dome beneath the Sparrow leasehold was not really true. 'Well, just what are the chances?' asked Sparrow.

'There isn't really any clear answer to that question,' Mr Heffern replied, 'because it depends on what else you know about the place where the sounding is made. If you have a site in a region where you know to start with that there are a lot of domes, and then a sounding indicates a dome, it might make sense to bet 9 to 1 or better that you've actually got a dome. But if you're in a basin where you know that domes are few and far between, you won't feel at all sure that you've got a dome even though a sounding does seem to say you have—you'll think it more likely that the sounding was misinterpreted.'

'That makes sense,' Mr Sparrow remarked, 'but how about this region and our site? If we have a sounding made and it seems to say there's a dome, what are the chances that we'll actually strike a dome if we drill?'

'I don't know,' Mr Heffern answered. 'There isn't a single instance I know of in this region where somebody has taken a sounding and then drilled and actually found out what was under the surface.'

'But you said the reliability studies carried out were encouraging,' Mr Sparrow rejoined somewhat impatiently. 'What do they tell you, if they don't tell you what the chances are that there's really a dome when the sounding says there is?'

Mr Heffern then explained that the studies did not deal with the dome question directly at all. What they did was to consider a larger number of cases where the known depth of a geological formation or stratum could be compared with an estimate of that same depth based on a seismic sounding, and their conclusions concerned the chances that seismic depth estimates would be incorrect by various amounts. Since the nature of the sounding and estimating process was such that errors of any given type were no more likely in one region than in any other, these results could be applied to a seismic made on the Sparrow leasehold even though the underlying data came from other regions. What the seismic expert would do if a sounding were made on the Sparrow site would be simply to look at the seismic trace and decide whether it looked more like what he would expect from a lime-shale formation at a 2500 foot depth, or more like what he would expect from a lime-shale formation about 5000 feet down. In the former case, they would interpret the seismic as indicating a dome, in the latter, as indicating no dome; and the findings of the studies were such as to lead Heffern to conclude that there was only about one chance in five that the seismic would indicate a dome if no dome existed and about the same chance that the seismic would indicate no dome if a dome did exist.

At this point Mr Sparrow decided to get down on paper all the relevant pieces of information in order to assess the relative values of the alternatives open to him. Assume that you are being retained by Mr Sparrow as adviser.

(*i*) Make an analysis of Mr Sparrow's decision problem that will be valid if Mr Sparrow accepts EMV as a complete guide to action, i.e. if Mr Sparrow wants to choose the immediate act that has the greatest EMV.

(*ii*) Assuming that Mr Sparrow understands the logic underlying the use of EMV, do you think that he would accept it as a complete guide in this problem?

(*iii*) Even if Mr Sparrow does not accept EMV as a complete guide in this problem, does any of the EMV analysis lead to useful conclusions concerning any parts of the complete decision problem?

(In answering these questions, assume that, if oil is struck, the ultimate recoverable reserves will be equal to Mr Heffern's 'most probable' estimate thereof.)

9 The assessment of probabilities

9.1 Introduction

In the various analyses that have been carried out in the last four chapters, we have developed an approach which attempts to separate judgments about pay-offs from judgments or assessments about probabilities. There are three basic elements that lie behind a decision concerning a particular project:

(*i*) The economic factors, e.g. costs, sales, speed of production, etc., leading to the pay-off.

(*ii*) The degree of uncertainty that lies behind the various factors included in (*i*).

(*iii*) The objectives, i.e. the decision-maker's resources and the relationship between the possible project outcomes and his desired objectives.

Consideration of the make-up of the first of these elements in any detail is outside the scope of this book, and we assume that the relevant costs and pay-offs concerned will be obtainable from the appropriate sources. The third element has so far been taken to be summarized correctly by the desire to maximize the EMV or expected monetary value. In Chapter 12 this basic premise will be examined further, and the concept of EMV extended to cover situations where EMV, in its straightforward form, is not felt to be appropriate.

In the present chapter we discuss the second of these elements. The discussion breaks into two parts. The first part (Sections 9.2 to 9.5) is concerned with estimating the appropriate probability for some defined event—that oil will be struck at site X before 31 December next, that the

H

demand for product Y will exceed 1000 units in the next twelve months, or that a new plant will be on stream within six months. The second part (Sections 9.6 and 9.7) deals with the formulation of a prior probability distribution for some unknown quantity—the proportion of married women who drive, the demand for product Y in the next twelve months, or the cost of installing and equipping a new chemical plant. Finally, some small experiments are described which illustrate some of the difficulties involved in probability assessments.

9.2 Categorization of assessments

We are all used to providing a categorization of our assessment of uncertain events. Thus, if we are asked about tomorrow's weather we may start by giving a (usually) rather long-winded description of what we are expecting to happen. We may try to summarize this description by using some evaluative phrases such as 'It is unlikely to rain' or 'It may rain' or 'It looks like rain' or even 'It seems pretty certain to rain'. This kind of evaluation is nothing new. Mr W. E. Cooke, the Government Astronomer for Western Australia at the turn of the century, advocated that each meteorological prediction be accompanied by a single number which would 'indicate, approximately, the weight or degree of probability that the forecaster himself attaches to that particular prediction'. The record of Cooke's forecasts is compiled in Table 9.1. The three categories used by Cooke are themselves ambiguous in

Table 9.1

Cooke's forecasts for Western Australia in 1905

Category	No. of predictions	Number correct	Proportion correct
1 Almost certain to be verified	685	675	0·985
2 Normal probability	970	910	0·938
3 Doubtful	296	233	0·787

meaning, but this ambiguity vanishes once we are aware of Cooke's performance record. A farmer who learns on a given day that Cooke forecasts rain with doubtful probability knows, once Cooke's record has been established, that in normal betting terms which most farmers understand, the odds are roughly 3 to 1 that it will rain. Cooke himself states:

> Those forecasts which were marked 'doubtful' were the best I could frame under the circumstances. I could see no way of improving them at the time and they would not have been expressed differently whether I weighted

them or not. If I make no distinction between these and others, I degrade the whole. But if, on the other hand, I attach a figure which practically says: 'I'm sorry, but this is the best I can do for you today—do not attach too much importance to it', I eliminate beforehand the adverse opinion which a great number of incorrect forecasts must produce and I raise the bulk of the predictions to their true value. In particular, I create a series, marked with my first category of certainty, which the public finds to be almost invariably correct, and thus raise the value of this particular series enormously.'

It is interesting to note how Cooke argues that by recognizing, and taming, the probabilistic nature of the forecast one is providing a better service than by merely ignoring its existence. Of course, one anticipates that Cooke would all the time be struggling to get more and more of his predictions from category 3 into category 2, and those in category 2 into category 1. As weather forecasting techniques become better we would expect this to happen and the consequence should be that, while the proportion correct in category 1 does not diminish, the proportion of forecasts put into category 1 will rise from its present level of 685/1951 or 35 per cent and the proportion of category 3 predictions will fall from its present level of 15 per cent.

We have, in this example, turned Cooke's three evaluative phrases into probabilistic assessments. Of course, the phrases themselves are sometimes replaced by rankings such as 'class I, II, III' or 'A, B, C, D', etc. But the trouble with such rankings, as with the evaluative phrases, is that they may well have different meanings for different people. Hence, it is worth trying to devise some system of scaling probabilistic judgments that will mean the same to different people.

9.3 A numerical scale

In the illustration just given using Cooke's data, he only allowed himself three categories and it might well be that in some instances he had a hard time deciding between placing his prediction into, say, category 2 (normal probability) or category 3 (doubtful). Indeed, Cooke's predilection might be for category 2·5 if it existed. In such a case, it might be easier for Cooke, and somewhat more meaningful and honest if, having noted that $0.84 = \frac{1}{2}(0.938 + 0.787)$, he were to say: 'It will rain tomorrow with probability 0·84', rather than to force himself to place his state of mind into either category 2 or category 3. This approach seems eminently plausible and straightforward but businesses do not commonly, however, ask their executives for numerical probabilities relating to future outcomes. The reasons for this omission are complex. The first objection raised seems to stem from the feeling that no number can reflect uncertainty. A number implies definiteness and predictability, and executives do not wish, nor will they trust (they may even fear) any such association of definiteness to a situation where the uncertainty is so great. Second, there is an instinctive feeling that probability is associated with the frequency interpretation, stemming back to the tossing of coins or throwing of dice. A probability of success of 0·1 or 1 out of 10 is assumed to be meaningless for drilling an oil well, because 10 wells will not be drilled under identical conditions.

A third objection is the fear that numbers—or any detailed analysis for that matter—will cause inaction or, at the very best, conservative action. Conservatism is associated with figure happy accountants or slide rule engineers, risk-taking with the non-numerical, intuitive, judgment-oriented end of the business. The intrusion of numbers is apparently thought to lead to analysis and, inexorably, to paralysis.

Not all executives agree with these objections and many accept that there has to be some scale of assessment for risk, just as there is for future costs of production. The use of a numerical, and understood scale, enables the different parts of a complex situation to be looked at, both separately and as a whole, in a manner that would not be otherwise possible. A scale permits evaluations of risk to be conveniently combined with other factors in the decision. In that way, the decision-maker can weight each event by the degree of likelihood with which he feels it will occur. Thereby a means of summarizing all the information and judgment that is available is provided. Such numbers do not imply objectivity or authority, although many people often try to read such magic into them. They are a form of language, permitting subjective views to be put into a more precise form which, in turn, provides a basis for comparison when relating one expert's evaluation with another. Thus, if you were to tell me that there is a 'fair' chance of rain tomorrow, there is rather less meaning to the statement than if you had said there was a 0·3 chance of rain tomorrow.

9.4 Fixed confidence levels

The previous section dealt with the idea of a numerical scale, a value from which was attached to the event or events concerned. Of course, the system can be operated by asking the evaluators to place a possible future event against defined probability levels. Thus, Williams, in 1951, reported the experience of eight professional Weather Bureau men who were regularly involved in making the Salt Lake City forecasts during December 1949 and January 1950. Each forecaster was asked to indicate the appropriate confidence number 0·6, 0·8 or 1·0 next to his twelve-hour forecasts of rain or no rain. Table 9.2 summarizes their overall joint performance. The proportions of correct predictions are fairly close to the confidence levels given to the forecasts, although the middle category could perhaps be recalibrated at 0·75.

Table 9.2

Rain–No rain forecasts for Salt Lake City 1949/50

Confidence level	Number of predictions	Number correct	Proportion correct
0·6	294	172	0·59
0·8	292	215	0·74
1·0	509	493	0·97

As consumers of such data, we should like probabilistic reports to be externally validated in the same way as these examples are done with empirical frequencies. Thus, we want our experts to calibrate themselves in such a way that if we were to group together a large number of forecasts in the 0·8 probability category (the forecasts being of weather, sales, prices, industrial output, etc.), then roughly 0·8 of the forecasts would turn out to be correct. The same should apply to other probability categories. Hence, overall, we are saying that it is better to try to separate out the components of a decision and to assess these separately than to try to make overall assessments incorporating all the elements. By this means, individual pieces of an analysis can be taken out and refurbished when fresh information becomes available, and the dependence of decisions on individual pieces of information made more apparent.

9.5 Assessment of probabilities

We have reaffirmed the need to assess probabilities on a numerical scale, but it is pertinent to discuss how such probabilities can be obtained. The first step, for most people, in assigning a probability to the occurrence of future outcomes, is to examine past experiences with similar or analogous outcomes. Thus, if a decision were to be made as to whether or not to drill a new well for natural gas in the North Sea, the probability of a strike is required. One set of figures readily available is that relating to previous drilling outcomes. These would probably have been compiled from drillings over a wide area of sea and may be of little use for the particular well under consideration. Indeed, the past success rate by itself is only likely to be acceptable for present purposes if, (*i*) the geologist concerned believed that such past experiences are pertinent to the current venture, (*ii*) he believes that the future will not differ in any way from the past, and (*iii*) he has no experience or evidence concerning the current venture which leads him to believe that it is very different from past experiences. In many situations, however, the geologist may not be willing to make these assumptions. He may not necessarily believe that the future will be the same as the past, and he may not wish to disregard the information that he has about the particular venture being considered—seismic maps, nearby drilling results, etc. All of this direct information, plus his personal past experience with similar situations and his personal judgment, may lead him to form a personal opinion or evaluation as to the chances of success for this particular venture. Thus, he will want to incorporate all the information about past success ratios, direct evidence for the particular prospect, his experience and his judgment when he makes the probability assignment. Such probability assignments are sometimes referred to as *personal probabilities*. In this way an individual incorporates all his experience, information and judgment. Such a probability can always be given, whether it be for the success of a gas strike or for rain tomorrow.

Because of the subjective nature of such probabilities, it does not follow that two persons will necessarily agree on the same probability for a particular outcome. Hence, it could happen that, of two geologists assessing a drilling venture, one would give a probability of success that leads to a decision to drill, while the other gives a probability that leads to the decision not to drill. This is not inconsistent and does not invalidate the theory. Decision theory is a way of capturing and utilizing judgment more effectively, not a method for replacing judgment as such. Thus, it is possible that personal probabilities may differ widely, as does judgment. However, reasonable men base the probabilities they assign to events in the real world on their information and experience with events in that world, and when two reasonable men are given the same information, and have had roughly the same experience with events of a given kind, they tend to assign to it roughly the same probability.

9.6 Estimation of fractiles

We turn now to the estimation of a prior probability distribution for some quantity, and approach this by estimating the fractiles of the distribution rather than the probabilities concerned. The method is illustrated around a marketing situation. Suppose that a marketing manager wishes to assess his prior probability distribution for the first year's demand for a new product which his company is proposing to market. (In some literature this distribution is referred to as the *judgmental probability distribution*.) As a start, he may feel that demand is more likely than not to be between, say, 600 and 1000 units, but that there is, nevertheless, a substantial chance that demand will turn out to be outside this range. Indeed, there is some small chance that demand will turn out to be very far outside this range, particularly on the high side. This suggests that the probability density function corresponding to demand has the general shape shown in Fig. 9.1. It is now necessary, however, to locate it rather more accurately and, to do this, we consider not the probability density function itself, but the cumulative density function.

The marketing manager will have little or no intuitive feeling for the chance that demand will be exactly equal to any one of the possible values but, by putting the problem in terms of cumulative probabilities, he will have some real intuitive feelings about the results. The following kind of procedure can be used:

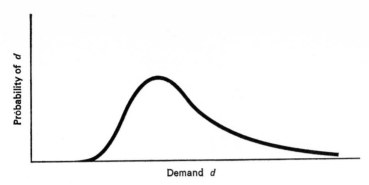

Fig. 9.1. Shape of demand distribution

(*i*) First, divide all the possible values of demand into equally likely halves. To do this, the manager looks for, and ultimately decides upon, some value of demand such that he would be just as ready to bet that demand will be below this value as he would be to bet that demand will be above. Suppose that he assesses this value at 750; it follows that 750 is the median, or 50th percentile, of the manager's distribution of demand.

(*ii*) Having divided his complete distribution into halves, the manager can go on to subdivide it into quarters by assessing his upper and lower quartiles from each of the halves. To assess the upper quartile (i.e. his 75th percentile) the manager focuses attention on those values of the demand distribution that lie above his assessed median, and decides upon a value which divides them into two equally likely halves. The lower quartile is treated similarly. We assume that, following this procedure, the manager decides upon 950 as the upper quartile, and 600 as the lower quartile.

(*iii*) Finally, the manager is asked to assess upper and lower limits between which demand will, in his opinion, almost certainly lie. This could be done by assessing, for example, a value that demand seems 99 times more likely to fall short of than to exceed. If the manager puts this value at 1500, then 1500 is denoted the 99th percentile of demand. Similarly, the manager may estimate the 1st percentile at 350.

Having divided the whole range for demand into six portions, by assessing five percentiles, the results can be plotted on a graph as in Fig. 9.2, and a smooth curve drawn through the five points. There is, of course, some personal latitude in the drawing of such a curve, particularly at the two extremes. Experience suggests, however, that when assessed probability distributions are actually used for the analysis of real decision problems, there is usually very little to be lost by the use of one particular curve rather than another, assuming both of them pass through the points representing the decision-maker's directly assessed percentiles. Hence, the decision-maker

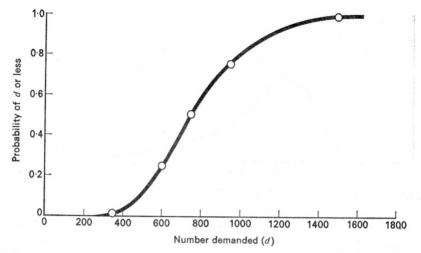

Fig. 9.2. Cumulative distribution for demand

need not take excessive pains with his first assessment of every probability
distribution required for the analysis of the particular problem concerned.
Once a preliminary analysis of the actual decision problem has been made,
based on these tentative probability assessments, a form of sensitivity analysis
can be carried out. The aim would be to decide which probability distributions,
and which parts of them, if any, are really worth the trouble of more careful
assessment.

It is, of course, perfectly possible to turn the cumulative density function of
Fig. 9.2 back into a probability density function of the type shown in
Fig. 9.1. To do this, we would first obtain from Fig. 9.1 the probabilities that

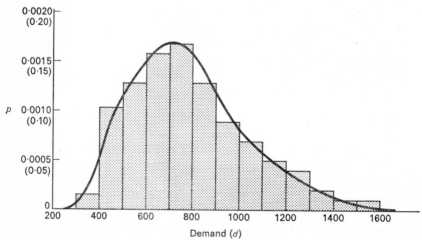

Fig. 9.3. Conversion to probability distribution

the demand *d* falls in a number of successive small intervals, e.g. 200–300, 300–400, 400–500, etc. These could then be plotted as a histogram and a smooth curve drawn through the flat levels of the histogram, as in Fig. 9.3, to produce the probability density function required. The vertical scale has been adjusted in that figure so that the area under the curve is equal to one, which requires a scale change of 100 as the original 'blocks' of demand had a width of 100 units. The histogram scale plots for *p* are given in brackets. In some situations the probability density function is the most useful form in which to have the information, but in most situations the cumulative density function is the more convenient form.

9.7 Experimental assessments

To illustrate some of the difficulties that people have in assessing probabilities, and concomitantly measuring odds, the author has carried out some experiments with executives and students. We describe here the results of an experiment with two groups of postgraduate students, some eighty in all, with an average age of about twenty-seven years and studying for degrees in business studies: virtually all the students had some business experience. They were each given a questionnaire which asked in part A for some information of their own habits and views and then, in more detail, for estimates of the percentiles of certain probability distributions. (The questionnaire is reproduced, in slightly abridged form, on page 225.)

The problems in part B of the questionnaire were picked so that, except for numbers 1 to 3 where the respondents as a group provided the answers themselves, virtually all the respondents would have some background knowledge but few, if any, would have complete knowledge and actually know the correct answers. Respondents would, accordingly, have to make estimates of the required quantities based on varying amounts of information. The problems were also such that the correct answers were ascertainable, and these could be made available immediately the exercise was completed. It could have been very revealing to have asked respondents to make judgments about future occurrences but, for teaching purposes, it was desirable to concentrate on problems for which the answers could be verified immediately.

9.8 Analysis of assessments

Each question asked the respondent to assess five percentiles, namely, 1st, 25th, 50th, 75th and 99th. These five percentiles divide the whole range of possible answers into six categories:

Category 1   All numbers below the 1st percentile.

Category 2   All numbers between the 1st and 25th percentiles.

Category 3   All numbers between the 25th and 50th percentiles.

Category 4   All numbers between the 50th and 75th percentiles.

Category 5   All numbers between the 75th and 99th percentiles.

Category 6   All numbers above the 99th percentile.

For any of the eight questions, once the respondent specifies his five percentiles, it is possible to indicate the category into which the true value falls. For example, suppose that Jones gave the following percentiles for question 5 on the National Debt (£ million):

Percentile	1st	25th	50th	75th	99th
Assessment	5000	10 000	20 000	30 000	40 000

The true value is 33 070 (£ million), and hence, Jones' answer is placed in category 5. This kind of analysis was now done for all respondents and all questions, with the results shown in Table 9.3, where the numbers in each row have been expressed as percentages for ease of understanding.

Table 9.3

Summary of assessment results

Question	Category						Total
	1	2	3	4	5	6	
1	0	0	12	22	41	25	100
2	6	3	16	34	32	9	100
3	6	9	12	22	29	22	100
4	31	9	25	16	0	18	100
5	0	3	6	19	9	63	100
6	6	13	9	19	28	25	100
7	12	12	6	17	13	40	100
8	0	3	3	6	6	82	100
Total	8	7	11	19	20	35	100

Look first at categories 3 and 4. In the aggregate, just as many true values should have fallen in these two categories as fell in all the others combined, since categories 3 and 4 refer to the range from the 25th to the 75th percentile. However, from the bottom row of the table rather more than twice as many fell outside than inside. But we also notice that there is a lot of variation from question to question, and also (although not shown by this table) from individual to individual. Table 9.4 shows, for each respondent, the number of questions for which he gave an answer that fell in either category 3 or category 4. In the final column is shown the corresponding expected numbers, on the assumption that there is a 0·3 chance that any category 3 or 4 range includes the true value, and that these responses are independent from question to question. The p value of 0·3 is selected since an overall proportion of 0·3 of the answers fell in one of these two categories. The reasonable agreement between the columns 2 and 3 suggests that each question is being considered independently by the respondents, even though there is clearly a general underestimate of the spread that should be given.

Table 9.4

Distribution of scores in categories 3 and 4

Category 3 and 4 score (1)	Observed no. of respondents with score in column (1) (2)	Expected* no. of respondents with score in column (1) (3)
0	0	5·8
1	27	19·7
2	27	29·7
3	27	25·4
4	7	13·6
5	6	4·8
6	6	1·0
7	0	0
Totals	100	100·0

* With $n=8$ and $p=0·3$.

Table 9.5 looks at the extremes as indicated by categories 1 and 6. We would expect such categories to occur only twice in a hundred times, but Table 9.5 gives the number of occasions, for each respondent, that he had a category 1 or a category 6 response. We actually had a total of 43 per cent of such responses, which is a shock figure when placed against the expected 2 per cent. The final column gives the 'expected' numbers for each score on the assumption of a $p=0·43$ and independence between questions. There is moderate agreement between the two columns, suggesting once again a degree of independence between answers given to the different questions by the respondents.

The results of the experiment, which broadly agree with those of other experiments that have been carried out, suggest that respondents do not always correctly appreciate the degree of uncertainty which exists in their knowledge of the quantities which they seek to estimate. As a consequence, the spread of the percentiles is rather too narrowly based.

Overall, respondents learn a great deal from this kind of experiment, and would no doubt improve considerably in further experiments of this kind (with different questions). Many respondents said in conversation afterwards

Table 9.5

Distribution of scores in categories 1 *and* 6

Category 1 and 6 score (1)	Observed no. of respondents with score in column (1) (2)	Expected* no. of respondents with score in column (1) (3)
0	0	1·1
1	10	6·7
2	21	17·8
3	22	26·8
4	18	25·2
5	22	15·3
6	7	5·7
7	0	1·4
Totals	100	100·0

* With $n=8$ and $p=0·43$.

that they were accustomed in business to think in terms of single estimates only, which we may equate to the 50th percentile. Hence, they really had no feel for assessing their degree of uncertainty and, thus, the probability levels other than evens. Yet it was generally agreed that this was largely a matter of training and experience.

9.9 Conclusions

The basic proposition in this book has been to suggest the use of weighted pay-offs as our method of choice between alternative decisions, where the weights are obtained from numbers representing the likelihood of the various outcomes. These numbers crystallize the decision-maker's past and current information, experience, judgment and intuition concerning the particular event involved. It is sometimes argued that results obtained through these numbers are valueless, because they require the decision-maker to attach numbers to the uncertain outcomes (even supposing he can fully enumerate them) and to the consequences. These numbers are, it is argued, so difficult to obtain as to make it hardly worth doing the subsequent calculations on the basis of so much vagueness. One eminent industrialist when asked to assess some probabilities as the basis for such an analysis stated: 'You give me the facts, I do the doubting.'

But what we are really trying to achieve throughout this kind of approach is consistency, so that the various decision problems faced by a decision-maker will hang together and make a coherent whole. In particular, a complex decision situation is effectively broken down into a number of smaller decision problems: once the small problems have been solved, consistency will enable these portions to be assembled together to provide a solution to the larger problem. We are not giving the decision behaviour of an idealized, rational and economic man. Rather we are concerned with an approach that will enable the ordinary person to reason and act more systematically and consistently than would otherwise be the case.

Experiments show that there are difficulties when individuals attempt to assess their degree of uncertainty in making estimates, but that these difficulties are probably linked to the habits of thought engendered by continually making point or single estimates rather than percentiles of a relevant probability distribution. Assessors when trained to think in terms of a probability distribution find, after a time, that the concept is a useful and relevant one in that it enables a consistent and uniform approach to uncertainty to be made.

REFERENCES

(These references provide further reading on the assessment of prior probability distributions)

Winkler, R. L. 1967. The assessment of prior distributions in Bayesian analysis. *Jl. Am. stat. Ass.*, pp. 1105–20.

Schlaifer, R. 1969. *Analysis of Decisions under Uncertainty*. McGraw-Hill, London, pp. 280–317.

Winkler, R. L. and Murphy, A. H. 1968. Good probability assessors. *Jl. appl. Met.*, pp. 751–8.

Shuford, E. H. *et al.* 1966. Admissible probability measurement procedures. *Psychometrika*, pp. 125–45.

Grayson, C. J. (Jr.). 1960. *Decisions under Uncertainty: Drilling Decisions by Oil and Gas Operators*. Boston, Division of Research, Harvard Business School.

Eisenberg, E. and Gale, D. 1959. Consensus of subjective probabilities. *Ann. math. Statist.*, pp. 165–8.

QUESTIONNAIRE FOR ASSESSMENTS OF PROBABILITIES

The purpose of this exercise is to see how well you, as an individual, and the group as a whole, can assess probability distributions for uncertain quantities. We list below eight items and you will be asked to assess the median, the lower and upper quartiles, and the first and ninety-ninth percentiles for each item. Because of the type of items used, we will be able subsequently to compare your assessments with the true values, and be able to see if you tend to be 'too tight', 'too loose', or biased upwards or downwards on certain types of questions.

Part A asks you to give your own answer to three questions. In Part B you are confronted with certain unknown (to you) quantities. Answer each question as best you can with your present knowledge.

Part A

(1) Do you take sugar with coffee?
(2) Do you currently favour Britain's entry into the Common Market?
(3) Would you personally accept a 50 : 50 gamble where you could lose £20 or win £40?

Part B

Estimate the percentiles shown on the answer sheet for the following quantities:

(1) The percentage of students (excluding those who never drink coffee) who take sugar with coffee.

(2) The percentage of students who favour entry into the Common Market.
(3) The percentage of students who would accept a 50 : 50 gamble to lose £20 or win £40.
(4) The distance (directly in miles) from London to Karachi.
(5) The size (in £ million nominal) of the British National Debt.
(6) The population of Brazil (in millions).
(7) The number of full-time students in British universities in the current academic year (in thousands).
(8) The number of qualified doctors on the Medical Register in Great Britain (in thousands).

ANSWER SHEET

Part A　Please check one response for each question.

(1) Coffee	Yes	No	Never drink coffee
(2) Common Market	Favour		Oppose
(3) Gamble	Accept		Refuse

(For questions 2 and 3, the answer 'Don't know' is not acceptable)

Part B　Please assess all five percentiles for the eight questions. The highest number on each line will be on the right. Decimals are acceptable, but note the units given. Where a percentage is required, write 27·5 for 27·5%, not 0·275, etc.

Percentile

	(1)	(25)	(50)	(75)	(99)
(1) Coffee					
(2) Common Market					
(3) Gamble					
(4) Distance					
(5) Debt					
(6) Population					
(7) Students					
(8) Doctors					

Exercises on Chapter 9

1 You have acquired a good deal of experience in sales forecasting, and you forecast that one of your company's new products will sell 4000 units next year. Your superior asks what you can say about the degree of uncertainty in your forecast. To answer this you examine your forecast performance in the past and feel that:

(*i*) In the long run sales would turn out to be greater than your forecast about as often as they would turn out to be less.

(*ii*) On about half of all occasions, sales would be between 20 per cent below and 30 per cent above forecast, and that when they did fall outside this range, they would be equally likely to fall above it as below it.

(*iii*) On only about one occasion in 100 would sales be less than half your forecast, and only about one occasion in 100 would they be more than twice your forecast.

Construct a suitable form of distribution to demonstrate to your superior the degree of uncertainty inherent in your forecast.

2 Assess prior probability distributions in cumulative density form for the following:

(*i*) The price of ICI ordinary shares six months hence.

(*ii*) The percentage change in the cost of living index over the next twelve months.

(*iii*) The consumption of electricity in your household over the next twelve months.

(*iv*) The number of new car registrations in Great Britain over the next twelve months.

(*v*) The number of months to the next General Election.

3 Compare the prior distributions you obtain in Question 2 with those obtained by two or three colleagues, and reach a group agreement as to a single prior distribution for each item. Is there any pattern of relationship between the combined prior distributions and the individual distributions from which they were formed?

10 The economics of binomial sampling

10.1 Introduction

In Chapter 5, Section 5.6, we introduced the idea of opportunity losses. It was demonstrated there that expected opportunity loss (EOL) and expected monetary value (EMV) both led to the same decision being made when deciding between a set of alternative courses of action. However, there are certain conceptual advantages in using EOL in place of EMV, when we are dealing with questions relating to the amount of sample information that it is worth purchasing prior to making a decision between alternative actions.

As a help in developing the argument we now introduce two new terms. The first is the expected value of perfect information (EVPI). This is equal, in cases of decision-making under uncertainty, to the EOL of the optimal action with the information currently available to the decision-maker. EVPI is thus equal to the cost of uncertainty in a decision-making situation. The magnitude of the EVPI thereby places an upper limit on the amount we would be willing to spend to gain additional information before making our initial decision. It does not, in itself, enable us to decide whether it is worth obtaining less than perfect information, and samples always provide less than perfect information. We can state with assurance, however, that if the sampling necessary to obtain the relevant information is more costly than the EVPI, then the sampling should not be undertaken. If, however, the cost of sampling is less than the EVPI, we need to carry out further investigations before we can evaluate the relative desirability of obtaining further sample information before a decision is made as opposed to making an immediate decision without obtaining further information.

228

To evaluate the desirability of obtaining sample information before a decision is made, we need to introduce a second concept, namely the expected value of the sample information (EVSI). For any given size of sample we define:

EVSI = EVPI (for use of best decision rule without sample information) −

   − EOL (for use of best decision rule with sample information).

Hence the EVSI may be regarded as the reduction in the cost of uncertainty brought about by the use of sampling procedures to obtain information. These two definitions will now be illustrated by an example.

Example 10.1

This example uses the same data as Example 5.5, page 108, which concerned a firm that was considering the addition of a new product to its range. There were two possible initial actions (ignoring the possibility of sampling for the moment), namely, 'Develop' or 'Don't develop'. The expected opportunity losses were as follows:

Develop   Expected opportunity loss   6 000

Don't develop   Expected opportunity loss   14 000

Hence the optimal action was to develop the new product, since this action had the lower expected opportunity loss. By definition, we can now state that the expected value of perfect information is equal to the expected opportunity loss of the optimal decision, or EVPI = 6000. In the extension of the discussion of the Example 5.5 the use of a random sample of twenty individual accounts to obtain further information was considered. It was shown that the optimal decision rule, using the sample information, was to carry out development if one or more of the sample accounts gave a favourable response, but otherwise not to develop. Furthermore, it was shown that the expected opportunity loss if this rule were followed is equal to 5281. Hence, we have

EVSI = EVPI (for use of best decision rule without sample) −

   − EOL (for use of best decision rule with sample)

   = 6000 − 5281 = 719.

Of course, this sample information value has taken no account of the cost of obtaining the sample itself. Suppose this cost was made up of two elements, a fixed cost of setting up the sampling procedure equal to 500 and a variable cost of 40 per sample unit investigated. Then the cost of sampling in this instance, with a sample size n of 20, would be 1300 and since this cost is greater than the EVSI of 719, the sample should not be taken.

   Note that the above discussion does not by itself indicate that every possible sample size is uneconomic, merely that the cost of a sample of 20 exceeds its expected value. Other sample sizes may yield expected values that are in excess of their cost, and this possibility is explored later.

It is typically true that as the sample size increases the expected monetary value of the information provided, which naturally increases, does so with decreasing marginal value. For example, the incremental value to be expected from increasing the sample size from 20 to 25 will be greater than that resulting from increasing it from 25 to 30. Consequently, there will come a time when the marginal increase is not worth the additional cost of sampling. The situation is shown schematically in Fig. 10.1, where the straight unbroken

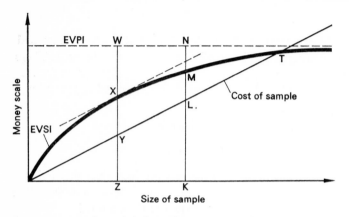

Fig. 10.1. Value of sample information

line shows a typical relationship between the size of sample and its cost, assuming that each item costs the same amount to inspect. The curved line shows the usual form for the expected value of the sample information (EVSI), such that it increases with sample size, but its rate of increase diminishes. The dotted horizontal line represents the expected value of perfect information (EVPI) or the EOL for the best decision without sample information. For a given sample size denoted by K, the distance KN represents EVPI, the distance LK the cost of the sample, the distance NM the expected opportunity loss for the best decision rule using the sample. ML+LK, or MK, then represents the value of EVSI and, finally, the distance ML represents the expected net gain from sampling, since it is EVSI minus the cost of sampling.

Let us denote the expected net gain from sampling represented by the distance ML, by the abbreviation ENGS. Then, the value of ENGS rises to a maximum and falls away to zero, eventually becoming negative. Its optimum or maximum value occurs when the tangent to the EVSI curve is parallel to the 'cost of sample' line. This is shown at point X, and Z therefore represents the optimum sample size in that the distance between the curve and the straight line is at a maximum. Beyond X, the increase in information value as shown by the curved line is not enough to overcome the extra cost of the sample as shown by the straight line. Hence, the ENGS starts to decrease and eventually, at point T, becomes zero.

The reader is left to consider for himself the situation where the cost of the sample is in two parts, a fixed cost and a variable cost per unit sampled. Here it will be found that ENGS is first of all negative and, then, depending on the precise situation, it may become positive rising to a maximum and then fall away to zero and turn negative once again for very large sample sizes. Of course, the sampling costs may be so high that, in the circumstances, ENGS never becomes positive at all. The various alternatives are discussed further in Section 11.9.

In the remainder of this chapter we will first study the effect of varying the decision rule for a given size, or quantum, of sample information, in terms of the conditional expected opportunity losses. This is done in Sections 10.2 and 10.3. Then, in the later sections, we will take up again the use of expected opportunity loss (or the Bayes' decision rule) and examine the effects of varying the sample size. The discussion in this chapter is confined to the binomial sampling situation, namely, where items of sample information either do or do not possess a certain characteristic, such as 'a purchaser' or 'not a purchaser'. The case of continuous measurable characteristics, such as the length of life of an electric light bulb, will be discussed in Chapter 11.

10.2 Opportunity losses and sample decision rule

We again use as our vehicle of discussion Example 5.5 which involved the development of a new product. The opportunity loss table formulated at that time is reproduced as Table 10.1.

Table 10.1

Opportunity loss table

Proportion of buyers	Decision	
	Develop	Don't Develop
$p < 0.05$	$1\,000\,000\,(0.05 - p)$	0
$p > 0.05$	0	$1\,000\,000\,(p - 0.05)$

The two possible decisions both have the same outcome when $p = 0.05$, but the opportunity losses rise steeply on either side of $p = 0.05$ if a wrong decision is made, as shown in Fig. 10.2. The value of p must be between zero and unity and, hence, the maximum possible opportunity loss under the

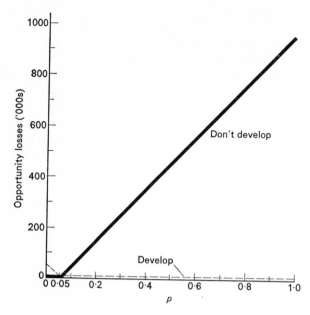

Fig. 10.2. Opportunity losses

decision 'develop' is 50 000, which occurs when p is equal to zero. If the decision made is 'don't develop', then the maximum possible loss is 950 000 which occurs when $p=1$. A choice between the decisions can be made at this stage, but an EMV approach would require some specification if a prior probability distribution for p, the proportion of buyers.

This analysis assumes so far that we have obtained no extra information by sampling the customers before making the decision. If we did decide to sample, a judgment could be made, on the basis of the sample results, as to whether it is likely that the batch has a proportion of defectives below, or above, the initial breakeven level of 0·05, Of course, we would, in the final analysis, have to take account of the costs involved in the sampling when formulating the amount of sampling we would be prepared to do but, once a sample has been obtained, that is a sunk cost and we must consider how best to use the sample information.

Suppose that a sample of size 20 has been randomly selected and we decide to develop the new product if more than c of the sample customers are stated to be definite buyers. Let the symbol $P(20, c|p)$ represent the probability that, when the population has a proportion p of potential buyers, the random sample contains c or fewer who will buy. Then $P(20, c|p)$ also represents the probability that we would decide not to develop the product when the population concerned has a proportion p of buyers.

Consider the case when p is less than the breakeven value of 0·05. Then the probability that we will decide to develop is $1-P(20, c|p)$ and the opportunity loss concerned is 1 000 000 $(0·05-p)$. Hence, the conditional expected opportunity loss incurred by following the sampling procedure is the product of these two quantities and is a function of p equal to

$$[1-P(20, c|p)] \times 1\ 000\ 000\ (0·05-p). \tag{10.1}$$

If p is greater than 0·05, the probability of making the wrong decision (i.e. not to develop) is $P(20, c|p)$ and the corresponding opportunity loss is 1 000 000 $(p-0·05)$. Hence, the conditional expected opportunity loss incurred by following the sampling procedure will be:

$$P(20, c|p) \times 1\ 000\ 000\ (p-0·05). \tag{10.2}$$

The two equations 10.1 and 10.2 give the conditional expected opportunity losses (CEOL) incurred by following the rule for any required value of p, and can be numerically evaluated using binomial tables such as those given in Appendix A. Notice that, in this instance, the word 'conditional' is included in the description, since the expected opportunity losses given are conditional on p and are only defined as a function of p, the proportion of buyers in the whole population.

Figure 10.3 shows the value of this conditional expected opportunity loss from Eqs. 10.1 and 10.2 plotted against p for three possible decision rules

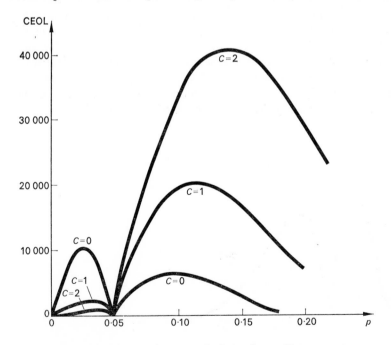

Fig. 10.3. Conditional expected opportunity losses for $n=20$

that have $c=0$, $c=1$ and $c=2$ respectively. For each rule, there are two distinct portions of the curves. The lefthand portion rises to a maximum, falls again, and vanishes when $p=0.05$; the righthand portion then rises to a fresh maximum which may be either higher or lower than the lefthand maximum. A quick study of the curves shows that it is not possible to pick any one of these three decision rules that is uniformly the best, i.e. one that has the lowest expected opportunity loss of the three rules whatever the value of p. For small values of p, under 0.05, the rule with $c=2$ seems best (of the three examined here), while for values of p above 0.05 the rule with $c=0$ seems to be best. If decision rules with c greater than 2 are considered, it is reasonable to conjecture that a marginal improvement in the minimum expected loss would be obtained for values of p below 0.05. However, above $p=0.05$, rules with c greater than 2 would have greater maximum expected losses, and hence the rule with $c=0$ is still to be preferred in that region. It should, of course, be re-emphasized that we have only been considering a sample of size 20.

If other values of n, the sample size, are considered the curves shown in Fig. 10.3 will change. In general terms, we would expect that as n increases the CEOLs will reduce and the value of c that gives the lowest CEOL over all values of p will also change. For example, in Fig. 10.4 are plotted the CEOLs for $n=100$ and $c=4$. The latter was chosen as being the value of c for which the maximum CEOL was the least, and it is interesting to note that the maximum CEOL is approximately 3800 when p is just below 0.04 as against a maximum of around 10 000 for $c=0$ when n was equal to 20. Hence, it could be said at this stage, without any prior probability distribution available for p, that having no sample available the maximum CEOL would be 950 000; with a sample of 20 it can be reduced to about 3800. This approach does not provide us with a satisfactory means to determine a desirable sample size, but it does illustrate straight away the intrinsic value of sample information.

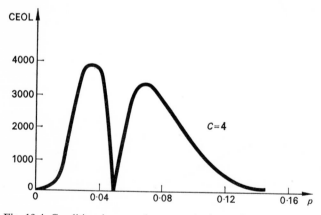

Fig. 10.4. Conditional expected opportunity losses for $n=100$

10.3 Varying sample sizes for Bayes' decision rules

A Bayes' decision rule can be brought into use when we have some prior probability distribution for p which enables us to weight the various alternatives and select that with the lowest expected opportunity loss. When the foregoing problem was discussed in Chapter 5, the weightings of Table 5.7 were such that they lead to the decision to develop the product. Furthermore we showed that, with a sample of 20, the optimal rule was to develop the new product if 1 or more of the sampled clients accepted the product, but that the ENGS, given certain sampling cost data, was -581. Hence, the sample should not be taken and the decision to develop should be taken without sample data.

This result does not automatically imply that no sample at all is worth taking. It could be that some other size is worthwhile. However, the precise size of sample that is most acceptable, which may be zero, is not obvious since the reduction in uncertainty resulting from sampling is, as we have seen, not necessarily proportional to the increase in sample size. Again, the cost of the sample is not necessarily proportional to size, generally having some fixed costs associated with taking any sample at all, and some variable costs more directly related to the size of sample taken. Determination of an optimal sample size can be accomplished only by subtracting the cost of obtaining the sample from the EVSI, thus obtaining the ENGS or expected net gain that is achieved with various sample sizes. Making this procedure even more cumbersome is the need for the EVSI calculation for each sample size to be based on the use of an optimal decision criterion, or c value, and this latter value will often change with sample size. Notice, therefore, that the determination of the optimal sample size in a practical situation is strictly a trial-and-error procedure, involving a number of calculations such as those shown earlier in Tables 5.10 and 5.12. We would need to determine the optimal decision criterion for each sample size, and then repeat this determination for all possible sample sizes. We can then combine the EVSI resulting from the use of various (n, c) combinations with the costs of obtaining the sample of n to obtain the ENGS, and hence determine the optimum size of sample that should be drawn.

This apparently laborious procedure is, however, not as tedious as it might seem at first sight. The optimum decision criterion as indicated by $\tilde{c}$ will change only occasionally, and in a systematic manner, as the sample size increases. For example, suppose it is found that $\tilde{c}=0$ represents the optimum criterion for some particular size of sample, as it does for $n=20$ in this example. Then for the next larger size sample ($n=21$ in this example), the optimal value of $\tilde{c}$ will either be 0 or 1. If this were not so, it would imply that the extra one unit in the sample could change the way in which the information from the original sample could best be used. It can also be demonstrated mathematically that if the EOL using the decision rule

($n=21$, $c=0$) is less than the EOL for the decision rule ($n=20$, $c=0$), then $\tilde{c}=0$ provides the optimum rule for $n=21$. If, alternatively, the EOL for the rule ($n=21$, $c=0$) is greater, then the optimum decision rule is given by ($n=21$, $c=1$). Thus, usually only one computation of an EOL for a given (n, c) combination need be made, and never more than two. Even if some sample sizes are omitted, the number of computations required can be strictly limited by proceeding in a systematic common sense manner along the lines just described.

At a practical level, it is not necessary to consider every possible sample size. Some very large values for the sample size n may be immediately ruled out, because the cost of obtaining such a sample would exceed the EVPI (the expected value of perfect information) for the particular decision problem concerned. This follows since sampling information of any sort must necessarily be less than perfect and there would clearly be no point in considering these sample sizes further. A rough idea of the optimum sample size may also be obtained by considering only a series of 'round' sample sizes and omitting from considering the possibilities that fall in between. For example, we could consider the values 20, 50, 100, 200, ... etc. As a first trial the optimum value of c will be approximately equal to np, where p is the breakeven proportion. Furthermore, it is generally true that the total cost curve (i.e. the sum of actual sampling costs and the remaining cost of uncertainty after sampling) will be rather flat in the region of the optimum sample size. Hence, even if we do not arrive at the true optimum size, a nearby value will lead to a total cost that is only marginally different from the optimum cost.

10.4 Net gain from sampling

We will now examine further the problem discussed in Example 5.5, and again in 10.1, and consider whether it would be economically desirable to purchase additional information before making a decision as to whether to develop or not. If it is, we need to establish how much information should be purchased. We saw in Section 10.1 that the use of a decision rule based on a sample of $n=20$ with $c=0$ was not desirable, since the EVSI of 719 was exceeded by the cost of obtaining the sample, namely, 1300. The latter cost was made up of a fixed cost of 500 and a variable cost of 40 per unit sampled. Now, using the method outlined earlier, we can calculate the EVSI, the sample cost and the expected net gain from sampling (ENGS) for other sample sizes. This information can then be used to determine the desirability of purchasing different quantities of information in the product development situation. The results of these calculations for various selected values of the sample size n, are given in Table 10.2. These results show that, for all values of n, the expected net gain from sampling, given in column 5, is negative.

Table 10.2

Net gain from sampling for various sample sizes

(1) Sample size n	(2) Optimum criterion number, $\tilde{c}$	(3) EVSI $600-$EOL for $(n, \tilde{c})$	(4) Sample costs $500+40n$	(5) Expected net gain from sampling (ENGS) (3)$-$(4)
10	—	0	900	-900
20	0	719	1300	-581
30	0	1345	1700	-355
40	1	1791	2100	-309
50	1	2174	2500	-316
100	4	3244	4500	-1256

The dash against a sample size of 10 indicates that no beneficial use can be made of the sample information in this situation, and that it is better to proceed as if the sample had not been drawn. In this instance, it would imply that we should develop the product. This result is independent of the sample cost so that, even if a sample of 10 were offered free of charge, the implication is that it would still be as good to make the decision without any consideration of the results obtained from the sample.

The costs of sampling are such that the net gain from sampling, shown in column 5, is always negative for all the sample sizes considered, even though the expected value of the sample information steadily rises in column 3 as the sample size increases. Hence, no size of sample is apparently worth purchasing, and we would do best to make the decision without any sample at all.

This result does, of course, depend in part upon the particular costs of sampling that are assumed. If the costs are changed, we may find a different

Table 10.3

Modified net gains from sampling

(1) Sample size, n	(4$'$) Sample costs $100+40n$	(5$'$) Expected net gain (3)*$-$(4$'$)
10	500	-500
20	900	-181
30	1300	$+45$
40	1700	$+91$
50	2100	$+74$
100	4100	-856

* Column 3 is taken from Table 10.2.

outcome even though all the other factors in the problem remain unchanged. Suppose, for illustration, that sampling involved a fixed cost of 100 and a variable cost of 40 per unit, in place of the previous 500 and 40 respectively. Then the relevant columns of Table 10.2 could be revised, still using the same optimum values of $\tilde{c}$, to give Table 10.3. There is now a non-zero optimum size of sample, which turns out to be around 40. Since the net gain is clearly only changing very slowly with sample size at around this point, there would be little danger in assuming that a sample size of 40 is the optimum.

10.5 General comments

We must emphasize again the earlier point made that the sampling gains that are shown in the foregoing analysis are all expected gains. As with all expected values, we have no assurance that this particular gain will be precisely realized, or even that the sampling procedure will automatically save us from a wrong decision in a particular situation. Remember, too, that the expected gains are based on possible opportunity losses that would flow from wrong decisions. These opportunity losses have no necessary relationship with accounting profits. Suppose that the optimum sized sample of 40 found in the previous section was taken, and the information thereby obtained led to the decision not to develop the product. We would then have nothing to show for our efforts in an accounting sense, except for an expense of 1700 due to the cost of the sample. The accounts will not, however, show that the 1700 investment may have saved the firm from a substantial loss. Furthermore, this does not imply that it always pays to sample, as the cost is only justified if the expected net gain is positive. Hence, with a consistent policy of always acting in this way the overall expected net gain will, in an accounting sense, provide a positive yield.

In this chapter and the next we assume that the sampling methods adopted are such that every item in the population concerned has the same chance of appearing in the sample. Sampling methods are discussed more generally in Chapter 14 in conjunction with the so-called classical approach to statistics.

The analysis in this chapter has been limited in two ways. First, the decision-maker's prior probability was taken to be discrete and only a few values of p were admissible. This is not necessarily a serious restriction in that, even if the true prior distribution is continuous, it is usually the case that a reasonable approximation could be made by a discrete distribution. Second, we have assumed that the sampling is of a binomial form, implying that each unit of information sampled either does or does not possess some stated property. In the next chapter we extend the economic analysis of sampling alternatives to the case where the information is measurable on a continuous scale with the restriction that the prior and sampling distributions are both assumed to be of the normal form.

Exercises on Chapter 10

(Some of these exercises, particularly the later ones, require a considerable amount of calculation and access to some form of computing equipment would be of considerable help.)

1 A large chain of supermarkets requires 15 000 fluorescent light bulbs for its stores, and the manager is looking for a source of supply. A supplier offers bulbs on two possible price tariffs. Tariff A offers the bulbs at a price of 80p per bulb, replacing any defective bulbs with guaranteed good bulbs at 80p each. Tariff B offers the bulbs at £1 per bulb, with a guarantee to replace all defective bulbs with bulbs drawn from the same source of supply free of charge. Assume that the proportion of defective bulbs in any batch purchased from the supplier is unknown.

(*i*) What defective rate would make the management indifferent as to the tariff it selects?

(*ii*) From past experience with fluorescent bulbs, the prior distribution of the proportion of defective bulbs in a batch is assessed as:

Proportion defective	0·15	0·20	0·25	0·30	0·35
Prior probability	0·1	0·2	0·3	0·3	0·1

Under which tariff should the manager purchase?

(*iii*) What is the expected value of perfect information (EVPI)?

(*iv*) The management is offered a random sample of 20 bulbs from the batch that the supplier is offering without cost. These 20 bulbs could be tested free of charge on a special machine to determine if they are defective. What is the expected value of the sample information (EVSI)?

(*v*) What is the maximum amount the supermarket would be willing to pay for testing the bulbs?

2 A publisher is considering the launching of a new specialized magazine. He estimates, on the basis of the best information available to him currently, that there is a 50 : 50 chance that the sales will be at the rate of 10 000 or alternatively 20 000 per month, all of which will come from a large club with 200 000 members. If the former sales rate emerges, his discounted pay-off from the launch is a loss of £15 000, while if the latter sales rate emerges, there is a profit of £40 000.

(*i*) Solely on the basis of this information, and using EMV as his criterion, should the publisher decide to launch?

(*ii*) A market research agency offers to carry out a test marketing operation for the publisher. This test marketing could be done at either of two levels, A or B. Level A involves a random sample of 250 members and costs £2000 to carry out. Alternatively, level B would look at a random sample of 500 members and cost £3000 to carry out. These costs include the setting up of a dummy magazine issue, etc., and could be assumed to to determine accurately whether or not each member of the club sampled will subscribe to the magazine should it be launched. Determine which, if either, of these two offers are worth considering by the publishing company.

3 A manufacturing process produces lots of 500 units each. Either 10 per cent or 30 per cent of the 500 items are defective in each lot manufactured. (This is a simplifying assumption for ease of analysis.) The quality control department inspects each lot before shipment. If accepted for sending out to a customer the lot generates a profit of £500 but, if rejected, the lot has to be sold for scrap at cost. If a 30 per cent defective lot is sent out, confidence in the company is lost and the firm estimates its expected loss in goodwill, and hence future orders, at £1500. In the past, 80 per cent of the lots produced were subsequently found to contain 50 defectives.

It costs £3 to test an item in the quality control department, but the test is non-destructive (i.e. the items can still be sold after testing). What is the best size of sample to take before making a decision and what is the corresponding decision rule? (Use the binomial distribution to compute the conditional probabilities required.)

4 A customer buys an electrical product in large lots, each of 1000 items. If a lot is accepted it costs 20p to correct each defective item subsequently found in the lot. However, rather than find the defectives as the items are used, an inspector could look through the entire lot on receipt and rectify all items found to be incorrect. To employ an inspector in this way costs £8 per lot, and experience shows that his activities will reduce the proportion of defectives in the lot to 0·01, but not any further. Note that he does not reject items in the sense of discarding them, but rectifies them so that they become satisfactory.

An examination of past records suggests that a reasonable assumption for the prior probability distribution of the proportion defective in the batch is given by:

Proportion defective	0·01	0·03	0·05	0·07	0·09	0·11	0·13	0·15
Prior probability		0·50	0·25	0·12	0·06	0·03	0·02	0·01	0·01

It would also be possible to sample and inspect items from the lot, before a decision is made as to whether or not to call in the inspector to examine the whole lot. This sampling and inspection costs 5p per item examined.

Determine whether or not sampling should be undertaken before making the decision on calling in the inspector. If sampling is recommended, what is the optimum size of the sample? (Assume that the lot is large enough to use the binomial distribution to determine the probabilities required.)

5 A large manufacturer of electronic office equipment is running a continuing programme of instruction to upgrade its 500 engineers who service the equipment owned or rented by customers. In the past the manufacturer has sent all qualified engineers to a special course that lasts 12 weeks and costs £500 per student. It is now proposed to send all engineers on a very intensive special one-week course that costs £50 per student. Those engineers who pass this course will be sent to a supplementary course at a cost of £300 per engineer, while those who fail will be enrolled in the regular £500 per engineer course. If the proportion of engineers who pass the intensive course is large enough, the manufacturer will save money, whereas if the proportion who pass is small, he will lose money.

Based on the manufacturer's training manager's previous experience of training his engineers, he places the following probability distribution on the proportion of engineers who will pass the intensive one-week course.

Proportion who will pass	0·15	0·20	0·25	0·30	0·35
Prior probability	0·2	0·3	0·2	0·2	0·1

(*i*) If the manufacturer has to make an immediate decision without running a pilot trial one-week scheme, should the special course be instituted or not?

(*ii*) Because of some uncertainty with respect to the prior distribution of the proportion who would pass the one-week course, the manufacturer decides to check on the validity of its decision by taking a random sample of engineers and putting them through the one-week special course to see how many will pass. Determine the optimum size of the sample and the decision rule to follow with respect to the sample information thereby obtained. Does it pay to carry out a sample investigation and why? (Assume initially that taking a sample does not deplete the population of engineers who have to be instructed.)

6 Elcon Limited purchases a machine part in lots of 4000 for use in electronic controllers that it produces. Most of the time only about 1 per cent of the purchased parts fail to meet specifications, but occasionally a bad shipment is received that may contain about 15 per cent defective parts. From the records available it appears that about 10 per cent of the shipments have been bad, as defined here.

Currently, incoming shipments are 100 per cent inspected for defectives at a cost of £100 per lot. Any defectives there may be in the lot are found in this way and returned to the manufacturer who replaces them free of charge. If the parts are not inspected, any defectives would eventually be discovered in the assembly process. To remove and replace them at this point involves a cost of £1·5 per defective part.

Elcon is considering the establishment of a sampling procedure to replace the 100 per cent inspection option. To set up the sampling procedure each time a lot is received would cost £17·5 and inspection of a random sample could then be accomplished at a cost of 5p per part included. Full (100 per cent) inspection of the remaining parts would still cost about £100 after sampling, if it were carried out.

Should the sampling procedure be instituted? If so, how large a sample should be taken, and what decision criterion should be used in conjunction with the sample?

11 The economics of normal sampling

11.1 Introduction

The previous chapter discussed the problem of whether or not to purchase additional information, through a sample, before making a decision. The analysis given there enabled us to compute the expected value of sample information (EVSI) for various sizes of samples. These values could then be compared with the cost of the various sizes of sample to determine the economic desirability of each sample size in a decision problem. The sample data available were of the form where each unit sampled either did, or did not, possess some defined characteristic. The purpose of this chapter is to take somewhat further the economic analysis of sampling alternatives in the normal case. The characteristic concerned is now assumed to be measurable on a continuous scale whilst both the prior and sampling distributions are assumed to be assessable in terms of a normal distribution.

As a first step in assessing the value of sample information, we examine the method for computing the value of perfect information (EVPI) where the probability distribution of the random variable is normal. It should be remembered that the EVPI in a decision problem is equal to the cost of uncertainty which is, in turn, defined as the expected opportunity loss (EOL) corresponding to the optimal action. To illustrate the procedure, a problem concerning the activities of a mining company will be described and examined in some detail.

11.2 Mining company problem

A mining company is investigating the desirability of buying and developing an ore body. The ore body is estimated to contain 5 million tons of ore. It will cost £1 million to purchase and develop the site, including the erection of a processing plant on the site. The variable cost of mining and processing is £25 per ton of ore. The selling price of the metal to be recovered is 12p per pound. The value of the site is clearly dependent upon the grade of the ore recovered, as defined by the percentage of the metal in the ore. All ore is recoverable and there are no other by-products of value.

There is, not unusually, some uncertainty as to the precise yield of metal that can be expected from the ore. On the basis of past experience and preliminary site evaluation, the manager estimates that the *average* grade of the ore body as a whole is 12 (per cent). If this is true, the total financial yield (£ million) will be:

$$0.12 \times 5 \times 0.12 \times 2240 - 25 \times 5 - 1 = 35.28.$$

Since this quantity is positive, it suggests that the purchase should be profitable. (Discounting of sums paid out, or yields, are ignored for purposes of illustration, but do not affect the principles on which the analysis is based.)

The managing director of the company asks his own management services department to study the various estimates and costs. While the analyst agrees, after an examination of the cost evidence, that these figures are acceptable, he points out that the 12 per cent grade or yield represents a reasonable 'best guess' and there is the possibility of considerable dispersion in the actual average yield achieved. Hence, he feels that there must be some uncertainty in the total net yield that can be achieved. There is, he points out, some chance that the yield might be negative. Pressed to provide some quantification of his views, he estimates after detailed discussions with the various experts concerned, that while the expected average grade of the ore is 12 per cent, there is an even chance that the actual average grade will fall outside the range of 12 ± 1 per cent.

With the background information now available, we can calculate the breakeven point for the grade of the ore. Suppose the grade is denoted by μ (per cent), while μ_b denotes the particular value of μ that is the breakeven point. Now the total fixed and variable costs of developing the ore body is

$$10^6 (1 + 5 \times 25) = 126 \times 10^6,$$

whilst the total revenue is

$$5 \times 10^6 \times 12 \times \mu \times 10^{-4} \times 2240 = 13.44\mu \times 10^6.$$

Hence, the breakeven percentage grade of the ore is given by:

$$13.44\mu_b \times 10^6 = 126 \times 10^6$$

or $\mu_b = 9.38$

Thus, should the true value of μ turn out to be greater than 9.38, the purchase of the ore body will be worth while. However, if μ is less than 9.38, a decision to purchase would in retrospect prove to have been a wrong decision and the firm would incur a loss.

The opportunity losses can now be evaluated. If μ is greater than μ_b, the optimal decision is to purchase, and the opportunity loss from not purchasing is $(13{\cdot}44\mu - 126) \times 10^6$. Similarly, if μ is less than μ_b, the optimal decision is not to purchase, and the opportunity loss from purchasing is $(126 - 13{\cdot}44\mu) \times 10^6$. These opportunity losses are summarized by the figures shown in Table 11.1. Note the symmetrical nature of the losses concerned,

Table 11.1

Opportunity losses

True value of μ	Correct decision	Incorrect decision	Opportunity loss of incorrect decision
$\mu \geq \mu_b$	Purchase	Do not purchase	$(13{\cdot}44\mu - 126) \times 10^6$
$\mu < \mu_b$	Do not purchase	Purchase	$(126 - 13{\cdot}44\mu) \times 10^6$

which indicates that errors in estimating μ are just as serious in one direction about μ_b as in the other. The values for the decision to purchase are illustrated in Fig. 11.1.

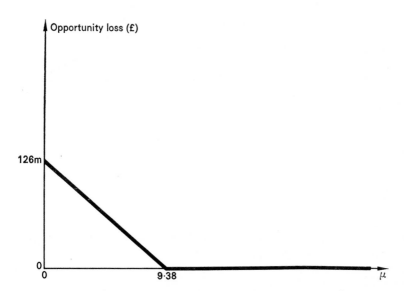

Fig. 11.1. Opportunity losses for decision to purchase

I

The procedure that has been used previously to evaluate the EOLs is to multiply the opportunity loss (conditional on each value of the random variable) by the probability that each value of the random variable occurs. These products are then summed over all possible values of the random variable to obtain the EOL for the decision concerned. We have the difficulty, in the present instance, that the random variable concerned is effectively continuous, being the average grade of the whole ore body. If we accept that it is reasonable to summarize the prior information we have in this situation in the form of a normal prior probability distribution, we have two relevant pieces of information to help us fix this normal distribution. First, the mean of the distribution, μ_0 say, should clearly be taken as 12. Second, there is an even chance that the average grade will fall outside the range of 12 ± 1 per cent. Figure 11.2 illustrates the situation, from which we note that

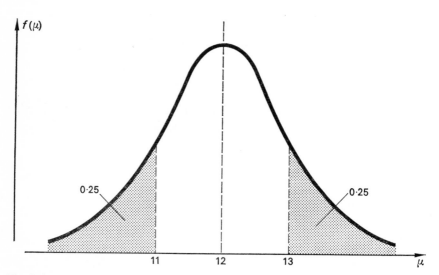

Fig. 11.2. The prior density function

$$P(\mu > 13) = 0 \cdot 25$$

or

$$F_N \left(\frac{13 - 12}{\sigma_0} \right) = 0 \cdot 25 = F_N(0 \cdot 675)$$

from inspection of the table given in Appendix B, where σ_0 is the standard deviation of the prior distribution. Hence

$$\frac{1}{\sigma_0} = 0 \cdot 675 \quad \text{or} \quad \sigma_0 = 1 \cdot 48 \text{ (per cent)}.$$

11.3 Computation of EOL

One method of computing the EOL in a straightforward, but tedious manner, would be to break up the continuous form of the normal distribution for μ into a number of discrete blocks or intervals. This is analogous to the method used to calculate the means and standard deviations of a grouped frequency distribution using the mid-point of each class interval to represent all the values in the class. Suppose, for example, that the range of values of μ is broken up into 0·25 intervals as shown in Fig. 11.3. Any interval, such as the

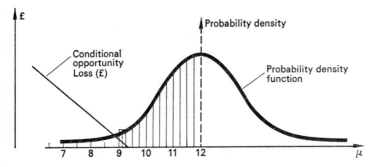

Fig. 11.3. Relationships for expected opportunity loss

shaded range from 9·0 to 9·25, would be represented by its mid-point, in this case 9·125. The conditional opportunity loss (or COL) for $\mu=9·125$ is equal to $(126-13·44\times9·125)\times10^6$ or $3·36\times10^6$. This COL would then be multiplied by the probability of the μ range (9·0 to 9·25) which the point $\mu=9·125$ represents. Probabilities for each interval such as $P(9·0<\mu<9·25)$ can, of course, be obtained from the unit normal distribution tables. Thus, 9·25 corresponds to a unit normal variable of $(9·25-12·0)/1·48=-1·856$ and 9·0 corresponds to $(9·0-12·0)/1·48=-2·025$. The required probability is then $F_N(-1·856)-F_N(-2·025)=0·0104$. The probabilities are multiplied by their respective mid-point COLs to give the contribution to EOL from that particular block. Intervals to the right of $\mu=9·375$, the breakeven point, can be ignored, since the COL term in the product is zero for all $\mu\geqslant9·375$. Likewise, at some point in the left tail of the distribution, the probability term for μ falling within the appropriate range becomes zero for practical purposes, even though the normal distribution theoretically extends to infinity. Thus, the calculations shown in Table 11.2 need only be made for μ values less than 9·375 and greater than, say, 6·75. Columns (1) and (2) give the μ groups and their mid-points. Column (3) gives the COL corresponding to the μ value in (2) and computed from the first line in Table 11.1. Column 4 gives the probability, deduced from the normal distribution tables in the manner

Table 11.2

Approximate computation of EOL for decision to purchase without further information

Interval (μ) (1)	Mid-point (2)	COL (£ million) (3)	Probability (4)	COL (£) × probability (5) = (3) × (4)
9·5–9·75	9·625	0	0·0188	0
9·25–9·5	9·375	0·84	0·0140	11 760
9·0–9·25	9·125	3·36	0·0104	34 944
8·75–9·0	8·875	6·72	0·0073	49 056
8·5–8·75	8·625	10·08	0·0050	50 400
8·25–8·5	8·375	13·44	0·0034	45 696
8·0–8·25	8·125	16·80	0·0022	36 960
7·75–8·0	7·875	20·16	0·0014	28 224
7·5–7·75	7·625	23·52	0·0009	21 168
7·25–7·5	7·375	26·88	0·0005	13 440
7·0–7·25	7·125	30·24	0·0004	12 096
6·75–7·0	6·875	33·60	0·0001	3 360
			Total (EOL)	£307 104

demonstrated above, that μ falls in the interval given in column (1). Column (5) is then the product of (3) × (4), and this column is finally summed to give an overall EOL of 307 104.

Now this EOL figure is known to be an approximation, owing to the breaking up of the continuous variable μ into a number of groups, and cutting off the calculation at $\mu = 6.75$. The degree of approximation is probably very small and the result could be made more accurate by using a narrower interval and extending the calculations below $\mu = 6.75$. This leads to a greater number of groups, and the volume of calculation would thereby be correspondingly increased. Fortunately, mathematics comes to our aid in this situation, and the use of calculus enables us to circumvent the numerical approximation used above and to obtain a precise result rather more easily than the approximation just obtained.

11.4 Normal loss integral

If (*i*) the prior probability distribution is normal, and (*ii*) the opportunity loss function is linear, then the EOL of the optimum act can be calculated by the use of an ancillary table that is described below. First, we describe the background to this table.

Suppose that the average grade of the ore is denoted by μ, and the prior probability distribution for this average is normal with mean μ_0 and standard deviation σ_0. We can write, for convenience, the probability that the average grade falls in the range μ to $\mu + \Delta\mu$ as $f(\mu)\Delta\mu$. Then, the expected opportunity loss conditional on μ is $(\mu - \mu_b)L$ where for $\mu < \mu_b$, L is negative, while for $\mu > \mu_b$, L is positive, and L is the absolute slope of the non-zero portion of the opportunity loss function (i.e. the rate of change of the opportunity loss with μ). Hence the expected opportunity loss, for the decision to purchase, corresponding to the shaded portion in Fig. 11.4 will be

$$(\mu - \mu_b)Lf(\mu)\Delta(\mu) \tag{11.1}$$

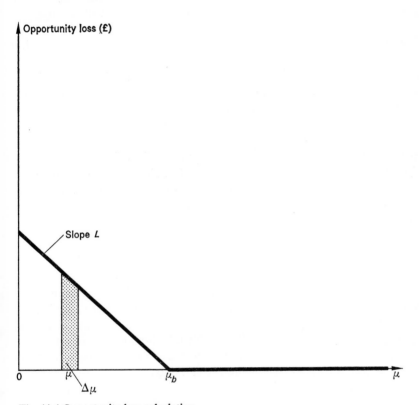

Fig. 11.4 Opportunity loss calculation

For any value of μ greater than μ_b, the corresponding expected opportunity loss will be zero. The total expected opportunity loss (EOL) will, therefore, be the quantity in Eq. 11.1 summed, or rather integrated, over all values of μ from $-\infty$ up to μ_b (the breakeven value of μ). Hence, we have

$$EOL = \int_{-\infty}^{\mu_b} (\mu - \mu_b)Lf(\mu)\,d\mu$$

$$= L\sigma_0 \int_{-\infty}^{\mu_b} \left(\frac{\mu - \mu_b}{\sigma_0}\right) f(\mu)\,d\mu$$

$$= L\sigma_0 N(D_0), \tag{11.2}$$

where

$$N(D_0) = \int_{-\infty}^{\mu_b} \left(\frac{\mu - \mu_b}{\sigma_0} \right) f(\mu)\, d\mu. \qquad (11.3)$$

The expression $N(D_0)$ depends upon the three quantities μ_0, μ_b and σ_0 and is referred to as the *unit normal loss integral*. Remember that $f(\mu)$ refers to a normal distribution with mean μ_0 and standard deviation σ_0. The quantity $N(D_0)$ has been numerically evaluated on a computer and tabulated using

$$D_0 = \frac{|\mu_0 - \mu_b|}{\sigma_0} \qquad (11.4)$$

as the argument. Extracts from one such table are reproduced as Appendix C.

We now illustrate this approach by using the previous problem relating to the purchase of the body of ore. First, we note that:

$$\mu_0 = 12\cdot0, \quad \mu_b = 9\cdot38 \quad \text{and} \quad \sigma_0 = 1\cdot48.$$

Hence $D_0 = |12\cdot0 - 9\cdot38|/1\cdot48 = 1\cdot77$. From Appendix C we find that $N(D_0) = 0\cdot01539$. Next, the value of L (the absolute slope of the COL line) is $13\cdot44 \times 10^6$. This can be seen from the first row in Table 11.1, which gives the opportunity loss as $(13\cdot44\mu - 126) \times 10^6$. Hence, the EOL for the optimum decision to purchase is:

$$L \times \sigma_0 \times N(D_0) = 13\cdot44 \times 10^6 \times 1\cdot48 \times 0\cdot01539$$

$$= 306\ 000.$$

This figure should be compared with the previous approximate figure of 307 104, a small difference of only about 0·3 per cent. The latest figure is to be preferred as being the more accurate. The consequence of either calculation is an indication that not more than about £306 000 should be spent on additional information, and even then the information needs to be such as to enable a decision to be made with complete certainty.

11.5 Reconciliation of definitions

Before we turn to the problem of evaluating less than perfect information, let us recapitulate the various definitions used so far in the analysis carried out for the ore-body purchase problem. In that problem, given the uncertainty regarding the grade of ore in the body, the decision-maker's expected profit (saving), or EMV, in £ million, is:

$$\text{EMV} = (0\cdot12 \text{ grade}) \times (5 \text{ size of ore body}) \times (0\cdot12 \text{ pence per lb}) \times$$

$$\times (2240 \text{ lb per ton}) - (25 \text{ cost per ton}) \times (5 \text{ size of ore body}) -$$

$$- (1 \text{ cost of purchase})$$

$$= 35\cdot28.$$

Now the EVPI (valued in this instance at £306 000) describes the amount of extra profit the decision-maker could expect to realize if he had available to him, free of charge, a perfect forecast of the uncertain random variable in his decision problem. Hence the sum of EMV+EVPI, i.e. the expected gain given uncertainty, plus the extra gain if that uncertainty can be resolved, equals the expected gain under conditions of absolute certainty. In this instance, in £ million:

$$EMV+EVPI = 35 \cdot 28 + 0 \cdot 31$$
$$= 35 \cdot 61$$

This figure, not to be confused with the EVPI by itself, describes the amount of profit that the decision-maker could expect to realize if he had available a perfect forecast of the uncertain random variable (in this instance, average grade of ore) in his decision problem and was therefore always able to make the correct decision. We need next to consider the valuation to be placed on any sample information obtained to assist in making of the decision concerned.

11.6 Expected value of sample information

The value to the decision-maker of a sample is shown by the reduction in the cost of uncertainty that it produces. The calculation of the value of the sample information for the discrete case discussed in Chapter 10 was somewhat tedious. The normal distribution analysis once again has a computational advantage of great simplicity.

So far we have been thinking of σ_0 as the standard deviation of the prior probability distribution for μ. There is, however, another source of variability within the body of ore itself in that the grade would vary from place to place in the body. Suppose we imagine that an infinite series of samples was taken from the ore body and that the standard deviation of the variation of grade between the samples is denoted by σ_w. We assume that we now randomly draw n samples of ore from the body and establish the grade in each of them. The sample information can be summarized by the sample mean grade, $\bar{x}$, which will have a standard deviation of:

$$\sigma_{\bar{x}} = \frac{\sigma_w}{\sqrt{n}}$$

Now, after the sampling has been carried out, the posterior distribution for μ will, from Eq. 7.9a (page 168), again be normal with a mean given by:

$$\mu_R = \frac{\mu_0 \sigma_1^2 + \bar{x} \sigma_0^2}{\sigma_1^2 + \sigma_0^2},$$

where $\sigma_1 = \sigma_w/\sqrt{n}$ in this context, giving:

$$\mu_R = \frac{\mu_0 \sigma_w^2 + n\bar{x}\sigma_0^2}{\sigma_w^2 + n\sigma_0^2}. \tag{11.5a}$$

The standard deviation is given, from Eq. 7.9b, by:

$$\sigma_R = \sqrt{\left(\frac{\sigma_0^2 \sigma_1^2}{\sigma_0^2 + \sigma_1^2}\right)},$$

where $\sigma_1 = \sigma_w / \sqrt{n}$, giving:

$$\sigma_R = \sqrt{\left(\frac{\sigma_0^2 \sigma_w^2}{n\sigma_0^2 + \sigma_w^2}\right)} \tag{11.5b}$$

We can now apply a similar procedure to that used before, for calculating the EVPI of the new information. If

$$D_R = \frac{|\mu_R - \mu_b|}{\sigma_R} \tag{11.6}$$

the expected loss, using the sample information in an optimum manner to decide whether or not to buy, will be given by the expression:

$$L \times \sigma_R \times N(D_R), \tag{11.7}$$

where L and $N(D)$ have the same connotations as before, namely L is the rate of change of opportunity loss with μ and $N(D)$ is the normal loss integral. Then the expected value of sample information, EVSI, is given by:

$$\text{EVSI} = \text{EVPI} - L \times \sigma_R \times N(D_R). \tag{11.8}$$

In order to apply this result to the ore purchase problem, we must first consider the form of sample that is taken. Suppose that the company finds it possible to take 10 random samples from the ore body and to determine the grade of each sample. We assume that the sampling is a truly random sample from the whole body of ore. Next, let us assume that the company's previous experience suggests that the standard deviation between grades found in such test areas would be about 3 per cent. Hence, we can put σ_w equal to 3. Furthermore, we assume for the moment, that the sample mean grade turns out to be 12·0, the same as the mean of the prior distribution. The posterior mean, μ_R, is then 12·0 as well. Then we have:

$$\sigma_1 = \frac{\sigma_w}{\sqrt{n}} = \frac{3}{\sqrt{10}} = 0.95$$

$$\sigma_R = \sqrt{\left(\frac{1.48^2 \times 0.95^2}{1.48^2 + 0.95^2}\right)} = 0.800$$

$$D_R = \frac{|\mu_R - \mu_b|}{\sigma_R} = \frac{|12 - 9.38|}{0.800} = 3.27$$

From Appendix C, we get $N(D_R) = 0.0001426$. Hence the expected opportunity loss will now be given by:

$$L \times \sigma_R \times N(D_R) = 13.44 \times 10^6 \times 0.800 \times 0.0001426$$

$$= 1535.$$

The expected value of the sample information is then given by:

$$EVSI = 306\ 000 - 1535$$

$$= 304\ 465.$$

It is noteworthy that the EVSI for a sample of only 10 in this ore purchase problem is as great as 304 465. This is surprisingly high and close to the EVPI of 306 000 found earlier. The question should be asked as to why the value of a modest-sized sample should be so great in this situation. The real key to this effect lies in the numerical result obtained for σ_R, which is the standard deviation of the posterior distribution. The value of σ_R enters in two ways. First, it appears directly in Eq. 11.7, so that the smaller the value of σ_R, the greater will be the value of EVSI. Second, it appears in the denominator of the expression in Eq. 11.6 for D_R, so that the smaller the value of σ_R the larger the value of D_R. However, an examination of Appendix C shows that $N(D)$ is inversely related to D; $N(D)$ decreases as D increases, so that the smaller the value of σ_R, the larger the value of D_R and the smaller the value of $N(D_R)$. Thus reductions in σ_R reduce the value of in Eq. 11.7, and, hence, increase the value of the EVSI.

Next we need to consider how we, as the decision-maker, should set about reducing the value of σ_R, if that is what will give us a high value for the EVSI. A study of Eq. 11.5b rearranged as:

$$\sigma_R = \sigma_0 \sqrt{\left(\frac{\sigma_w^2}{\sigma_w^2 + n\sigma_0^2}\right)} \tag{11.9}$$

reveals three things. First, that, for fixed n and σ_w, we will make the biggest proportionate reduction in σ_R when σ_0 is itself large. This implies that the sample information is of most value when the decision-maker has little prior information. Second, if we fix σ_0 and σ_w, an increase in sample size improves the value of the sample information, which is logical, but the rate of improvement is rather less than proportional to the increase in sample size. Third, a reduction in σ_w, keeping σ_0 and n fixed, reduces the value of σ_R and, hence, improves the expected value of the sample information. These results are all in agreement with intuitive considerations of the sampling process, and should help to make the apparently magical features of the earlier formulae more understandable.

We should note one further point at this stage: D_R (from Eq. 11.6) depends not only on σ_R, but also upon $|\mu_R - \mu_b|$, the absolute difference between the posterior estimate of the mean and the breakeven point. The larger this difference, the larger the value of D_R, and the smaller the value of $N(D_R)$. The EVSI will then be more than would have been the case if the value of D_R had been much smaller and μ_R thus closer to the breakeven value of μ_b. This again agrees with intuition. Sample information is more valuable when it gives a result that is some distance away from the breakeven value.

11.7 Actual versus expected values

We mentioned earlier that the expected value of sample information does not generally turn out to be precisely equal to its actual value when the sample is obtained. The latter depends upon how much it reduces the cost of uncertainty. The EOL of the optimal decision, given the revised information, must be compared with EOL of the optimal decision that would be made on the basis of the prior information alone. This difference, only available to us with the benefit of hindsight, is not necessarily precisely equal to the value the sample is expected to have beforehand. Thus, in the ore purchase problem, the cost of uncertainty (EVPI) based on prior information was 306 000. Now suppose that the 10 ore samples had produced not a mean grade of 12·0 (agreeing precisely with the mean of the prior distribution), but a mean grade of 11·0 and a standard deviation between samples of 2·0. Then the revised cost of uncertainty is $L \times \sigma_r \times N(D_r)$, where the subscript r refers to the sample results actually achieved. Substitution gives the revised cost of uncertainty as:

$$13\cdot44 \times 10^6 \times 2\cdot0 \times N\left(\frac{11\cdot0 - 9\cdot38}{2/\sqrt{10}}\right)$$

$$= 13\cdot44 \times 10^6 \times 2\cdot0 \times 0\cdot00161$$

$$= 43\ 277.$$

Thus the actual reduction in the cost of uncertainty, and hence the value of the sample, once this particular sample was actually taken was 306 000 − 43 277 or 262 723. This compares with the originally estimated value for the EVSI of 304 465. The sample simply turned out, in this instance, in retrospect, to be less valuable than anticipated.

11.8 Optimum sample size

To date, we have analysed the expected benefit of only one sample size, namely, $n = 10$. Although the EVSI was impressively high, this was in part due to our omitting from consideration any question of the cost of obtaining the sample. If we ignore costs completely, it is obvious that the larger the sample, the larger the EVSI. Once we include the inescapable costs of obtaining the sample, it is not obvious where the optimum size of sample will lie. Certainly it is not necessarily at $n = 10$ for the particular example we have examined here. The optimum sample size will be given by that value of n for which the expected net gain from sampling (ENGS) is a maximum, where:

ENGS = EVSI − cost of obtaining sample.　　　　　　　　　　(11.10)

Suppose that, in the ore-purchase problem, the samples from the ore body can be obtained at a cost which consists of two parts. There is an initial outlay of £5000 in order to set up the equipment, etc., at the site, together with a variable cost at the rate of £2000 per test core (sample) that is taken. Thus, the sample cost can be expressed as:

Sample cost $= 5000 + 2000n$.

Table 11.3 lays out a systematic approach for computing the net gain from sampling for various sizes of sample. The various columns in Table 11.3 are self-explanatory and use the same definitions as the earlier calculation for the sample size of 10 by itself. Since $n = 10$ came so close to the EVPI, it is prudent to consider lower sample sizes first, and for this reason the table is worked from $n = 1$ upwards. The final column of Table 11.3 gives the ENGS for each sample size. The various key quantities are illustrated in graphical form in Fig. 11.5.

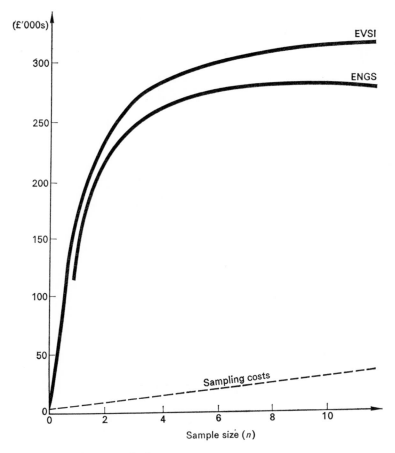

Fig. 11.5. Optimum sample size

Table 11.3

Determination of optimum sample size

Sample size n (1)	$\sigma_1 = \dfrac{3}{\sqrt{n}}$ (2)	σ_R (3)	$D_R = \dfrac{12 \cdot 0 - 9 \cdot 38}{\sigma_R}$ (4)	$N(D_R)$ (5)	$(13 \cdot 44 \times 10^6) \times \sigma_R N(D_R)$ (6)	EVSI = EVPI $-$(6) (7)	Sample cost $5000 + 2000n$ (8)	ENGS (7)$-$(8) (9)
1	3	1·350	1·95	0·009698	175 961	130 039	7 000	123 039
2	2·13	1·215	2·16	0·005472	89 356	216 644	9 000	207 644
3	1·73	1·128	2·33	0·003352	50 700	255 300	11 000	244 300
4	1·50	1·050	2·50	0·002004	28 300	277 700	13 000	264 700
5	1·34	0·995	2·63	0·001330	17 900	288 100	15 000	273 100
6	1·23	0·943	2·78	0·000841	10 100	295 900	17 000	278 900
7	1·14	0·900	2·91	0·000523	6 340	299 660	19 000	280 660
8	1·06	0·862	3·04	0·000332	3 840	302 160	21 000	281 160
9	1·00	0·828	3·16	0·000215	2 390	303 610	23 000	280 610
10	0·95	0·800	3·27	0·000143	1 535	304 465	25 000	279 465

As a result of these calculations, we can see that the optimum sample size actually occurs for $n=8$. Notice, too, that the net gain for sample sizes near the optimum is relatively insensitive to small changes in the sample size. This also implies that the original subjective estimate for σ_0, which had to be made in order to carry out the calculations, could be somewhat in error without any serious effect on the decision as to the quantity of additional information that should be purchased. For this problem, as in many instances, sampling is very valuable in itself, but the exact size of the sample is not a crucial issue. It is, however, perhaps worth pointing out that in this particular problem the EOL is small relative to the EMV of the decision to purchase without obtaining further information. Hence the company might feel that the gain from sampling is small relative to the delays which would inevitably occur with sampling and which have not been brought into the assessment.

11.9 Existence of an optimum

The shape and location of the curve for ENGS exhibited in Fig. 11.5 is not a general situation. The relationship of the EVSI and the sampling costs may be such that ENGS is negative for all sample sizes (above zero). Such a situation is shown in Fig. 11.6, and here it is clear that there is no sample size for

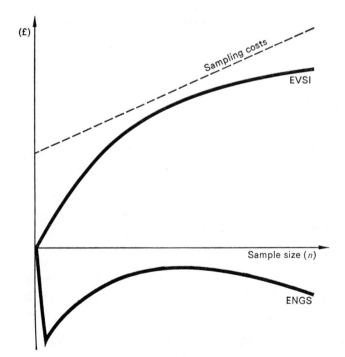

Fig. 11.6. Sampling gain relationship

which the ENGS is positive, and hence no sample should be taken.
Figure 11.7 illustrates a rather different situation, and it is instructive to
consider, in general terms, how such a situation could arise.

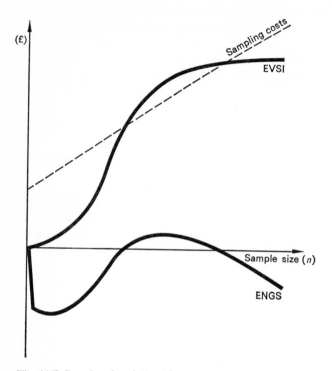

Fig. 11.7. Sample gain relationship

If the prior distribution very definitely favours one of the possible decisions
that can be made, it is very improbable that a small sample will affect the
decision. Accordingly, the expected value of sample information starts by
increasing very slowly with *n*. As *n* becomes large enough for the sample to
have a real chance of affecting the decision, the value increases more rapidly;
but as the value approaches the expected value of perfect information the
marginal rate of increase again becomes small and eventually approaches
zero. Since the variable cost of sampling increases directly with *n*, it is not
obvious that there will be any value of *n* for which the expected value of the
sample is greater than its cost. This depends upon whether the EVSI curve is
above the sampling costs for any value of *n*. Figure 11.7 shows the situation
where there is a non-zero optimum value of *n*. If the EVSI curve is at all
times below the dotted line representing the sampling costs the optimum
sample size is *n* equal to zero.

11.10 Summary of procedure

The procedure outlined in this chapter to determine the optimum level of information to purchase involved a number of steps, which have been explained one at a time. It is probably useful at this point to give a summary of the procedure that has been followed to calculate the ENGS. The steps are as follows:

(*i*) Calculate EVPI. (Use Eqs. 11.2 and 11.4.)
(*ii*) Calculate the standard deviation of the posterior distribution. (Use Eq. 11.5b.)
(*iii*) Calculate the expected loss using the sample information. (Use Eq. 11.7.)
(*iv*) Calculate the EVSI by subtracting the quantity found in (*iii*) from that found in (*i*). (Use Eq. 11.8.)
(*v*) Calculate the ENGS by subtracting the cost of obtaining the sample from the EVSI found in (*iv*). (Use Eq. 11.10.)

Finally, we should point out that the normal distribution may not provide an exact representation of the prior distribution. Indeed, in many instances the prior distribution may have been specified in terms of some discrete distribution. It would be perfectly possible to analyse such a problem along the lines used in Section 11.3 with obvious extensions to deal with the information derived from various sample sizes. However, the use of the normal distribution as an approximation is usually completely adequate for problems of the discrete type and will almost always provide a useful starting point. If the expected net gain from sampling is relatively insensitive to changes in sample size around the optimum, it is not likely that a more complete analysis on the discrete data will change the optimum sample size. If the net gain does change rapidly, a complete decision analysis should be carried out in the region of the optimum. Even in this case, the normal analysis will at least have helped to locate the region of the optimum.

Exercises on Chapter 11

1 A paper mill with coal-fired boilers is considering whether or not to change its coal from the existing grade A to a new grade B. The key consideration is cost per unit of calorific value. The factory purchases 5 million calorific units per annum. Data supplied on grade B leads the manager to suppose that the average cost per unit of calorific value is £0·65 against the known £0·67 for grade A. However, there are some doubts about grade B which his staff express by putting the prior probability distribution for cost with a mean of £0·65 and a standard deviation of £0·03.

(*i*) On an EMV basis, would the paper mill go ahead with the change?
(*ii*) The coal is provided in wagons and samples can be drawn from a wagon to determine calorific value. This costs £150 per wagon examined, and the

standard deviation between samples taken from different wagons (for a given coal) is believed to be around £0·04. Would it be worthwhile to examine 25 wagons selected at random before making a final decision or not?

(Assume a one year time horizon only, as the decision could be reversed after each year.)

2 A chemical company is considering the introduction of a new paint. The cost of the paint to the company is in three parts. First, a royalty payment of £22 000 per annum; second, an annual overhead cost of production of £40 000 and, third, a variable manufacturing cost of £1 per gallon. The paint would be sold (ex works) at £1·5 per gallon.

The sales manager estimates that the average demand per outlet per annum would be 150 gallons per annum and there are 1000 outlets. There is some uncertainty about the average demand figure and the sales manager expresses this doubt in the form of a probability distribution for average demand per outlet with mean 150 gallons per annum and standard deviation 30 gallons per annum.

(*i*) On an EMV basis, would the chemical company go ahead?
(*ii*) Suppose that a test could be made by buying in similar paint at £1·6 per gallon and selling it (at £1·5 per gallon) to *n* outlets for a year. The figure of £1·6 includes all marketing, etc. Would this be worthwhile if first, *n* is equal to 40 outlets or second, if *n* is equal to 80 outlets? What do you deduce about the optimum value of *n*?

(You should assume previous experience suggests that the standard deviation of paint sales per annum of a given type of paint between outlets is approximately 40 gallons, and that the population of outlets can be regarded as sufficiently large to be able to ignore any non-independence of outlets sampled.)

3 An insurance company with 600 branches is contemplating the installation of a centralized data-processing system in its head office with tape input units in each of the branch agencies. The system is designed to provide a more efficient debtors ledger and better cash control. The total system, including the inputs, can be rented from the computer manufacturer for a two-year period at a cost of £60 000 per month. Since the firm believes that its current practices are providing satisfactory levels of customer service, economic justification for the facility must be made on the basis of a saving in clerical effort. The management team believes that the elimination of some clerical labour could be accomplished without creating serious personnel problems. Some of the effort is now provided by part-time and temporary employees, and normal wastage among the clerical force could be expected to take care of the remaining reductions.

There is, not unusually, some uncertainty as to the precise financial saving that will be achieved by the computer system. The computer manufacturer's sales representative has estimated that average monthly savings of £125 in clerical costs could be achieved for each agency. For the two-year period of the hire arrangement, the estimated savings would be £75 000 × 24 = £1 800 000. Since the total hire costs are £1 440 000, this estimate suggests that the installation would be quite profitable. (Discounting of sums paid out, or savings made, are ignored.)

The managing director asks his own operational research specialist to study the validity of the manufacturer's claims and estimates. While the specialist agrees, after an examination of the cost evidence readily available, that £125 per month per agency represents a reasonable 'best guess' as to the clerical cost reductions, including wages, fringe benefits and reducible overheads, he points out the possibility of considerable dispersion in the savings likely to be achieved for each individual agency. Hence, he feels that there must be some uncertainty in the total cost savings figure that has been quoted. There is, he points out, even a remote chance that the total labour costs could be increased as a result of the change. Pressed to provide some quantification of his views, he estimates that there is an even chance (0·5) that the *average* cost savings (per agency per month) lie between the figures £75 and £175 (i.e. £125 ± £50). He also reports that the two-year period is a reasonable one for decision-making purposes, in that technology changes are fairly rapid.

The company finds it possible to make a one month's trial run, at a randomly selected sample of its agencies, to determine the cost savings that are possible. The company estimates, on the basis of the experience of the computer manufacturer and other information, that the standard deviation of the savings per agency per month is approximately £150. The cost of carrying out such a sampling procedure for a month is a fixed cost of £50 000 together with £1000 per branch examined.

(*i*) If no sampling of branches is undertaken, what decision would be reached?

(*ii*) Determine whether it is worthwhile to undertake sampling and, if so, the optimum number of branches to be sampled.

4 A firm with a great deal of experience in the car hire business in the UK is considering opening an agency in Cyprus. During a special visit to the island to survey the possibilities, the managing director found that he could buy suitable new cars at a fleet rate of £1000 each and sell them after one year of use at £500. He also examined the possibilities of operating a fleet of 50 cars based in ten locations in the island, five cars at each location. His estimate of average usage per car per year at each location was 225 days, with a 0·5 chance that the mean rental days per car at any one location would be within the band of ± 60 days, i.e. 165 to 285 days. The estimated average daily rental was £4 per car and the annual operating expenses of the organization, excluding the depreciation expenses, would be £11 000.

(*i*) Should the firm start the car hire agency?

(*ii*) The managing director decided to conduct a test for one month which consisted of having available five cars for renting in each of two random selected locations from among the ten being considered. It was found that the mean rental days per car in the month was 14 with a variance of 12. Would this influence the managing director's decision as reached under (*i*)? It can be assumed that the demands at the ten possible locations are independent of each other.

5 A pharmaceutical company is evaluating the feasibility of introducing and marketing a new product in a large town of 45 000 families. A marketing programme to launch the product is expected to cost £75 000. The company estimates that, if the new product is sold at £2 per unit, the profit will be £0·75 per unit. At this price, the company believes that it will be able to sell an average of two units per family per year and that there is a 50 : 50 chance that the average sales per family will lie between 1·6 and 2·4. Past experience with similar products has suggested that this product can be successfully marketed for one year. At the end of that time, it is expected that intense competition from the rest of the pharmaceutical industry will destroy the profitability of marketing this product.

(*i*) Should the new product be introduced and what is the EVPI?

(*ii*) Assume that the cost of sampling a family to establish their likely purchases is £1·5 per family sampled and that it is estimated, from previous experience of a similar nature that the standard deviation of purchases per year as between families is 0·4 units. Find the optimum size of sample that should be taken.

6 An investment advisory company is proposing to launch a new weekly market newsletter as a supplement to an existing monthly subscription mail magazine service. The latter currently has a circulation of about 11 000 copies. The chairman thinks that about half the subscribers will take the supplement, at a cost of £12·5 per year, but concedes that there is a 10 per cent chance that the proportion may be one quarter or less, and the same chance that it may be three quarters or more.

The variable cost of producing this newsletter is estimated at £7 per subscriber per year, but it would involve initial development costs of £40 000. The chairman wants these development costs to be recovered quickly since competition will copy the newsletter, probably forcing him to lower the price within two years.

One of the executives in the company suggests including, in a current number of the existing monthly magazine, a circular about the newsletter, and extracts from a possible number, together with an invitation to subscribe.

By keeping to a sample the company's image would not be tarnished, should the response not be sufficiently favourable to go ahead with the newsletter. The cost of sampling subscribers in this way is a fixed cost of £500, together with £1·5 per subscriber included.

(*i*) What is the maximum number of subscribers that could economically be sampled?

(*ii*) What is the optimum number of subscribers that should be sampled?

(*Note:* the standard deviation of the proportion of success in a random sample of size n from a population with a proportion p of successes is $\sqrt{\{p(1-p)/n\}}$.)

12 The concept of utility

12.1 Introduction

In earlier chapters we have laid a great deal of stress on the maximization of expected monetary value for making a choice between alternative decisions. This approach was shown to have an intuitive validity when similar decision situations were to be repeated again and again, or in situations where expected profit could be interpreted as the long-run average profit.

In other situations, which occur only once and will never be repeated, the rationality of the procedure has been defended partly on the way in which it allows large problems to be broken down into smaller problems, and partly on the grounds of consistency. It is not clear, however, that the procedure is necessarily optimum when the probabilities do not have the frequency interpretation associated with repeated decisions.

Let us first, however, consider an illustration to show that cases do exist where the maximization of expected monetary value is an inappropriate decision rule, in that some of the consequences of decisions cannot readily be expressed in terms of a monetary pay-off.

Example 12.1

A manufacturer has to decide whether or not to pay excess carriage charges to ship a consignment of heavy engineering goods abroad by air to meet a customer deadline. If he sends the goods by sea there is an appreciable chance that they will arrive late but, on the other hand, the shipping charges are low. If he sends the goods by air they are virtually certain to arrive on time, but he incurs higher freight charges. Should the goods arrive late he may lose both customer goodwill and have a possible claim for damages for late delivery. His decision/pay-off matrix can be summarized as shown in Table 12.1.

Table 12.1

Pay-offs for decision as to choice of shipment

Decision	Outcome	
	E_1 Goods arrive on time	E_2 Goods arrive late
D_1 Send by sea	Low cost of shipment Satisfied customer R_{11}	Low cost of shipment Customer not satisfied Loss of goodwill Possible claim for damages R_{12}
D_2 Send by air	High cost of shipment Satisfied customer R_{21}	High cost of shipment Customer not satisfied Loss of goodwill Possible claim for damages R_{22}

Suppose that the consequences of the various combinations of decisions (or actions) and outcomes to the manufacturer are denoted on some numerical scale by R_{ij}. Then the value R_{11} will clearly be the highest since the manufacturer will have got the goods to the customer on time, without having incurred the extra costs of air freight. R_{22} is clearly the least satisfactory, and the lowest value, as the manufacturer has incurred extra cost, but still not satisfied the customer. R_{12} and R_{21} lie in between and may be in either order, since the extra cost of shipment may or may not be balanced by customer satisfaction and possible damages. Hence, the manufacturer is likely to be in a quandary. If he knows that the sea freight (D_1) would arrive on time, he would obviously prefer it; if he is uncertain about it, he is also uncertain about whether to switch from D_1 to D_2 as the ranking of R_{12} and R_{21} is uncertain.

At this stage we go back to the probabilities involved. Suppose the manufacturer attaches the probability P_{11} to the outcome that goods sent by sea arrive on time. Now if P_{11} were near unity, the manufacturer would almost certainly choose D_1 and send by sea. If P_{11} were very close to zero, he would be reasonably sure he was going to be late on delivery and would change to decision D_2 and send his goods by air. Somewhere along the scale as P_{11} decreases from near unity to near zero, he should presumably change from decision D_1 to decision D_2, but where is the point of change? Obviously the point of changeover is not only dependent on the ranking of the consequences, but also on how much better one consequence is than another. For example, if R_{12} is close to R_{22} because customer goodwill is very important, then P_{12}, the chance of late delivery by sea, will not have to be so large before shipment by air begins to be preferred in order to try to avoid the unpleasant consequences of late delivery. One way in which the manufacturer might seek to mitigate these effects and make his decision would be to seek insurance to cover the risk of late arrival. However, he would still have to assess the amount of financial loss to insure against and this will again involve assessment of the value to be placed on goodwill and damages for late delivery.

The next example demonstrates how the use of a probability measure, allied to the notion of long-run frequencies, may make the maximization of expected monetary value an inappropriate criterion to follow.

Example 12.2

The owner of a small business, Smalbiz Ltd, is deciding whether or not to undertake one of two contracts. A and B, that have been offered to him. He cannot undertake both and there is some uncertainty about the outcome of either. To simplify the illustration, we assume that there are only three possible outcomes in each instance, with the pay-offs and associated probabilities that are shown in Table 12.2. It is assumed that the EMV for rejecting both contracts is zero.

Table 12.2

Summary of two contracts under consideration

Outcome	Contract A		Contract B	
	Pay-off	Probability	Pay-off	Probability
E_1	80 000	0·6	50 000	0·5
E_2	10 000	0·1	30 000	0·3
E_3	− 30 000	0·3	− 10 000	0·2

On the usual bases the calculations for EMV give:

$$EMV(A) = 0·6 \times 80\,000 + 0·1 \times 10\,000 + 0·3 \times (-30\,000) = 40\,000,$$

$$EMV(B) = 0·5 \times 50\,000 + 0·3 \times 30\,000 + 0·2 \times (-10\,000) = 32\,000,$$

and since the former EMV exceeds the latter, and exceeds the EMV for rejecting both contracts, the owner should accept contract A.

But it is by no means certain that all businessmen who found themselves in this situation would choose A rather than B. The reason is that under A there is some possibility of a loss of 30 000, and such a loss might wipe out the business completely. Hence, they might not be willing to undertake any contract which held out come possibility of so large a loss, regardless of the fact that there was some possibility of gaining 80 000 and that the EMV of accepting the contract was as high as 40 000. If such a businessman had to choose between A and B he might well choose B because the maximum loss of − 10 000 is much smaller, even though the EMV is now rather lower. However, other businessmen for whom the loss of − 30 000 would not be such a serious event, or who need desperately to obtain more than 50 000 to keep the business going, would probably prefer contract A. What this means is that expected monetary values do not always accurately reflect a decision-maker's true feelings about situations. This is particularly true when the losses or gains involved are large compared with the decision-maker's resources.

12.2 Measure of consequences

The foregoing discussion suggests that our next task is to provide something more than just a ranking of the monetary consequences; we have to put the *R*s of Example 12.1 on some scale of measurement. What we need is some more global numerical measure for the merit of each decision/outcome combination, just as we attach a probability figure to indicate the chances of uncertain events. We do this with reference to some standard and make comparisons with that standard. The figures so obtained are referred to as *utilities*. Let us, therefore, return to Example 12.2 concerning Smalbiz Ltd, and demonstrate a possible procedure through this example.

Example 12.2 (*continued*)

Considering both the contracts together, plus the alternative of not undertaking either of them, there are seven outcomes corresponding to the seven possible pay-offs. These are (in decreasing order of monetary pay-off):

80 000, 50 000, 30 000, 10 000, 0, − 10 000, − 30 000.

If the businessman does not accept either contract, then he will venture nothing and get a return of 0. This is the reason for the inclusion of 0 in the list. We will assume that there are in this instance no other intangibles, e.g. customer goodwill, that need to be considered, and that these pay-offs reflect the full monetary story of each outcome. Denote the highest outcome 80 000 by R_1 and the lowest outcome of − 30 000 by R_7. Then we will define the utility of R_1 as unity and that of R_7 as zero. That is:

$$u(R_1)=1 \qquad u(R_7)=0$$

where $u(R_i)$ is a shorthand for 'the utility corresponding to the outcome denoted by R_i'.

To determine the utilities of the other outcomes, consider a lottery in which there are only two prizes, namely, R_1 and R_7. For each other monetary outcome in the list, R_i, we now ask the decision-maker to select for us that value of u for which he would be indifferent between (*i*) playing a lottery defined by

prize $R_1 = 80\ 000$ probability u

prize $R_7 = -30\ 000$ probability $1 - u$, or

(*ii*) receiving the sum of R_i with certainty.

The value of u so obtained is then the utility of the event concerned. Note that under (*i*) the lottery could be simulated by a drum with 100 tickets. On $100u$ of the tickets the figure 80 000 is written, on $100(1-u)$ the figure $-30\ 000$ is written. One ticket is drawn at random and the number on it is the result of playing the lottery. Suppose we consider outcome R_4, for which the associated pay-off is 10 000. Then, for high values of u, the decision-maker might prefer to go in for the lottery rather than take 10 000 on a certain basis. For low values of u, however, the opposite would be true and he would prefer to have 10 000 with certainty rather than a chance at the lottery. The value of u where he is indifferent between the two options is the utility corresponding to 10 000.

Note that, if the decision-maker merely equates expectations, he would find the value of u, u' say, such that

$$u' \times 80\ 000 + (1 - u') \times (-30\ 000) = 10\ 000,$$

leading to a value of $u' = 4/11$. However, the decision-maker might not be willing to go in for the lottery unless u was at least equal to 0·5. Hence, 0·5 is the utility corresponding to R_4. The decision-maker now proceeds on similar lines for the other four outcomes, and we will suppose that the overall list he compiles of his utilities runs as follows:

$u(80\ 000) = 1$ $u(50\ 000) = 0.9$

$u(30\ 000) = 0.8$ $u(10\ 000) = 0.5$

$u(0) = 0.3$ $u(-10\ 000) = 0.2$

$u(-30\ 000) = 0$

We should point out that, while we have spoken of the decision-maker, this is because the firm and the decision-maker are synonymous in this example. In a larger firm, it would be the firm's utility function, and not that of any individual, is required.

Having obtained the utilities, we must now decide how to use them. The basis is very simple, namely, we judge between decisions on the basis of expected utility (EUV) in place of expected monetary value (EMV). If the utility scales correctly represent the decision-maker's preferences, it can be shown that the optimum method of rational procedure in a decision problem is for the decision-maker to choose that action for which expected utility is maximized. Such a procedure will be in accordance with his rational preferences.

Returning to the example, we can use the utility information to compute the expected utility for each contract, using the probabilities given earlier, as follows:

Contract A $EUV = 0.6 \times 1 + 0.1 \times 0.5 + 0.3 \times 0 = 0.65$;

Contract B $EUV = 0.5 \times 0.9 + 0.3 \times 0.8 + 0.2 \times 0.2 = 0.73$.

The utility of not undertaking either contract is $u(R_5) = 0.3$. The largest of these three utilities is 0·73, and thus the businessman should accept contract B as preferable either to contract A, or the alternative of not undertaking either contract. The reason why he now prefers B to A no doubt stems from the fact that the largest possible loss is less for contract B than for A, and he is willing to accept a smaller expected profit to avoid some possibility of a large loss.

12.3 Utility function

In the example just discussed, the decision-maker gave the utilities he thought corresponded to a number of monetary outcomes. He gave these utilities on behalf of his firm or business and we discuss the problem of estimating utilities in more detail in Section 12.8 below. The utilities obtained can be plotted on a graph, as shown in Fig. 12.1, and a freehand curve drawn

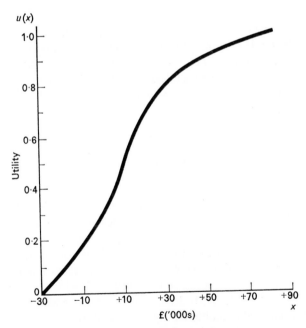

Fig. 12.1. Utility curve for contracts problem

through the points available. Such a curve would be called a utility curve. If x denotes the realizable assets of the firm concerned and $u(x)$ the associated utility, then the function $u(x)$ can be looked upon as the utility function of the firm, and the curve drawn in Fig. 12.1 as a representation of this function.

There are a few general properties that we would expect any utility function $u(x)$ to possess. First, we would expect an increase in x to cause an increase in utility, or formally that $u(x)$ increases with x. Most of us would prefer to have the higher of two levels of assets. Hence, the larger assets must have the larger utility. Note that if this were not the case, we would find, contrary to our experience, people or businesses literally throwing money away.
A second feature of $u(x)$ concerns its form for very large values of x. Suppose you, as an individual, are contemplating two outcomes, one of which has a monetary value of £1 million and the other of £1·05 million. You would find it hard to distinguish between these outcomes in utility terms. Both would enable you to do all the things that you have ever dreamt of doing, and the extra £0·05 million would probably not have any real effect on your expectations. Hence, there comes a point where utility ceases to increase without limit as x increases. A third feature, which is not so inevitable, but a reasonable attribute of a decision-maker's approach, concerns the effect that a change, say c, in x has on utility. Suppose our decision-maker is looking at the utilities corresponding to x and $x+c$ and calculates the difference in utilities, namely:

$$u(x+c) - u(x) \qquad (12.1)$$

This difference is likely to depend upon x and not be invariant whatever the value of x, whether we be talking of an individual or of a firm. Suppose that c is £1000 and x is £5000. Then the difference in Eq. 12.1 represents the satisfaction the decision-maker gains from an additional £1000. If, on the other hand, x is £500 000 and c is still £1000, we would not expect that the gain in satisfaction as measured by

$$u(501\ 000) - u(500\ 000)$$

to be as great as that measured by

$$u(6000) - u(5000).$$

In other words, the increase in utility is a diminishing function of the initial realizable assets as measured by x. This principle is often referred to as the principle of the diminishing marginal utility of money, marginal utility being the term used for the increase in utility due to a unit increase in the assets x.
Commonly, we put the bounds for utility, as mentioned earlier, at zero and unity. This is purely a convention and we could equally well work with a scale from 0 to 100, or from -1 to $+1$, etc. Indeed, if a constant is added to each utility value and each utility value multiplied by a constant, the properties of the utility function remain unaltered. Thus, if a is constant and

b a positive constant, and x is an amount of money $u_2(x) = a + bu_1(x)$ is as legitimate a measure scale of utility as $u_1(x)$. Utility units in this more general sense are sometimes referred to as *utiles*.

Example 12.3

An individual has a utility function that can be expressed in the form

$$u(X) = X - 0 \cdot 1 X^2 \quad 0 \leqslant X \leqslant 20,$$

where X is the individual's assets. Currently, his assets are 2 units. How would the individual rank a proposal to receive 1 unit for certain as an outright gift, against the alternative possibility of taking part in a lottery whose prize is given by $X = y - 2$ units where y is a random variable that follows a Poisson distribution with parameter 3.

For either option, his utility starts at 1·6. For the former option his revised utility is

$$u(3) = 3 - 0 \cdot 1 \times 9 = 2 \cdot 1.$$

For the latter, we need to evaluate the expected value of the utility which is

$$E(X + 2) - 0 \cdot 1 E(X + 2)^2$$

$$= E(y) - 0 \cdot 1 E(y)^2$$

Now y is distributed as a Poisson variable and the mean or expected value of y is (from Eq. 3.13a, page 57) 3 and hence the utility, which is equal to

$$E(\bar{y} - 3 + 3) - 0 \cdot 1 E(\bar{y} - 3 + 3)^2$$

can be expanded in the form

$$E(y - 3) + E(3) - 0 \cdot 1 E(y - 3)^2 - 0 \cdot 2 E(y - 3) - 0 \cdot 1 E(3)^2$$

$$= 0 + 3 - 0 \cdot 1 \times 3 - 0 - 0 \cdot 1 \times 9$$

$$= 1 \cdot 8. \qquad \text{(Using Eq. 3.13b)}$$

Hence, the proposal to receive 1 unit certainly is the more attractive proposition for the individual.

12.4 Utility curves

In Fig. 12.1 we showed a utility curve corresponding to the utilities obtained from particular monetary pay-offs that we were concerned with in the contracts problem. Of course, the curve is particular to both the decision-maker and the range of monetary values with which the decision-maker is concerned. If we were to generalize, similar curves could be established for other decision-makers and Fig. 12.2 shows graphically three typical utility functions that could occur.

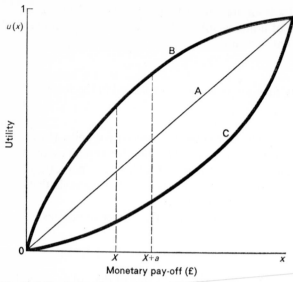

Fig. 12.2. Typical utility functions

The utility function represented by A is appropriate for the decision-maker who is prepared to operate precisely on an EMV basis and is neutral to risk. For him, the extra gain in utility $u(x)$ for a change of assets from X to $X+a$ does not depend upon the value of X. Thus, there is for A a precise linear relationship between monetary value and utility of the form:

$$u(x)=ax+b,$$

where a and b are constants (in this instance b is zero).

The line denoted B corresponds to a decision-maker who is more risk-averse than the strict EMV man. He does not like, or cannot afford, big risks and is a risk-avoider. We can see this from a study of the form of curve B. Suppose the decision-maker has a capital of X and is given the choice between a certain gain in assets of a or a gain of a together with an equal chance of winning or losing an amount b, where b is positive. While decision-maker A would have no particular inclination towards either of these two possibilities, decision-maker B would prefer the former. This follows from looking at the utilities. The first alternative will leave B with $u(x+a)$. The second will leave him with an *expected* utility of:

$$\tfrac{1}{2}u(x+a+b)+\tfrac{1}{2}u(x+a-b),$$

and this quantity is less than $u(x+a)$ because of the concave nature of the utility function. On the basis of utility, the gamble will therefore be refused, even though it is fair from a straightforward expected monetary pay-off point of view. The upshot of this discussion is that a decision-maker with concave utility for money will refuse a monetarily fair bet and is thus said to be risk-averse. The degree of aversion depends upon the curvature of the utility function and, in our illustration, is greater for the smaller values of x than for the larger values.

The line denoted by C corresponds to a decision-maker who prefers a risk, instead of being averse to it. For such a man, the expected utility of a monetarily fair bet exceeds the utility of not gambling and hence a fair bet will always be taken. The utility function is said to be convex. It is doubtful if many persons would have such a utility function, although they might have it over a limited range of values of x, and certainly some businesses might have such a utility function at particular moments in time.

It is sometimes suggested that a number of individuals have a sigmoid form of utility function, as illustrated by Fig. 12.3. Thus, the individual is a risk-preferer for very small values of x, but a risk-avoider for larger values. To substantiate this we can cite the case of stake money placed on football pools, etc., where gamblers take part even though the odds are against them, but there is some chance of a very large return.

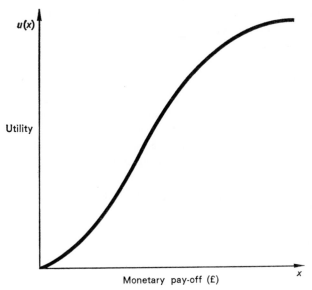

Fig. 12.3. Sigmoid utility function

12.5 Expected utility

We have now introduced a concept whereby action A will be preferred to action B if its expected utility is the higher. Generalizing, we select the best decision from among a set of decisions by choosing that decision in which the expected utility is the highest. So far this is straightforward, but the objection that is raised to the whole procedure is that it is often impossible because of the difficulty of obtaining the utilities themselves. But the great benefit of the approach is that it allows a complex decision situation to be effectively broken down into a number of smaller decision problems. Once each of these smaller problems has been solved, the argument of consistency, on which utility rests, then enables these smaller problems to be pieced together to provide a solution to the larger problem. This can be seen in Example 12·1 where the manager had to decide between ship or plane for a consignment of machinery. Here, the proposed procedure breaks down the problem into a number of simpler problems by considering, first, the probability that the consignment arrives late (which can be done by considering a gamble between a prize obtainable with probability p and the same prize only obtainable if the consignment arrives on time). Second, the utility of the consequences of the various outcomes is considered. Again, the utility of the customer's dissatisfaction at the late arrival of his goods can be assessed by considering an appropriate gamble and hence obtaining a figure for the utility. The pieces are then assembled together to solve the original, rather larger, problem. Hence the reply to the man who accuses us of guessing at the whole problem is: 'If you can't do simple problems, how can you do big ones?' A chain is only as strong as its weakest link, and if a component of the original situation is fragile, so may be the whole.

12.6 Illustration of procedure

We now demonstrate the procedure suggested above by adapting Example 8.2 (page 185) concerning the oil wildcatter. The decision he had to make was one of three possible actions, namely whether to withdraw, to drill without a seismic sounding, or take a seismic sounding before making his final decision. Suppose now that it has been possible for the oil wildcatter to establish his utility function as in Fig. 12.4. We can then substitute the appropriate utilities in place of his various monetary pay-offs as follows:

Monetary pay-off	Utility
− 130	0
− 100	0·16
− 30	0·38
0	0·44
70	0·58
100	0·64
470	0·99
500	1

The revised decision tree is shown in Fig. 12.5, utilities being given in place of monetary pay-offs at the ends of the various branches. The probabilities remain as before.

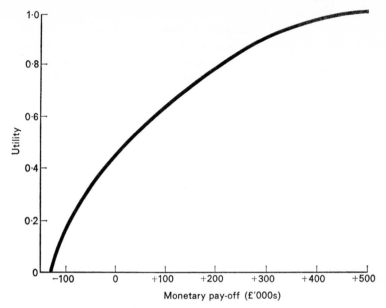

Fig. 12.4. Oil wildcatters utility function

We can now evaluate each branch in turn. For the upper branch at point W the expected utility corresponding to decision D is:

$$EUV = 0·5 \times 0·16 + 0·25 \times 0·64 + 0·25 \times 1 = 0·49.$$

Hence, D is a better decision than $\bar{D}$, with its utility of 0·44. At decision point W, the utility of 0·49 is now entered and decision rate $\bar{D}$ is barred.

For the middle branch at point X the decision D, to drill, leads to an expected utility of:

$$EUV = \tfrac{2}{9} \times 0 + \tfrac{3}{9} \times 0·58 + \tfrac{4}{9} \times 0·99 = 0·63.$$

This is preferable to the utility of 0·38 corresponding to decision $\bar{D}$ and hence we enter 0·63 at point X and bar decision $\bar{D}$.

For the lower branch of the tree at point Y the expected utility corresponding to D is:

$$EUV = 0·0 \times 0·727 + 0·58 \times 0·182 + 0·99 \times 0·091 = 0·196.$$

This is lower than the utility of 0·38 corresponding to decision $\bar{D}$, and, hence, the latter figure is entered at point Y and decision D is barred.

Our next step is to combine the middle and lower branches into one expected utility as before, giving:

$$0·45 \times 0·63 + 0·55 \times 0·38 = 0·4925.$$

The initial comparison now is between an expected utility of 0·49 for the initial decision to proceed without a seismic sounding, 0·4925 to proceed with a seismic sounding and 0·44 to withdraw. The seismic sounding result is the highest, albeit very marginally, leading to a decision that is contrary to the one found in Chapter 8. Probably in this particular instance the decision-maker would argue that the first two results are so close that he really has no

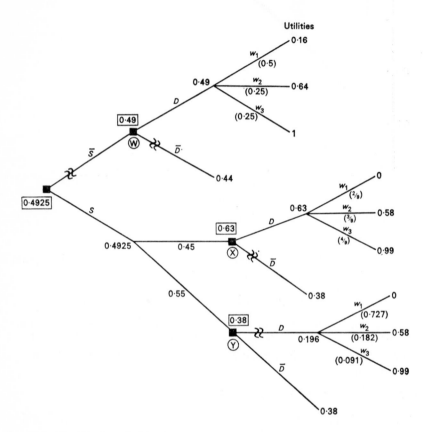

Fig. 12.5. Oil wildcatters decision tree

preference for either of the two possibilities, and other factors, e.g. convenience might influence his decision. This, again, is different from the situation in Chapter 8, and shows the effect of being risk-averse, in that the oil wildcatter now finds the purchase of extra information before making a final decision more worthwhile than previously. If this utility curve were of the opposite form, namely, a concave curve, showing him to be a risk-seeker, then he would find his desire to purchase extra information diminished by a change from monetary values to utilities.

12.7 Insurance

We next consider the position, in practice, where we have some risk situation and consider disposing of it, as this illustrates well the unconscious use of utilities in practice. The common way of disposing of a risk is through insurance and we select as an illustration the common fire insurance for a house. Here, in return for an annual premium from the house-owner, the insurance company will compensate him in the event of such a calamity. The decision situation which faces the owner is shown in Table 12.3. Let C be the house-owner's total assets, m the amount of the annual premium for fire insurance, and h the cost of reinstating the house if it is destroyed by fire. Insurance is assumed to leave the owner where he would have been financially without the fire, but if he does not insure and there is a fire, he could be much worse off, since m is considerably less than h. (In what follows we simplify by considering only the total loss, as opposed to a partial loss, situation.)

Table 12.3

Decision outcomes from fire insurance

	Outcome	
Decision	Fire	No fire
Insure	Inconvenience, but no real loss $(C-m)$	Loss of premium $(C-m)$
Not insure	Loss of capital $(C-h)$	No losses (C)

(House-owner's capital shown in brackets)

The decision 'Not insure' leads to a situation whose consequences are probabilistic. Clearly, part of the decision whether or not to insure is governed by the premium quoted by the insurance company, and part by the risk of fire as the owner assesses it. Suppose that he assesses the probability of a fire during the year at p. Now the individual is likely to be a risk-avoider, and, hence, have a concave utility function such as B in Fig. 12.2. Thus, the change in utility between $C-h$ and $C-m$ is greater than would be anticipated on a true expected monetary principle for an owner who is neutral to risk. Furthermore, he would be invariant between the two possible decisions if p is the probability of a fire and

$$u(C-m)=pu(C-h)+(1-p)u(C). \tag{12.2}$$

K

Let us first suppose that the owner's utility function is given by $u(x)=x$, or, in other words, that he is neutral towards risk. Then we have, from Eq. 12.2, that

$$C-m=p(C-h)+(1-p)C$$

or

$$m=ph.$$

This is the premium to be expected from a straight expected monetary value approach. Now if the owner's utility function over the relevant range is concave as indicated by curve XY in Fig. 12.6, rather than linear as previously, this must give

$$u(C-m)>pu(C-h)+(1-p)u(C).$$

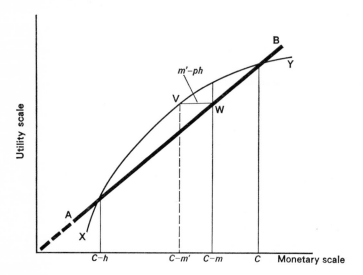

Fig. 12.6. Insurance premiums

and the corresponding acceptable premium is greater than before. If Eq. 12.2 is solved to give this revised premium, m' say, then the difference $m'-ph$ represents the excess that the decision-maker is prepared to pay above the strict expected monetary value cost for insuring his house. Alternatively, the premium can be found graphically by projecting a horizontal line from point W on Fig. 12.6 until it cuts the utility function at point V. The length VW then represents the excess premium $m'-ph$ which the owner is willing to pay.

The situation from the insurance company's point of view is rather different. If their assets are K, then the possible asset positions for the company after offering the insurance, are $K-h+m$, K, and $K+m$, according to whether or not a claim is made and/or the policy is taken out. These three quantities will be not very different from one another in relative terms as the company's assets, K, will be very large. Furthermore, on the company's utility curve, the position will be such that a very close approximation to the utility curve can be obtained if we assume it to be linear over the range from $K-h+m$ to $K+m$. Now if the utility curve is linear, this is equivalent to taking utility to be the same as money, albeit with a scale factor. Hence, the company will be quite content to work with expected monetary value as its decision criterion. Consequently, a 'pure' premium of $m=ph$ as calculated earlier would be acceptable to the company, plus a loading to cover expenses and profit. Thus, a premium in excess of the pure premium ph is acceptable to both the policy-holder and the insurance company, provided the excess covers the company's expenses and profit. This attractiveness of insurance applies because of the concave nature of the owner's utility function. It follows as a corollary that if the curvature of the individual's utility function is very small. or even reversed in direction, he will not be able to obtain attractive premiums. Again, the argument demonstrates that it does not pay an individual to insure against small losses, only against large ones, because over a small range of an individual's utility function the latter is effectively linear. Hence, the insurance company cannot then offer the individual an attractive premium.

12.8 Assessing utility

The earlier discussion in this chapter exposes the need for assessing utility, for individuals or for firms, according to the nature of the decision involved. We will first discuss some of the problems for individual assessments of utility and comment later on the manner in which such assessments can be extended to firms.

We have already mentioned, in Section 12.2, a possible way of obtaining utility by posing a series of hypothetical gambles. In practice, it is commonly found that individuals presented with a series of these gambles are inconsistent. If this is the case, the appraiser must ask the individual which of the inconsistent estimates really represents his preference. After thought, the individual will usually be able to bring the estimates into line. The main trouble, however, is usually that individuals do not relate these forms of gamble to business situations and regard them as something special, outside the real world of business activity. This may lead to somewhat artificial results.

To counteract this difficulty, we might try to simulate more closely real-world situations. For example, we could concentrate on oil drilling and present to the individual a series of hypothetical drilling deals. For each deal we present three items of information: the cost of the investment in the deal, the pay-off to the individual if oil is struck, and the probability of finding oil. The individual is asked to think of these as actual deals, implying that if it is accepted the money is tied up until the well pays out, which may, typically, be several years. For example, we might offer a deal with an investment of £30 000, a pay-off (or present value of any oil found) of £100 000 and a 70 per cent chance of success. Would the individual accept this deal? If he accepts, we then ask if he would accept it with a 50 per cent chance of success, or a 30 per cent chance and so on, until we find a point where he is on the borderline between acceptance and rejection. Once this point is found, we forget the deal and go on to another one. Each deal is separate, but gives one point on the utility function.

Similar types of deal could be devised for most situations, and different individuals asked the same series of questions in order to see how the utility curve is affected by the individual's background and responsibilities in the organization concerned. The next section describes the main difficulties encountered.

12.9 Difficulties with assessments

Probabilities undoubtedly create the greatest difficulty in experiments such as those just described. First, many individuals do not normally use numerical probabilities in their decisions, and they find it strange to try to reach a decision on the basis of probabilities. Explanation can usually smooth the path. It is alternatively possible to re-design the experiment to keep the probabilities constant at 50 per cent and change the pay-offs to find the indifference point. However, this is even further removed from reality and would tend to introduce yet another element of artificiality.

Second, some difficulties are experienced in interpreting the pay-off figure. Ventures presented in the real world have many factors (e.g. interactions with other projects) that are collapsed into the present value pay-off figure, and some time needs to be spent in discussing with the individual the precise content of the pay off figure.

Third, it is important to use deals that are within the normal range of operational activity of the individual concerned. We cannot expect individuals to construct consistent utility curves over a wide range of deals that are outside their normal experience.

If such curves are plotted for different individuals from a firm, there will still remain varying risk-taking preferences. While manager A might undertake a deal at certain probabilities, manager B might refuse. As the decision-making in the firm is likely to be split between the two (or even between more managers), there is the possibility that the firm, as a whole, is taking risks on an inconsistent basis in the sense that they are not maximizing any one utility function. More consistent action would result if the managers concerned would look at the functions, talk over their objectives, preferences, the asset position and so on and draw up a new utility function that captures selected features of the individual's functions. Alternatively, they could decide to adopt one of the existing functions to guide all their decisions.

One general criticism remains—namely, that the whole system of utilities is too complex and time-consuming. However, any decision problem faced by senior management is already complex, and while utility procedures may be strange at first, they are not unworkable. Once formulated, decisions can be made easier, faster and—what is perhaps most important—more consistently. Even if such procedures are not adopted in totality, the mere discussion of them will help managers to recognize that they are already considering problems informally, and how to think about them more formally. This may, by itself, produce a high pay-off for the decision theory approach.

REFERENCES

(These references provide additional reading on the assessment and use of utilities.)

Hammond, J. S. 1967. Better decisions through preference theory. *Harvard Business Review.*
Swalm, R. O. 1965. Utility theory—better insights into risk taking. *Harvard Business Review.*
Grayson, C. J. (Jr.) 1960. *Decisions under Uncertainty; Drilling Decisions by Oil and Gas Operators.* Boston, Division of Research, Harvard Business School, pp. 279–319.
Raiffa, H. 1968. *Decision Analysis*, Addison-Wesley, pp. 51–103.

Exercises on Chapter 12

1 A decision-maker has the following utilities over the relevant portion of his overall assets scale:

Assets (£'000s)	5	6	7	8	9
Utility	0·32	0·46	0·59	0·67	0·72

(*i*) The decision-maker currently possesses total assets of £7000. He is offered a place in the lottery where he has a chance of 0·6 of winning £1000, together with a complementary chance of 0·4 of losing £1000. Should the decision-maker accept the offer?

(*ii*) If the decision-maker were offered participation in a series of two independent plays of the same lottery with the same prizes and probabilities in each play, would this affect his decision to enter (or not to enter) the lottery? (Note that entry implies participation in both plays of the lottery.)

2 Mr X states that he would prefer a single-stage lottery to a two-stage lottery, even when the overall probabilities of the prizes are the same in the two situations. The reason he gives is that the single-stage lottery is easier on his nerves, involving only one chance mechanism rather than two.

(*i*) Does this appear to be a reasonable attitude? Is this man what we commonly call a *rational decision-maker*?

(*ii*) In what ways is Mr X's approach likely to be emulated by businesses in their approach to decision-making?

3 Two insurance companies, A and B, have the same utility function given by:

$$U = \tfrac{1}{2}W^{1/2}$$

where W represents the assets of the company in £m. Company A currently has assets of £100m, and company B assets of £60m. The two companies are each asked to quote for the insurance of a ship worth £20m. against the risk of total loss in a particular year, the probability of which is assessed by both companies at 0·01.

(*i*) What is a reasonable premium for company A to quote for the whole risk?

(*ii*) What is a reasonable premium for company B to quote for the whole risk?

(*iii*) Suppose the risk is shared equally between the two companies A and B. What premium should each company charge? Hence obtain the total premium required.

(*iv*) Comment on the differences, if any, between the premiums the insured would pay under the three alternatives. Why do these differences arise?

(Ignore office expenses and insurance company profit loadings in your calculations and assume that the premium is small in comparison with the minimum assets possible should the companies accept the risk.)

4 An international mining company with substantial assets is faced with decisions on a large number of separate projects each year.

(*i*) For what sorts of decisions on projects would it seem reasonable to maximize the expected monetary value?

(*ii*) How might one set about determining how large the sums of money involved have to be before expected monetary value is no longer a suitable criterion for choice amongst projects?

5 Reconsider the problem described in Exercise 8.1 (page 205). Suppose that M. Borel has total assets of 100mNF and that the relevant portion of his utility function is as follows:

Assets (mNF)	50	75	100	125	150	175
Utility		0·47	0·57	0·66	0·72	0·77	0·81

What is M. Borel's present optimum initial decision, i.e. should he decide upon acceptance of the contract without further inspection, and if he does inspect, how many ships should he inspect?

6 Mr Bull currently has assets of £10 000 and is presented with a deal which, in his opinion, has probability $\tfrac{1}{3}$ of resulting in a loss of £10 000, but probability $\tfrac{2}{3}$ of resulting in a profit of £10 000. Mr Bull's utility function is as follows:

Assets (£'000s)	0	2·5	5	10	15	20
Utility		0	0·45	0·65	0·85	0·95	1·00

(*i*) Show that Mr Bull should refuse the deal.
(*ii*) Suppose that five people with utility functions exactly like Mr Bull's, and each with assets of £10 000, all assign the same probabilities to the possible consequences of this deal. If they all agree to share the profit or loss equally, does the deal become attractive for all of them as a syndicate?

7 A businessman is considering which of two contracts his firm should undertake. Both contracts yield precisely the same expected profit. He decides to select the contract which minimizes the variance of the profit.

(*i*) Is this procedure consistent with the maximization of expected utility?
(*ii*) If your answer to (*i*) is yes, what is the form of the firm's utility function? Is there anything unusual about it?

8 A firm is offered a contract to develop a special turbine engine. The contract stipulates that if the engine is not developed within two years from date of contract, the contract is void. If the engine is developed in time, the expected profit is £0·25 million; if not, the expected loss is £1·25 million. The firm's current assets are £1·5 million. The research and development department assesses the probability of successful development within the two year period as 0·90.

(*i*) If the firm uses expected monetary value as its criterion what is the optimal action?
(*ii*) The firm has the following utility function for its assets, x (in £ million), namely $u(x) = x - 0·2x^2 + 150$,
What is the optimal action? For what range of values is this utility function likely to be reasonable?
(*iii*) What would you expect to be the difference in reaction to this contract as between a large firm (e.g. Vickers) and a small research and development engineering firm?

9 Imagine that you personally are invited either to take part in a gamble having a prize of 200 with probability p, or a loss, b, with probability, $1 - p$, or, alternatively, to receive a cash sum X with certainty. Give the value of p (for yourself) at which you would be indifferent between these two alternatives for the values of b and X specified below, and hence draw out a portion of your own utility function. (For purposes of this exercise you should abandon any moral scruples you may sensibly have against gambling.) All figures are in £.

$X = 25, 50, 100, 150$

combined with each b_i value listed

$b_1 = -5$

$b_2 = -10$

$b_3 = -25$

$b_4 = -50$

$b_5 = -100$

13 Classical statistics—Hypothesis testing

13.1 Introduction

It will be found that problems of the type discussed in Chapters 5 to 12 of this book are often given only a very brief discussion in most statistics books. Indeed, many students might see only a vague connection between the bulk of the material discussed in this book and that in many standard statistical texts. The main difference is that while we have been discussing what is termed the *Bayesian approach* to statistical decision-making, most standard texts are concerned with the so-called *classical approach* to statistics through the testing of hypotheses and the problems of estimation. This chapter and the next will be devoted to a necessarily concise discussion of the classical approach, which enables us to point out some of the basic differences between it and the Bayesian approach. We do not give a complete account of hypothesis testing and estimation, but sufficient detail is included to make possible a meaningful comparison with Bayesian methods. We should point out at this stage that we have already been concerned with problems of estimation, but the approach and interpretation through classical statistics is somewhat different from that adopted so far.

13.2 Hypotheses

Statisticians are commonly concerned with random variables whose probability distributions are not known in complete detail. For example, suppose that a manufacturing process is turning out electric light bulbs. Let x be the random variable representing the length of life of the bulbs produced. It is never

285

possible to know exactly the distribution of x. The best we can do is to determine its approximate form. Thus, we might assume that, to an adequate degree of approximation, x has a normal distribution which is completely defined by its mean and standard deviation. Any conjecture made about the distribution of a random variable x is referred to in classical statistics as a *hypothesis*. For example, we might make the hypothesis that the random variable x has a normal distribution with mean 1000 hours and standard deviation 100 hours.

We now ask the question as to whether, and how, we can prove that a hypothesis about some random variable is true or false. By carrying out investigations which, in one way or another, involve the random variable concerned, we can gather data which may strongly indicate that the hypothesis is false or true, but normally no procedure exists by which we can ever demonstrate incontrovertibly that the hypothesis is true or false. Thus, in the above example, we could in principle prove or disprove the hypothesis by simply checking every lamp produced by the process and determining the length of life of each lamp. This situation is, however, likely to be unacceptable in practice (with no bulbs left for sale), and thus no practical means usually exists for complete verification of the hypothesis concerned. It is important to realize that in general there is no way in which such verification can be incontrovertibly made.

For a more detailed illustration that points up the asymmetry in the testing procedure, suppose we are concerned with π, the proportion of households in the county of Kent which possess a refrigerator. The hypothesis that we wish to test is that $\pi = 0.5$. To test this hypothesis we select, at random, a sample of 100 households from Kent and find out whether or not they each possess a refrigerator. If x is the random variable corresponding to the number of households possessing a refrigerator, then earlier work in Chapter 3 shows that x will be a binomial variable with parameters $n = 100$ and π, where the hypothesis we want to test is that $\pi = 0.5$. Note that, technically speaking, we have here a hypergeometric distribution (see Section 3.8, page 59), but the population size is clearly so large, compared with the sample size of $n = 100$, that the binomial distribution will provide a more than adequate approximation.

Let us suppose that our sample of 100 households produces 75 with a refrigerator. Although this could happen with a random sample drawn from a population with $\pi = 0.5$, in the sense that there is some minute possibility of that particular sample result occurring, most analysts would feel that the outcome of this sample provided sufficient evidence to abandon the hypothesis that $\pi = \frac{1}{2}$. What is the justification for reaching this conclusion? It cannot be based on the fact that the probability of obtaining exactly 75 households with refrigerators is very small, since the probability of obtaining exactly 50 households with a refrigerator is also very small. Rather it is based on a chain of reasoning as follows. The expected value or mean of x when

$n=100$ and $\pi=\frac{1}{2}$ is $n \times \pi = 50$, and the standard deviation of x is $\sigma = \sqrt{\{n\pi(1-\pi)\}} = 5$. Now, for the values of n and π that we have here, the normal distribution provides an effective numerical approximation and, from Appendix B, we know that the probability that $|x - n\pi|$ exceeds 3σ or $3 \times 5 = 15$ is about 0·003. Hence, in only about 3 times out of 1000 would x be greater than 65 or less than 35. The observed value for x of 75 lies well outside this range. On the other hand, if $\pi = 0·70$, for example, the probability that x exceeds 75 would no longer be effectively zero, but would be much larger (approximately 0·163). Hence, we are led to suspect that our observed result is incompatible with $\pi = 0·5$, but is compatible with some other undefined value of π greater than 0·5. Thus, an argument along these lines illustrates how the outcome of some experiment can lead to an individual abandoning some hypothesis about the value of π.

On the other hand, could the outcome of an experiment of this type ever convince us that the hypothesis was correct? Here we must regretfully state that the answer is generally no. Suppose we obtained 53 households with refrigerators, does this convince us that $\pi = \frac{1}{2}$? There is no reason why it should, since obtaining 53 households with refrigerators is quite consistent with $\pi = 0·50$ or $\pi = 0·48$ or $\pi = 0·52$, etc., the respective probabilities being 0·066, 0·048 and 0·078. We could not differentiate between these probabilities with just one value of x. By carrying out larger and larger investigations, we could progressively narrow down the range of π values which we felt were consistent with the information obtained, but it would never be possible to decide with complete assurance that one particular value of π was indeed the true one to the exclusion of all other values. This points up the asymmetrical nature of the process for getting information about, or testing the hypothesis that $\pi = \frac{1}{2}$. The experimental information may very well convince us that the hypothesis is false. This is commonly the situation. The reader may therefore well wonder at this stage what is to be gained by formulating a hypothesis and then testing it by gathering information. We will return to this question later after discussing the procedure for testing hypotheses in a little more detail.

13.3 Significance test

Before making a formal statement of what is meant by a test of a statistical hypothesis, we will describe in some detail another example to illustrate the concepts.

Example 13.1

The tensile strength of steel rods made by a standard process is believed to follow a normal distribution with mean strength 400 kg and standard deviation 12 kg. The manufacturing process is modified by the engineer in charge in order, it is hoped by the management, to increase the expected tensile strength without changing the normality of the distribution or the standard deviation. The company has to decide whether the engineer's claim is justified or not.

We have here a hypothesis about the distribution of the tensile strengths; namely, that, with the standard process they are normal with mean 400 kg and standard deviation 12 kg, and that if the modified process has no effect they will still be distributed in the same way. To examine this hypothesis we want to obtain some information from the modified process. If this information is shown to be very unlikely to come from the original process, but is rather more likely to have come from some modified process, then we would reject the former in favour of the latter and agree to the engineer's claim. If not, there is no reason to discard the original assumptions and the engineer's claim might either be rejected, or the matter set aside for further study.

Since our interest lies in the mean tensile strength, the logical statistic to use in order to examine the claim is the mean value of tensile strength of a sample drawn from the modified process. Suppose that 25 sample rods are randomly drawn and their average tensile strength is 409 kg. Now, *if* the sample were drawn from the original unmodified process, the sample mean would have a normal distribution with a mean of 400 kg and a standard deviation of $12/\sqrt{25}=2\cdot4$ kg. Hence, the statistic

$$u=\frac{\bar{x}-400}{2\cdot4}$$

would follow a unit normal distribution. We have observed a sample mean $\bar{x}$ of 409 kg. This corresponds to a value of u of

$$u=\frac{409-400}{2\cdot5}=3\cdot6.$$

The probability of getting $u=3\cdot6$, or a more extreme value, is $1-F_N(u)=0\cdot0004$ from the table in Appendix B. In other words, what we have observed (i.e. $\bar{x}=409$) would be very unlikely indeed to have arisen if the process mean had remained at 400 kg. However, if the process mean has increased after the modification, a sample mean of 409 would not necessarily be so unusual. We accordingly conclude that the sample observations give strong evidence that the modification has increased the mean tensile strength of the rods.

Such a testing procedure, as the one we have just described, is usually referred to as a *significance test*, and we are now in a position to lay out a formal approach to such tests, listing the four main elements which constitute a significance test.

(*i*) *Null hypothesis*, commonly denoted by H_0. The null hypothesis is the hypothesis that is under test. Thus, in Example 13.1, the null hypothesis was that the tensile strength was distributed normally with mean 400 kg and standard deviation 12 kg. Note, that while the procedure described can lead to our rejecting the null hypothesis, it cannot lead us to accept formally that the null hypothesis is true.

(*ii*) *Alternative hypothesis*, commonly denoted by H_1. In testing whether the sample information is consistent with the null hypothesis H_0, some alternative hypothesis is stated or implied. In example 13·1, H_1 stated that the tensile strengths were normally distributed with standard deviation 12 kg, but with a mean that is greater than 400 kg.

(*iii*) *Test statistic*. From the sample information, some statistic is calculated which is used to test the null hypothesis H_0. In Example 13.1 this was the sample mean $\bar{x}$. Generally speaking, the test statistic is chosen so that as its value gets larger and larger (or smaller and smaller) the truth of the null hypothesis becomes more and more unlikely, i.e. there is a direct relationship between the value of the test statistic and the relative likelihood of the hypothesis concerned. The basic problem then reduces to one of deciding how large (or how small) the value of the test statistic ($\bar{x}$ in this case) must be in order that the null hypothesis is to be rejected.

(*iv*) *Significance level of the test*. The probability that the observed value, or a more extreme value, of the test statistic occurs under the null hypothesis can be calculated. If this probability, call it α, is extremely small the null hypothesis is rejected in favour of the alternative hypothesis H_1. We have to decide just how small α has to be before we take this decision. The critical value of the probability α is referred to as the significance level of the test. The classical theory of statistics provides us with no hard and fast rules for the selection of α, but it is often selected to have the value of 0·01 or 0·05. Then when α turns out to be lower than the value selected, the null hypothesis is rejected.

Figure 13.1 illustrates the situation. It gives the original distribution of the individual results for x under the null hypothesis H_0, where the mean is θ_0,

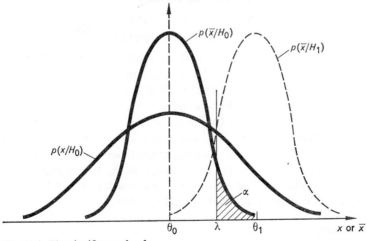

Fig. 13.1. The significance level

the distribution of the test statistic $\bar{x}$, also under the null hypothesis H_0, and the point λ on the x scale such that if $\bar{x} > \lambda$ the null hypothesis H_0 will be rejected. The significance level α is the probability that $\bar{x}$ exceeds λ under the null hypothesis, H_0 and is equivalent to the shaded area in the figure. Note, of course, that the significance level is synonymous with the probability that the null hypothesis H_0 is rejected, when it is in fact true. If the alternative hypothesis H_1 is true, and the mean is θ_1, then the probability of rejecting H_0 in favour of H_1 will be the area under the dotted curve to the right of the vertical line at the point λ. As θ_1 increases this area will tend to unity, the total area under the dotted line.

We now give two further examples to illustrate the principles that have just been enunciated.

Example 13.2

A machine is packaging nominal 8 oz packets of sugar, and it has been found that, over a long period, the actual weight of sugar put in the packet has been normally distributed with a mean of 8·1 oz and a standard deviation of 0·04 oz. The setting on the machine which regulates the amount of sugar put in is thought to have been accidentally altered, and to discover whether this is so, a random sample of ten packets is examined, and the sugar weighed. For the sample the mean weight of sugar in the ten packets is found to be 8·123 oz.

First of all it seems a reasonable assumption that, even if the average amount of sugar per packet has been altered, the standard deviation of such amounts will be unchanged. It is therefore assumed that the standard deviation of the amounts is 0·04 oz, irrespective of the mean. The null hypothesis H_0, is then that the population mean is 8·1 oz, with the alternative hypothesis, H_1, that the mean is different from 8·1 oz. The appropriate test statistic to use is the sample mean, and the quantity

$$\frac{\text{Sample mean} - \text{Population mean}}{\text{Standard deviation of sample mean}} = \frac{\bar{x} - 8 \cdot 1}{0 \cdot 04 / \sqrt{10}} = \frac{0 \cdot 023}{0 \cdot 0126} = 1 \cdot 818$$

is a unit normal variable. From Appendix B the probability of exceeding $u = 1 \cdot 818$ is 0·0345. This could be regarded as quite an unlikely occurrence, and hence it would be reasonable to say that there is some more likely population from which these samples were drawn, e.g. with the population mean somewhat higher than 8·1 oz. One other consideration must, however, be borne in mind. The value of 8·123 oz has been taken as a significant result, significant in the sense that it shows some departure from the standard weight of 8·1 oz. But suppose that the mean weight of the ten sample packages had come to be 8·077 oz which is as far below 8·1 oz as 8·123 is above. In this case the appropriate unit normal variable is

$$\frac{\bar{x} - 8 \cdot 1}{0 \cdot 04 / \sqrt{10}} = -1 \cdot 818,$$

and from Appendix B the probability of getting the observed value of $\bar{x}$ or a more extreme value, that is a lower value, is again equal to 0·0345. Since this is indicative of an unlikely event, the null hypothesis would again be rejected. This shows that getting a mean of 8·123 oz, and rejecting the null hypothesis, is indicative of an unlikely event, the null hypothesis would again be rejected. also implies in this instance that a mean of 8·077 oz or less will similarly lead to a rejection of the null hypothesis. Hence, overall, the significance level of the test is not 0·0345 but $2 \times 0·0345$ or 0·069. This is not so small as before and we might hesitate before rejecting the null hypothesis that the population mean is still 8·1 oz.

Note the different alternative hypotheses H_1 in Examples 13.1 and 13.2. In Example 13.1 it was that the mean was *greater* than 400 kg; in Example 13.2 it was that the mean was *different* from 8·1 oz. The significance level calculation was accordingly different in the two instances.

Example 13.3

Two plantations in Malaya are supplying rubber in batches to a factory. The factory has, over a period of years, been checking the tensile strength in kilograms per square centimetre of samples from each plantation, and has found that the standard deviations between samples of the tensile strengths are 6 kg for the first plantation and 8 kg for the second. The factory is interested to know whether the mean tensile strength of the rubber in a certain batch is the same for the rubber from each of the two plantations, and examines twelve randomly selected samples from the first plantation and sixteen from the second with the following results (in kilograms per square centimetre):

| First plantation | 201 | 201 | 181 | 193 | 179 | 183 |
| | 188 | 182 | 197 | 185 | 204 | 198 |

| Second plantation | 183 | 189 | 201 | 174 | 194 | 169 | 181 | 199 |
| | 178 | 174 | 198 | 188 | 196 | 171 | 195 | 170 |

From these figures the following values are obtained:

$$\bar{x}_1 = 191, \qquad \bar{x}_2 = 185.$$

Now the null hypothesis H_0 that we wish to test is that $\mu_1 - \mu_2 = 0$, where μ_1 and μ_2 are the two respective population means. The alternative hypothesis, H_1, is that $\mu_1 - \mu_2 \neq 0$.

To test H_0, we use as our test statistic $d = \bar{x}_1 - \bar{x}_2$ and, from Chapter 3, we have that:

$$\text{var}(d) = \text{var}(\bar{x}_1) + \text{var}(\bar{x}_2) = \frac{\sigma_1^2}{n_1} + \frac{\sigma_2^2}{n_2}$$

where σ_i is the variance in the ith population and n_i the size of sample drawn from that population. Hence, in this instance, the quantity

$$\frac{d}{\text{standard deviation of } d} = \frac{\bar{x}_1 - \bar{x}_2}{\sqrt{\left(\frac{\sigma_1^2}{n_1} + \frac{\sigma_2^2}{n_2}\right)}} = \frac{6}{2 \cdot 646} = 2 \cdot 268$$

is distributed as a unit normal variable. From Appendix B, the area beyond $2 \cdot 268$ is $0 \cdot 0117$. However, a two-tailed test is required here, since the problem involves an alternative hypothesis that implies both positive and negative values of the test criterion will be judged as significant evidence for disproving H_0. This gives the appropriate significance level as $2 \times 0 \cdot 0117$ or $0 \cdot 0234$. This result is very small, and hence would probably be regarded as evidence to reject hypothesis H_0 in favour of H_1, i.e. reject that the plantation population means are the same in favour of the alternative that the first plantation has a higher mean value of tensile strength than the second plantation.

13.4 Inference for means

Both in this and in earlier chapters, we have made use of the statistic

$$u = \frac{\bar{x} - \mu}{\sigma / \sqrt{n}} \tag{13.1}$$

as a unit normal variable where a random sample size n with mean $\bar{x}$ has been drawn from a normal population having mean μ and standard deviation σ. For the purpose of testing hypotheses, the population standard deviation σ has been tacitly assumed to be known. This, however, is commonly not the case. Thus, even in Example 13.1, we assumed the standard deviation to be unaltered after the process had been modified and this may not necessarily be a true assumption. For large samples, say n greater than 40, the sample estimate

$$s = \sqrt{\left\{\frac{1}{n-1} \sum_{i=1}^{n} (x_i - \bar{x})^2\right\}}, \tag{13.2}$$

where x_i represents the sample observations, can be used in place of the unknown σ, and little error is then involved by assuming the expression in Eq. 13.1 to be a unit normal variable. However, for smaller samples from populations of unknown variability, the sample statistic s in Eq. 13.2 may itself be subject to considerable sampling error. The probable amount of error is, of course, related to the sample size n: for small values of n the average error in the estimate may be quite large, while as n increases, the average error decreases. In statistical jargon, we say that s is an estimate of the population standard deviation σ based on $(n-1)$ *degrees of freedom*. This is the only occasion in this book that we use the statistical concept of degrees of freedom, but it has quite wide currency in other situations than the one we are now concerned with. The degrees of freedom for a statistic give a measure of the number of independent pieces of information used to calculate that statistic. In calculating s from Eq. 13.2 above, the sample information is in the form of n pieces of information $(x_i - \bar{x})$. Since

$$\bar{x} = \sum_{i=1}^{n} x_i,$$

we find that only the first $(n-1)$ of the n terms $(x_i - \bar{x})$ are independent, i.e. the nth difference $(x_n - \bar{x})$ can be written as a linear combination of the first $(n-1)$ differences $(x_i - \bar{x})$ for $i = 1, 2, \ldots n-1$. Hence, we say that s is an estimate based on $(n-1)$ degrees of freedom.

To return to the original argument, suppose that we have a small sample of n observations from a population with unknown standard deviation σ. Then we are unable to use Eq. 13.1 and the nearest that we can manage is

$$\frac{\bar{x} - \mu}{s/\sqrt{n}} \tag{13.3}$$

where σ has been replaced by s from Eq. 13.2. Equation 13.3 is referred to as a t-statistic and has a distribution referred to as the t-*distribution*. In this particular instance it has $(n-1)$ degrees of freedom.

The t-distribution with f degrees of freedom (commonly written as t_f) is symmetrical about zero, there being a different member of the family of distributions for each value of f. As f increases, the distribution tends to the unit standard normal form, as illustrated by Fig. 13.2. For small values of f, the distribution is a rather flattened form of the unit normal distribution, its

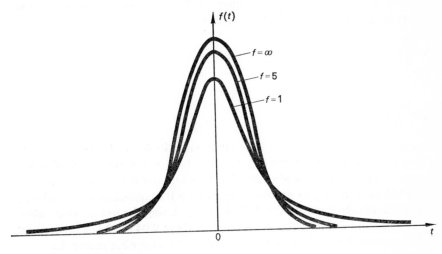

Fig. 13.2. The t-distribution

standard deviation being greater than 1 as for the unit normal distribution. This flattening effect is illustrated by looking at the table of the significance points of the *t*-distribution shown in Appendix D. If we look at the column headed by the probability level 0·025, we notice that the appropriate *t*-value falls from 12·71 for $f=1$, to 2·57 for $f=5$, to 2·23 for $f=10$ and eventually to 1·96 for $f=\infty$. The last-named is the same value as for a unit standard normal variable corresponding to a tail probability of 0·025. This progression is what we would expect. For small values of f we have a larger value of t than of u to reach a given level of significance. When f tends to infinity it is equivalent to having an estimate of σ based on an s value with infinite degrees of freedom. This estimate would certainly be precisely accurate, leading us to a significance test of form Eq. 13.1 rather than Eq. 13.3 and, hence, we would expect the *t*-value to approach the *u*-value as f tends to infinity.

Example 13.4

The production manager wishes to test whether the tensile strength of a large batch of corrugated cases is up to the average production standard of 26·4 units. (The precise nature of the units here are immaterial; they are actually in terms of a constant times the pounds per perimeter inch pressure required to crush the case.) To test the batch a random sample of 8 cases is taken and tested. The strengths are:

26·3   25·5   25·9   25·5   26·5   25·9   28·5   25·9.

From this sample we calculate that the sample mean $\bar{x}$ is 26·0 and the sample estimate, s, of the population standard deviation is 0·4.

The sample mean is below the process norm. But is it significantly below the norm? To examine this we set up the null hypothesis H_0 that $\mu=26\cdot4$, with the alternative hypothesis H_1 that $\mu<26\cdot4$. Our test statistic is $\bar{x}=26\cdot0$ and to judge this test statistic we calculate:

$$t_f=\frac{\bar{x}-\mu}{s/\sqrt{n}}$$

or

$$t_7=\frac{26\cdot0-26\cdot4}{0\cdot4/\sqrt{8}}=-2\cdot83.$$

We now look up this *t*-value in the tables given in Appendix D, which only provides probabilities for positive values of t. However, the distribution is symmetrical so that, instead of looking up the probability of getting an observed value of $-2\cdot83$ or lower, we look up the equivalent probability of getting an observed value of $+2\cdot83$ or higher. Using the row corresponding to $f=7$, we can estimate this probability at about 0·04 (2·83 lies between the columns given for $p=0\cdot05$ and for $p=0\cdot025$ and somewhat nearer the former). The significance level is accordingly 0·04. We now have to make a judgment, namely, how small a significance level we accept to provide evidence that H_0 should be rejected in favour of H_1, and, that a real change (diminution) in strength has occurred. Probably in this case we would feel that the evidence justified some action. Whether the action would be a formal complaint, or just an examination of a further sample, would clearly depend upon the circumstances surrounding the purchase of this particular batch of corrugated cases.

The test we have just carried out in Example 13.4 is another example of a one-tailed test. If the alternative hypothesis, H_1, had not been that $\mu < 26 \cdot 4$, but that $\mu \neq 26 \cdot 4$, we would now reject H_0 in favour of H_1 if $\bar{x}$ was either significantly above $\mu = 26 \cdot 4$ or below it. Hence, if we are prepared to reject H_0 when $t_7 = -2 \cdot 83$ or lower, we would also logically have to reject H_0 if $t_7 = +2 \cdot 83$ or higher. This is now a two-tailed test. The corresponding probability of this joint possibility is not $0 \cdot 04$ as before, but $2 \times 0 \cdot 04$ or $0 \cdot 08$. Our action now might be different.

13.5 Types of errors

The various examples discussed in this chapter so far enable us to define formally the two types of error that can occur in a statistical test of a hypothesis. Let us note at once that these are errors of inference, not errors of arithmetic or algebra. To fix our ideas, we will discuss them through an illustrative problem. Suppose that an electrical manufacturer has brought out a new electric light bulb which he claims will give an increased length of life as compared with that of his standard bulb. To decide whether the claim is justified, a large commercial user carries out an experiment whereby he uses the new bulb at a number of positions in his factory at each of which the length of life can be readily determined and uses this data to decide upon the manufacturer's claim. Let us define our null hypothesis H_0 that $\mu = 1000$ hours (the assumed known average length of life of the population of standard bulbs). We further define the alternative hypothesis H_1 that $\mu > 1000$ hours and for the moment concentrate upon a particular portion of H_1, namely, that $\mu = 1020$ hours. If we now reject H_0 or not according to whether or not $\bar{x}$ is greater than some quantity λ, the latter being determined in the manner used in Example 13.4, there are two types of possible error:

Type 1: The null hypothesis H_0 is rejected when it is in fact true.
Type 2: The null hypothesis H_0 is accepted when it is in fact false, and the
        alternative hypothesis H_1 is true.

Now the type 1 error is equivalent to the significance level, α, that we decide to use for the test that we carry out. This level is, of course, under our control and we can raise or lower it as much as we desire. In theory, we could make it negligible. This would imply setting λ at some very large level indeed. However, the effect of so doing would be to increase the type 2 error because if H_1, i.e. that the mean μ is actually 1020 hours, is true then the probability that $\bar{x}$ exceeds λ will diminish the larger the value of λ. This is illustrated in Fig. 13.3 where the distributions of the sample mean when the

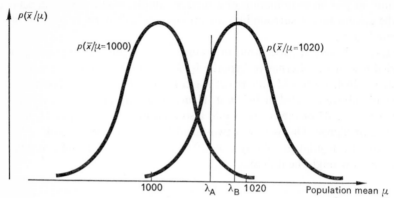

Fig. 13.3. Decision criteria and statistical errors

population mean is 1000 or, alternatively 1020 hours are given. Furthermore, two possible values of λ, namely, λ_A and λ_B, are marked. (The actual values are illustrative only.) For λ_A there is a 0·10 level of type 1 error and a 0·40 level of type 2 error. When the value is changed to λ_B, this has the effect of reducing the type 1 error, but at the same time it increases the type 2 error. The latter is commonly denoted by β. Hence, we may generalize to say that, for a given quantity of information, we will always have to make a trade-off between the two types of error. If one type of error is too high, we can only reduce it by allowing the other type of error to increase. This is a fundamental point, from which we cannot escape, that lies behind the whole concept of statistical hypothesis testing; it dominates a full understanding of the use of sample information in problems of inference.

The value of $1-\beta$ measures the probability that we reject the null hypothesis H_0 in favour of the alternative hypothesis H_1. This value, $1-\beta$, is commonly referred to as the *power* of the test. Obviously, when we are considering various possible tests for a given situation we aim to find the most powerful test available in this sense, that is we seek to maximize $1-\beta$ for a fixed value of α. This is why, for example, the illustration just discussed used the sample mean rather than the sample median to test hypotheses relating to the population mean μ.

13.6 Level of information

The discussion in the previous section shows that, once the type 1 level of error is fixed, so also is the type 2 level of error for a completely defined alternative hypothesis H_1. It is common practice to fix the type 1 level of error at α say, and then to see what level of error is implied for the type 2 error. Suppose that we then want to make the latter error, denoted by β, smaller? How can this be done? One way in which it can be done is to select a larger sample size such that, while keeping α fixed, the value of β can be reduced to the desired level. Figure 13.4 shows the same situation as in Fig. 13.3, but

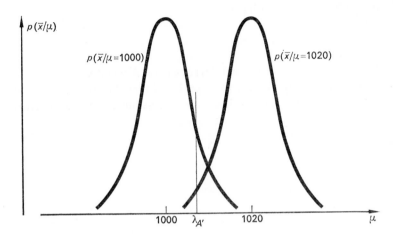

Fig. 13.4. Changed decision criteria

with a larger sample size than before. It is clear that, if α is kept constant, λ_A will be smaller than before. If this is changed to say $\lambda_{A'}$, the value of β is automatically decreased. Hence it would seem that by suitably selecting the sample size one can reduce β as much as is desired while keeping α at some specified value. The following example illustrates this concept.

Example 13.5

The purity of a chemical manufactured on a large scale has, in the past, shown a mean of 68 per cent, with a standard deviation among the individual determinations of 2·3 per cent. A new process is proposed which will, it is estimated, produce a purity yield of 70 per cent. How many samples should be examined from the new process in order to be sure that the purity has, in fact, improved?

To estimate the required sample size n, we first specify that the null hypothesis H_0 is that the population mean μ is equal to 68, with the alternative hypothesis H_1 that the population mean is 70. In each case we assume a normal distribution of observations with a standard deviation of 2·3 per cent. We now have to set a suitable level for the two errors. For the significance level, or type 1 error, we will specify 0·02, while for the type 2 error we will specify 0·05. We emphasize that these errors are at choice and must be dictated by the circumstances of the investigation.

Suppose that the critical value of $\bar{x}$ is λ, i.e. if $\bar{x}$ exceeds λ we reject H_0 in favour of H_1, while if $\bar{x}$ falls short of λ we accept H_0. Then, for the type 1 error, we will have

$$u_1 = \frac{\lambda - 68}{2 \cdot 3 / \sqrt{n}} = 2 \cdot 05,$$

while for the type 2 error we will have

$$u_2 = \frac{70 - \lambda}{2 \cdot 3 / \sqrt{n}} = 1 \cdot 65,$$

where 2·05 and 1·65 are the unit normal deviates from Appendix B corresponding to tail probabilities for the type 1 and type 2 errors of 0·02 and 0·05 respectively. Eliminating λ from these two expressions for u_1 and u_2 gives

$$\lambda = \frac{2 \cdot 05 \times 2 \cdot 3}{\sqrt{n}} + 68, \quad \text{and also} \quad \lambda = 70 - \frac{1 \cdot 65 \times 2 \cdot 3}{\sqrt{n}}.$$

Hence

$$70 = \frac{1 \cdot 65 \times 2 \cdot 3}{\sqrt{n}} + \frac{2 \cdot 05 \times 2 \cdot 3}{\sqrt{n}} + 68,$$

or

$$2\sqrt{n} = 2 \cdot 3 \times 3 \cdot 70,$$

or

$$n = 18 \cdot 1 \quad \text{(or 19 to the next highest integer)}.$$

Hence, we should take a sample of at least 19 to achieve a test with the required or lower levels of error.

13.7 Summary and comparison

This chapter has outlined the way in which classical statistics defines hypotheses and seeks to test them. It has introduced the notion of the null and alternative hypotheses, and the errors associated with rejecting these hypotheses falsely. Table 13.1 summarizes the situation in terms of a pay-off

Table 13.1

Pay-offs for alternative situations

		Outcomes	
	Action	r_0 H_0 true	r_1 H_1 true
a_0	Accept H_0	u_{00}	u_{01}
a_1	Reject H_0	u_{10}	u_{11}

table as used earlier in Chapter 5, with u_{ij} to represent the pay-off for the ith action and the jth outcome. Under classical statistics, the choice between action a_0 and action a_1 is linked directly to the probabilities of the two kinds of error. However, we should point out that although when these errors are very small the investigator commonly makes an immediate choice of actions, when they are not so small he commonly suggests that we should collect more information before making a final decision. In the approach adopted in this book, the third alternative (collect more information) would be formally inserted as a further possible action, and all actions evaluated on the basis of the pay-offs and estimated relative likelihoods of the possible hypotheses. Hence, we can see that classical statistics:

(*i*) does not formally take into account any prior beliefs of the truth of the outcomes r_0 and r_1 concerned;

(*ii*) does not formally take into account the respective pay-offs u_{ij};

(*iii*) does not formally allow a trade-off to be made between the errors α and β and forces the setting of α at what may be an arbitrary level.

These contrasts show up the differences between the two approaches starkly, but it must be realized that there are also great similarities, and that in many situations the classical approach is the only approach possible, for example, in many forms of scientific experimentation. When the formal theory of statistical significance tests was being developed in the 1920s, the approach adopted was governed very much by the view that the prior probabilities would not be available, and neither would be the pay-offs. Today, while this is still the case in many instances, this is not universally so and an approach which considers them explicitly, even if they are incapable of precise evaluation, seems better than an approach which ignores them.

Exercises on Chapter 13

1 The purity of a chemical manufactured on a large scale varies slightly from batch to batch. In the past the purity per batch has had a mean value of 68·4 per cent and a standard deviation between batches of 2·3 per cent. A small modification of the manufacturing process is made and the purity of the first eleven batches produced is:

66·1, 71·3, 75·2, 64·3, 76·4, 75·6, 66·3, 63·2, 65·8, 62·4, 73·4

Assuming that the standard deviation between batch purities is unchanged, has the modification improved the process?

2 Cement mortar briquettes are being made and the breaking strength of the briquettes measured. The standard deviation of the breaking strength of samples from the same batch has been found to be 17 lb. Random samples, each of ten briquettes, are available from two different batches and the breaking strengths are:

Batch A   518   508   554   555   536   544   532   530   554   542

Batch B   544   538   554   540   506   534   548   530   525   522

Test whether there is any significant difference between the mean strengths of the two batches.

3 A company is concerned about the amount of time required for clerical personnel to file a certain kind of record. A random sample of 150 observations gave the following results:

Mean time per record filed   68·2 seconds

Standard deviation of time per record filed   18·0 seconds

Test, at the 5 per cent significance level, the hypothesis that the population mean time per record filed is 70, against the alternative hypothesis that it is less than 70 seconds.

4 Rotating disc electricity meters are adjusted, as part of the manufacturing process, to make them operate synchronously with a standard meter. After this adjustment has been made to a large batch of meters, ten are selected at random and their accuracy measured against a norm of 1·000 for the standard meter. The ten meters have accuracies of:

0·983, 1·002, 0·998, 0·996, 1·002, 0·983, 0·994, 0·991, 1·005, 0·986.

Can the deviations from 1·000 be regarded as random fluctuations, or do the results indicate that the accuracies of the meters deviate systematically from 1·000?

5 A manufacturer of television colour tubes was disturbed by reports from the field that the new 'improved' tube currently being manufactured had a shorter service life than the tubes being made formerly. It found that its research division was already testing a random sample of twenty television sets for component failures by plugging them in and letting them run continuously until some failure occurred. The manufacturer ordered that records be kept on tube life and that the sets be operated until tube failure. It was known from past experiences that the mean length of life for old process tubes was 9000 hours. After a considerable time the test was completed, with the following results:

Sample size=20.

Mean life=8700 hours.

Sample estimate of standard deviation of tube life=1200 hours.

Test the hypothesis that the new tubes have a true mean length of life equal to or greater than 9000 hours.

6 An investigation into the performance of two machines in a factory each manufacturing large numbers of nominally the same product gives the results shown in Table 13.2.

Table 13.2

Machine performances

Machine	No. of articles examined	No. of articles defective
A	750	42
B	900	36

(*i*) Apply a statistical test in order to determine whether there is any significant difference in the performance of the two machines as measured by the number of defective articles produced.

(*ii*) What action would you recommend if the firm concerned was considering replacing machine A, which is old, by another machine of type B which is, however, quite costly to install?

7 The standard set for the maximum proportion of defective items involving a complicated assembly in a production process is 0·20. The company has an order for 10 000 items and, on testing 100 items selected at random from the first 1000, finds 25 defective items. Test the hypothesis that the overall proportion of defectives for the lot is 0·20 against the alternative hypothesis that the proportion is greater than 0·20. (Use the normal approximation to the binomial distribution to evaluate probabilities in the sample.)

8 The price fetched for iron ore depends critically upon the iron content which has to be decided by chemical analysis of ore samples. The standard

Table 13.3

Iron ore determinations

Ore no.	Per cent iron method A	Per cent iron method B
1	28·22	28·27
2	33·95	33·99
3	38·25	38·20
4	42·52	42·42
5	37·62	37·64
6	37·84	37·85
7	36·12	36·21
8	35·11	35·20
9	34·45	34·40
10	52·83	52·86

method A uses dichromate, while a new method B using thioglycolate is proposed. Samples taken from ten widely different ores are examined by the two methods and the results are shown in Table 13.3. Test the hypothesis that the new method B is unbiased with respect to the standard method A.

9 A brewer believes that he has developed a beer which can clearly be distinguished by taste from his competitor's brand. To test this assertion he selects twenty-five individuals at random and allows them to sample his beer. Later he gives them each two unlabelled glasses, one containing his beer and one containing his competitor's beer, and asks them to select the glass which contains his beer. It turns out that seventeen of them correctly identify his beer.

- (*i*) What are the null hypotheses and the alternative hypotheses for the appropriate statistical test in this instance?
- (*ii*) If the type 1 error (significance level) is set at $\alpha = 0.05$, would you agree that the tests show that it is possible to achieve some discrimination by taste?

10 The management of the Regency Aircraft Company are examining their welding operations. Currently the mean time per weld is 11·5 minutes with a standard deviation of 2·5 minutes. A new process is introduced for which, it is claimed, the mean time is 10·4 minutes. Assuming that the company sets its type 1 error at 0·05 and its type 2 error at 0·01, how large a sample of welds under the modified system should be taken to determine whether the expected improvement has occurred?

11 A chemist has developed a new synthetic rubber, Y, for a tyre company, which he believes is better than the synthetic rubber, X, currently in use. Extensive testing over the years on X has shown that the useful mileage for a tyre made from X can be regarded as a normally distributed random variable with a mean of 15 000 miles and a standard deviation of 2000 miles.

Suppose a test is to be set up and a random sample of n tyres made with the new rubber Y are to be tested. How large should n be if the type 1 error is to be kept to 0·01 and the type 2 error, when the true (but unknown) mean of Y is 15 500 miles, is to be kept to 0·05? Comment on the rate of change of the value of n with changes in the value of the type 2 error.

(Assume that the standard deviation of tyre life for rubber Y is the same as for rubber X.)

14 Classical statistics—estimation

14.1 Introduction

A fundamental task of statistical work is to devise sample statistics which provide suitable estimators of corresponding population parameters. For example, it is common practice to use the sample mean $\bar{x}$, calculated from a random sample of size n from some population with unknown mean μ as an estimator of μ itself. We do this all the time—the average length of life of car tyres, the average petrol consumption per gallon in a car, the time taken for a journey, etc. But we could use other estimators, for example, the sample median $\tilde{x}$. Why do we commonly use $\bar{x}$ in preference to $\tilde{x}$? It is not computational ease, as $\tilde{x}$ can very often be calculated rather more simply than can $\bar{x}$. To answer this question we need to consider the basic properties that we would like all estimators to possess. The three main such properties are absence of bias, efficiency and consistency. To illustrate a discussion of these properties suppose that the manufacture of a random sample of 5 cartons for some product has been timed and costed in a works and the costs (in £) are:

0·37, 0·28, 0·33, 0·30, 0·27.

The problem is then to estimate the mean and variance of the cost per carton for the complete population of cartons being made in the works. The three properties are now discussed in turn.

14.2 Bias of estimators

To estimate the population mean we might reasonably decide to use a number of estimators, such as the sample mean $\bar{x}$ (0·31, in this instance) or the sample median $\tilde{x}$ (0·30, in this instance). We would, however, be unlikely to use the highest observation (0·37). The reason is that we would like our estimator to be unbiased; that is we want

$E(\text{Estimate}) = \text{population value},$

and, while it is true, and to be expected from general considerations, that

$E(\bar{x}) = E(\tilde{x}) = \mu,$

it is to be expected that

$E(\text{highest observation}) \neq \mu,$

since a moment's reflection will suggest that the average 'highest observation' in a series of samples of size n will be considerably higher than μ. Nevertheless, to choose between $\bar{x}$ and $\tilde{x}$, we must consider some other property of the estimators which we do in the next section but, before doing so, we consider the estimation of the population variance σ^2. If we calculate

$$s_1^2 = \frac{1}{n} \sum (x_i - \bar{x})^2$$

from the sample, we find that

$$E(s_1^2) = \frac{n-1}{n} \sigma^2 \neq \sigma^2.$$

In other words, s_1^2 would on average underestimate the population variance. This arises because, with the calculation of $\bar{x}$ from the sample itself, there are in reality only $n-1$ independent deviations $(x_i - \bar{x})$, as discussed in Section 13.4. To form an unbiased estimate we need to take

$$s^2 = \frac{1}{n-1} \sum (x_i - \bar{x})^2,$$

since we then have

$E(s^2) = \sigma^2.$

Hence, s^2 is referred to as an unbiased estimator of σ^2, while s_1^2 is referred to as a biased estimator.

14.3 Efficient estimators

In general, we would choose to use an unbiased estimator rather than a biased one. It is often the case, however, that more than one unbiased estimator can be defined for estimating a particular parameter, e.g. $\bar{x}$ and $\tilde{x}$ above both provide unbiased estimators for μ. A question of choice then arises.

The sampling variances of the possible estimators provides a basis for choice between them. The estimator whose sampling distribution has the least spread (or variance) is to be preferred, since the numerical estimates provided by that estimator will cluster more closely round the population parameter value than will those derived from an estimator which has a larger sampling variance. We state formally that the smaller the sampling variance of the estimator, the more *efficient* is the estimator. If the set of all possible unbiased estimators of some parameter is considered, then the one with the smallest variance is called the *most efficient*, or *best*, esitmator. The others are sometimes said to be *inefficient* estimators.

Reverting to the example discussed earlier, we had two possible unbiased estimators of μ, namely, $\bar{x}$ and $\tilde{x}$. The variance of $\bar{x}$, from Chapter 4, is given by

$$\text{var}\,(\bar{x}) = \frac{\sigma^2}{n},$$

while that of $\tilde{x}$ is given by

$$\text{var}\,(\tilde{x}) = \frac{\pi}{2} \cdot \frac{\sigma^2}{n}.$$

(This result is stated and will not be derived; it does, unlike var $(\bar{x})$, assume that the sampling is from a normal population.) Since var $(\bar{x})$ is less than var $(\tilde{x})$, $\bar{x}$ is more efficient than $\tilde{x}$ as an estimator of μ. We can go further than this since it can be proved mathematically that of all possible estimators of μ, $\bar{x}$ is the one with the smallest variance. Therefore, $\bar{x}$ is the most efficient estimator of μ.

It can also be shown that s^2 is the most efficient estimator of σ^2, i.e. no other estimator of σ^2 has a lower sampling variance. It may be asked what other unbiased estimators exist for σ^2, and there are, in fact, plenty. For example, the range (highest observation minus lowest observation in the sample) can be used to estimate σ (and hence σ^2) and is so used for this purpose in many quality-control schemes in industry. Although it is not as efficient an estimator as using the sample variance, it nevertheless has two advantages. First, in small samples the relative loss of efficiency in terms of the sampling variance of the estimator is low; it is only in large samples that the loss is a dramatic one. Second, the speed and ease of computation of range is vastly superior to that for sample variance, and the scope for numerical error on the factory floor thereby minimized. Hence, range does find a ready use in such situations: it is better to have a readily usable estimator with slightly less than 100 per cent efficiency than an intractable estimator having 100 per cent efficiency.

14.4 Consistent estimators

In addition to the two properties of estimators that have already been discussed, it would be desirable to use estimators whose precision of estimation increases as the sample size increases. The ultimate in precision would obviously be for the numerical estimate to coincide with the parameter value for every sample drawn. This would imply that the estimator would be unbiased and have zero sampling variance. This state of affairs is impossible in practice, but the precision of many, if not most, estimators tends to this ideal as the sample size increases. We call such estimators *consistent*. In the example discussed it can be seen that var $(\bar{x})$ and var $(\tilde{x})$ both tend to zero as n tends to infinity. Hence, both are consistent estimators.

Table 14.1 summarizes the main properties of an estimator, b

Table 14.1

Properties of estimators

Property	Bias	Efficiency	Consistency
Definitions	b is unbiased if $E(b) = \beta$	b is efficient if it is unbiased and var (b) is minimized	b is consistent if it is unbiased and var $(b) \to 0$ as $n \to \infty$
Examples: (i) For μ	$\bar{x}$ and $\tilde{x}$ are both unbiased estimators of μ	$\bar{x}$ is efficient $\tilde{x}$ is inefficient	$\bar{x}$ and $\tilde{x}$ are both consistent
(ii) For σ^2	s_1^2 is biased s^2 is unbiased	s^2 is efficient	s^2 is consistent
(iii) For σ	Range (with appropriate multiplier) is unbiased	Inefficient	Inconsistent

When choosing between estimators, the properties just described should all be considered. As mentioned earlier, the ideal estimator may be sacrificed on grounds of expediency, as in using sample range to estimate population standard deviation, but in making such a choice it is important to realize just what is being sacrificed.

14.5 Point estimates by maximum likelihood

In the preceding sections we have been discussing what are termed *point estimates*—namely, some sample statistic that can be used to provide an estimate of a corresponding population parameter. A very useful way in which such point estimators can be derived is the method of *maximum likelihood*. The general approach is to choose as the estimator of some population parameter θ, that function of the sample observations which will, when substituted for θ itself, make the probability of the sample a maximum. In other words, for the chosen value of θ the observed sample is the most likely sample. To illustrate the method we discuss two examples.

Example 14.1

A large population of electronic components has an unknown proportion p defectives. A random sample of n components is selected and k of these are found to be defective. What is the maximum likelihood estimator of p?

Here we have

$$f = p\{n, k | p\} = \binom{n}{k} p^k (1-p)^{n-k}.$$

As a function of p, this expression is a maximum when

$$\frac{df}{dp} = 0 \quad \text{and} \quad \frac{d^2f}{dp^2} < 0.$$

By differentiation, we obtain

$$\frac{df}{dp} = \binom{n}{k} [kp^{k-1}(1-p)^{n-k} - (n-k)p^k(1-p)^{n-k-1}],$$

giving the critical value $\hat{p}$ of p as

$$\hat{p} = \frac{k}{n}.$$

It is easy to verify that this value, which is the sample proportion of defectives, does indeed correspond to a maximum for f and not a minimum, and this estimator is the same as the intuitive estimator used earlier in Chapter 3.

† *Example* 14.2

The length of life x (hours) of television tubes in a large batch is assumed to follow the probability distribution

$$f(x|\theta) = \frac{1}{\theta} e^{-x/\theta} \qquad x > 0.$$

A random sample of n tubes is drawn from the batch and the lengths of life of the tubes are

$x_1, x_2, x_3, \ldots x_n$ respectively.

What is the maximum likelihood estimator for θ?

Here, the joint probability of the observed results is:

$$\frac{1}{\theta} e^{-x_1/\theta} \cdot \frac{1}{\theta} e^{-x_2/\theta} \ldots \frac{1}{\theta} e^{-x_n/\theta} = \left(\frac{1}{\theta}\right)^n e^{-\sum_{i=1}^{n} x_i/\theta} = L$$

We want to find the value, $\hat{\theta}$, say, that maximizes L. In practice, the logarithm of L is often more convenient to deal with than L itself. Since $\log L$ is a monotonic-increasing function of L, a value of θ which maximizes L also maximizes $\log L$. Hence, we need to find θ to satisfy

$$\frac{d}{d\theta}(\log L)=0 \quad \text{and} \quad \frac{d^2}{d\theta^2}(\log L)<0.$$

Now

$$\log L = -n\log\theta - \frac{1}{\theta}\sum_{i=1}^{n}x_i \text{ and}$$

$$\frac{d}{d\theta}(\log L) = -\frac{n}{\theta} + \frac{1}{\theta^2}\sum_{i=1}^{n}x_i,$$

giving

$$\theta = \frac{1}{n}\sum_{i=1}^{n}x_i = \bar{x},$$

and $(d^2\log L)/d\theta^2)$ is less than zero. Hence, the sample mean provides us with the appropriate estimator.

14.6 Properties of maximum likelihood estimators

The following are the main reasons for recommending the use of maximum likelihood (ml) estimators:

(*i*) The ml estimator is consistent.
(*ii*) The ml estimator tends to be normally distributed as the sample size n increases (and, in some instances, is normally distributed for any value of n).
(*iii*) The ml estimator is the most efficient estimator for large values of n. It does not follow, incidentally, that ml estimators are necessarily the most efficient for small values of n.

It is worth noting that ml estimators are not necessarily automatically unbiased. Many are, but some are not, and this is a point that sometimes needs close watching. Any bias that exists can generally be corrected fairly readily.

14.7 Interval estimates—attributes

It is quite likely that a statistician or anyone else recognizing the possibility of sampling error will wish to hedge his point estimate of some population parameter θ on the basis of a sample. The statistician, at least, would typically prefer to express his estimates as an interval which contains the point estimate, but allows for some error on either side. A statement of the type that the true proportion of defective bulbs in a large batch, based on the information contained in a sample of 500 bulbs from the batch, lay between, say, 0·04 and 0·08 would represent an interval estimate.

Now if a statistician estimating the population proportion p were to assert 'p lies between 0 and 1' he would be very safe indeed. In fact, we could say that he is then 100 per cent confident that his interval estimate contains the true value of p. Of course, such an estimate really says nothing that is not obvious, and is of little use to anyone. A much more meaningful statement would instead establish an interval that was reasonably sure to contain the true value of p. With 6 per cent defective bulbs in the sample of 500 bulbs, intuition suggests, for instance, that it is highly unlikely that the true value of p for the population is as high as 90 per cent, or 50 per cent or even 25 per cent. The interval estimate need not therefore contain these values. But what values should be included? It turns out that it is possible to ascertain specifically how wide the interval should be to provide us with an interval such that, at any stated level of *confidence*, the true but unknown value of p is contained within it.

Suppose we desire to construct what is called a 95 per cent confidence interval for estimating p. This means that we need to find an interval which we are 95 per cent confident contains the true p. This could be interpreted as implying that, if we followed this procedure on a very large number of separate occasions, possibly with samples from a number of populations, we would find in retrospect that we had been right on 95 per cent of these occasions. It will also be true that there is a 5 per cent chance that each interval does not contain the true p. The customary procedure is to split this 5 per cent equally and to assume that there is a 2·5 per cent chance that the stated interval is too high to include the true p and a 2·5 per cent chance that it is too low. The problem is to find the limits of such an interval. This can be accomplished by using the binomial tables in a reverse fashion, and we illustrate the necessary procedure through an example.

Example 14.3

From a large batch of new electric washing machines, a random sample of fifty machines were selected and carefully examined. As a result, six machines were found to have one or more faults. A 95 per cent confidence interval for the proportion of all machines with one or more faults is required.

To find the limits of this interval, we reproduce in Table 14.2 a portion of the binomial table for $n = 50$, namely, portions of the rows of the table for $r \geqslant 6$ and $r \geqslant 7$. (The need for these particular rows is related to the fact that exactly 6 defectives were found in the sample of 50.) The entries in this abbreviated table give the probabilities of 6 or more, or alternatively 7 or more, defectives for various values of p. Ideally, the lower limit of a 95 per cent confidence interval could be found by searching across the $r \geqslant 6$ row for a probability equal to 0·025. The column in which we find this value is

L

associated with a particular p value. In other words, the trick is to locate the p value such that

$$P(r \geqslant 6 | n = 50, p) = 0.0250.$$

Table 14.2

Binomial table excerpt, n $= 50$

p	0·02	0·03	0·04	0·05	0·06			
$r \geqslant 6$	0·0005	0·0037	0·0144	0·0378	0·0776			
$r \geqslant 7$	0·0001	0·0007	0·0036	0·0118	0·0289			
p	0·22	0·23	0·24	0·25	0·26	0·27	0·28	0·29
$r \geqslant 6$	0·9767	0·9841	0·9893	0·9930	0·9954	0·9970	0·9981	0·9988
$r \geqslant 7$	0·9445	0·9603	0·9720	0·9806	0·9868	0·9911	0·9941	0·9961

It needs a detailed table with more p columns to locate such a p value exactly, but an approximate result can be obtained by interpolation in Table 14.2. The value of p is seen to fall approximately midway between $p = 0.04$ and $p = 0.05$, say for $p = 0.045$.

For the upper limit of the interval we need the probability

$$P(r \leqslant 6 | n = 50, p) = 0.0250$$

or

$$P(r \geqslant 7 | n = 50, p) = 0.9750,$$

since these two probabilities must add to unity. Again, inspection of Table 14·2 shows that this value occurs between $p = 0.24$ and 0.25 and the approximate value, by linear interpolation, will be $p = 0.243$. We can now state that the 95 per cent confidence interval for p is from 0·045 to 0·243. The reader is left to experiment with other degrees of confidence, say 90 per cent or 99 per cent, to see the effect that this would have on the confidence interval.

14.8 Interval estimates—variables

The previous section dealt with the case of attributes, deducing an appropriate confidence interval for the unknown proportion in the population possessing that attribute. We now turn to the case of a measured variable, where we have a random sample of observations from some normal population and wish to put confidence limits on the mean for that population. First, we assume that the population standard deviation is known and, second, that it is unknown. Both situations will be illustrated through examples.

Example 14.4

The average wear on make A of tyres after 1000 miles travelling is to be estimated. Twenty-five tyres are selected at random from a large batch and the wear measured (in thousands of an inch). The mean wear of the sample is 17.4. Previous experience suggests that the standard deviation of wear within a large batch of tyres is 3·2 (using the same units). It is required to find confidence limits for the average wear of the batch on the basis of the sample results.

First, the sample mean, $\bar{x}$, say, is normally distributed (exactly if the population itself is normal, otherwise approximately) with unknown mean μ and standard deviation $\sigma/\sqrt{n}$. In this instance the latter quantity is $3·2/\sqrt{25}=0·64$. Hence, the shape of the probability distribution of the sample mean is known, but its expected value, μ, is not. Next, we have to define the level of confidence or reliability with which we are concerned. Suppose we decide upon a 95 per cent confidence level. Now we know that the chance that the true mean is more than 1·96 standard deviations above the observed mean is 0·025, and similarly for the same distance below the observed mean. (The figure of 1·96 is obtained from the tables of the unit normal distribution, to cut off an area 0·025 in each tail of the distribution.) Then, equivalently, we can state that there is a 95 per cent chance that the interval $17·40\pm1·96\times0·64$ or $17·40\pm1·25$ contains the true mean μ, i.e. the interval 16·15 to 18·65 is the required 95 per cent confidence interval.

It is perhaps worth noting that the width of the interval here, i.e. $18·65-16·15$ or 2·50, is inversely proportional to the square root of the sample size. Thus, had the sample been of 100 tyres, then the width of the interval with the same level of confidence would have been, not 2·50, but $2·50\times\sqrt{25}/\sqrt{100}$ or 1·25. Hence, to halve the interval width, it is necessary to quadruple the sample size.

Example 14.5

In a socio-economic survey, the average monthly expenditure on food for families of two adults and two children was £27·50 among a random sample of thirty such families. Using the sample data, the estimated population standard deviation of expenditure was £3·55. Find 90 per cent confidence limits for the average expenditure on food amongst the population of such families.

The calculation proceeds along similar lines to those of the previous example, except that we now have to use the t-distribution in place of the unit normal variable to find the appropriate limits. The required interval for μ, in symbolic form, will be

$$\bar{x}\pm t_{n-1,\ \alpha/2}\frac{s}{\sqrt{n}},$$

where $\bar{x}$ is the sample mean (27·50 in this instance)

n is the sample size (30)

$1-\alpha$ is the confidence level required ($\alpha=0\cdot10$)

$t_{n-1, \ \alpha/2}$ is the value of the t-distribution with $n-1$ degrees of freedom that cuts off $\frac{1}{2}\alpha$ at the upper end of the distribution (1·70).

Substituting in this particular instance, we find

$$27\cdot50 \pm 1\cdot70 \times \frac{3\cdot55}{\sqrt{30}}$$

or

$$27\cdot50 \pm 1\cdot10$$

giving £26·40 to £28·60 as the appropriate 90 per cent confidence interval.

14.9 Comments on confidence intervals

An informal interpretation of the type of confidence interval constructed above would be as follows: if a very large number of 95 per cent confidence interval estimates were constructed on the basis of successive samples, possibly from different populations, at least 95 per cent of these intervals would contain the true value of the population parameter concerned; the other 5 per cent (or less) would fail to include it. We are simply saying we are 95 per cent certain that the true parameter value falls somewhere between the limits specified in the confidence interval. Although this statement is intuitively appealing, and forms a cornerstone of classical statistics, some classical statisticians object to it on the grounds that it is simply not proper to make probability statements about a population parameter. They argue that the parameter is a fixed quantity and that a statement giving the probability that it is more or less than some limit is meaningless. While it is quite all right to talk of the probability of obtaining a given sample result via some sampling procedure the population parameter, even if unknown, is fixed.

However, it is certainly useful to the decision-maker to view unknown population parameters as if they were random variables, even if they are already fixed or determined if only one knew the details. Indeed, the betting odds that the decision-maker assigns to possible values of such parameters become the weights which, along with conditional pay-offs, determine the optimal action and has been the basis of the approach adopted in this book.

The debate can be highlighted by the following illustration. Suppose you and a friend had no knowledge whatsoever of the outcome of last year's Grand National steeplechase, but a videotape re-run of the race was available. There is no reason why you and your friend could not engage in some spirited betting on the race, even though the outcome is unknown to you while known to others. You could then decide upon the consequences of your bets by showing the re-run.

To the business manager, the probability or odds that some key decision variable lies within specified limits is a meaningful concept. The confidence interval—at least the subjective interpretation of it—is a convenient way of summarizing the state of available knowledge concerning an unknown quantity. However, its direct usefulness in decision problems is not obvious. Does one use the point estimate or the extremes of the limits, and, if so, what level of confidence does one choose? Such choices are essentially arbitrary and such inputs are certainly to be avoided in decision-making. Nevertheless, confidence intervals are widely used to convey a certain kind of information, but *per se* they are of little value in the decision-making process. This is not to say that sample information has no use in decision-making as has already been made clear in earlier chapters.

14.10 Sampling procedures

We have made a great deal of use of sample information both in this chapter and in the book as a whole, particularly in Chapters 11 and 12, and a few remarks are therefore in order on the nature and procedures of sampling. The obvious advantages of a sample survey over a complete enumeration are a reduction in the cost of the survey, and the greater speed with which the data and results are obtained. Indeed, in some circumstances where destructive testing is required to assess quality, it is essential to sample in order to have any product left for normal use. By using specially qualified personnel, carefully supervising the field work, and thoroughly scrutinizing the data, one can aim at a greatly increased accuracy of the results obtained through a sample survey, because the reduced number of units to be considered enables greater care to be taken per unit. In any sample survey there is always a sampling error, which arises from the drawing of inferences about the whole population on the basis of observation of only a part of it (the sample). The statistician tries to reduce this error by choosing a 'good' technique of sampling. However, it should be pointed out that, although the complete enumeration survey is void of sampling error, there are other types of error that can creep in both at the stage of the survey design and in the collection and processing of the data. These errors are termed *non-sampling errors*, and can occur whether complete enumeration or a sample survey is used to gather information.

We discuss the latter types of non-sampling errors first. These errors are of various kinds: bias in measurement; omission or duplication of units in the population to be sampled; faulty enumeration methods; inaccurate questionnaires and schedules; lack of trained personnel; inadequate supervision and scrutiny; non-response of some of the units sampled; errors in tabulation, data-processing or presentation; etc. Bias arises when the measuring method itself is wrong for the purpose in hand, and thus leads to an erroneous result.

As a simple illustration, suppose that the lengths of steel rods were measured with a tape measure that had stretched, with the consequence that all lengths were unknowingly 2 per cent below the true figure. Then, even if every steel rod in a batch were measured, the result would be wrong by some 2 per cent. The same phenomenon applies to opinion polls. In a political poll taken, for example, a fortnight before an election, a bias may occur because the question cannot be linked to what is actually going to happen in the polling booth, but only to what people admit that they think they will do at the time they are polled. The poll could elicit an honest reply from the entire population and still be wrong as measured by the actual outcome of the election concerned. It is important to emphasize that this bias has nothing to do with sampling as such; it is entirely connected with the measuring instrument that has been used for the problem in hand, and would occur whether the sample used were 1 per cent, 10 per cent or 100 per cent of the population concerned. Other forms of non-sampling errors can be assessed and controlled by certain internal checks of consistency, by post-survey checks and a careful study (in market research polls) of non-response. There are well-tried techniques for using an interpenetrating network of subsamples, consisting of drawing the sample in the form of two or more subsamples, selected in an identical manner, which are then surveyed and processed by different groups of persons. Agreement in the subsample estimates clearly provides some check on the quality of the data, but not a complete check.

14.11 Sampling methods

We turn now to errors or discrepancies that arise because we have only looked at a sample and not at the complete population. In considering these sampling errors we must first distinguish between alternative ways in which a sample can be selected from a defined population. While there are many variations, the choice of sample method used rests basically upon either the *quota* method or the *random* method, and we discuss these in turn.

First, let us consider the quota method. Here, the sample is selected so as to fill a previously defined quota of individuals. For example, suppose a quota sample of 2000 individuals is to be selected from the whole of the United Kingdom, the precise purpose for which the sample is required being unspecified. If no restrictions were placed on the composition of the quota, then it could be selected in any manner we please; the first 2000 people coming out of Waterloo Station at 8.30 in the morning, for example. For some purposes this might be a relevant frame of reference—perhaps for asking on which day of the week a person's birthday fell—but not if we were trying to find out the voting intentions of the United Kingdom population, or its travelling habits. Hence, some form of quota restrictions could be put on to try to remedy any possible bias. For example, it might be specified that 1000 of the individuals were to be male and 1000 female. This would almost certainly improve the situation, but would not necessarily completely eliminate the bias. For example, suppose one were asking questions designed to find out what people ate for breakfast. By asking both men and women in fixed proportions from among the individuals leaving Waterloo Station, one would undoubtedly get a better answer than one could with an unrestricted sample, which might well contain too many men. But there are still problems, e.g. age distribution, or occupational or geographical variations, which may need to be taken into account to get a better picture of breakfast habits. This could lead to further quota restrictions, e.g. that half the sample should be under thirty five years of age, that there should be some specified geographical breakdown, and possibly also a social class restriction as well.

Taking all the restrictions into account, a particular interviewer may now need to find, for the complete sample, ninety men, each over thirty-five years of age, living in the South-East, falling in a particular social class, and so on. Within the quota controls, the individuals can be found in any way the interviewer pleases, and it would still be permissible to go back to Waterloo Station for the appropriate portion of the sample. Clearly, the more restrictions that are placed on the sample, the more representative it becomes, but the more difficult and costly it is to find the individuals to fill the various portions of the quota. Quota sampling completely eliminates the common problem of non-response: if a person is not available, you choose another one to fit the quota. There is, however, no way beyond the quota restrictions of guaranteeing freedom from any personal choice preferences that interviewers may have. Thus, one particular interviewer may have a predilection for neatly dressed, congenial or conveniently available respondents. Quota sampling involves a conscious choice by the interviewer which means that the sample is not random. One consequence of this lack of randomness is that an evaluation of the error due to sampling is, in general, not possible from the results of the sample itself. We can examine, when possible, over time and with a number of similar surveys, the discrepancies that arise between the survey result and what subsequently turns out to be the true result from the population as a whole, and then use these to help us to estimate the limits of sample error. However, we are forced to conclude that the reliability of quota samples is a difficult quantity to evaluate.

The alternative method of selecting the sample is through some random choice procedure, whereby each individual in the population concerned has a known chance of appearing in the sample. For the latter reason this method is sometimes referred to as probability sampling. In simple random sampling there would be an equal chance. Suppose, for example, that we wanted a simple random sample of 1000 electors to be selected from a constituency which has a total of 70 000 electors for a market research survey. One straightforward but tedious way in which the selection could be made would be to put all the names of the 70 000 individual electors on separate slips of paper, shuffle them all up and draw out, blindfold, 1000 of the slips. The names appearing on the slips drawn out would then constitute the sample. Those electors, and only those electors, who had been selected must then be tracked down and the relevant information obtained from them.

This method of selection is clearly more time-consuming and costly than quota sampling; why, then, should we be put to all this trouble and expense to get the 1000 persons required? The answer lies in the way in which we can, from the sample itself, estimate in probabilistic terms the possible range of error in using our sample result to generate information about the population. Our earlier discussions have shown us that, if we are sampling with respect to some attribute (say, possession of a refrigerator in the electors' household) in an infinite population, then the precision of the random sample is proportional to $\sqrt{(p(1-p)/n)}$ where $100\,p$ is the percentage of electors with refrigerators and n is the sample size. The precision is a term to describe the width of the confidence interval for p based on a sample of a given size and a given level of confidence.

What happens to this precision if the population size is not infinite but finite? This question can be tackled mathematically, but we give in Table 14.3 an indication of the consequential results in arithmetical terms. The table assumes two levels of population size, N, and a variety of sample sizes. The correction factor is the quantity by which the standard deviation of the population estimate of p in sampling from an infinite population has to be multiplied in order to obtain the standard deviation allowing for the sampling having come from a finite population. In other words,

$$\begin{pmatrix} \text{Standard deviation for} \\ \text{finite population} \\ \text{sampling} \end{pmatrix} = \begin{pmatrix} \text{Standard deviation for} \\ \text{infinite population} \\ \text{sampling} \end{pmatrix} \times \begin{pmatrix} \text{Correction} \\ \text{factor} \end{pmatrix}$$

Table 14.3

Correction factors for finite populations

	$N=1000$			$N=100\,000$	
n	$100n/N$	Correction factor	n	$100n/N$	Correction factor
10	1·0	0·995	10	0·010	1·000
25	2·5	0·987	25	0·025	1·000
50	5·0	0·975	50	0·050	1·000
100	10·0	0·949	100	0·100	0·999
200	20·0	0·894	200	0·200	0·999
500	50·0	0·707	500	0·500	0·997

From the table it is clear that, provided we are not sampling more than about 10 per cent of the population, the size of that population is irrelevant to the precision achieved by a sample of given size. Furthermore, if we assume the population is infinite and select the sample size accordingly, we will actually achieve a higher precision than we originally expected.

There is one other consequence of the dependence of precision on the size of the sample that merits attention. This is the effect on precision of splitting a population into smaller subpopulations. Table 14.4 shows a situation where a global random sample of 1000 has been drawn from a population which can subsequently be subdivided into four regions or subpopulations. Suppose that a 5 per cent sample is drawn from each region, and that the (unknown) proportion in each region with the character concerned is 0·2. Then the precisions of the regional and total population estimates of p are shown by the figures in the final column which gives the values of $\pm 2\sqrt{(p(1-p)/n)}$ where $p = 0·2$ and n is the sample size concerned. This is broadly equivalent to the 95 per cent confidence limits about the sample proportion. The widths of the confidence intervals vary enormously and it would be totally incorrect to place the width (or precision) from the whole population around each regional estimate. Of course, if it were known that the proportion were the same in each region, we would only be interested in overall precision. If the proportion differed, however, we would be very much interested in the relative precisions in the different regions which depend heavily upon the sample sizes concerned.

Many surveys are carried out by considering a complete population divided into non-overlapping groups, usually called *strata* and samples drawn independently from each stratum would constitute what is known as *stratified sampling*. A weighted combination of the estimates from the various strata gives the overall estimate for the population. The more homogenous the strata are within themselves, the more precise would be the estimates from each stratum, and the greater the gain from the stratification.

There are many other methods of conducting sample surveys and a statistician always tries to choose a sampling and estimation procedure which

Table 14.4

Precision of regional estimates

Region	Population (N_i)	Sample (n_i)	Sample proportion (n_i/N_i)	Precision of sample estimate of p
A	2 000	100	0·05	±0·080
B	5 000	250	0·05	±0·050
C	10 000	500	0·05	±0·036
D	3 000	150	0·05	±0·066
Total population	20 000	1000	0·05	±0·024

is the most 'efficient', subject to the inevitable budget restrictions which inevitably limit the amount which can be spent on his survey. Indeed, in business, just as in research and everyday life, sampling is in constant use and, properly handled, it is an extremely powerful tool.

14.12 Summary and comparison

This chapter has been largely concerned with problems of estimation, using the maximum likelihood approach to estimate the parameters of populations and confidence intervals to determine limits within which population parameters can be expected to lie with a given degree of confidence. These problems are essentially what classical statisticians refer to as problems of *inference*. Such statisticians would, in general, avoid getting themselves involved in making probability statements about unknown population parameters. So far as they are concerned, the true proportion of defectives (say) in some population of electronic valves is either greater than 0·1 or it is not. Probabilities for them can only be interpreted from a relative frequency point of view.

The follower of the methods adopted in this book, colloquially referred to as a *Bayesian*, would seek to answer the kinds of problems treated in this chapter in a different kind of way. He might report something like this: 'On the basis of my formerly held beliefs, which I outlined previously, and taking into account the current sample information, I now believe that there is a probability of 0·4 that p exceeds 0·1, a probability of 0·6 that p exceeds 0·08, and a probability of 0·8 that p exceeds 0·07. I have synthesized these figures to produce the posterior probability distribution for p shown in the attached diagram.' We have, of course, in this book gone further and incorporated such concepts as cost, loss, profit, value, etc., but this must not obscure the fundamental distinction concerning unknown population parameters between the classical approach to inference and the Bayesian approach to decision that has been highlighted by this chapter.

To illustrate these differences of approach, suppose that we wish to estimate the mean breaking strength θ of cartons and randomly test a sample of four cartons, obtaining a mean strength of 22 (the units are immaterial for this illustration). We further assume that the measurements, which are made by a physical testing device, are subject to some random error being normally distributed about the true carton value with a standard deviation of 1 unit. Under the classical approach, the 95 per cent confidence limits for the unknown population mean would be $22 \pm 1·96 \times 1/\sqrt{4}$ or $22 \pm 0·98$.

Under the Bayesian approach, we start from some assumption about the prior distribution for the mean. Suppose that past information suggests that the means of batch strength, θ, have been normally distributed with mean 20 and standard deviation 2. Then, from Eqs. 7.9a and 7.9b, the posterior distribution for θ using both the prior and the sample information will be

$$\text{Mean} = \frac{20 \times \frac{1}{4} + 22 \times 4}{4 + \frac{1}{4}} = 21 \cdot 5$$

$$\text{Standard deviation} = \sqrt{\frac{4 \times \frac{1}{4}}{4 + \frac{1}{4}}} = 0 \cdot 485$$

The comparative position is illustrated in Fig. 14.1. The posterior distribution overlaps that part of the prior distribution that is close to the observed sample mean of 22. The standard deviation is also much reduced. Compared with the classical confidence interval, the location of the Bayesian estimator is slightly different (centre of interval at 21·5 compared with 22) and the width of the comparable intervals is marginally lower (1·90 compared with 1·96 for 95 per cent probability). Of course, the differences depend very much upon the sample size, as this increases the results derived from the two approaches expectedly merge imperceptibly into each other. Nevertheless, for small samples Bayesian methods will often yield more credible point estimates and shorter interval estimates as in this illustration.

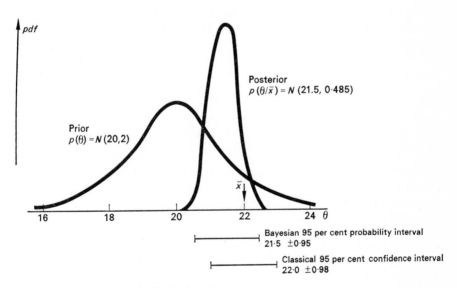

Fig. 14.1. Bayesian versus classical estimation

The major criticism of Bayesian methods would lie with their subjective element, particularly in regard to the formation of the prior probability distribution and the appropriate pay-offs (or losses). It should be pointed out, however, that classical methods are by no means free of the same subjective elements. Indeed, one of the major contributions that Bayesian methods have made is to lay bare the implicit assumptions in classical techniques.

Exercises on Chapter 14

1 The lifetime x of electric light bulbs has probability density function $\lambda e^{-\lambda x}$ for $x > 0$. A random sample of n bulbs is tested. After time x_0, the test is stopped and r bulbs have failed, with lifetimes $x_1, x_2, \ldots x_r$. The remaining $(n-r)$ bulbs have not failed at time x_0. Find an expression for the maximum likelihood estimate of λ.

2 A random variable x has a probability density function

$$f(x) = \frac{1}{\beta} e^{-(x-\alpha)/\beta} \qquad \text{for } \alpha < x < \infty, \ \beta > 0.$$

$\qquad = 0$ elsewhere.

Find the maximum likelihood estimators of α and β from a random sample of n observations $x_1, x_2, \ldots x_n$. Comment on the estimation of α from this example.

3 An electronic counter records the number of vehicles passing a checkpoint on a road in successive intervals of one minute. The counter records the actual number except that, when it exceeds 4 the counter only registers 4.

In 100 such intervals the counter records the following:

No. of vehicles	0	1	2	3	4
No. of intervals	14	26	28	17	15

Assume that the number of vehicles passing per minute follows a Poisson distribution with parameter λ. Use the maximum likelihood procedure to estimate λ. (Hint: an iterative procedure may be necessary to solve the appropriate maximum likelihood equation numerically.)

4 Nine hundred cigarettes were taken at random off a mass production line, and of these forty-five were found to be defective. Make an estimate of the population proportion defective, and obtain 95 per cent confidence limits for the population proportion.

5 The manager of a factory producing rotary pumps is contemplating the introduction of a new model. The pump, like others in the line on offer, would be sold mainly to industrial customers. It is desired to estimate the proportion of customers currently using other models in the line who would also find the new pump useful. How many customers would you recommend should be questioned if it is desired that the probability that the estimate will deviate from the true proportion by more than five percentage points should not exceed 0·1? The manufacturer has about 2000 customers currently using other models. Would it help to take the sample in two stages and, if so, why?

6 A sample poll of 100 ratepayers, chosen at random in a given district, indicated that 60 per cent of them were in favour of a proposed town development scheme. Find 95 per cent confidence limits for the proportion of all ratepayers in the district who would indicate that they are in favour of the scheme.

7 Measurements of the diameters of a random sample of 150 from the ball-bearings made by a machine in one week showed a mean of 0·436 inches and a standard deviation of 0·022 inches. Find (*i*) 90 per cent and (*ii*) 95 per cent confidence limits for the mean diameter of the population of ball-bearings.

8 A manufacturer of a particular model of a colour television set wishes to estimate the mean time until sets first suffer a failure. It is desired that the probability of the estimate differing from the true mean by more than 10 hours should be not more than 0·05. The standard deviation of the time to failure is believed, from evidence on similar models, to be 100 hours. How many sets should be tested?

9 A chemist is using a particular method to determine the sulphur content of a given organic chemical. Studies on other substances with a known sulphur content using the method have shown that the results can be considered normally distributed with a mean equal to the true sulphur content (expressed as a percentage by weight) and a standard deviation of 0·5 (expressed as a percentage by weight). To improve the estimate of the sulphur content, determinations are made on a number of samples from the chemical. How many determinations should be made if it is desired that the probability that the estimate of sulphur content deviates from the true content by more than 0·1 (percentage by weight) is not greater than 0·05?

10 A manufacturer of refrigerators asks a consumer research group to test a sample of a particular model of refrigerators. It particularly wants to find the 99 per cent confidence limits for the temperature of the freezer box in their refrigerators. Experience with other models suggests that the temperature of the freezer box in the refrigerators has a standard deviation of 1·5°F. What size of sample should the researchers be recommended to take if the manufacturer wants the 99 per cent limits to be no more than 0·5°F wide?

11 A national daily newspaper tells its advertisers that a recent audit shows that 1·5 million copies were sold daily, whilst the proprietors estimate that they were read by a total of 2·7 million people. One of the major advertisers in the paper on a particular day undertakes his own survey and finds that, from a randomly selected 300 bought copies of the paper on that day, only 204 people had noticed his advertisement, whilst the standard deviation of 'advertisement readers' per copy sold is 0·85. Estimate 90 per cent confidence limits for the total number of people who had read the advertisement.

15 Overview and critique

15.1 Introduction

We have attempted to outline in this book a framework for decision-making under uncertainty. It is not so much a statement as to how decisions under uncertainty are currently made in practice, but more a development of the manner in which such decisions could and (hopefully) should be made, given the various prerequisites for any particular application. The major contribution, from the decision-maker's point of view lies in the systematic treatment and subsequent control of decision errors, in a probabilistic sense, which should inherently lead to better decisions. Although we have developed the methods discussed here from a theoretical and conceptual base, applications have been brought in at virtually every stage, and it is reasonable to anticipate that the methods described can be applied to an even wider range of problems than those discussed here. The kernel of the suggestions lay in Chapters 5 to 12 inclusive. Chapters 1 to 4 provided a lead-in to these central chapters, and Chapters 13 to 14 provided a link with classical statistics. What the reader should have obtained is an understanding of the logical structure which supports the concepts of statistical decision-making, giving rise to the expectation that the reader will thereby become a better and more consistent decision-maker.

It is worth noting that the classical statistics approach, as exemplified in Chapters 13 and 14, is not so much opposed to the decision analysis approach adopted as the theme of this book as is sometimes averred to be the case. J. Neyman and E. S. Pearson, the progenitors of the formal concepts of statistical hypothesis testing, said 'the probabilities *a priori* of the admissible hypothesis . . . must enter into the problem' and yet they 'can only rarely be expressed in precise numerical form'. The difficulty has been one of quantification, rather than one of principle. For example, a test of the hypothesis of extra-sensory perception would be rather different from a test of the hypothesis that a coin is unbiased, though the mathematical analysis would be similar. Again, a jury would demand higher probability of guilt in a murder case than for a relatively minor motoring charge. Classical statistics sought procedures that were insensitive to prior concepts: decision analysis seeks to confront such problems directly.

In this final chapter we deal, in turn, with four areas of debate. First, the role of the analyst in assisting in the analysis of decision problems. Second, the selection of the correct problem for analysis. Third, the assessment of the overall gain by following this approach. This leads, finally, to a listing of the overall pros and cons of the decision analysis approach. Any self-styled expert is liable to claim, or be accused of claiming, an exaggerated degree of importance for the methods he professes, and see them as a complete cure to all the ills of an organization. In this chapter we will endeavour to hold the scales fairly and give both sides of the argument.

15.2 Role of the analyst

It is generally assumed that the most important part of the analysis of any decision comes at the stage where the qualitative logic and anatomy of the problem is considered in detail. However, this presupposes that the problem exists and has readily been identified as such. But this is not always the case, nor is the precise identity of the decision-maker always obvious. To illustrate this, suppose that Mr Cutler is an executive in a large chemical company. He is what we would term a senior manager in charge of a major operating division, but is in turn responsible to a member of the main board of directors. The company calls in an analyst to help Mr Cutler with a specific problem. Mr Cutler wants to know what he should do in a particular situation. So far as the analyst is concerned, Mr Cutler is the decision-maker and the analyst must use Mr Cutler's values and judgments in order to help him to solve his problem. Of course, Mr Cutler's values and judgments might derive from the expertise of others. Again Mr Cutler is not synonymous with the company and his motivations may not be the same as that of the chairman, or the shareholders, or society at large. An analysis of the same problem from the point of view of a shareholder, for example, might well be quite different—the assessments of components, such as probabilities and utilities, may change. Still, Mr Cutler is the decision-maker. In analysing his problem, it may or may not be appropriate to bring into consideration the motivations and feelings of others; this is a function of the problem at hand.

Suppose that Mr Cutler does not himself decide upon actions, but recommends action to be taken by Mr Lawson, another manager in the company in a different division. The analyst, however, is working for Mr Cutler and not Mr Lawson. Here Mr Cutler and the analyst must now be concerned not only with what Mr Cutler thinks, but also with what Mr Lawson is likely to do, and the analyst might be wise to carry out an uncertainty analysis of Mr Lawson's reactions to Mr Cutler's specific recommendations. In addition, the analyst must help Mr Cutler to assess preferences or utilities for consequences that are a composite of what Mr Cutler recommends, what Mr Lawson is likely to do, and what actually happens.

Alternatively, suppose that Mr Cutler asks an analyst to study a company problem in a context where Mr Cutler does not think of himself as the decision-maker—in fact, no one seems to admit to taking the ultimate responsibility. Here, the identity of the decision-maker is in limbo. In some mysterious way, a decision will eventually be made, and after everybody learns how it has turned out, the identity of the decision-maker will suddenly come to the surface. In such a situation the analyst himself may be the fall guy if the recommended strategy turns out to be a poor choice after the event; and equally he will not gather much glory if the strategy turns out well.

We have assumed throughout that the analyst helps to organize the decision-maker's thought processes, elicits judgmental information from him and from his delegated experts, checks the internal inconsistencies of judgmental inputs, assists the decision-maker in bringing these judgments together into a coherent whole and, finally, processes this information and identifies a best strategy for action. Nowhere in these functions is the analyst supposed to inject his personal views or biases. Of course, this demarcation of the role of the analyst is not always so clear-cut. In some circumstances, for example, the decision-maker may directly or indirectly ask his analyst to incorporate his own judgments. More importantly than this, however, the analyst can influence the outcome in a myriad of subtle ways; by what he chooses to incorporate in the analysis, how he phrases questions, the grimaces he makes in dialogue with the expert, the tone of voice he uses in an oral presentation, the issues he may conceal behind a barrage of mumbo-jumbo. Indeed, in some circumstances, it can turn out that the analyst is himself the real decision-maker and the alleged decision-maker is just the front man. It is therefore crucial for management to comprehend and intimately involve itself in the process of analysis, whether we be talking about decision analysis as presented in this book or in any other form.

A further point arises when the analyst finds himself unable to accept the probabilities, utilities, or even alternatives that Mr Cutler postulates. This is the not infrequent role of experts and there is no unique answer. The barrister's answer to this dilemma is that his client comes foremost and, having pointed out why he cannot personally accept the premises, he nevertheless goes ahead as the client's adviser and accepts his values and judgments.

15.3 Analysing the correct problem

In large organizations there is commonly a tremendous status gap between the decision-maker and the analyst. More than one analyst (including at times this author) has made a very complete study of the wrong problem, because of a lack of close liaison and continuous feedback between the decision-maker and the analyst. Sometimes it is due to a lack of frankness on the part of the decision-maker who does not wish to reveal all the relevant information, or indeed all the organizational constraints upon alternative solutions. All decision makers have, at some time or other, been guilty also of these failings.

Usually the analyst's work will not have been entirely wasted, but a precise answer to the wrong question is not nearly so desirable as an incomplete answer to the right one. In some circumstances, also, the analyst may isolate the real problem only to find that the decision-maker is not sophisticated enough to recognize it, or to find that the decision-maker is no longer emotionally involved in the problem and is not prepared to meet the analyst half way. The communications gap must be closed if an effective relationship is to be established between decision-maker and analyst. At each stage of the analysis, it is critical that the analyst checks and rechecks to see that he is working on the real problem required by the decision-maker.

In the initial stages of an investigation the analyst should acquaint himself with the general perspective and sensitivity of the problem area. He might write out descriptions of the consequences and implications that certain paths through the decision tree would have for the company, its competitors and society in general. At the end of this initial stage, and before he assigns any hard numbers or probes experts for their judgments or worries about critical trade-offs and so forth, the analyst and the decision-maker should review the analysis done thus far to see that it is addressed to the real problem. Accordingly, this preliminary qualitative investigation should be viewed as a communication vehicle for the analyst to get on the same wave-length as the decision-maker. Once this descriptive stage has been agreed, it is easier for both parties to choose jointly the facets of the problem they wish to incorporate in a more formal quantitative analysis, and to set priorities for the analysis of different sub-problems. After they have completed the formal analysis, they can then investigate informally whether certain qualitative considerations that have been omitted from the formal quantitative analysis tend to reinforce or weaken the general conclusions. Good documentation is important at each stage of the analysis because it serves to facilitate the communication process, to crystallize agreements, to invite constructive criticism from impartial outsiders, to record the development of the analysis for the use of others who may have the same or a similar problem at a later date. Finally, a critical ingredient that determines whether or not management will ever implement an analysis is the quality of the involvement of the decision-maker in the analytical process at every stage right from the start.

15.4 Overall gain

A decision-maker will often ask whether it is really worthwhile carrying out a formal decision analysis for his problem. Can we demonstrate that it is worthwhile? Obviously it is difficult to demonstrate the benefits one way or the other in individual situations. Generally speaking, however, it is clear that in a problem involving hundreds of thousands of pounds, it is worth spending a few pounds, say a fraction of 1 per cent, on a systematic review and analysis of all facets of the problem. At the other end of the scale, if a problem involves choices whose difference in monetary pay-offs could not pay for the time involved in the analysis, it is not worthwhile to carry out such a formal analysis. There are, of course, many intermediate situations that need to be resolved. Consider, for example, a situation in which a decision-maker has three alternative branches to choose from at the very start of the analysis of a decision tree. Suppose he has formally investigated two of these branches and the question under review is whether it is worthwhile to analyse formally the third branch. The analyst may believe that, in a formal analysis, the third will prove to be worse than the better of the other two branches. However, he may also think that, even if he is wrong, the possible merits of the third cannot be large enough to warrant the expense of the analysis. In this case, surely, he should simply prune this third branch unless he believes he can gain some insight into its evaluation by a cruder and less costly mode of analysis. Is it worth analysing this; perhaps it is or perhaps it is not. It is probably better to handle such matters outside the formal decision theory in a pragmatic and informal manner.

Of course it may be argued that, while we have developed a procedure of how really coherent (or rational) men should act, we have not attempted to describe how people actually make decisions. Observation suggests that people do not always maximize expected pay-offs. They tend to act in a conservative way towards data. That is, they do not take as much account of information as they ought to. In extreme cases we are all aware of the phenomenon—'Don't bother me with the figures, my mind is made up', or 'Give me the facts, I'll do the doubting'. This suggests that men are, in the main, incoherent decision-makers. Perhaps it is that, while mankind has not yet fully accepted the expected pay-off approach, it has not yet been able to explain it away and fall back on a conservative approach.

The examples in this book have mainly been concerned with business and commercial problems. However, the concepts described have been much used in other fields, for example in medical diagnosis where great strides have been made in recent years. In the realm of public social policy the Roskill Commission report in 1970 of the siting of the third London Airport represents the most sustained attempt that will be seen for a long time to apply the principles of rational decision-making discussed in this book to a major public problem. The fact that the methods used failed to win complete recognition by public and politicians was a setback but demonstrated, albeit rather expensively, the need for the analysts to have carried out rather fuller discussions of the trade-off rates between, for example, expenditure on roads and the preservation of Norman churches. Where a decision rests on a number of different attributes and one course of action is not superior to all others on each possible attribute a difficulty arises. In such circumstances those most directly involved must express their views as to the relative importance of the various factors. Furthermore, even when the costs can simply be measured in money terms it will often be useful to translate them into terms of benefits foregone, since few people can otherwise really appreciate the meaning of the large sums involved. Just as Atlas units are used as a rough measure of computer power, so one might use in social policy the cost of building and running a new District General Hospital as a unit for capital and for recurrent costs. The differences between the alternatives facing the Roskill Commission represented several such units and one wonders whether, had the costs been expressed in such terms, there would have been as widespread a welcome for the final Government decision as there was at the time.

15.5 Pros and cons

No score card can provide a complete summary of the merits and demerits of decision analysis, but some rough evaluation can be made. First the favourable items:

(*i*) The decision-maker is forced to come to quantitative grips with the interactions between the various facets of the problem he faces.

(*ii*) Each relevant expert can give evidence on the problem relating to his area of expertise in an unambiguous manner.

(*iii*) The value of information in a decision context is formally assessed which helps in the gathering, compiling and analysis of that data.

(*iv*) The decision-maker's preferences for alternative consequences are sharply distinguished from his judgments about uncertainties.

(*v*) The decision-maker and his staff are stimulated to think hard, at the appropriate time, about new and viable alternative actions.

(*vi*) A complete analysis helps the decision-maker to emphasize that the decision has not been made on frivolous grounds; it can be used to communicate the rationale of the adopted strategy and rally support for it.

(*vii*) A decision analysis enables attention, in cases of disagreement, to be focused on those issues where there really are fundamental disagreements.

(*viii*) Decision analysis provides a coherent framework for contingency planning.

Against these favourable items must be put a number of unfavourable items:

(*i*) To relinquish control of a business enterprise to analysts, albeit competent ones, who have no direct experience of managing the business concerned, creates a dangerous precedent.

(*ii*) The spirit of decision analysis is to divide and conquer. Experts are not asked complicated, fuzzy questions, but crystal clear, unambiguous, elemental, hypothetical questions. The trouble is, however, that these basic questions are often the most difficult to answer, and many decision-makers shudder at the idea of thinking about these starkly simple, hypothetical situations.

(*iii*) Decision analysis requires the explicit articulation of a thought process. This requirement may inhibit analysis of complex situations. The human brain can be a magnificent synthesizer of disparate pieces of nebulous information, whilst formal techniques and procedures often thwart and inhibit this mysterious mechanism from operating efficiently.

(*iv*) Many high-level decisions are finally taken on 'political' grounds; that is, several conflicting interests have to be taken into account, and hence optimization is inapplicable because no single 'optimizer' exists. Quantification is inapplicable to many of the problems involved and, furthermore, there is a reluctance to base decisions on mathematical analyses that the decision-maker does not fully comprehend.

(*v*) Critics allege that the breed of man who desires to tackle decisions in this kind of way lacks heart; analysts are so concerned with putting numbers on everything that they automatically bias a study in a direction that leaves out many human and aesthetic aspects.

Clearly you, the reader, have to make your own judgment as to where the balance of gains and losses occurs. The present book has striven to show that the balance is already in favour of decision analysis. However, the methodology is not as yet fully developed, and much work remains to be done before a generally applicable theory is available to cope with all possible practical situations.

15.6 Conclusions

Two centuries have elapsed since the time when, after his death, the Reverend Thomas Bayes's famous paper was presented in London to the Royal Society, on 23 December 1763. In the paper's preface (written by Richard Price, author of the *Northampton Life Table*, one of the very earliest of such tables and a basis on which modern life assurance principles were established in the second half of the eighteenth century), the following paragraph occurs:

Every judicious person will be sensible that the problem now mentioned is by no means merely a curious speculation, but necessary to be solved in order to provide a sure foundation for all our reasonings concerning past facts, and what is likely to be hereafter. Common sense is indeed sufficient to show us that, from the observation of what has in former instances been the consequence of a certain cause or action, one may make a judgment what is likely to be the consequence of it another time, and that the larger the number of experiments we have to support a conclusion, so much the more reason we have to take it for granted. But it is certain that we cannot determine, at least not to any nicety, in what degree repeated experiments confirm a conclusion . . . which proves that the problem enquired into in this essay is not less important that it is curious.

The paper itself then goes on to formalize a method of blending probability judgments which are rooted in frequency observations—in observations creating the presumption that frequency ratios converge on definite values— with probability judgments derived from mere hunches of the decision maker or from his ignorance. The present book has attempted to develop a theme that is both 'positive' and 'normative' at the same time: that is a decision theory which develops principles according to which reasonable and well-informed individuals observably tend to behave when facde with decision problems which they take seriously and which they have properly understood.

Any approach to decision-making must be judged, not so much as to whether it provides the right answer every time, but whether it is 'right' more often than would otherwise be the case. It is common to act in many forms of planning as if the most likely outcome will occur; a course of action that can lead to frightful consequences if the unexpected arises. The benefits of the procedure outlined in this book are that it forces consideration of alternatives, probabilities, outcomes and criteria of choice in a way that serves to clarify the problem structure and relates probabilities to values of alternative outcomes. The author's experience of putting these ideas to executives is that they tend to temporize, to say they will wait for more information, etc. But this is commonly not possible (and anyway can often be shown to be not worth the money involved), but the starkness with which the final decision has to be made commonly intimidates. More factors are thought of, the criterion for choice changed, etc., so that finally the decision-maker, is able to say, 'We will use our judgment', which really means more or less that we will do the same as before. Yet you, the decision-maker, have to decide, and it is fair to ask how you will decide between alternative courses of action if you do not use a systematic approach such as that described in this book.

The author believes that the concept of probability lies at the heart of problems of decision-making (which are almost invariably under uncertainty). In particular, it must be regarded as the central theme of any adequate theory of profit maximization, whether profit be in terms of money or any other scale of measurement. For this reason the approach given here must inevitably lead to a great deal of rethinking among accountants, economists, engineers, etc., who have not been naturally used to thinking in these terms. Until recently, study of the decision-making process has been left to lawyers, historians, economists and the like. Their contributions have been, and remain, important. But now the quantitative approach, the ability to measure things and work in numbers, has something to say. It does not provide a panacea that will answer all problems; it has nothing to say at all in some circumstances. But there are many problems where its mode of thinking can make a contribution, clarifying and offering viable solutions to the problems at hand. If business decisions did not involve elements of risk, there would be no dearth of managerial talent. That there is such a dearth, illustrates well the need to attempt a systematic approach to the relationship between risk and business decision.

Appendix A
Cumulative binomial probabilities

The following table lists cumulative binomial probabilities for values of p (by increments of 0·05) for values of n from 5 to 25 (with increments of 5) and 50. For values of $p \leqslant 0\cdot50$, the table shows the probability of x *or more* successes in n trials. For values of $p > 0\cdot50$, the same table can be used to find the probability of x *or less* successes in n trials.

Values of p are given to two places of decimals, probabilities to four places. The use of the tables will be illustrated with some examples.

(*i*) For $n=5$ and $p=0\cdot10$, find the probability of two or more successes. Find the section of the table for $n=5$. Since $p \leqslant 0\cdot50$, look down the x column in the lefthand margin to find $x=2$. Then look across this row to find the cell below $p=0\cdot10$. The value of 0·0815 in this cell is the binomial probability of two or more successes, given $n=3$ and $p=0\cdot10$.

(*ii*) For $n=5$ and $p=0\cdot90$, find the probability of three or less successes. Find the section of the table for $n=5$. Since $p > 0\cdot50$, look down the x column in the righthand margin to find $x=3$, and look across this row to the cell below a $(1-p)$ value of 0·10 (since if $p=0\cdot90$, $1-p=0\cdot10$). The value in this cell is 0·0815 and is the probability of three or less successes, given $n=5$ and $p=0\cdot90$.

(*iii*) For $n=5$ and $p=0\cdot90$, find the probability of four or more successes. This probability is simply 1 minus the probability of obtaining one or fewer successes, given $n=5$ and $p=0\cdot10$. Hence from (*iii*) it is $1-0\cdot0815$ or 0·9185.

Binomial probabilities, *n* = 5

x	*p* = 0·05	0·10	0·15	0·20	0·25	0·30	0·35	0·40	0·45	0·50 = (1 − *p*)	*x*
1	0·2262	0·4095	0·5563	0·6723	0·7627	0·8319	0·8840	0·9222	0·9497	0·9688	4
2	0·0226	0·0815	0·1648	0·2627	0·3672	0·4718	0·5716	0·6630	0·7438	0·8125	3
3	0·0012	0·0086	0·0266	0·0579	0·1035	0·1631	0·2352	0·3174	0·4069	0·5000	2
4		0·0005	0·0022	0·0067	0·0156	0·0308	0·0540	0·0870	0·1312	0·1875	1
5			0·0001	0·0003	0·0010	0·0024	0·0053	0·0102	0·0185	0·0313	0

Binomial probabilities *n* = 10

x	*p* = 0·05	0·10	0·15	0·20	0·25	0·30	0·35	0·40	0·45	0·50 = (1 − *p*)	*x*
1	0·4013	0·6513	0·8031	0·8926	0·9437	0·9718	0·9865	0·9940	0·9975	0·9990	9
2	0·0861	0·2639	0·4557	0·6242	0·7560	0·8507	0·9140	0·9536	0·9767	0·9893	8
3	0·0115	0·0702	0·1798	0·3222	0·4744	0·6172	0·7384	0·8327	0·9004	0·9453	7
4	0·0010	0·0128	0·0500	0·1209	0·2241	0·3504	0·4862	0·6177	0·7340	0·8281	6
5	0·0001	0·0016	0·0099	0·0328	0·0781	0·1503	0·2485	0·3669	0·4956	0·6230	5
6		0·0001	0·0014	0·0064	0·0197	0·0473	0·0949	0·1662	0·2616	0·3770	4
7			0·0001	0·0009	0·0035	0·0106	0·0260	0·0548	0·1020	0·1719	3
8				0·0001	0·0004	0·0016	0·0048	0·0123	0·0274	0·0547	2
9						0·0001	0·0005	0·0017	0·0045	0·0107	1
10								0·0001	0·0003	0·0010	0

Binomial probabilities, $n = 15$

x	$p = 0.05$	0.10	0.15	0.20	0.25	0.30	0.35	0.40	0.45	$0.50 = (1-p)$	x
1	0·5367	0·7941	0·9126	0·9648	0·9866	0·9953	0·9984	0·9995	0·9999	1·0000	14
2	0·1710	0·4510	0·6814	0·8328	0·9198	0·9647	0·9858	0·9948	0·9983	0·9995	13
3	0·0362	0·1841	0·3958	0·6020	0·7639	0·8732	0·9383	0·9729	0·9893	0·9963	12
4	0·0055	0·0556	0·1773	0·3518	0·5387	0·7031	0·8273	0·9095	0·9576	0·9824	11
5	0·0006	0·0127	0·0617	0·1642	0·3135	0·4845	0·6481	0·7827	0·8796	0·9408	10
6	0·0001	0·0022	0·0168	0·0611	0·1484	0·2784	0·4357	0·5968	0·7392	0·8491	9
7		0·0003	0·0036	0·0181	0·0566	0·1311	0·2452	0·3902	0·5478	0·6964	8
8			0·0006	0·0042	0·0173	0·0500	0·1132	0·2131	0·3465	0·5000	7
9			0·0001	0·0008	0·0042	0·0152	0·0422	0·0950	0·1818	0·3036	6
10				0·0001	0·0008	0·0037	0·0124	0·0338	0·0769	0·1509	5
11					0·0001	0·0007	0·0028	0·0093	0·0255	0·0592	4
12						0·0001	0·0005	0·0019	0·0063	0·0176	3
13							0·0001	0·0003	0·0011	0·0037	2
14									0·0001	0·0005	1
15										0·0002	0

Binomial probabilities, $n = 20$

x	p=0.05	0.10	0.15	0.20	0.25	0.30	0.35	0.40	0.45	0.50=(1−p)	x
1	0.6415	0.8784	0.9612	0.9885	0.9968	0.9992	0.9998	1.0000	1.0000	1.0000	19
2	0.2642	0.6083	0.8244	0.9308	0.9757	0.9924	0.9979	0.9995	0.9999	1.0000	18
3	0.0755	0.3231	0.5951	0.7939	0.9087	0.9645	0.9879	0.9964	0.9991	0.9998	17
4	0.0159	0.1330	0.3523	0.5886	0.7748	0.8929	0.9556	0.9840	0.9951	0.9987	16
5	0.0026	0.0432	0.1702	0.3704	0.5852	0.7625	0.8818	0.9490	0.9811	0.9941	15
6	0.0003	0.0113	0.0673	0.1958	0.3828	0.5836	0.7546	0.8744	0.9447	0.9793	14
7		0.0024	0.0219	0.0867	0.2142	0.3920	0.5834	0.7500	0.8701	0.9423	13
8		0.0004	0.0059	0.0321	0.1018	0.2277	0.3990	0.5841	0.7480	0.8684	12
9		0.0001	0.0013	0.0100	0.0409	0.1133	0.2376	0.4044	0.5857	0.7483	11
10			0.0002	0.0026	0.0139	0.0480	0.1218	0.2447	0.4086	0.5881	10
11				0.0006	0.0039	0.0171	0.0532	0.1275	0.2493	0.4119	9
12				0.0001	0.0009	0.0051	0.0196	0.0565	0.1308	0.2517	8
13					0.0002	0.0013	0.0060	0.0210	0.0580	0.1316	7
14						0.0003	0.0015	0.0065	0.0214	0.0577	6
15							0.0003	0.0016	0.0064	0.0207	5
16								0.0003	0.0015	0.0059	4
17									0.0003	0.0013	3
18										0.0002	2

Binomial probabilities, $n = 25$

x	$p=0.05$	0.10	0.15	0.20	0.25	0.30	0.35	0.40	0.45	$0.50=(1-p)$	x
1	0·7226	0·9282	0·9828	0·9962	0·9992	0·9999	1·0000	1·0000	1·0000	1·0000	24
2	0·3576	0·7288	0·9069	0·9726	0·9930	0·9984	0·9997	0·9999	1·0000	1·0000	23
3	0·1271	0·4629	0·7463	0·9018	0·9679	0·9910	0·9979	0·9996	0·9999	1·0000	22
4	0·0341	0·2364	0·5289	0·7660	0·9038	0·9668	0·9903	0·9976	0·9995	0·9999	21
5	0·0072	0·0980	0·3179	0·5793	0·7863	0·9095	0·9680	0·9905	0·9977	0·9995	20
6	0·0012	0·0334	0·1615	0·3833	0·6217	0·8065	0·9174	0·9706	0·9914	0·9980	19
7	0·0002	0·0095	0·0695	0·2200	0·4389	0·6593	0·8266	0·9264	0·9742	0·9927	18
8		0·0023	0·0255	0·1091	0·2735	0·4882	0·6939	0·8464	0·9361	0·9784	17
9		0·0005	0·0080	0·0468	0·1494	0·3231	0·5332	0·7265	0·8660	0·9461	16
10		0·0001	0·0021	0·0173	0·0713	0·1894	0·3697	0·5754	0·7576	0·8852	15
11			0·0005	0·0056	0·0297	0·0978	0·2288	0·4142	0·6157	0·7878	14
12			0·0001	0·0015	0·0107	0·0442	0·1254	0·2677	0·4574	0·6550	13
13				0·0004	0·0034	0·0175	0·0604	0·1538	0·3063	0·5000	12
14				0·0001	0·0009	0·0060	0·0255	0·0778	0·1827	0·3450	11
15					0·0002	0·0018	0·0093	0·0344	0·0960	0·2122	10
16						0·0005	0·0029	0·0132	0·0440	0·1148	9
17						0·0001	0·0008	0·0043	0·0174	0·0539	8
18							0·0002	0·0012	0·0058	0·0216	7
19								0·0003	0·0016	0·0073	6
20								0·0001	0·0004	0·0020	5
21									0·0001	0·0005	4
22										0·0001	3

Binomial probabilities, $n = 50$

x	p=0·05	0·10	0·15	0·20	0·25	0·30	0·35	0·40	0·45	0·50=(1−p)	x
1	0·9231	0·9948	0·9997	1·0000	1·0000	1·0000	1·0000	1·0000	1·0000	1·0000	49
2	0·7206	0·9662	0·9971	0·9998	1·0000	1·0000	1·0000	1·0000	1·0000	1·0000	48
3	0·4595	0·8883	0·9858	0·9987	0·9999	1·0000	1·0000	1·0000	1·0000	1·0000	47
4	0·2396	0·7497	0·9540	0·9943	0·9995	1·0000	1·0000	1·0000	1·0000	1·0000	46
5	0·1036	0·5688	0·8879	0·9815	0·9979	0·9998	1·0000	1·0000	1·0000	1·0000	45
6	0·0378	0·3839	0·7806	0·9520	0·9930	0·9993	0·9999	1·0000	1·0000	1·0000	44
7	0·0118	0·2298	0·6387	0·8966	0·9806	0·9975	0·9998	1·0000	1·0000	1·0000	43
8	0·0032	0·1221	0·4812	0·8096	0·9547	0·9927	0·9992	0·9999	1·0000	1·0000	42
9	0·0008	0·0579	0·3319	0·6927	0·9084	0·9817	0·9975	0·9998	1·0000	1·0000	41
10	0·0002	0·0245	0·2089	0·5563	0·8363	0·9598	0·9933	0·9992	0·9999	1·0000	40
11		0·0094	0·1199	0·4164	0·7378	0·9211	0·9840	0·9978	0·9998	1·0000	39
12		0·0032	0·0628	0·2893	0·6184	0·8610	0·9658	0·9943	0·9994	1·0000	38
13		0·0010	0·0301	0·1861	0·4890	0·7771	0·9339	0·9867	0·9982	0·9998	37
14		0·0003	0·0132	0·1106	0·3630	0·6721	0·8837	0·9720	0·9955	0·9995	36
15		0·0001	0·0053	0·0607	0·2519	0·5532	0·8122	0·9460	0·9896	0·9987	35
16			0·0019	0·0308	0·1631	0·4308	0·7199	0·9045	0·9780	0·9967	34
17			0·0007	0·0144	0·0983	0·3161	0·6111	0·8439	0·9573	0·9923	33
18			0·0002	0·0063	0·0551	0·2178	0·4940	0·7631	0·9235	0·9836	32
19			0·0001	0·0025	0·0287	0·1406	0·3784	0·6644	0·8727	0·9675	31
20				0·0009	0·0139	0·0848	0·2736	0·5535	0·8026	0·9405	30
21				0·0003	0·0063	0·0478	0·1861	0·4390	0·7138	0·8987	29
22				0·0001	0·0026	0·0251	0·1187	0·3299	0·6100	0·8389	28
23					0·0010	0·0123	0·0710	0·2340	0·4981	0·7601	27
24					0·0004	0·0056	0·0396	0·1562	0·3866	0·6641	26
25					0·0001	0·0024	0·0207	0·0978	0·2840	0·5561	25
26						0·0009	0·0100	0·0573	0·1966	0·4439	24
27						0·0003	0·0045	0·0314	0·1279	0·3359	23
28						0·0001	0·0019	0·0160	0·0780	0·2399	22
29							0·0007	0·0076	0·0444	0·1611	21
30							0·0003	0·0034	0·0235	0·1013	20
31							0·0001	0·0014	0·0116	0·0595	19
32								0·0005	0·0053	0·0325	18
33								0·0002	0·0022	0·0164	17
34								0·0001	0·0009	0·0077	16
35									0·0003	0·0033	15
36									0·0001	0·0013	14
37										0·0005	13

Appendix B
Unit normal distribution

x	$f_N(x)$	$F_N(x)$	x	$f_N(x)$	$F_N(x)$
0·00	0·3989	0·5000	1·75	0·0863	0·9599
0·05	0·3984	0·5199	1·80	0·0790	0·9641
0·10	0·3970	0·5398	1·85	0·0721	0·9678
0·15	0·3945	0·5596	1·90	0·0656	0·9713
0·20	0·3910	0·5793	1·95	0·0596	0·9744
0·25	0·3867	0·5987	2·00	0·0540	0·9772
0·30	0·3814	0·6179	2·05	0·0488	0·9798
0·35	0·3752	0·6368	2·10	0·0440	0·9821
0·40	0·3683	0·6554	2·15	0·0396	0·9842
0·45	0·3605	0·6736	2·20	0·0355	0·9861
0·50	0·3521	0·6915	2·25	0·0317	0·9878
0·55	0·3429	0·7088	2·30	0·0283	0·9893
0·60	0·3332	0·7257	2·35	0·0252	0·9906
0·65	0·3230	0·7422	2·40	0·0224	0·9918
0·70	0·3123	0·7580	2·45	0·0198	0·9929
0·75	0·3011	0·7734	2·50	0·0175	0·9938
0·80	0·2897	0·7881	2·55	0·0154	0·9946
0·85	0·2780	0·8023	2·60	0·0136	0·9953
0·90	0·2661	0·8159	2·65	0·0119	0·9960
0·95	0·2541	0·8289	2·70	0·0104	0·9965
1·00	0·2420	0·8413	2·75	0·0091	0·9970
1·05	0·2299	0·8531	2·80	0·0079	0·9974
1·10	0·2179	0·8643	2·85	0·0069	0·9978
1·15	0·2059	0·8749	2·90	0·0060	0·9981
1·20	0·1942	0·8849	2·95	0·0051	0·9984
1·25	0·1826	0·8944	3·00	0·0044	0·9987
1·30	0·1714	0·9032	3·10	0·0033	0·9990
1·35	0·1604	0·9115	3·20	0·0024	0·9993
1·40	0·1497	0·9192	3·30	0·0017	0·9995
1·45	0·1394	0·9265	3·40	0·0012	0·9997
1·50	0·1295	0·9332	3·50	0·0009	0·99977
1·55	0·1200	0·9394	3·60	0·0006	0·99984
1·60	0·1109	0·9452	3·70	0·0004	0·99989
1·65	0·1023	0·9505	3·80	0·0003	0·99993
1·70	0·0940	0·9554	3·90	0·0002	0·99995
			4·00	0·0001	0·99997

The functions tabulated are $f_N(x) = \dfrac{1}{\sqrt{(2\pi)}} e^{-x^2/2}$ and $F_N(x) = \displaystyle\int_{-\infty}^{x} f_N(x)\, dx$

Appendix C
Unit normal loss integral

The values in the table $N(D)$ are expected opportunity losses for linear loss functions and a normal distribution with a mean of 0 and a standard deviation of 1. The value D represents the absolute value of the standardized deviation of the breakeven value μ_b from μ, the mean of the distribution.

D	0·00	0·01	0·02	0·03	0·04	0·05	0·06	0·07	0·08	0·09
0·0	0·3989	0·3940	0·3890	0·3841	0·3793	0·3744	0·3697	0·3649	0·3602	0·3556
0·1	0·3509	0·3464	0·3418	0·3373	0·3328	0·3284	0·3240	0·3197	0·3154	0·3111
0·2	0·3069	0·3027	0·2986	0·2944	0·2904	0·2863	0·2824	0·2784	0·2745	0·2706
0·3	0·2668	0·2630	0·2592	0·2555	0·2518	0·2481	0·2445	0·2409	0·2374	0·2339
0·4	0·2304	0·2270	0·2236	0·2203	0·2169	0·2137	0·2104	0·2072	0·2040	0·2009
0·5	0·1978	0·1947	0·1917	0·1887	0·1857	0·1828	0·1799	0·1771	0·1742	0·1714
0·6	0·1687	0·1659	0·1633	0·1606	0·1580	0·1554	0·1528	0·1503	0·1478	0·1453
0·7	0·1429	0·1405	0·1381	0·1358	0·1334	0·1312	0·1289	0·1267	0·1245	0·1223
0·8	0·1202	0·1181	0·1160	0·1140	0·1120	0·1100	0·1080	0·1061	0·1042	0·1023
0·9	0·1004	0·09860	0·09680	0·09503	0·09328	0·09156	0·08986	0·08819	0·08654	0·08491
1·0	0·08332	0·08174	0·08019	0·07866	0·07716	0·07568	0·07422	0·07279	0·07138	0·06999
1·1	0·06862	0·06727	0·06595	0·06465	0·06336	0·06210	0·06086	0·05964	0·05844	0·05726
1·2	0·05610	0·05496	0·05384	0·05274	0·05165	0·05059	0·04954	0·04851	0·04750	0·04650
1·3	0·04553	0·04457	0·04363	0·04270	0·04179	0·04090	0·04002	0·03916	0·03831	0·03748
1·4	0·03667	0·03587	0·03508	0·03431	0·03356	0·03281	0·03208	0·03137	0·03067	0·02998
1·5	0·02931	0·02865	0·02800	0·02736	0·02674	0·02612	0·02552	0·02494	0·02436	0·02380
1·6	0·02324	0·02270	0·02217	0·02165	0·02114	0·02064	0·02015	0·01967	0·01920	0·01874
1·7	0·01829	0·01785	0·01742	0·01699	0·01658	0·01617	0·01578	0·01539	0·01501	0·01464
1·8	0·01428	0·01392	0·01357	0·01323	0·01290	0·01257	0·01226	0·01195	0·01164	0·01134
1·9	0·01105	0·01077	0·01049	0·01022	$0{\cdot}0^2 9957$	$0{\cdot}0^2 9698$	$0{\cdot}0^2 9445$	$0{\cdot}0^2 9198$	$0{\cdot}0^2 8957$	$0{\cdot}0^2 8721$
2·0	$0{\cdot}0^2 8491$	$0{\cdot}0^2 8266$	$0{\cdot}0^2 8046$	$0{\cdot}0^2 7832$	$0{\cdot}0^2 7623$	$0{\cdot}0^2 7418$	$0{\cdot}0^2 7219$	$0{\cdot}0^2 7024$	$0{\cdot}0^2 6835$	$0{\cdot}0^2 6649$
2·1	$0{\cdot}0^2 6468$	$0{\cdot}0^2 6292$	$0{\cdot}0^2 6120$	$0{\cdot}0^2 5952$	$0{\cdot}0^2 5788$	$0{\cdot}0^2 5628$	$0{\cdot}0^2 5472$	$0{\cdot}0^2 5320$	$0{\cdot}0^2 5172$	$0{\cdot}0^2 5028$
2·2	$0{\cdot}0^2 4887$	$0{\cdot}0^2 4750$	$0{\cdot}0^2 4616$	$0{\cdot}0^2 4486$	$0{\cdot}0^2 4358$	$0{\cdot}0^2 4235$	$0{\cdot}0^2 4114$	$0{\cdot}0^2 3996$	$0{\cdot}0^2 3882$	$0{\cdot}0^2 3770$
2·3	$0{\cdot}0^2 3662$	$0{\cdot}0^2 3556$	$0{\cdot}0^2 3453$	$0{\cdot}0^2 3352$	$0{\cdot}0^2 3255$	$0{\cdot}0^2 3159$	$0{\cdot}0^2 3067$	$0{\cdot}0^2 2977$	$0{\cdot}0^2 2889$	$0{\cdot}0^2 2804$
2·4	$0{\cdot}0^2 2720$	$0{\cdot}0^2 2640$	$0{\cdot}0^2 2561$	$0{\cdot}0^2 2484$	$0{\cdot}0^2 2410$	$0{\cdot}0^2 2337$	$0{\cdot}0^2 2267$	$0{\cdot}0^2 2199$	$0{\cdot}0^2 2132$	$0{\cdot}0^2 2067$
2·5	$0{\cdot}0^2 2004$	$0{\cdot}0^2 1943$	$0{\cdot}0^2 1883$	$0{\cdot}0^2 1826$	$0{\cdot}0^2 1769$	$0{\cdot}0^2 1715$	$0{\cdot}0^2 1662$	$0{\cdot}0^2 1610$	$0{\cdot}0^2 1560$	$0{\cdot}0^2 1511$
3·0	$0{\cdot}0^3 3822$	$0{\cdot}0^3 3689$	$0{\cdot}0^3 3560$	$0{\cdot}0^3 3436$	$0{\cdot}0^3 3316$	$0{\cdot}0^3 3199$	$0{\cdot}0^3 3087$	$0{\cdot}0^3 2978$	$0{\cdot}0^3 2873$	$0{\cdot}0^3 2771$
3·5	$0{\cdot}0^4 5848$	$0{\cdot}0^4 5620$	$0{\cdot}0^4 5400$	$0{\cdot}0^4 5188$	$0{\cdot}0^4 4984$	$0{\cdot}0^4 4788$	$0{\cdot}0^4 4599$	$0{\cdot}0^4 4417$	$0{\cdot}0^4 4242$	$0{\cdot}0^4 4073$
4·0	$0{\cdot}0^5 7145$	$0{\cdot}0^5 6835$	$0{\cdot}0^5 6538$	$0{\cdot}0^5 6253$	$0{\cdot}0^5 5980$	$0{\cdot}0^5 5718$	$0{\cdot}0^5 5468$	$0{\cdot}0^5 5227$	$0{\cdot}0^5 4997$	$0{\cdot}0^5 4777$

Appendix D
Percentage points of the *t*-distribution

f \ α	0·25	0·1	0·05	0·025	0·01	0·005
1	1·000	3·078	6·314	12·706	31·821	63·657
2	0·816	1·886	2·920	4·303	6·965	9·925
3	0·765	1·638	2·353	3·182	4·541	5·841
4	0·741	1·533	2·132	2·776	3·747	4·604
5	0·727	1·476	2·015	2·571	3·365	4·032
6	0·718	1·440	1·943	2·447	3·143	3·707
7	0·711	1·415	1·895	2·365	2·998	3·499
8	0·706	1·397	1·860	2·306	2·896	3·355
9	0·703	1·383	1·833	2·262	2·821	3·250
10	0·700	1·372	1·812	2·228	2·764	3·169
11	0·697	1·363	1·796	2·201	2·718	3·106
12	0·695	1·356	1·782	2·179	2·681	3·055
13	0·694	1·350	1·771	2·160	2·650	3·012
14	0·692	1·345	1·761	2·145	2·624	2·977
15	0·691	1·341	1·753	2·131	2·602	2·947
16	0·690	1·337	1·746	2·120	2·583	2·921
17	0·689	1·333	1·740	2·110	2·567	2·898
18	0·688	1·330	1·734	2·101	2·552	2·878
19	0·688	1·328	1·729	2·093	2·539	2·861
20	0·687	1·325	1·725	2·086	2·528	2·845
21	0·686	1·323	1·721	2·080	2·518	2·831
22	0·686	1·321	1·717	2·074	2·508	2·819
23	0·685	1·319	1·714	2·069	2·500	2·807
24	0·685	1·318	1·711	2·064	2·492	2·797
25	0·684	1·316	1·708	2·060	2·485	2·787
26	0·684	1·315	1·706	2·056	2·479	2·779
27	0·684	1·314	1·703	2·052	2·473	2·771
28	0·683	1·313	1·701	2·048	2·467	2·763
29	0·683	1·311	1·699	2·045	2·462	2·756
30	0·683	1·310	1·697	2·042	2·457	2·750
40	0·681	1·303	1·684	2·021	2·423	2·704
60	0·679	1·296	1·671	2·000	2·390	2·660
120	0·677	1·289	1·658	1·980	2·358	2·617
∞	0·674	1·282	1·645	1·960	2·326	2·576

The value tabulated is $t_{f,\alpha}$ where

$$\alpha = \int_{t_{f,\alpha}}^{\infty} f(t)\, dt$$

and $f(t)$ is the probability density function for the t-distribution having f degrees of freedom.

Appendix E
Glossary of symbols

The normal use made in this book of the various symbols is given below. When use is made of any of them in a different manner, a modified definition is given in the text.

$\neq$	Not equal to
$\doteq$	Approximately equal to
$>$	Greater than
$\geqslant$	Greater than or equal to
$<$	Less than
$\leqslant$	Less than or equal to
$!$	Factorial; i.e. $x! = x(x-1)(x-2)\ldots 3.2.1.$
$\lvert a \rvert$	Absolute value of a, i.e. $\lvert a \rvert = \lvert -a \rvert = a$
$\mid$	Given
dy/dx	Derivative of y with respect to x
$\displaystyle\int f(x)\,dx$	Integral of $f(x)$ with respect to x
$\cap$	Intersection
$\cup$	Union
∞	Infinity
a_i	Action or decision i
α	Significance level (or type 1 error) of a statistical test
β	Type 2 error of a statistical test
b_x	Binomial probability of a random variable x
cdf	Cumulative density function
CEOL	Conditional expected opportunity loss

COL	Conditional opportunity loss
Δx	Delta x, meaning a small change
e	The constant $2 \cdot 71828 \ldots$
E	Expectation
EMV	Expected monetary value
ENGS	Expected net gain from sampling
EOL	Expected opportunity loss
EUV	Expected utility value
EVPI	Expected value of perfect information
EVSI	Expected value of sample information
Exp	Exp $x = e^x$
$f(x)$	pdf of a random variable x
$f_N(x)$	pdf of a unit normal variable
$F_N(x)$	cdf of a unit normal variable
H_0	Null hypothesis
H_1	Alternative hypothesis
h_x	Hypergeometric probability for a random variable x
$\log a$	Logarithm of a
ml	Maximum likelihood
μ	Mean of population
n	Number of trials: size of sample
N	Size of population or universe
$\binom{n}{r}$	Binomial coefficient
$N(D)$	Normal loss integral
$N(\mu, \sigma)$	Normal variable with mean μ, standard deviation σ
p	Population proportion: probability of success in a binomial probability situation.
$P(A)$	Probability of event A
$P(AB)$	Joint probability of events A and B
$P(A\|B)$	Conditional probability of event A, given event B
pdf	Probability density function
π	The constant $3 \cdot 14159 \ldots$
r_j	Outcome or event j
s	Sample estimate of population standard deviation
s^2	Sample estimate of population variance
σ	Standard deviation of population
σ^2	Variance of population
$\sum$	Summation
t_f	Standardized deviate for t-distribution with f degrees of freedom
u	Unit normal variable
u_{ij}	Pay-off or profit from action a_i and outcome r_j
Var (x)	Variance of a random variable x
$\bar{x}$	Mean of a sample of n observations $x_1, x_2, \ldots x_n$

Appendix F
Glossary of statistical terms

This list gives descriptions, but not formal definitions, of the distinctive statistical terms used in this book. Further information on the terms can be obtained from the text, and the number given in brackets with each term relates to the page where the term concerned is first mentioned in detail.

Alternative hypothesis (289)	Any admissible hypothesis alternative to the hypothesis under test
Arithmetic average (46)	The mean value of a set of observations
Bayes' theorem (154)	A fundamental theorem which revises prior probabilities in the light of further information to form posterior probabilities
Bias (303)	An effect which deprives a statistical result of representativeness by systematically distorting it
Binomial probability distribution (51)	A probability distribution for the probability of a defined number of successes in a series of independent trials at each of which the probability of success is the same
Confidence interval (309)	A range within which it can be asserted that an unknown population parameter lies with some defined probability
Confidence limits (309)	The values at the two extremes of a confidence interval (q.v.) for some unknown parameter

Consistency of estimator (306)   A desirable property of an estimator such that, as the sample size increases, the estimator converges on the unknown population parameter

Continuous random variable (68)   A random variable which can, theoretically, take any value between defined limits

Criterion (95)   Principle to be followed in choice between alternatives

Cumulative density function (68)   Function expressing the probability that a continuous random variable is less than or equal to some defined value

Cumulative probability distribution (43)   Function expressing the probability that a discrete variable is less than or equal to some defined value

Decision tree (121)   A method of displaying the flow of possible courses of action in the form of a branching network

Degrees of freedom (292)   The number of independent values in a sample set, given the constraints placed on it, e.g. that the mean is equal to some defined value

Discrete random variable (41)   A random variable which can only take certain values, e.g. positive integers

Discounting (136)   Method of calculating the present worth of future payments

Efficiency of estimators (304)   One estimator is regarded as more efficient than another if it has a smaller sampling variance

Error, Type 1 (295)   The rejection of a statistical hypothesis when it ought to be accepted

Error, Type 2 (295)   The acceptance of a statistical hypothesis when it is false and ought to be rejected

Estimator (303)   A rule or method for estimating a parameter in a parent population from a random sample drawn from that population

Expected value or expectation (45)   The mean value in repeated sampling

Exponential distribution (71)   A probability density function of the form ae^{-ax} where a is a constant and x is the random variable

Frequency distribution (41)   An arrangement of data specifying the number of items of each category included in the data

Histogram (42)	A form of diagram in which the elements of a frequency distribution are represented by rectangles whose areas are proportional to the frequency of the observations
Hypothesis (285)	A statistical hypothesis concerns the parameters or form of the probability distribution (or pdf) for a designated population
Incremental analysis (103)	Optimum sought through examining effects of series of small changes in variables concerned
Independence (21)	Events are said to be independent in a probability sense if the occurrence of one does not affect the occurrence of others and vice versa
Inference (318)	The deduction of information concerning a population using a sample taken from that population
Intersection (19)	Composite event $A \cap B$ is occurrence of both events A and B
Judgmental probability distribution (218)	A probability distribution in whose estimation some element of human judgment directly enters
Likelihood (307)	The probability of a sample set, expressed as a function of the population parameters
Maximum likelihood (306)	A method of estimating a parameter of a population by that value which maximizes the likelihood of the sample
Mean (46)	An arithmetic average
Median (219)	A location average, being the central value of a variable when the values are ranged in order of magnitude
Minimax loss (or maximin gain) (95)	A principle of choice whereby the maximum loss in taking a wrong decision is minimized
Minimax regret (96)	A principle of choice whereby the maximum regret (q.v.) in taking a wrong decision is minimized
Mutually exclusive (20)	Two events A and B are mutually exclusive if they cannot occur simultaneously
Node (122)	A point in a decision tree where a choice of action has to be made
Normal distribution (77)	A continuous probability distribution defined for all values by its mean and standard deviation and arising very commonly in practice

Normal loss integral (248)	The overall expected loss when combining a linear loss function with the probabilities arising from a defined normal distribution
Null hypothesis (288)	A particular hypothesis under test, in contrast to the alternative hypothesis
Opportunity loss (107)	The cost of a lost opportunity, or alternative goods or services foregone or alternative opportunity for investment
Parameter (51)	Some quantity that is one element in defining a probability distribution (e.g. the mean for a normal distribution)
Percentiles (87)	The set of location values which divide the total frequency ordered by value into one hundred equal parts
Permutation (51)	The number of ways of choosing a subset from a set of objects, the order of choice being immaterial
Personal probabilities (218)	See judgmental probability distribution
Poisson probability distribution (56)	The limiting form of the binomial probability distribution when n is very large and p is very small
Population (86)	The whole of the material from which a sample is taken. Synonymous with universe
Posterior probability (151)	The revised probability assigned to some event when the prior probability is modified in the light of further information
Power (296)	Probability that a statistical test rejects the null hypothesis when the alternative hypothesis is true—it is the complement of the error of the second kind
Prior probability (150)	The probability assigned to some event at a particular moment in time
Probability (classical) (13)	The probability of an event regarded as being obtainable from a consideration of the physical conditions under which the event can occur, e.g. a penny has two sides, hence the probability of a head on tossing is a half
Probability (relative frequency) (14)	The probability of an event is regarded as the limit of the frequency of occurrence of that event in a series of n trials as n tends to infinity
Probability density function (42)	Function expressing the probability that a continuous random variable takes any defined value

Probability distribution (42)	Function expressing the probability that a discrete random variable takes any defined value
Quartiles (upper and lower) (89)	Three variable values separate the total frequency of a distribution, in ranked order of magnitude, into four equal parts: the lower quartile, the median and the upper quartile
Quota sampling (314)	A method of selection by which the sample is divided into quotas which indicate the number of units of a particular type to be sampled, the choice of the actual units being left to the sampler
Random sample (314)	A method of selection in which every unit of a population has exactly the same chance of being included in the sample as any other unit
Regret (96)	The difference between the pay-off achieved under a given action and that which could have been achieved if the best action had been taken for the outcome which subsequently resulted
Roll-back (129)	A principle of analysing decision trees which involves proceeding from the latest action/ outcomes to the initial action choice
Sample (313)	A part of a population, which is obtained by some process or other, usually by way of planned selection, with the object of investigating the properties of the population
Sample space (17)	Geometric representation of the set of sample points corresponding to all possible samples
Significance level (289)	The probability in a test of a hypothesis, that the observed sample value of the test statistic or a more extreme one, is obtained when the null hypothesis is true
Significance test (287)	A statistical test of a null hypothesis against one or a set of alternatives
Standard deviation (49)	A measure of the dispersion of the values of a series of observations from their arithmetic mean
Statistic (52)	A summary value calculated from a sample of observations, usually but not necessarily, as an estimator of some population parameter

Stratification (317)   The division of a population into parts, especially for the purpose of drawing a sample, an assigned proportion of the sample being selected from each stratum

Subjective probability (218)   See judgmental probability distribution

t-distribution (293)   A distribution that is, among other things, that of the ratio of a sample mean (measured from the population mean) to a sample standard deviation in samples from a normal population

Test statistic (289)   A function of a sample of observations which provides a basis for testing a statistical hypothesis

Union (18)   Composite event $A \cup B$ is the occurrence of either A or B alone, or both events together

Universe (86)   The whole of the material from which a sample is taken; synonymous with population

Utiles (271)   A generalized utility (q.v.) measurement, not necessarily in the scale zero to unity

Utility (267)   A scale of values for the possible outcomes of a decision (or series of decisions) taking into account the preferences of the decision maker; usually expressed on a scale of zero to unity

Variance (48)   The square of the value of the standard deviation (q.v.)

Venn diagram (17)   Representation of a set of possible and alternative outcomes in a diagrammatic form

Appendix G
Bibliography

The short list below gives a few books that could usefully be studied to follow up and expand upon the material presented in this book. They are additional to the (mainly journal or monograph) references given on specific topics at the end of certain chapters. Items in Section G.1 are concerned with statistical description (not formally covered in this book) and classical statistics. Items in G.2 are concerned with statistical decision analysis methods. Finally, the items in G.3 provide useful sets of statistical and mathematical tables.

G.1 Statistical Description and Classical Statistics

Yeomans, K. A. 1968. *Introducing Statistics: Statistics for the Social Scientist*. 2 volumes. Penguin.

Moore, P. G. 1969. *Principles of Statistical Techniques*. 2nd Edition. Cambridge Unversity Press.

Yamane, T. 1969. *Statistics, An Introductory Analysis*. Harper & Row.

The first two items require O level mathematics only, the third requires A level mathematics. The books are concerned with practical applications and do not attempt a formal mathematical approach.

G.2 Statistical Decision Analysis

Hadley, G. 1967. *Introduction to Probability and Statistical Decision Theory*. Holden-Day.

Schlaifer, R. 1969. *Analysis of Decisions under Uncertainty*. McGraw-Hill.

Raiffa, H. 1968. *Decision Analysis, Introductory Lectures on Choices under Uncertainty*. Addison-Wesley.

Aitchison, J. 1970. *Choice against Chance*. Addison-Wesley.
Jedamus, P. and Frame, R. 1971. *Business Decision Theory*. McGraw-Hill.
Lindley, D. V. 1971. *Decision Making*. Wiley–Interscience.

The second item is the most comprehensive of these references. The first and fourth require a good mathematical comprehension, the former covering a great deal of ground systematically and rigorously, both in Bayesian and classical statistics. The latter is notable for the wide range of problem types that are discussed in entertaining style. The third item gives a fascinating development of the ideas of subjective probabilities and utilities. The fifth item is a basic textbook that is readable with only a moderate mathematical background, while the last requires a slightly higher mathematical background.

G.3 Statistical Tables

Pearson, E. S. and Hartley, H. O., eds 1954. *Biometrika Tables for Statisticians, Part I*.
    Cambridge Unversity Press.
Lindley, D. V. and Miller, J. C. P., eds. 1953. *Cambridge Elementary Statistical Tables*.
    Cambridge Unversity Press.
Comrie, L. J., ed. 1959. *Shorter Six-figure Mathematical Tables*. Chambers.

The first item is a reference work, the second and third are useful ancillaries for all serious students of this subject.

Answers to exercises

Chapter 2 (p. 36)

1 (*i*) 0·346; (*ii*) 0·077.

2 30.

3 18.

4 8640.

5 0·6.

6 (*i*) 0·75; (*ii*) 0·10; (*iii*) 0·15; (*iv*) 0·35; (*v*) 1·00; (*vi*) 0·85.

7 (*i*) 0·53; (*ii*) 0·92.

8 50/81.

9 (*i*) 0·546; (*ii*) 0·071.

10 0·344.

11 P (picking 4 cards at random with 2 errors) = 0·0136; this is approximately one chance in 74 and would suggest that work is substandard.

12 5.

13 0·656.

14 $\binom{10}{7}$ $7! \, (1/10)^7$.

15 (*ii*) 3 per cent; (*iii*) 0 per cent.

16 (*i*) 0·10; (*ii*) 0·05.

17 1/3 : 1/3 : 1/3.

18 $p(1-p)^{k-1}/(1-(1-p)^n)$.

19 $q > 1/3$.

20 (*i*) 0·027; (*ii*) 0·20.

21 $2k/\pi d$.

22 $(a-c)^2/(a+b)^2$.

Chapter 3 (p. 61)

2 (*i*) $1·95 \times 10^{-3}$; (*ii*) 1·745; (*iii*) No, since $E(x) <$ cost of postage.

3 (*i*) £2·3875; (*ii*) £2387·5, No.
  (*iii*) No, since revenue per unit is now £2·1775.

4 (*i*) $E(x) = 0·47$, st. dev. $(x) = 0·875$.
   (*ii*) y represents loss on one batch with x defectives;
   (*iii*) $E(y) = £1·88$, st. dev. $(y) = £3·50$.

5 (*i*) 0·739; (*ii*) 0·941; (*iii*) 0·164.

6 0·0035.

7 £32·10.
  £321·00
  £32·20.

8 (*i*) 0·642; (*ii*) 0·378; (*iii*) 0·736.

9 $(\frac{1}{2})^{2n} \sum\limits_{r=0}^{n} (^nC_r)^2$.

10 £97·70.

11 0·11.

12 0·019.

13 (*i*) (*a*) $1-(1-p)^4$;
      (*b*) $p(1-p)^4$;
      (*c*) $(1-p)^5$;
   (*ii*) $1/p$, $\sqrt{\{(1-p)/p\}}$.

14 (*i*) 0·223; (*ii*) 0·191.

15 0·0115.

16 (*i*) 0·3235; (*ii*) 0·0025.

17 (*i*) 0·348; (*ii*) ½; (*iii*) 0·474.

18 0·139.

19 45, 11·0.

Chapter 4 (p. 86)

1 (*i*) $F(x) = 0, x \leqslant 0$
$$= x^3, 0 \leqslant x \leqslant 1$$
$$= 1, x \geqslant 1;$$
   (*ii*) 1/27, 0·729, 0·088; (*iii*) 0·63; (*iii*) 3/4, 3/80.

2 8/27.

3 66·1p, 68·7p; first contract is better.

4 173 lb.

5 0·50.

6 (*i*) 272·4 lb, 2·82 lb; (*ii*) 4358·4 lb, 11·28 lb.

7 (*i*) 50·13 per cent; (*ii*) 0·25, 13·36 per cent.

8 (*i*) 0·933; (*ii*) 0·174.

9 (*i*) 1638·5; (*ii*) 0·975.

10 2·28 per cent.

11 8·75, 1·64.

12 (*i*) $b\{[\log(16)]^{1/2} - [\log(16/9)]^{1/2}\}$;
   (*ii*) $b[(4-\pi)/2]^{1/2}$;
   (*iii*) $\{[\log(16)]^{1/2} - [\log(16/9)]^{1/2}]/[(4-\pi)/2]^{1/2}$.

13 $f(x_{(1)}) = 2 - 2x_{(1)}$ mean $= 1/3$, st. dev. $= 1/18$.

14 (*i*) 0·089; (*ii*) 577; (*iii*) 0·247.

15 $\dfrac{R}{M+1}\left(\dfrac{M}{M+2}\right)^{1/2}.$

16 31.

17 (*i*) (*a*) 6·68 per cent, (*b*) 2·275 per cent; (*ii*) 32·7 per cent.

18 1/8.

19 (*i*) Poisson, mean$=3$; (*ii*) 0·35.

20 (*i*) Mean$=$st. dev.$=\beta$; (*ii*) 0·11; (*iii*) 0·38.

Chapter 5 (p. 115)

1 (*i*) Operate as always (maximum profit 20);
  (*ii*) Operate as always or expand current operation (minimax regret 40 in each case);
  (*iii*) Expand current operation (expected monetary value 42).

2 (*i*) Hire new employees (minimax loss 450);
  (*ii*) Selective retraining (minimax regret 10);
  (*iii*) Expected costs: General retraining 426·5;
  Selective retraining 421·0;
  Hire new employees 434·0.

Minimum expect cost strategy is selective retraining.

3 4.

4 (*i*) $k=4\times10^{-6}$;
  (*ii*) Optimum number to order is 2500.

5 2.

6 (*i*) On given information, best action is to purchase foreign bulbs (EOL$=$£250);
  (*ii*) Best rule is to reject foreign bulbs if 3 or more of the sample of 50 are faulty (EOL$=$£168·56).

7 (*i*) Use old machine (EOL$=$£112);
  (*ii*) Optimum decision rule using sample is to change to new machine if 2 or fewer defectives in sample of 50. The expected gain from sampling is 31·6 against a cost of 20. Hence sampling is worthwhile.

8 (*i*) Use testing device (expected cost is £28·25 per unit).

Chapter 6 (p. 145)

1 Sell in UK (EMV £1500, EMV of going to Rome £950).

4 (*iii*) $\alpha<0\cdot482$.

5 Build large plant initially (EMV £3·4m.).

6 Initial Decision as before, build large plant (EMV £0·904m.).

7 Indifferent (on EMV basis) between re-adjusting on arrival and testing each component. For testing: if test shows bad adjustment then re-adjust, if test shows good adjustment, then pass (EMV of either strategy$=$£50 per sub-assembly).

8 Optimal Strategy: Cut 2—If both ruined sell rest;
—If one or two not ruined, then cut the rest.

(EMV of this strategy £802.)

9 Optimal Strategy—Accept offer to try to sell A;
—If sell A then try to sell C;
—If sell C then try to sell B.

(EMV of this strategy £781·25.)

Chapter 7 (p. 174)

1 0·75, 0·25.

2 0·909.

3 5/6.

4 0·796.

5 Problem 2.3: (*i*) 0·5; (*ii*) 0·97; (*iii*) 0·965.
Problem 2.4: One test, 0·345; Two tests, 0·84.

6 (*i*) 0·525; (*ii*) 0·342.

7 (*i*) No—expected proportion in favour $=0.47$;
(*ii*) $P(30\%)=0.023$
$P(40\%)=0.231$
$P(50\%)=0.514$
$P(60\%)=0.232.$

8 $P(0)=0.8$; $P(1)=0.2$; $P(2)=0.$

9 Posterior distribution has mean 8·75 per cent, standard deviation 0·473 per cent; Expected profit of buying mine is $-£8.4$m. and hence unprofitable.

10 (*i*) Posterior distribution is $=1.1 f_N(x)$ for $10<x<12$
$=0$ for $10>x>12$

where $f_N(x)$ is the distribution N (11·5, 2·25), i.e. posterior distribution is a truncated normal distribution;
(*ii*) With normal prior, posterior is N (11·06, 0·106).

11 (*i*) 0·72, 0·01; (*ii*) 0·009; rises sharply as P falls.

Chapter 8 (p. 205)

1 (*i*) With no further information M. Borel should reject the offer.
(EMV$=-5$m. NF.)

(*ii*) Given the opportunity of obtaining more information, M. Borel should inspect one ship and accept the offer if it passes, and reject otherwise (EMV of this strategy = 17·9m. NF).

2 Optimal strategy is to examine the two machines.

If both are alright—accept the offer.

If one is alright—accept the offer.

If neither is alright—reject the offer.

The EMV of this strategy is £186.

3 EMV of sampling is $1·26 \times 10^4$ (rule is to accept offer if two or more customers purchase); EMV of not sampling is $1·25 \times 10^4$: hence it is marginally best to take sample before deciding whether or not to accept offer.

4 Optimum strategy is to pull left-hand arm the first time; if a win is registered, pull it again otherwise pull the right hand arm (EMV is 0·2p).

5 (*i*) Best strategy, using EMV, is to drill without seismic (EMV is $64 800).

(*ii*) Note that chance of finding oil is less than one in five, and there is a 4/5 chance of making a loss of $100 000 or more.

Chapter 10 (p. 239)

1 (*i*) 0·25;

(*ii*) Without sampling—tariff B;

(*iii*) £240;

(*iv*) With the following decision rule:

Use Tariff A if 4 or less out of 20 are defective, or Tariff B if 5 or more out of 20 are defective, the EVSI is £118·20;

(*v*) Maximum amount is the EVSI in (*iv*) or £118·20.

(*i*) Yes, the publisher should decide to launch;

(*ii*) Both offers are worth considering.

Best rule with level A is to launch if 17 or more members are favourable.

Best rule with level B is to launch if 35 or more members are favourable.

ENGS (A) is £2000 and ENGS (B) is £3591.

Hence the best overall offer is level B.

3 Best sample size is 23 and the decision rule is to reject batch if 5 or more are defective; ENGS (with population depletion) is £164·29.

4 Sampling is not an economic proposition; EOL of best initial decision (not using inspector) is £1·08.

5 (*i*) Without pilot scheme the best decision is to send all the men on the £500 course;

    (*ii*) With sampling (and assuming the sample depletes the population) best sample size is 8; best decision rule is then to send all the men on the £50 course if 3 or more out of the 8 pass, and to send all the men on the £500 course if 2 or less pass.

6 Sampling should be instituted; the best sample size is 67 and the best decision rule is:
Inspect batch if 4 or more are defective.
ENGS (with this rule) is £14·47.

Chapter 11 (p. 259)

1 (*i*) Worth going ahead with change as prior EOL is £22 700;
    (*ii*) Worthwhile sampling: ENGS is £18 890.

2 (*i*) On EMV, it is worth going ahead (EOL = £1600);
    (*ii*) For $n = 40$ or 80, the EOL is approximately zero. Hence a sample size of 40 gives a larger ENGS (£1000). The analysis clearly shows that the optimum sample size is likely to be less than 40.

3 (*i*) Best decision without sampling is to go ahead with installation of the computer;
    (*ii*) It is worth sampling; optimum number of branches to be sampled is 34, when ENGS is £141 850.

4 (*i*) Yes, as expected annual revenue is £9000;
    (*ii*) Still go ahead with agency because, whilst the expected gain has been reduced it is still positive, namely £4600.

5 (*i*) Yes, EVPI is £4800;
    (*ii*) Optimum is for sample of 20 when ENGS is approximately £4764. Note that the value of any sample is extremely high, and the precise sample size is therefore not critical.

6 (*i*) Max economic sample size is 506;
    (*ii*) Optimum sample size is 41, when EOL is £14 and ENGS is £684·5.

Chapter 12 (p. 281)

1 (*i*) No; he should not accept;
    (*ii*) Yes; it will affect his decision and he should accept.

3 (*i*) £216 000;
    (*ii*) £219 000;
    (*iii*) A, £102 000; B, £103 400; Combined, 205 400;

(*iv*) As ratio of risk to assets of company becomes smaller we expect ratio of premium to actuarial premium to become closer to unity. Hence we expect premium A to be less than premium B, and the premiums charged by the companies when risk is shared to be each less than half the original individual premiums.

5 Optimum initial decision without considering inspection is to reject as expected utility charge is negative. If inspection is allowed, he should inspect one aircraft, and accept if it is satisfactory and reject if it is not; expected utility increase is then 0·035.

6 (*i*) Mr Bull should refuse deal as expected end utility is 0·33 (compare with initial utility of 0·85);

(*ii*) The deal becomes attractive to the syndicate; expected end utility for each individual is 0·86.

8 (*i*) Accept the contract;

(*ii*) Accept the contract, although the decision is now more marginal. The utility function has a maximum at £2·5m., and hence it is not likely to be valid beyond this point;

(*iii*) The utility function for the large firm is likely to be more nearly linear over the relevant range than for the smaller firm; hence the contract is more attractive to the former.

Chapter 13 (p. 299)

1 Modification has not significantly changed parity (significance level is 0·16).

2 No significant difference between mean strengths of the two batches.

3 Observations not inconsistent with hypothesis that mean time has remained 70 seconds.

4 Results indicate significant systematic deviations from norm of 1·000 (at 5 per cent level).

5 New tubes not significantly different from mean of 9000 hours.

6 (*i*) Significant difference at 4 per cent level (2-tailed test).

7 Results not inconsistent with an overall proportion defective of 0·20.

8 Method B is not significantly biased with respect to method A.

9 (*i*) H_0: Proportion of individuals who can correctly identify a particular beer is 0·5.

H_1: Proportion is $>0·5$;

(*ii*) Results just not significant at 5 per cent level.

10 Sample size required is 82.

11 Sample size required is 254.

Chapter 14 (p. 320)

1 $\hat{\lambda} = \dfrac{r}{\left(\sum\limits_{i=1}^{r} x_i + (n-r)x_0\right)}$.

2 $\hat{\beta} = \dfrac{\left(\sum\limits_{i=1}^{n} x_i - n\alpha\right)}{n}$.

α is arbitrary.

3 1·93.

4 95 per cent confidence limits for the population proportion defective are 0·038 to 0·066.

5 Maximum possible sample size required is 273; however, the sample size required depends on p, the proportion who would find the new pump useful. It would be helpful to take the sample in two stages; the first to obtain an approximate estimate of p, the second to complete the sample size based on this estimate.

6 95 per cent confidence limits are 0·497 to 0·687.

7 (*i*) 90 per cent confidence limits in inches are $0·436 \pm 2·85 \times 10^{-3}$;
   (*ii*) 95 per cent confidence limits in inches are $0·436 \pm 3·39 \times 10^{-3}$.

8 Minimum number of sets for required accuracy is 385.

9 Minimum number of determinations is 96.

10 Solution requires sample size n to be such that
   $2 \times 2·58 \times 1·5/\sqrt{n} \leqslant 0·5$
   or n to be at least 240.

11 The 90 per cent confidence limits for 'advertisement readers' per copy sold is $0·68 \pm 1·645 \times 0·85/\sqrt{300}$. Hence the 90 per cent limits for all 1·5m. copies sold are 0·90m. to 1·14m. Note that, due to the large sample, the normality assumption of readers is not of great importance.

1.

$$\left(\sum w + (a - \mu_0)^2\right)^{\frac{1}{2}}$$

$$\left(\frac{\sum (x - \bar{x})^2}{n}\right)^{\frac{1}{2}}$$

2.

3. 1965.

4. ...

5. ...

6. 28 per cent confidence limits are 0.612 to 0.688.

7. (i) 90 per cent confidence limit. In metres the 0.826 g 1995 to 1976;
(ii) 95 per cent confidence limits, metres are 0.826, 1.975 to 1.976.

8. Minimum number required for required sample is 1.45.

9. Minimum number of iterations line is 45.

10. ...

11. The 90 per cent confidence limits ... sample ...

Index